YOUR STUDY OF

THE BOOK OF MORMON

• MADE EASIER •

FOR TEENS

PART THREE: 3

HELAMAN THROUGH MORONI

BOOKS BY DAVID J. RIDGES

THE GOSPEL STUDIES SERIES

- *Isaiah Made Easier, Second Edition*
- *The New Testament Made Easier, Part 1, Second Edition*
- *The New Testament Made Easier, Part 2, Second Edition*
- *Your Study of The Book of Mormon Made Easier, Part 1*
- *Your Study of The Book of Mormon Made Easier, Part 2*
- *Your Study of The Book of Mormon Made Easier, Part 3*
- *Your Study of The Doctrine and Covenants Made Easier, Part 1*
- *Your Study of The Doctrine and Covenants Made Easier, Part 2*
- *Your Study of The Doctrine and Covenants Made Easier, Part 3*
- *The Old Testament Made Easier, Part 1*
- *The Old Testament Made Easier—Selections from the O.T., Part 2*
- *The Old Testament Made Easier—Selections from the O.T., Part 3*
- *Your Study of the Pearl of Great Price Made Easier*
- *Your Study of Jeremiah Made Easier*
- *Your Study of The Book of Revelation Made Easier, Second Edition*
- *Gospel Studies Series Deluxe Sets*

ADDITIONAL TITLES BY DAVID J. RIDGES

- *Our Savior, Jesus Christ: His Life and Mission to Cleanse and Heal*
- *Mormon Beliefs and Doctrines Made Easier*
- *The Proclamation on the Family: The Word of the Lord on More Than 30 Current Issues*
- *100 Signs of the Times Leading Up to the Second Coming of Christ*
- *Doctrinal Details of the Plan of Salvation: From Premortality to Exaltation*
- *To This End Was I Born: Walking with the Savior in His Final Week*
- *Temples: Sacred Symbolism, Eternal Blessings*
- *Priesthood Power Unlocked*
- *Using the Signs of the Times to Strengthen Your Testimony*
- *The Red Porsche*
- *The Righteous Role of a Father*
- *A Mother's Perfect Hope*
- *Seasons of a Mother's Love*
- *Born to the Virgin Mary*
- *Gospel Questions, Gospel Answers*

YOUR STUDY OF

THE BOOK OF MORMON

• MADE EASIER •

FOR TEENS

PART THREE: 3

HELAMAN THROUGH MORONI

DAVID J. RIDGES

CFI

An imprint of Cedar Fort, Inc.
Springville, Utah

ISBN 13: 978-1-4621-3685-8 (Volume 3)
ISBN 13: 978-1-4621-3579-0 (Set)

Published by CFI, an imprint of Cedar Fort, Inc.
2373 W. 700 S., Springville, UT 84663
Distributed by Cedar Fort, Inc., www.cedarfort.com

LIBRARY OF CONGRESS CATALOGING-IN-PUBLICATION DATA

Names: Ridges, David J., author.
Title: The Book of Mormon made easier for teens / David J. Ridges.
Description: Springville, Utah : CFI, an imprint of Cedar Fort, Inc., [2019] | Includes bibliographical references.
Identifiers: LCCN 2019018562 (print) | LCCN 2019020853 (ebook) | ISBN 9781462135790 (perfect bound : alk. paper)
Subjects: LCSH: Book of Mormon--Commentaries. | Mormon youth--Religious life.
Classification: LCC BX8627 .R533 2019 (print) | LCC BX8627 (ebook) | DDC 289.3/22--dc23
LC record available at https://lccn.loc.gov/2019018562
LC ebook record available at https://lccn.loc.gov/2019020853

Cover design by Shawnda T. Craig

Edited by Nicole Terry

Printed in the United States of America

10 9 8 7 6 5 4 3 2 1

Printed on acid-free paper

CONTENTS

THE JST REFERENCES IN STUDY GUIDES BY DAVID J. RIDGES

Note that some of the JST (The Joseph Smith Translation of the Bible) references I use in my study guides are not found in our LDS Bible in the footnotes or in the Joseph Smith Translation section in the reference section in the back. The reason for this, as explained to me while writing curriculum materials for the Church, is simply that there is not enough room to include all of the JST additions and changes to the King James Version of the Bible (the one we use in the English-speaking part of the Church). As you can imagine, as was likewise explained to me, there were difficult decisions that had to be made by the Scriptures Committee of the Church as to which JST contributions were included and which were not.

The Joseph Smith Translation of the Bible in its entirety can generally be found in or ordered through LDS bookstores. It was originally published under the auspices of the Reorganized Church of Jesus Christ of Latter Day Saints in Independence, Missouri. The version of the JST I prefer to use is a parallel column version, Joseph Smith's "New Translation" of the Bible, published by Herald Publishing House, Independence, Missouri, in 1970. This parallel column version compares the King James Bible with the JST side by side and includes only the verses that have changes, additions, or deletions made by the Prophet Joseph Smith.

By the way, some members of the Church have wondered if we can trust the JST since it was published by a breakaway faction from our Church. They worry that some changes from Joseph Smith's original manuscript might have been made to support doctrinal differences between us and the RLDS Church. This is not the case. Many years ago, Robert J. Matthews of the Brigham Young University Religion Department was given permission by leaders of the RLDS Church to come to their Independence, Missouri, headquarters and personally compare the original JST document word for word with their publication of the JST. Brother Matthews was thus able to verify that they had been meticulously true to the Prophet's original work.

INTRODUCTION

Welcome to the Book of Mormon Made Easier for Teens (and adults who would like a bit more help studying the Book of Mormon). These three study guide volumes combined contain every verse in the Book of Mormon. So, as you read and study, you will be reading the entire Book of Mormon word for word.

This study guide series was written for you. It is designed to help you learn to see applications in your own life from what you are reading and learning in the Book of Mormon. That way, it will be more interesting for you to read and study.

One of the things that typically stands in the way of understanding the scriptures is the vocabulary and overall language used in the scriptures. And so, I am going to help you learn "Scriptureze," or, in other words, the language of the scriptures, as we go along. In effect, you will learn a new language. Especially at first, I will define many words as we come to them. As you get to the point that you no longer need some of the words defined, you can ignore my definitions, realizing that you are actually making good progress in learning the language of the scriptures.

The Prophet Joseph Smith taught that we can get closer to God by living according to the teachings of the Book of Mormon than through any other book. The exact quote is, "I told the brethren that the Book of Mormon was the most correct of any book on earth, and the keystone of our religion, and a man would get nearer to God by abiding by its precepts, than by any other book." (See Book of Mormon, Introduction, paragraph 6.) So, there is probably nothing more valuable that you can do than to read and study the Book of Mormon.

The difference between this version and the regular Book of Mormon Made Easier study guides published several years ago is that these three volumes have many more definitions of scriptural terms that can be difficult for younger readers and also for many adults. They also contain a number of additional explanations of the teachings and principles taught in the Book of Mormon, and some longer and more technical notes and commentary have not been included.

You will see as we go along that I have used bold for many words and phrases. You can use this as a guide to mark your own scriptures with colored pencils, or highlight them if you are using digital scriptures. Also, you will see that by marking certain key words and phrases in a verse, you can, in effect, make brief notes as to what the verse is about. Later, as you re-read and study your Book of Mormon, you can glance at a verse and quickly see what it is about because of what you have marked in it.

Most important of all, the Book of Mormon is true. It is the word of God. And it is a sure way to bring the Spirit into your heart and mind whenever you choose to read and study it.

—David J. Ridges

THE BOOK OF HELAMAN

Welcome to volume three of *Your Study of the Book of Mormon Made Easier for Teens (And Others Who Want More Help)*. This volume covers the books of Helaman through Moroni. Let's briefly review and set the stage for what we will be studying.

We first met Alma the Elder as a young man in wicked King Noah's court as the prophet Abinadi was testifying and teaching (Mosiah 17). Alma was converted and eventually became the leader of the Church under the direction of King Mosiah II (Mosiah 25:19).

King Mosiah's four sons, along with Alma's son, Alma the Younger, were rebellious when we first met them but were converted when an angel appeared to them (Mosiah 27). Alma the Younger went on to become the next leader of the Church as well as the chief judge or leader of the Nephite nation (Mosiah 29:42).

The four sons of Mosiah asked to go on a mission to the Lamanites (Mosiah 28:5–9) and helped bring thousands of Lamanites into the Church over the fourteen years of their missionary service. These Lamanite converts were first known as Anti-Nephi-Lehies (Alma 23:17), but later were known as the people of Ammon (Alma 27:26). They were driven out of their own lands by the unbelievers among their people, stirred up by apostate Nephites (Alma 24:1).

Over the years, the Lamanites, often stirred up by apostate Nephites, came to war against the Nephites and the converted Lamanites (Alma 43–62). During this time of war, Captain Moroni led the Nephite Armies with the help of many righteous chief captains under his command. Captain Moroni is one of the great leaders in the Book of Mormon. We learned much from him about how to conduct war when war cannot be avoided. Among other things, we learned how to remain righteous and keep the Spirit of the Lord with us under extremely difficult circumstances. It was during these wars that we met the two thousand stripling warriors who were led into numerous battles by their beloved Helaman. They were later joined by sixty more sons of the people of Ammon (Alma 57:6).

As we came to the end of the Book of Alma, Captain Moroni turned the defense of the Nephite nation over to his son, Moronihah (Alma 62:43). Captain Moroni died at about age 42–43 (Alma 63:3), which we calculated by using the chronology in the chapter headings for that part of the Book of Mormon. Alma the Younger's son, Helaman, who led the 2000 stripling soldiers, died as reported in Alma 62:52. Helaman's brother, Shiblon, had been keeping the records and other sacred things of the Nephites. Before he died, he turned that responsibility over to Helaman's son, who was also named Helaman (Alma 63:11).

Thus, the Book of Helaman begins as the record of Helaman, son of Helaman, grandson of Alma the Younger, and great-grandson of Alma the Elder.

Helaman will have two sons that he will name Nephi and Lehi (Helaman 3:21). Helaman will die, and his oldest son Nephi will become the chief judge (Helaman 3:37). Nephi and Lehi face the same issues that we face in these last days, and we will learn much about spiritual survival and happiness from them.

Finally, we will meet Samuel the Lamanite in the last four chapters of Helaman. His teachings have many applications to us and to people living in our day.

As we begin the Book of Helaman, we will see more warfare between the Lamanites and the Nephites, but these wars will not be the main focus. Rather, Mormon will show us that internal dissension and corruption are far more dangerous to a nation than outside enemies. Going hand in hand with this is the extreme danger of what we refer to as "secret combinations" or groups who meet secretly to plot assassinations and the destruction of the righteous. In our day we could well refer to such people as "terrorists."

This point in the Book of Mormon is only fifty-two years before the birth of Christ to Mary in Bethlehem and about eighty-five years before the destruction of the wicked in America, after which the resurrected Lord appears to the Nephites. We will find amazing parallels between the conditions among the Nephites leading up to the Savior's appearance to them and the conditions in our day, which will ultimately lead up to the Second Coming of Christ, with the righteous being caught up to meet Him and the wicked being destroyed.

The table below summarizes some of these parallel conditions, including (1) conditions beyond the Book of Helaman and into Third Nephi, and (2) signs of the times for our day. "Signs of the times" are prophecies that will be fulfilled in the last days to alert people that the Second Coming is near.

Comparison between Book of Mormon conditions and our day

Book of Mormon	Our Day
Helaman 1:1–13. Political turmoil and overthrow of governments, including political assassinations.	D&C 87:6; 88:91. Same thing happening throughout the world today.
Helaman 1:14; 3 Nephi 3:26. Wars and rumors of wars.	D&C 45:26; Matt. 24:6. Wars and rumors of wars.
Helaman 4:4. Many dissenters and apostates leave personal righteousness and join the enemies of the righteous.	Many people abandoning the Bible and God's commandments and seeking to undermine laws and governments that strive to preserve righteous principles.
Helaman 4:12. Widespread personal wickedness and corruption.	2 Timothy 3:1–7. Widespread personal wickedness and corruption.
Helaman 5:14–19. Great success in reactivating members, plus large numbers of converts to the Church.	Activation efforts are leading to increased activity and retention rates, plus large numbers of converts to the Church.
Helaman 6:12–14. Members of the Church prosper as a whole and have great joy and much revelation from God, in spite of the gross wickedness all around them.	Same thing happening among faithful members today.
Helaman 6:15–16. Increasing wickedness and more political assassinations.	Same thing happening throughout the world today.
Helaman 6:17. Materialism and pride take over the majority of society.	Same thing happening throughout the world today.
Helaman 6:22–23. Secret combinations are formed to commit acts of terrorism against society.	Terrorists, gangs, etc., are doing the same things throughout the world today.
Helaman 6:31. The majority of society turns away from God and embraces wickedness.	Same thing happening throughout the world today.
Helaman 6:35. The Spirit of the Lord begins to withdraw from the Nephites.	D&C 63:32. "I am holding my Spirit from the inhabitants of the earth."
Helaman 6:38. Government policies and laws, etc., are changed to support personal wickedness.	Laws are passed that support abortion, adultery, homosexuality, etc., and remove God from public meetings and prohibit prayers in government, etc.
Helaman 7:4–6. Rapid take–over of government by unprincipled leaders who set God's commandments, etc., aside.	Same thing happening throughout the world today.
Helaman 11:1. Wars everywhere.	Same thing happening throughout the world today.
Helaman 11:4–6. People have ignored the gospel preaching, so famine is sent to humble them and reclaim as many as possible back to God.	D&C 88:88–90. Natural disasters happening throughout the world today for the same purpose.
Helaman 13:27–28. Many teach that there is no such thing as right and wrong. They gain popularity and large followings.	Same thing happening throughout the world today.
Helaman 14:6. Many signs and wonders in heaven.	D&C 45:40. Many signs and wonders in heaven and on the earth.
3 Nephi 1:22. Satan tempts people to re-fuse to believe obvious signs and wonders.	2 Peter 3:3–4. Many people will refuse to believe obvious signs and wonders in the last days.
3 Nephi 1:23. Much peace among faithful members of the Church.	Much peace and happiness among faithful members of the Church.

3 Nephi 2:14–16. Many Lamanites joined the Church.	D&C 49:24. Lamanites "blossom as the rose." Large numbers join the Church.
3 Nephi 3:9–10. The wicked claim that their evil works are good works.	Same thing happening throughout the world today.
3 Nephi 6:11. Many lawyers were employed in the land.	Same thing happening throughout the world today.
3 Nephi 7:2. Society divided up into ethnic groups who were against each other.	Same thing happening throughout the world today.
3 Nephi 7:16. Nephi testified boldly to the people.	Church leaders today testify boldly to the world as well as to members.
3 Nephi 7:17–20. People got so wicked that they became angry at Nephi for doing miracles. 3 Nephi 7:22. Many miracles and great outpourings of Spirit among the faithful.	The wicked get angry at the leaders of the Church as the Church continues its miraculous growth and service. The righteous today experience many miracles and great outpourings of the Spirit.
3 Nephi 7:26. Many baptisms just before the coming of the Lord (recorded in Third Nephi, chapter 8).	Convert baptisms continue to increase in unprecedented numbers.

We will now proceed to study the Book of Helaman.

HELAMAN 1

You will see that this chapter moves along quickly through national elections, a rebellion, a political assassination, an attack by outside military forces, surprise attacks within the Nephite nation, a temporary loss of the nation's capital, and then regaining it. It sounds similar to world events today.

We will continue to use **bold** text to suggest possible things for you to choose from if you underline or mark in your own Book of Mormon. You will obviously find additional things to mark for emphasis. Also, the bold text often becomes a brief "note" showing briefly what the verse is about. In a way, the bold text often becomes a brief outline of what a verse or series of verses is about.

1 AND now behold, it came to pass **in** the commencement of **the fortieth year** of the reign of the judges over the people of Nephi [*about 52 BC, meaning about 52 years before Christ was born*], **there began to be a serious difficulty among** the people of **the Nephites** [*internal divisions and attacks on their own government*].

2 For behold, **Pahoran** [*the chief judge or "president" of the Nephite nation during Captain Moroni's time*] **had died**, and gone the way of all the earth; therefore **there began to be a serious contention** [*debate; fight; argument*] **concerning who should have the judgment-seat** [*in other words, over who should be the next president (chief judge) of the Nephite nation*] **among** the brethren [*brothers*], who were **the sons of Pahoran**.

3 Now these are their names who did contend for [*fought for*] the judgment-seat, who did also cause the people to contend: **Pahoran, Paanchi, and Pacumeni**.

4 Now these are not all the sons of Pahoran (for he had many), but these are they who did contend for the judgment-seat; therefore, **they did cause three divisions among the people**.

5 Nevertheless, it came to pass that **Pahoran was appointed by the voice of the people** to be chief judge and a governor over the people of Nephi. [*In other words, they held an election as a democratic nation and Pahoran won.*]

6 And it came to pass that **Pacumeni**, when he saw that he could not obtain the judgment-seat, he **did unite with the voice of the people** [*peacefully joined with his brother who won the election*].

7 But behold, **Paanchi**, and that part of the people that were desirous that he should be their governor, **was exceedingly wroth** [*angry*]; therefore, he was about to flatter away those people to rise up in rebellion against their brethren [*was about to commit treason—a very dangerous attack on their democratic form of government*].

8 And it came to pass as he was about to do this, behold, **he was taken** [*arrested*], and was **tried** according to the voice of the people [*he was given an open

and fair trial], **and condemned unto death**; for **he had** raised up in rebellion and **sought** [*tried*] **to destroy the liberty of the people**.

Next comes a serious downward step for the Nephite nation. We will be introduced to a wicked man named Kishkumen. This is the beginning of secret combinations (secret groups) among the Nephites in this particular era of Nephite history. These secret combinations were inspired by the devil and promoted murder and destruction in order to gain power and disrupt peace.

9 Now when **those people who were desirous that he should be their governor** saw that he was condemned unto death, therefore they **were angry**, and behold, **they sent** forth one **Kishkumen**, even to the judgment-seat of Pahoran, and **murdered Pahoran as he sat upon the judgment-seat**.

10 And **he was pursued by the servants of Pahoran**; but behold, so speedy was the flight of Kishkumen that **no man could overtake him**.

We shudder, next, at the blasphemy (complete disrespect and blatant mocking of sacred things) of using the name of God in making this evil covenant to keep this murder secret. Perhaps you've noticed that Satan seems to have an evil counterfeit for every good thing sponsored by the gospel of Christ. For example, non-Christian worship has often included human sacrifice, which is a devil-sponsored mockery of the Savior's voluntary sacrifice to save His people from sin.

11 And he went unto those that sent him, and **they all entered into a covenant** [*a secret combination*], yea, **swearing by their everlasting Maker** [*making a covenant in the name of God*], **that they would tell no man that Kishkumen had murdered Pahoran**.

Watch, next, how the behavior of Kishkumen and his band follows the same pattern that we see among terrorists today.

12 Therefore, **Kishkumen was not known** among the people of Nephi, **for he was in disguise** at the time that he murdered Pahoran. And **Kishkumen and his band, who had covenanted with him, did mingle themselves among the people, in a manner that they all could not be found**; but as many as were found were condemned unto death.

13 And now behold, **Pacumeni** [*the brother of Pahoran, the murdered chief judge*] **was appointed**, according to the voice of the people [*by public election*], **to be** a **chief judge** and a **governor** over the people, to reign [*rule*] in the stead of [*in place of*] his brother Pahoran; and it was according to his right. And all this was done **in the fortieth year** of the reign of the judges; and it had an end.

We have been dealing with internal problems caused by rebellious citizens. Next, we deal with the threat from outside enemies to the nation, who are led by a rebellious Nephite who hates his own people and country.

14 And it came to pass in the **forty and first year** of the reign of the judges, that **the Lamanites had gathered together an innumerable** [*so many that they couldn't count them*] **army of men**, and armed them with swords, and with cimeters [*curved swords*] and with bows, and with arrows, and with head-plates, and with breastplates, and with all manner of shields of every kind.

15 And **they came down** again that they might pitch battle **against the Nephites**. And they were **led by a man whose name was Coriantumr**; and he was a descendant of Zarahemla; and **he was a dissenter** [*one who wanted to undermine and destroy the Nephite government and democracy*] **from among the Nephites**; and he was a large and a mighty man.

16 Therefore, the **king of the Lamanites**, whose name was **Tubaloth, who was the son of Ammoron** [*the apostate Nephite who had become king of the Lamanites; remember that "apostate" means one who leaves the Church and fights against its values*], supposing that Coriantumr, being a mighty man, could stand against the Nephites, with his strength and also with his great wisdom, insomuch that by sending him forth he should gain power over the Nephites—

17 Therefore he did stir them up to anger, and he did gather together his armies, and he **did appoint Coriantumr to be their leader**, and did cause that they should march down to the land of Zarahemla to battle against the Nephites.

Next, we see that internal dissension and divisions among the citizens had seriously weakened the Nephite nation's defense.

18 And it came to pass that **because of so much contention and so much difficulty in the government**, that **they had not kept sufficient guards** in the land of Zarahemla; for they had supposed that the Lamanites durst not [*didn't dare*] come into the heart of their lands to attack that great city Zarahemla.

19 But it came to pass that **Coriantumr did march forth at the head of his numerous host** [*large army*], **and came upon the inhabitants of the city**, and their march was with such exceedingly great speed [*so fast*] that **there was no time for the Nephites to gather together their armies** [*a surprise attack*].

20 Therefore **Coriantumr** did cut down the watch [*the men positioned to watch and warn of coming enemies*] by the entrance of the city, and did march forth **with his whole army** into the city, and they did slay [*kill*] every one who did oppose them, insomuch that they **did take possession of the whole city**.

21 And it came to pass that **Pacumeni**, who was the chief judge, **did flee** before Coriantumr, even **to the walls of the city**. And it came to pass that **Coriantumr did smite him against the wall, insomuch that he died**.

And thus ended the days of Pacumeni.

Perhaps you can see some symbolism in what is happening to the Nephites here in these verses. If we look at Coriantumr as a "type" of Satan, or in other words, as symbolic of Satan, we see him going straight for Zarahemla, the capital city of the Nephite democracy. As we continue to see symbolism, we can see Lucifer going straight for our "capitals" of media and entertainment as well as our "capitals" of government in order to do maximum damage to our nation.

While we do not want to become pessimistic and negative, we would be foolish to ignore the education from the past that Mormon is pointing out to us in these verses.

22 And now **when Coriantumr** saw that he was in possession of the city of Zarahemla, and saw that the Nephites had fled [*run away in fear*] before them, and were slain, and were taken, and were cast into prison, and that he **had obtained the possession of the strongest hold in all the land**, his heart took courage insomuch that he was about to go forth against all the land.

23 And now **he did not tarry** [*remain*] **in the land of Zarahemla, but he did march forth with a large army, even towards the city of Bountiful**; for it was his determination [*plan*] to go forth and cut his way through with the sword, that he might obtain the north parts of the land.

Just as Coriantumr is moving very quickly, taking advantage of the disorganization of the people, so also Satan is moving very quickly in our day, taking advantage of the spiritual and moral disorganization among people who have abandoned the Bible and other standards that could keep them organized against evil.

24 And, supposing that their greatest strength was in the center of the land, therefore **he did march forth, giving them no time to assemble themselves together** save [*except*] it were in small bodies; and in this manner they did fall upon them and cut them down to the earth.

Next, we see Moronihah (Captain Moroni's son who is now the chief of the Nephite armies; see Alma 62:43) develop a strategy to defeat Coriantumr and the Lamanite armies.

25 But behold, **this march of Coriantumr through the center of the land gave Moronihah great advantage over them**, notwithstanding [*in spite of*] the greatness of the number of the Nephites who were slain.

26 For behold, **Moronihah had supposed that the Lamanites durst not** [*would not dare*] **come into the center of the land**, but that they would attack the cities round about in the borders as they had hitherto done [*as they had done up to this time*]; therefore Moronihah had caused that their strong armies should maintain those parts round about by the borders.

27 **But** behold, **the Lamanites** were not frightened according to his desire, but they had come into the center of

the land, and had taken the capital city which was the city of Zarahemla, and **were marching through the most capital parts of the land**, slaying the people with a great slaughter, both men, women, and children, taking possession of many cities and of many strongholds.

The Lamanites' marching through the main parts of the country, in verse 27, above, could be compared to Satan's marching through our most prominent and influential media personalities, etc., and the resulting spiritual slaughter that is taking place.

28 But **when Moronihah had discovered this, he immediately sent forth Lehi with an army** round about **to head** [*stop*] **them** before they should come to the land Bountiful.

29 And thus he did; and **he did head them** [*cut them off*] **before they came to the land Bountiful, and gave unto them battle**, insomuch that **they began to retreat** back towards the land of Zarahemla.

30 And it came to pass that **Moronihah did head them** [*cut them off*] **in their retreat**, and did give unto them battle, insomuch that [*so that*] it became an exceedingly bloody battle; yea, **many were slain, and among the number who were slain Coriantumr was also found**.

31 And now, behold, **the Lamanites could not retreat either way**, neither on the north, nor on the south, nor on the east, nor on the west, for they were surrounded on every hand by the Nephites.

32 And thus had Coriantumr plunged the Lamanites into the midst of the Nephites, insomuch that they were in the power of the Nephites, and he himself was slain, and the **Lamanites did yield themselves** [*surrender*] **into the hands of the Nephites**.

33 And it came to pass that **Moronihah took possession of the city of Zarahemla again**, and caused that the Lamanites who had been taken prisoners should depart out of the land in peace.

34 And **thus ended the forty and first year** of the reign of the judges.

HELAMAN 2

Next, Helaman (the son of Helaman, who is the son of Alma the Younger) will be voted in as chief judge (basically, the president of the nation) to replace Pacumeni, who was killed by Coriantumr. Helaman is a righteous man. He is keeping the record of the Nephites, and the Book of Helaman was named after him. He will serve as chief judge for about eleven years.

In this chapter, we will again meet Kishkumen (who had murdered Pahoran) as he tries to assassinate, in other words, kill Helaman. We will also meet an evil man by the name of Gadianton who will become the leader of Kishkumen's secret band of murderers and robbers. This band will become known as the Gadianton robbers and will cause terrible damage to the Nephite nation. In fact, they seem to represent the exact opposite of good in everything they do, so much that we sometimes refer to modern-day groups such as this (who fight good and call evil good and good evil) as "modern-day Gadianton robbers."

1 AND it came to pass in the **forty and second year** of the reign of the judges, **after Moronihah had established again peace** between the Nephites and the Lamanites, behold **there was no one to fill the judgment-seat**; therefore there began to be a contention [*argument, strong debate*] again among the people concerning who should fill the judgment-seat.

2 And it came to pass that **Helaman**, who was the son of Helaman, **was appointed to fill the judgment-seat, by the voice of the people** [*in a general election in which the citizens voted*].

3 But behold, **Kishkumen**, who had murdered Pahoran, **did lay wait** [*was hiding*] **to destroy Helaman also**; and he was upheld [*supported*] by his band [*friends*], who had entered into a covenant that no one should know his wickedness [*a secret combination*].

4 For **there was one** [*a man named*] **Gadianton**, who was exceedingly [*very*] **expert in many words** [*was good at flattering people into following him*], and also in his craft, **to carry on the secret work of murder and of robbery**; therefore **he became the leader of the band of Kishkumen**.

As you will see in verse 5, next, the same motives that drive Satan are the motives that drove Gadianton; namely, to have unrighteous power and control over people. In other words, he "sought to destroy the agency of man" (Moses 4:3). And just as Satan seeks to tempt others to follow him by promising them power, glory, and unrighteous dominion, so also Gadianton promised his followers the same. To the greedy and selfish, these are flattering promises.

5 Therefore **he did flatter them**, and also Kishkumen, that if they would place him in the judgment-seat **he would grant** [*give*] **unto those who belonged to his band that they should be placed in power and authority among the people**; therefore Kishkumen sought to destroy Helaman.

6 And it came to pass **as he went forth towards the judgment-seat to destroy Helaman**, behold **one of the servants of Helaman**, having been out by night, and having obtained, through disguise, a knowledge of those plans which had been laid by this band to destroy Helaman—

7 And it came to pass that he **met Kishkumen**, and he gave unto him a sign; therefore Kishkumen made known unto him the object of his desire, desiring that he would conduct him to the judgment-seat that he might murder Helaman.

Again, in verse 8, next, Mormon points out what the real goals and motives of those who belong to secret combinations are. These remain the same throughout the ages. We will bold them to point them out.

8 And when the servant of Helaman had known all the heart of Kishkumen, and how that it was his object to murder, and also that it was the object of all those who belonged to his band **to murder**, and **to rob**, and **to gain power**, (and this was their secret plan, and their combination) the servant of Helaman said unto Kishkumen: Let us go forth unto the judgment-seat.

9 Now **this did please Kishkumen exceedingly, for he did suppose that he should accomplish his design** [*plot*]; but behold, **the servant of Helaman**, as they were going forth unto the judgment-seat, **did stab Kishkumen even to the heart, that he fell dead** without a groan. And **he ran and told Helaman all the things which he had seen, and heard, and done**.

10 And it came to pass that **Helaman did send forth to take** [*capture*] **this band of robbers and secret murderers**, that they might be executed according to the law.

11 But behold, **when Gadianton had found that Kishkumen did not return he feared lest that** [*for fear that*] **he should be destroyed**; therefore he caused that his band should follow him. **And they took their flight** [*they fled*] **out of the land**, by a secret way, into the wilderness; and thus when Helaman sent forth to take them they could nowhere be found.

Next, Mormon prepares us for what is yet to come concerning the dark and destructive power of the Gadianton band, often referred to today as "the Gadianton robbers," and all such secret combinations.

12 And **more of this Gadianton shall be spoken hereafter**. And thus ended the forty and second year of the reign of the judges over the people of Nephi.

13 And behold, **in the end of this book** [*the Book of Mormon*] **ye shall see that this Gadianton did prove** [*cause*] **the overthrow, yea, almost the entire destruction of the people of Nephi**.

14 Behold I [*Mormon*] do not mean the end of the book of Helaman, but **I mean the end of the book of Nephi** [*the Large Plates of Nephi, in other words, the whole Book of Mormon*], from which I have taken all the account which I have written.

HELAMAN 3

In this chapter, Mormon will take us quickly through ten more years of Nephite history, from 49 to 39 years BC. So it will only be a relatively short time before the sign of the Savior's birth in Bethlehem will be given here in America—namely, a day and a night and a day with no darkness.

Mormon will summarize several details of history, but will focus mainly on how people who want to be righteous can remain close to God. So, by paying close attention, you can learn much about remaining spiritually healthy yourself. He will warn about pride among members of the Church and then report the death of Helaman. Nephi will then take over the judgment-seat in place of his father.

Perhaps this is a good place for you to notice an important thing: namely, that the Book of Mormon is not mainly a history book about the ancient inhabitants of the Americas. Rather, as stated by Moroni in the title page of the Book of Mormon, it is sacred scripture which bears witness to us of Christ and shows how the Lord deals with people to save them.

The contents of the Book of Mormon are intentionally selected to give us hope and encouragement, to warn us against evil, and to continually remind us of the power of the Savior's Atonement to cleanse and heal us from sin as He invites us to return safely to Him and the Father. Chapter three, here, is a good example of this important fact.

As you know by now, Mormon is an inspired master teacher. As he begins in verse one, he will casually mention pride as if it were just a side issue, but before this chapter is over, he will demonstrate how it can grow into a spiritually devastating illness among members.

1 AND now it came to pass in the **forty and third year** of the reign of the judges [*49 BC*], there was **no contention** among the people of Nephi **save** [*except*] it were **a little pride** which was in the church, which did cause some little dissensions [*arguing and debating*] among the people, which affairs were settled in the ending of the forty and third year.

2 And there was **no contention among the people in the forty and fourth year; neither was there much contention in the forty and fifth year**.

In the next several verses, Mormon provides many brief historical details, including northward migrations of large numbers of people.

3 And it came to pass in the forty and sixth, yea, **there was much contention and many dissensions; in the which there were an exceedingly great many who departed out of the land of Zarahemla, and went forth unto the land northward to inherit the land**.

4 And **they did travel to an exceedingly** [*very*] **great distance**, insomuch that they came to large bodies of water and many rivers.

5 Yea, and even **they did spread forth into all parts of the land**, into whatever parts it had not been rendered desolate and without timber, because of the many inhabitants who had before inherited the land [*the Jaredites; see Mosiah 8:8*].

6 And now **no part of the land was desolate** [*barren*], **save it were for timber** [*except for the lack of trees*]; but because of the greatness of the destruction of the people who had before inhabited the land it was called desolate.

7 And there being but little timber [*very few trees*] upon the face of the land, nevertheless **the people who**

went forth became exceedingly expert in the working of cement; therefore **they did build houses of cement**, in the which they did dwell.

8 And it came to pass that **they did multiply** [*increase in population*] **and spread**, and did go forth from the land southward to the land northward, and did spread insomuch that they began to cover the face of the whole earth, from the sea south to the sea north, from the sea west to the sea east.

Next, we are told that because of the scarcity of trees, caused by a previous civilization (the Jaredites, see Mosiah 8:8; 21:26), these settlers of the northlands were very protective of any tree that they found growing.

9 And the people who were in the land northward did dwell in tents, and in houses of cement, and **they did suffer** [*allow*] **whatsoever tree should spring up upon the face of the land that it should grow up, that in time they might have timber** [*lumber*] to build their houses, yea, their cities, and their temples, and their synagogues, and their sanctuaries, and all manner of their buildings.

10 And it came to pass as **timber was exceedingly scarce** in the land northward, they did send forth much by the way of shipping.

11 And thus **they did enable the people** in the land northward that they might **build many cities, both of wood and of cement**.

Next, Mormon mentions the people of Ammon (the Lamanite converts who joined the Church during the fourteen-year mission of the four sons of Mosiah and their companions) who were originally known as the Anti-Nephi-Lehies (Alma 23:17). The two thousand stripling soldiers, led by Helaman approximately thirteen to fifteen years earlier, were sons of these converts.

12 And it came to pass that there were **many of the people of Ammon, who were Lamanites by birth, did also go forth into this land**.

Next, Mormon tells us of a great many Nephite records that had been handed down through the generations to his day. There is an interesting quote from Brigham Young in which he tells of the equivalent of several wagonloads of metal plates used in record keeping by the Nephites, which were in a room in the Hill Cumorah when Joseph Smith and Oliver Cowdery returned the plates to it. We will include this quote here:

"I believe I will take the liberty to tell you of another circumstance that will be as marvelous as anything can be. This is an incident in the life of Oliver Cowdery, but he did not take the liberty of telling such things in meeting as I take. I tell these things to you, and I have a motive for doing so. I want to carry them to the ears of my brethren and sisters, and to the children also, that they may grow to an understanding of some things that seem to be entirely hidden from the human family. **Oliver Cowdery went with the Prophet Joseph when he deposited these plates**. Joseph did not translate all of the plates; there was a portion of them sealed, which you can learn from the Book of Doctrine and Covenants. When Joseph got the plates, **the angel instructed him to carry them back to the hill Cumorah**, which he did. Oliver says that when Joseph and Oliver went there, the hill opened, and they walked into a cave, in which there was **a large and spacious room**. He says he did not think, at the time, whether they had the light of the sun or artificial light; but that it was just as light as day. They laid the plates on a table; it was a large table that stood in the room. **Under this table there was a pile of plates as much as two feet high, and there were altogether in this room more plates than probably many wagon loads**; they were piled up in the corners and along the walls. The first time they went there the sword of Laban hung upon the wall; but when they went again it had been taken down and laid upon the table across the gold plates; it was unsheathed, and on it was written these words: 'This sword will never be sheathed again until the kingdoms of this world become the kingdom of our God and his Christ'" (*Journal of Discourses*, 19:38–39).

13 And now **there are many records kept of the proceedings of this people,** by many of this people, which are particular [*very detailed*] and very large, concerning them.

14 But behold, **a hundredth part of the proceedings of this people**, yea, the account of the Lamanites and of the Nephites, and their wars, and contentions, and dissensions [*apostasies; Nephites joining the Lamanites, etc.*], and their preaching, and their prophecies, and their shipping and their building of ships, and their building of temples, and of synagogues [*houses of worship*] and their sanctuaries [*churches*], and their righteousness, and their wickedness, and their murders, and their robbings, and their plundering [*destroying and takings from others*], and all manner of abominations [*extreme wickedness*] and whoredoms [*sexual immorality*], **cannot be contained in this work** [*the plates being engraved by Mormon, which Joseph Smith will receive from Moroni*].

15 But behold, **there are many books and many records of every kind**, and they have been kept chiefly [*mainly*] by the Nephites.

16 And **they have been handed down from one generation to another by the Nephites**, even until they have fallen into transgression and have been murdered, plundered, and hunted, and driven forth, and slain, and scattered upon the face of the earth, and mixed with the Lamanites until they are no more called the Nephites, becoming wicked, and wild, and ferocious, yea, even becoming Lamanites.

17 And **now I** [*Mormon*] **return again to mine account** [*of Helaman and the Nephites, about 45 BC*]; therefore, what I have spoken had passed after there had been great contentions, and disturbances, and wars, and dissensions [*apostasies; leaving the Church*], among the people of Nephi.

The reason we consider the word "dissensions" (verse 17, above) to mean "apostasies" is that Mormon seems to almost always use this word in connection with people leaving the Church and/or adopting wicked lifestyles. See Helaman 4:4, Mosiah 26:5, and 3 Nephi 2:18.

18 The **forty and sixth year of the reign of the judges ended**;

19 And it came to pass that there was **still great contention** [*fighting and arguing among themselves*] in the land, yea, even **in the forty and seventh year**, and also in the **forty and eighth year**.

A repeating theme of the Book of Mormon is that righteousness brings prosperity and growth not only spiritually, but also in terms of physical and financial well-being to the righteous as a whole. Mormon will teach this principle again in the next verses.

20 Nevertheless **Helaman** did fill the judgment-seat with justice and equity [*fairness*] yea, he did observe to keep the statutes, and the judgments, and the commandments of God; and he **did do that which was right in the sight of God** continually; and he did walk after the ways of his father [*Helaman, son of Alma the Younger*], insomuch that **he did prosper in the land**.

21 And it came to pass that **he had two sons.** He gave unto the eldest the name of **Nephi**, and unto the youngest, the name of **Lehi**. And they began to grow up unto the Lord.

In Helaman 5:6 we are told why Helaman gave his two sons those names.

Next, we see the gradual return of a degree of peace to the Nephite nation. However, the secret combination of the Gadianton robbers is beginning to quietly and secretly grow in number among the people. This will eventually cause terrible trouble.

22 And it came to pass that **the wars and contentions began to cease** [*stop*], **in a small degree,** among the people of the Nephites, in the latter end of the **forty and eighth year** of the reign of the judges over the people of Nephi.

23 And it came to pass in the forty and ninth year of the reign of the judges, there was **continual peace established in the land, all save it were** [*except*] **the secret combinations which Gadianton the robber had established** in the more settled parts of the land, which at that time **were not known unto those who were at the head of government**; therefore they were not destroyed out of the land.

24 And it came to pass that in this same year there was exceedingly **great prosperity in the church**, insomuch that there were **thousands** who did join themselves unto the church and **were baptized** unto repentance.

This great increase in Church membership among the Nephites before the coming of the Savior to them is similar to the great increase in members of the Church in our last days before the Second Coming of Christ. This prosperity and growth of the Church is almost startling to many of us, and the rapid growth in the days of Helaman surprised the leaders of the Church in his day.

25 And **so great was the prosperity of the church**, and so many the blessings which were poured out upon the people, **that even the high priests and the teachers were themselves astonished** beyond measure.

26 And it came to pass that **the work of the Lord did prosper** unto the **baptizing** and uniting to the church of God, many souls, yea, even **tens of thousands**.

Some years ago, I was able to attend a stake presidents' training meeting, which was taught by a member of the Quorum of the Twelve Apostles. In it we were told, by way of prophecy, to stop thinking in terms of ten or fifteen million members of the Church. Rather, we were counseled to raise our sights to fifty or one hundred million and beyond as we prepare for modern-day growth in the Church.

Next, we again find Mormon's phrases "thus we may see," "thus we see," and "we see," which alert us to the fact that Mormon is now going to tell us what he hopes we will learn from what he is about to say. You may want to put a little note in your scriptures by each of these phrases to indicate that Mormon is making, as it were, an editorial comment.

27 **Thus we may see** that the Lord is merciful unto all who will, in the sincerity of their hearts, call upon his holy name.

28 Yea, **thus we see** that the gate of heaven is open unto all, even to those who will believe on the name of Jesus Christ, who is the Son of God.

In verses 29 and 30, next, Mormon will use many gospel phrases that are familiar to those who know the scriptures. We will **bold** a number of them and define them. Verse 29 begins with Mormon's editorial comment phrase "we see."

29 Yea, **we see** that whosoever will [*wants to*] may **lay hold upon the word of God** [*take the gospel into their lives*], which is **quick and powerful** [*alive; lively and strong*], which shall **divide asunder** [*cut down; destroy*] all the cunning [*deception*] and the snares [*traps*] and the wiles [*tricks*] of the devil, and **lead the man of Christ** [*the faithful follower of Christ*] in a **strait and narrow course** [*the path which leads to celestial exaltation*] **across that everlasting gulf of misery** [*the torment which awaits the unrepentant wicked*] **which is prepared to engulf the wicked**—

30 And land their souls, yea, their immortal souls, at **the right hand of God** [*the "covenant" hand; symbolic of those who make and keep covenants with God; meaning saved in celestial glory*] in the kingdom of heaven, **to sit down with Abraham, and Isaac, and with Jacob** [*to join Abraham, Isaac, and Jacob, who have already become gods; see D&C 132:37*], and with all **our holy fathers** [*righteous ancestors who have earned exaltation*], **to go no more out** [*to live in celestial glory and exaltation forever*].

31 And **in this year there was continual rejoicing** [*happiness and enjoying life*] in the land of Zarahemla, and in all the regions round about, even in all the land which was possessed by the Nephites.

32 And it came to pass that there was peace and exceedingly great joy [*the result of personal righteousness among large numbers of people*] in the remainder of the **forty and ninth year**; yea, and also there was continual **peace and great joy** in the **fiftieth year** of the reign of the judges.

As mentioned in the note earlier in this chapter, pride is a most dangerous thing to allow into our lives. Next, it works its way into the hearts of some Church members. Note also how Mormon separates the Church as an inspired organization from the faults and shortcomings of the members themselves. Many critics of the Church do not see or make this separation.

33 And in the **fifty and first year** of the reign of the judges there was peace also, save it were [*except for*] the **pride** which **began to enter into the church—not into the church of God, but into the hearts of the people who professed** [*claimed*] **to belong to the church of God**—

34 And they were **lifted up in pride**, even to the persecution of many of their brethren [*other members of the Church*]. Now this was a great evil, which did cause the more humble part of the people to suffer great persecutions, and to wade through much affliction [*have many troubles and problems*].

Next, we are counseled how to remain faithful when other members of the Church ridicule our firm commitment to gospel standards. We are also told what the result of such commitment is, right now, during our daily lives.

35 Nevertheless they did **fast and pray oft**, and did wax [*grow*] stronger and stronger in their **humility**, and **firmer and firmer in the faith of Christ**, unto the **filling their souls with joy and consolation** [*comfort*], yea, even to the **purifying and the sanctification** [*making them holy and fit to have the Spirit with them constantly*] **of their hearts**, which **sanctification cometh because of their yielding their hearts unto God**.

Next, Mormon points out one of the most common causes of pride.

36 And it came to pass that the fifty and second year ended in peace also, save it were the **exceedingly great pride** which had gotten into the hearts of the people; and it was **because of their exceedingly great riches** [*wealth*] **and their prosperity in the land**; and it did grow upon them from day to day.

Next, we say goodbye to Helaman, and the stage is set for the ministry of Nephi in chapters 4 through 11.

37 And it came to pass in the **fifty and third year** of the reign of the judges [*39 BC*], **Helaman died**, and his eldest son **Nephi began to reign in his stead** [*in his place*]. And it came to pass that he did fill the judgment-seat with justice and equity [*fairness*]; yea, **he did keep the commandments of God**, and did walk in the ways of his father.

HELAMAN 4

Chapters 4–6 could be called "the anatomy of the downfall of a nation" or "how a righteous nation gets destroyed." It could also be called "how the devil destroys the spirituality of believers in Christ and then goes on to destroy the nation."

We will be warned against many things, and will see the destructive power of Satan. But we will also see the power of the word of God in bringing people back to Christ.

As we begin chapter 4, we will see much of apostasy (leaving the Church) and weakening of the Nephite nation through internal arguing, disagreements, and infighting. Also, you may wish to pay attention to a gradual shifting of the definitions of the terms "Nephites" and "Lamanites." You may already have noticed that the word "Nephites" is coming to mean anyone who is a member of the Church and is trying to be righteous, regardless of race or origin. On the other hand, Mormon is using the term "Lamanites" to mean those who have left the Church and who are worldly and caught up in wickedness. Thus, the "Lamanites" include many Nephites who have gone over to the wicked ways of the world.

1 AND it came to pass in the **fifty and fourth year** [*38 BC*] there were **many dissensions** [*much apostasy, falling away*] **in the church**, and there was **also a contention** [*fighting*] **among the people**, insomuch that there was much bloodshed.

2 And **the rebellious part were slain** [*killed*] **and driven out of the land, and they did go unto the king of the Lamanites**.

3 And it came to pass that **they did endeavor** [*attempt*] **to stir up the Lamanites to war against the Nephites; but** behold, **the Lamanites were exceedingly** [*very*] **afraid**, insomuch that they would not hearken to [*go along with*] the words of those dissenters [*apostates*].

4 But it came to pass in the **fifty and sixth** year of the reign of the judges [*two years later; 36 BC*], there were **dissenters** who **went up from the Nephites unto the Lamanites; and they succeeded with those others in stirring them up to anger against the Nephites**; and they were all that year preparing for war.

Again, we see similarities between the things going on among the Nephites relatively shortly before the destruction of the wicked at the coming of Christ to them, and what is happening to us in our day as we get closer to the Second Coming of Christ. Next, we will see the taking over of the land of Zarahemla by those who have abandoned the teachings of Christ. So also in our day, much of the doings in our country have been taken over by those who no longer try to live according to God's standards, including His commandments in the Bible.

5 And in the **fifty and seventh year** [*35 years before the Savior's birth to Mary in Bethlehem*] **they did come down against the Nephites to battle, and they did commence the work**

of death [*they started killing the Nephites*]; yea, insomuch that [*so that*] in the **fifty and eighth year** of the reign of the judges [*34 BC*] **they succeeded in obtaining possession of the land of Zarahemla**; yea, and also all the lands, even unto the land which was near the land Bountiful.

6 And **the Nephites and the armies of Moronihah** [*Captain Moroni's son who is now the commander-in-chief of the Nephite armies*] **were driven even into the land of Bountiful**;

7 And **there they did fortify against the Lamanites**, from the west sea, even unto the east; it being a day's journey for a Nephite, on the line which they had fortified and stationed their armies to defend their north country.

8 And **thus those dissenters of the Nephites, with the help of a numerous** [*large*] **army of the Lamanites, had obtained all the possession of the Nephites which was in the land southward**. And all this was done in the fifty and eighth and ninth years of the reign of the judges.

9 And it came to pass in **the sixtieth year** of the reign of the judges, **Moronihah did succeed with his armies in obtaining many parts of the land; yea, they regained many cities** which had fallen into the hands of the Lamanites.

10 And it came to pass in the sixty and first year of the reign of the judges **they succeeded in regaining even the half of all their possessions**.

Next, Mormon points out to us how internal dishonesty and wickedness weaken a nation. This wickedness also includes wickedness among the members of the Church, whose lives should be strengthening the nation, rather than helping destroy it.

11 Now **this great loss of the Nephites**, and the great slaughter which was among them, **would not have happened had it not been for their wickedness and their abomination** [*extreme wickedness*] which was among them; yea, and **it was among those also who professed** [*claimed*] **to belong to the church of God**.

As you read Mormon's detailing of various forms of wickedness in verses 12–13, next, you may wish to see how many of these you can spot in society today. We would all be wise to make sure they are not in our own lives.

12 And it was because of the **pride of their hearts, because of their exceeding riches**, yea, it was because of **their oppression to the poor, withholding** [*keeping*] **their food from the hungry, withholding their clothing from the naked** [*those who did not have enough clothing*], and smiting their humble brethren upon the cheek [*ridiculing members who try to live the gospel*], **making a mock of that which was sacred, denying the spirit of prophecy and of revelation, murdering, plundering** [*robbing and destroying*], **lying, stealing, committing adultery, rising up in great contentions** [*fighting among themselves*], and **deserting away** [*apostatizing; in other words, leaving the true gospel and Church*] into the land

of Nephi, among the Lamanites [*including becoming like the world in our fashions, speech, priorities, etc.*]—

13 And because of this their **great wickedness**, and their **boastings in their own strength**, they were left in their own strength [*God withdrew His blessings from them*]; therefore **they did not prosper**, but were afflicted and smitten, and driven before the Lamanites, until they had lost possession of almost all their lands.

> Next, we see how the power of preaching the gospel helps bring those who were once active but have fallen away back into activity.

14 But behold, **Moronihah did preach** many things unto the people because of their iniquity, and also **Nephi and Lehi**, who were the sons of Helaman, **did preach** many things unto the people, yea, and did prophesy many things unto them concerning their iniquities [*their sin and wickedness*], and what should come unto them if they did not repent of their sins.

15 And it came to pass that **they did repent**, and **inasmuch as** [*when*] **they did repent they did begin to prosper** [*things started going well for them*].

16 For **when Moronihah saw that they did repent he did venture to lead them forth from place to place, and from city to city, even until they had regained the one-half of their property and the one-half of all their lands**.

17 And thus ended the **sixty and first year** of the reign of the judges.

18 And it came to pass in the **sixty and second year** of the reign of the judges [*30 BC*], that **Moronihah could obtain no more possessions over the Lamanites**.

19 **Therefore they did abandon** [*give up*] **their design** [*plans*] **to obtain the remainder of their lands**, for so numerous were the Lamanites that it became impossible for the Nephites to obtain more power over them; **therefore Moronihah did employ** [*use*] **all his armies in maintaining** [*keeping*] **those parts which he had taken**.

20 And it came to pass, because of the greatness of the number of the Lamanites **the Nephites were in great fear, lest** [*for fear that*] **they should be overpowered, and trodden down, and slain, and destroyed**.

> Next, Mormon will point out what had happened to the Nephite democracy, which had been founded upon the laws and commandments of God as King Mosiah II set it up in Mosiah, chapter 29. The constitution of the United States was also founded upon the laws of God (see D&C 101:77–80). We will briefly outline the steps in the downward spiral taken by the Nephite democracy, as detailed by Mormon in verses 21–25, next. You will no doubt see the same thing happening in our government today.
>
> **Step 1.** The majority of people in the nation become wicked (verse 21).
>
> **Step 2.** Wicked people cannot stand righteous laws; therefore, they get rid of the original laws of the nation, which were based on

righteous principles, and they change, by legislation or by court decisions and interpretations, to laws which allow their personal wickedness to continue, including being legal (verse 22).

Step 3. Corrupt laws corrupt people, because they no longer ask, "What does God say?" Rather, they ask, "Is it legal?"

Step 4. Some members of the Church begin to join the world in behaviors, thinking, fashions, language, etc., thinking all the time that because they belong to the Church, go to church on Sunday, pay tithing, etc., that they "are not as bad as the world." Thus, being just a bit behind the world, they don't realize that they are spiraling down at the same rate of speed as the rest of society (verses 23 and 24).

Step 5. The downward spiral continues in the nation until a nation which was once strong and God-fearing becomes corrupt and wicked like other nations (verses 24 and 25).

These steps are pointed out in **bold** in verses 21–25, next.

21 Yea, they began to remember the prophecies of Alma, and also the words of Mosiah; and they saw that they had been a stiffnecked people, and that **they had set at naught** [*ignored*] **the commandments of God**;

22 And that **they had altered** [*changed*] **and trampled under their feet the laws of Mosiah, or that which the Lord commanded him to give unto the people** [*they had changed and corrupted the "constitution" given them by their "founding fathers," especially King Mosiah II, in Mosiah 29*]; and they saw that **their laws had become corrupted**, and that **they had become a wicked people**, insomuch that **they were wicked even like unto the Lamanites** [*the unbelievers*].

23 And **because of their iniquity** [*wickedness*] **the church had begun to dwindle** [*gradually have less and less strong, faithful members*]; and **they began to disbelieve in the spirit of prophecy and in the spirit of revelation**; and the judgments of God [*punishments of God*] did stare them in the face.

24 And they saw that **they had become weak, like unto their brethren, the Lamanites**, and that **the Spirit of the Lord** did no more preserve them; yea, it **had withdrawn from them because the Spirit of the Lord doth not dwell in unholy temples** [*will not stay with us if we keep being wicked*]—

25 Therefore **the Lord did cease to preserve them** by his miraculous and matchless power, for **they had fallen into a state of unbelief and awful wickedness**; and they saw that the Lamanites were exceedingly more numerous than they, and except [*unless*] they should cleave unto the Lord their God [*hold onto the Lord and His gospel tightly*] they must unavoidably perish.

We have seen many examples of how the Lord protects His people, even when they are badly outnumbered by enemies. However, as Mormon points out next, when

God's people forget the gospel and no longer apply it in their lives, they no longer have His protection and become as other nations.

26 For behold, they saw that **the strength of the Lamanites was as great as their strength**, even man for man. **And thus had they fallen into this great transgression**; yea, **thus had they become weak, because of their transgression**, in the space of not many years [*in a short time*].

HELAMAN 5

You have probably heard the term "born again." It is used many times in the scriptures and means becoming a new, more righteous person through repentance and baptism. After baptism, we receive the gift of the Holy Ghost, which helps us throughout our lives to keep being born again. In other words, the Holy Ghost inspires and directs us to keep improving by repenting and becoming better and better at living the gospel. And so, in a very important and real way, on a daily basis, we are born again and again as we come closer to Christ.

In Alma, chapter 5, Alma taught us how to be "born of God" and how to receive "his image in [*our*] countenances," which is part of progressing toward celestial exaltation in the kingdom of God. One of the things he taught us in Alma 5:6 is the importance of remembering past blessings from the Lord. "Remembering" is an important part of living the gospel successfully and thus being constantly "born again."

Chapter 5, next, could well be called "the remember chapter." It has the word "remembered" once and "remember" at least fourteen times as Mormon shares with us the counsel given by Helaman to his sons Nephi and Lehi.

In this chapter, we will see great success in bringing inactive members back into activity in the Church who had fallen away. There will also be thousands of converts who join the Church. Nephi and Lehi will be miraculously protected from wicked men and more conversions will result. One of the major messages is the fact that the Lord does not give up easily in His merciful attempts to bring His wayward children back to being faithful members of His church.

As we begin the chapter, Nephi will do as his great-grandfather Alma the Younger did (Alma 4:18–20), namely, give up the office of chief judge or president of the Nephite nation in order to spend his full time and energy to preaching the gospel.

1 AND it came to pass that in this same year, behold, **Nephi delivered up** [*gave*] **the judgment-seat to a man whose name was Cezoram**.

Next, we see that the situation among the Nephites had become much worse to a very dangerous point. As mentioned in chapter 4, wicked people cannot stand righteous laws, so the national laws of the Nephites had been changed by the majority, who chose to abandon God's laws.

2 For as their laws and their governments were established by the voice

of the people [*by the voters in elections*], and **they who chose evil were more numerous than they who chose good,** therefore they were **ripening** [*getting ready*] **for destruction**, for **the laws had become corrupted** [*changed in a bad way*].

3 Yea, and **this was not all**; they were a stiffnecked [*stubborn, wicked*] people, insomuch that **they could not be governed by the law nor justice**, save it were to their destruction.

> The conditions described at the end of verse 3, above, would lead a nation to have to build more and more prisons, which still would not solve the problem.

4 And it came to pass that **Nephi had become weary because of their iniquity** [*wickedness*]**; and he yielded up** [*gave up*] **the judgment-seat, and took it upon him to preach the word of God** [*the gospel*] **all the remainder of his days, and his brother Lehi also**, all the remainder of his days;

> Remember, as we said before, that the words "remembered" and "remember" appear at least fifteen times in this chapter. They are in **bold and underlined** so you can pick them out.

5 For they **remembered** the words which their father Helaman spake [*spoke*] unto them. And these are the words which he spake:

> Next, Helaman is quoted as he explains why he gave his sons the names "Nephi" and "Lehi."

6 Behold, my sons, I desire that ye should **remember** to keep the commandments of God; and I would that ye should declare unto the people these words. Behold, **I have given unto you the names of our first parents** [*our first ancestors, Lehi and Nephi*] who came out of the land of Jerusalem; and this I have done **that when you remember your names ye may remember them; and when ye remember them ye may remember their works** [*the good things they did*]; and when ye **remember** their works ye may know how that it is said, and also written, **that they were good**.

7 **Therefore**, my sons, **I would that ye should do that which is good, that it may be said of you, and also written, even as it has been said and written of them**.

8 And now my sons, behold I [*Helaman*] have somewhat more to desire of you, which desire is, that ye may not do these things that ye may boast, but that ye may **do these things to lay up for yourselves a treasure in heaven, yea, which is eternal** [*will last forever*], and which fadeth not away; yea, **that ye may have that precious gift of eternal life**, which we have reason to suppose hath been given to our fathers [*Lehi and Nephi*].

> As used in the scriptures, the term "eternal life" (verse 8, above) always means exaltation in the highest degree of glory in the celestial kingdom. Or, in other words, becoming gods and living in a family unit forever.

9 O **remember**, **remember**, my sons, the words which king Benjamin spake unto his people [*in Mosiah, chapters 2 through 5*]; yea, **remember** that **there is no other way nor means whereby man can be saved, only** [*except*] **through the atoning blood of Jesus Christ**, who shall come; yea, **remember** that he cometh to redeem the world.

In verse 10, next, we are once again reminded that we cannot be saved "in" our sins, rather, "from" our sins. As you no doubt are noticing, many Christian churches in our day are "changing the rules" so that people can be saved in their sins rather than requiring them to keep the laws of God as given in the Bible. It doesn't work. God makes the rules.

10 And **remember** also the words which Amulek spake unto Zeezrom, in the city of Ammonihah [*Alma 11:34–37*]; for he said unto him that **the Lord surely should come to redeem his people**, but that **he should not** [*would not*] **come to redeem them in their sins, but to redeem them from their sins**.

11 And he [*Christ*] hath power given unto him from the Father to redeem them **from** their sins **because of repentance**; therefore he hath sent his angels to declare [*teach and explain*] the tidings [*news*] of the conditions of repentance [*the requirements of repentance*], which bringeth unto [*which brings people to*] the power of the Redeemer, unto the salvation of their souls.

Next, Helaman uses powerful imagery to describe the spiritual safety that comes to us when we build our lives upon the sure foundation of Christ and His gospel. When we do, we are absolutely guaranteed that Satan will never be able to take us away from God and salvation. Remember, we are not promised that there will not be strong temptations. That is part of our schooling here on the earth. Rather, we are promised that if we "bind" ourselves (D&C 43:9) to Christ, by making and keeping covenants, and by constantly studying His words, Satan cannot succeed against us.

12 And now, my sons, **remember**, **remember** that **it is upon the rock of our Redeemer**, who is Christ, the Son of God, **that ye must build** your foundation; **that when** [*not "if" but "when"*] **the devil shall send forth his mighty winds** [*temptations*], **yea, his shafts in the whirlwind, yea, when all his hail and his mighty storm shall beat upon you, it shall have no power over you to drag you down to the gulf of misery** [*hell*] **and endless wo**, because of the rock upon which ye are built, which is a sure foundation, **a foundation whereon if men build they cannot fall**.

13 And it came to pass that **these were the words which Helaman taught to his sons**; yea, he did teach them many things which are not written, and also many things which are written.

14 And **they did remember his words**; and therefore **they went forth, keeping the commandments of God, to teach the word of God**

among all the people of Nephi, beginning at the city Bountiful;

Mormon will now show us how powerful the pure gospel of Christ can be when preached effectively.

15 And from thenceforth **to the city of Gid; and** from the city of Gid to the city of **Mulek**;

16 And even **from one city to another**, until they had gone forth **among all the people of Nephi** who were in the land southward; **and from thence** [*there*] into the land of Zarahemla, **among the Lamanites**.

In verse 17, next, we are given a brief course on how people can repent and return to activity and commitment in the true Church of Jesus Christ.

17 And it came to pass that **they did preach with great power**, insomuch that [*so that*] they did confound [*straighten out the false thinking of*] many of those dissenters [*people who had left the Church*] who had gone over [*to the Lamanites; see Helaman 4:4*] from the Nephites, insomuch that **they came forth and did confess their sins and were baptized unto repentance**, and immediately returned to the Nephites to endeavor [*try*] to **repair unto them the wrongs which they had done.**

This is the "law of restitution," which is an important part of true repentance. In other words, where possible you must repair and fix the wrongs you have done.

Next, Nephi and Lehi preach among Lamanites who live in and around the land of Zarahemla. Mormon emphasizes the necessity of being inspired by the Holy Ghost while preaching.

18 And it came to pass that **Nephi and Lehi did preach unto the Lamanites with** such **great power and authority**, for they had power and authority given unto them that they might speak, and **they also had what they should speak given unto them—**

19 **Therefore they did speak unto the great astonishment** [*surprise*] **of the Lamanites, to the convincing them**, insomuch that there were **eight thousand of the Lamanites** who **were** in the land of Zarahemla and round about **baptized** unto repentance, and were **convinced of the wickedness of the traditions of their fathers.**

The last lines of verse 19, above, are an amazing miracle. Righteous traditions can be a powerful influence for good, whereas wicked traditions can often hold an entire family or ethnic group down for generations.

Next, Nephi and Lehi will go among the Lamanites in the land of Nephi to preach. They will end up in the same prison that Limhi put Ammon and his companions in when they came from Zarahemla to see if any Nephites had survived among the Lamanites. (See Mosiah 7:6–7. This refers to the first Ammon in the Book of Mormon, not the missionary Ammon who was one of the four sons of King Mosiah.)

One of the things we will be taught in the next verses is that there are often many of the "noble and great ones," in other words, the great, righteous spirits from premortality (Abraham 3:22) among the wicked who have not yet been taught the gospel in circumstances that they can truly understand and accept it. Once they feel the Spirit and understand what is going on, they are converted, and their premortal goodness and righteousness quickly take over. This is certainly one of the reasons that the Lord on, occasion, has the leaders of the Church cautiously and carefully send missionaries into seemingly dangerous settings to preach.

20 And it came to pass that **Nephi and Lehi did proceed from thence** [*there*] **to go to the land of Nephi**.

21 And it came to pass that **they were taken** by an army of the Lamanites **and cast into prison**; yea, even in **that same prison in which Ammon and his brethren were cast by the servants of Limhi**.

22 And **after they had been cast into prison many days without food, behold, they went forth into the prison to take them that they might slay** [*kill*] **them**.

The following is one of the more famous accounts from the Book of Mormon. It is a tender story of complete dedication in the face of death. It appears that Nephi and Lehi did not expect to be saved from being executed. It was not until they saw that they were surrounded by fire (verse 24) that they began to hope that they might not die.

23 And it came to pass that **Nephi and Lehi were encircled about as if by fire**, even insomuch that they [*the Lamanites*] durst not [*did not dare*] lay their hands upon them for fear lest they should be burned. Nevertheless, **Nephi and Lehi were not burned**; and they were as standing in the midst of fire and were not burned.

24 And **when they** [*Nephi and Lehi*] **saw that they were encircled about with a pillar of fire, and that it burned them not, their hearts did take courage**.

25 For **they saw that the Lamanites durst not lay their hands upon them**; neither durst they come near unto them, but stood as if they were struck dumb with amazement.

What happens in verse 26, next, shows the depth of character and Christlike goodness deep in the souls of Nephi and Lehi. Whereas lesser men would take satisfaction in the fear upon the faces of these Lamanites who came to kill them, Nephi and Lehi immediately seek to calm their fears and explain what is happening.

26 And it came to pass that **Nephi and Lehi** did stand forth and **began to speak** unto them, **saying: Fear not**, for behold, it is God that has shown unto you this marvelous thing, in the which is shown unto you that ye cannot lay your hands on us to slay us.

27 And behold, when they had said these words, **the earth shook** exceedingly, and **the walls of the prison did shake** as if they were about to tumble to the earth; **but behold,**

they did not fall. And behold, they that were in the prison were Lamanites and Nephites who were dissenters [*apostate Nephites who had left the teachings of the gospel*].

These Nephites had rejected the gospel many years earlier when Alma, Amulek, Zeezrom, and others had taught them the gospel (see Alma 31 and Helaman 5:41). What is happening here is another reminder that the Lord does not easily give up on trying to help people use their agency to return to Him. Rather, He keeps trying, over and over again. Perhaps you have friends or loved-ones who are inactive in the Church and you are glad that the Lord has not given up on them.

28 And it came to pass that **they were overshadowed with a cloud of darkness**, and an **awful solemn fear came upon them**.

Perhaps you have noticed that things often come in threes in the scriptures. Perhaps something does not work on the first attempt, nor on the second, but does on the third. The number three often has symbolic meaning in the cultures of ancient scripture. In one aspect of numerical symbolism, three represents "God" or "Godhead." It may be that this is the reason that the voice, which these soon-to-be converts hear in the next verses, comes three times.

As we read about it, we will be given a somewhat detailed description of the voice of the Lord.

29 And it came to pass that **there came a voice** as if it were above the cloud of darkness, **saying: Repent ye, repent ye, and seek no more to destroy my servants whom I have sent unto you to declare good tidings**.

30 And it came to pass when they heard this voice, and beheld that **it was not a voice of thunder, neither was it a voice of a great tumultuous noise**, but behold, it was **a still voice of perfect mildness**, as if it had been **a whisper, and it did pierce even to the very soul**—

As we continue, we see how the elements themselves (Moses 6:63) bear witness of the Lord to these people who were about to execute Nephi and Lehi.

31 And notwithstanding the mildness of the voice, behold **the earth shook exceedingly**, and **the walls of the prison trembled again**, as if it were about to tumble to the earth; and behold **the cloud of darkness, which had overshadowed them, did not disperse** [*go away*]—

32 And behold **the voice came again, saying: Repent ye, repent ye, for the kingdom of heaven is at hand** [*your chance to repent and live the gospel is here*]; and **seek no more to destroy my servants**. And it came to pass that **the earth shook again, and the walls trembled**.

33 And also again **the third time the voice came, and did speak unto them marvelous words** which cannot be uttered [*spoken out loud*] by man; and **the walls did tremble again**, and **the earth shook** as if it were about to divide asunder [*tear apart*].

34 And it came to pass that **the Lamanites could not flee** [*run away*] **because of the cloud of darkness** which did overshadow them [*perhaps symbolic of the extreme spiritual darkness in which they were living*]; yea, and **also they were immovable because of the fear** which did come upon them [*perhaps symbolic of the fear which would come upon them at the day of judgment if they did not repent of their wickedness*].

Again, in the next verses, we are reminded of the kindness and mercy of the Lord as He continues to reach out to His children who have gone astray and left the Church. In this case, a man by the name of Aminadab (verse 39), who had left the Church, is allowed to see Nephi and Lehi in their true role as messengers from God. He is thus enabled to understand what is happening and counsels these frightened people (verse 41) as to what they need to do to get the darkness to leave.

35 Now there was **one among them** who was a **Nephite by birth**, who **had once belonged to the church of God** but had dissented [*apostatized; left the Church*] from them.

36 And it came to pass that he turned him about, and behold, **he saw through the cloud of darkness the faces of Nephi and Lehi**; and behold, **they did shine** exceedingly, even **as the faces of angels**. And he beheld [*saw*] that **they did lift their eyes to heaven**; and they were in the attitude **as if talking or lifting their voices to some being whom they beheld**.

37 And it came to pass that **this man did cry** [*shout*] **unto the multitude, that they might turn and look**. And behold, there was **power given unto them** [*perhaps symbolic of the power the Atonement gives us to turn from darkness toward the light of the gospel*] that **they did turn and look**; and they did behold [*see*] the faces of Nephi and Lehi.

38 And **they said unto the man: Behold, what do all these things mean**, and who is it with whom these men do converse [*speak*]?

39 Now **the man's name was Aminadab**. And Aminadab said unto them: **They do converse with the angels of God**.

Next, these people ask the "right" question. Note the gospel symbolism in their question and in the answer they are given.

40 And it came to pass that **the Lamanites said** unto him: **What shall we do, that this cloud of darkness may be removed from overshadowing us?**

41 And **Aminadab said** unto them: **You must repent, and cry unto the voice** [*pray to God*], **even until ye shall have faith in Christ**, who was taught unto you by Alma, and Amulek, and Zeezrom; and **when ye shall do this, the cloud of darkness shall be removed from overshadowing you**.

42 And it came to pass that **they all did begin to cry unto the voice of him who had shaken the earth;**

yea, they did cry even until the cloud of darkness was dispersed.

43 And it came to pass that **when they** cast their eyes about [*when they looked around*], and **saw that the cloud of darkness was dispersed** [*went away*] **from overshadowing them** [*the result of praying and faith in Christ*], behold, they saw that **they were encircled about** [*surrounded*]**, yea every soul, by a pillar of fire.**

Fire is often used symbolically in the scriptures to mean the Holy Ghost and the testimony of the Father and Son which comes to us from Him.

44 And **Nephi and Lehi** were in the midst of them; yea, they **were encircled about; yea, they were as if in the midst of a flaming fire, yet it did harm them not**, neither did it take hold upon [*burn*] the walls of the prison; and **they were filled with that joy** [*the result of repenting and turning to Christ*] **which is unspeakable** [*cannot be described in words*] **and full of glory.**

45 And behold, **the Holy Spirit of God did come down from heaven**, and did **enter into their hearts** [*the center of feeling*], and they were **filled as if with fire** [*filled with the Holy Ghost*], and **they could speak forth marvelous words.**

Next, these humbled people hear the kind and pleasant voice of Heavenly Father.

46 And it came to pass that **there came a voice** unto them, yea, a **pleasant** voice, **as if it were a whisper**, saying:

47 **Peace, peace be unto you, because of your faith in my Well Beloved** [*Christ*], **who was from the foundation of the world** [*who was chosen in premortality to be your Redeemer*].

48 And now, **when they heard this they cast up their eyes** as if to behold from whence [*where*] the voice came; and behold, **they saw the heavens open; and angels came down out of heaven and ministered unto them.**

49 And **there were about three hundred souls** [*people*] **who saw and heard these things**; and they were bidden [*requested*] to go forth [*leave the prison*] and marvel not [*don't second-guess this*], neither should they doubt.

Next, we see a great conversion among the Lamanites. Notice the things they give up in order to truly accept the gospel and start living it.

50 And it came to pass that **they did go forth, and did minister unto the people**, declaring throughout all the regions round about all the things which they had heard and seen, insomuch that **the more part of the Lamanites were convinced of them, because of the greatness of the evidences which they had received.**

51 And **as many as were convinced did lay down their weapons of war**, and also **their hatred** and **the tradition of their fathers** [*the false traditions and customs of their people which would stand in the way of living the gospel*].

52 And it came to pass that **they did yield up** [*give back*] **unto the Nephites the lands of their possession.**

They gave the Nephites back the land the Lamanites had taken from them as a result of wars; this is the law of "restitution" in action.

HELAMAN 6

Before this chapter is over, we will see a rather complete switch between the Lamanites and the Nephites. The Lamanites will become righteous and wise. The Nephites will become wicked and foolish.

To begin with, the Lamanites will preach the gospel to the Nephites, and many will be converted. There will be a time of wonderful peace and prosperity for both the Nephites and the Lamanites. But then there will be political assassinations—in other words, killings and murders—the Gadianton robbers will gain strength and power, many people will apostatize from the Church, and the majority of the Nephites will join the Gadianton robbers.

At this point, the Lamanites will repent and remove the Gadianton robbers from among them, whereas the Nephites will support these robbers and vote them into political offices until the entire Nephite government is under their wicked and corrupt control.

Mormon will take time in this chapter to point out the history of some of Satan's temptations in times past, including with Cain and with the Tower of Babel. He will teach us and warn us against the cunning, tricky, and sly methods of the devil as he shows how Lucifer (another name for Satan) puts his plots and plans into the hearts of people.

One major message in this chapter that we all need to pay close attention to is to avoid personal wickedness, which blinds us to Satan's ways. Righteous people see them clearly. Wicked people adopt them and consider the righteous to be foolish and blind.

1 AND it came to pass that when the **sixty and second year** of the reign of the judges had ended [*29 BC, in other words, 29 years before the coming birth of Christ to Mary in Bethlehem*], all these things had happened and **the Lamanites had become, the more part** [*the majority*] **of them, a righteous people**, insomuch that **their righteousness did exceed** [*was more than*] **that of the Nephites**, because of their firmness and their steadiness in the faith [*the gospel*].

2 For behold, there were **many of the Nephites who had become hardened** [*insensitive to spiritual things*] **and impenitent** [*unrepentant*] **and grossly** [*very*] **wicked**, insomuch that **they did reject the word of God and all the preaching and prophesying which did come among them**.

Next, Mormon points out that faithful members of the Church can still have joy and happiness during such times.

3 Nevertheless [*in spite of the wickedness going on among the majority of people*], **the people of the church did have great joy** because of the conversion of the Lamanites, yea, because of the church of God, which had been established among them. And **they did fellowship one with another, and**

did rejoice one with another, and did have great joy.

4 And it came to pass that **many of the Lamanites** did come down into the land of Zarahemla [*where the majority of the Nephites lived*], and **did declare unto the people of the Nephites the manner of their conversion, and did exhort** [*teach and counsel*] **them to faith and repentance.**

These Lamanite missionaries had great success among the Nephites.

5 Yea, and **many did preach with exceedingly great power and authority**, unto the bringing down many of them [*the Nephites*] into the depths of humility, to be the humble followers of God and the Lamb.

Nephi and Lehi, the sons of Helaman, are also involved in this great preaching effort.

6 And it came to pass that many of the Lamanites did go into the land northward; and **also Nephi and Lehi went into the land northward, to preach unto the people.** And thus ended the **sixty and third year.**

One thing the Lord has Mormon do over and over again throughout the Book of Mormon is to remind us of the contrast between a society in which high standards of righteousness exist and societies in which wickedness prevails. We see this lesson again in the next several verses. First, he points out the benefits of a righteous society.

7 And behold, **there was peace in all the land**, insomuch that **the Nephites did go into whatsoever part of the land they would** [*wherever they wanted to go*], whether among the Nephites or the Lamanites.

8 And it came to pass that **the Lamanites did also go whithersoever** [*wherever*] **they would** [*wanted to*], whether it were among the Lamanites or among the Nephites; and thus they did have free intercourse [*associations, friendships; business transactions, etc.*] one with another, to buy and to sell, and to get gain [*make a living*], according to their desire.

9 And it came to pass that **they became exceedingly rich**, both the Lamanites and the Nephites; and they did have an exceeding **plenty of gold**, and of **silver**, and of all manner of **precious metals**, both in the land south and in the land north.

Next, Mormon adds a note about geography in the Book of Mormon and gives a bit of history about Mulek to go along with it.

By way of quick review, Mulek was one of the sons of wicked King Zedekiah, who was the King of Judah (1 Nephi 1:4) at the time Lehi and his family left Jerusalem in 600 BC. Zedekiah refused to listen to the prophets, especially Jeremiah (see Jeremiah, chapter 38). We know from Jeremiah, chapter 39, that Nebuchadnezzar, King of Babylon, attacked Jerusalem and captured Zedekiah as he was trying to escape. Zedekiah was forced to watch as his sons were killed (Jeremiah 39:6), but they obviously missed his son, Mulek. Mulek and others were brought by the Lord to the Americas, where they settled north of where Lehi and his people settled.

10 Now **the land south was called Lehi and the land north was called Mulek**, which was **after the son of Zedekiah**; for **the Lord did bring Mulek into the land north, and Lehi into the land south**.

11 And behold, there was **all manner of gold in both these lands**, and of **silver**, and of **precious ore of every kind**; and there were also curious workmen [*skilled craftsmen, workers*], who did work all kinds of ore and did refine it; and thus they did become rich.

12 **They did raise grain in abundance** [*much grain*], both in the north and in the south; and they did **flourish exceedingly** [*do very well*], both in the north and in the south. And they did multiply and wax [*grow*] exceedingly strong in the land. And they did **raise many flocks** and **herds**, yea, many **fatlings** [*young, healthy animals*].

13 Behold **their women did toil and spin, and did make all manner of** [*all kinds of*] **cloth**, of fine-twined **linen** and cloth of every kind, to clothe their nakedness. And thus the **sixty and fourth year** did pass away in **peace**.

14 And in the sixty and fifth year [*27 BC*] they did also have **great joy** and **peace**, yea, **much preaching** and **many prophecies** concerning that which was to come. And thus passed away the **sixty and fifth year**.

Next, we see the beginning of a sad transition back toward wickedness. First, we see political assassinations, in other words, killings in which some citizens who did not like some of the government rulers began killing them.

15 And it came to pass that in the **sixty and sixth year** of the reign of the judges [*which began sixty-six years earlier when the Nephite government switched from a kingdom to a democracy under King Mosiah II; see Mosiah, chapter 29*], behold, **Cezoram** [*the chief judge or "president" of the democracy*] **was murdered** by an unknown hand as he sat upon the judgment-seat. And it came to pass that in the same year, that **his son**, who had been appointed by the people in his stead [*to replace him as chief judge*], **was also murdered**. And thus ended the sixty and sixth year.

16 And in the commencement of the sixty and seventh year **the people began to grow exceedingly wicked again**.

Perhaps you've noticed what is often referred to as the "Cycle of Apostasy" in the Book of Mormon. We have seen it many times already and will yet see it many more times. Briefly, it is as follows: Almost every time the people become humble and repent, they prosper. Things start going well for them. As they prosper, they become rich. After a time with wealth, they get prideful. Pride leads to wickedness. Wickedness leads to destruction. Destruction leads to poverty and humility. Humility leads to repenting and keeping God's commandments, which leads to prosperity. And around the cycle they go again and again.

Perhaps one of our major challenges, as a people and as individuals, is to avoid the cycle of apostasy. It can be done. People who remain humble and faithful despite prosperity are able to avoid going through the cycle repeatedly. They seem to be able to follow the counsel of the Lord found in Jacob 2:16–19 as follows:

Jacob 2:16–19

16 O that he would rid you from this iniquity and abomination. And, O that ye would listen unto the word of his commands, and **let not this pride of your hearts destroy your souls!**

17 **Think of your brethren like unto yourselves**, and be familiar [*friendly and kind*] with all and free with your substance [*be generous*], that they may be rich like unto you.

18 But **before ye seek for riches, seek ye for the kingdom of God** [*keep your priorities straight*].

19 And after ye have obtained a hope in Christ ye shall obtain riches, **if ye seek them**; and **ye will seek them for the intent to do good—to clothe the naked, and to feed the hungry, and to liberate the captive, and administer relief to the sick and the afflicted**.

We will now continue with Helaman, chapter 6, as Mormon explains how wealth can become a problem to the spirituality of people. We will see the search for wealth become the master rather than the servant.

17 For behold, the Lord had blessed them so long with the riches of the world that they had not been stirred up to anger, to wars, nor to bloodshed; therefore **they began to set their hearts upon their riches** [*getting money and wealth became the thing they wanted most, their main goal in life*]; yea, **they began to seek to get gain that they might be lifted up one above another** [*they wanted wealth so that they could appear better than others*]; therefore **they began to commit secret murders, and to rob and to plunder, that they might get gain** [*wealth and money*].

Next, we see rapid growth of Gadianton's band, commonly called the Gadianton robbers.

18 And now behold, **those murderers and plunderers were a band who had been formed by Kishkumen and Gadianton**. And now it had come to pass that **there were many**, even **among the Nephites, of Gadianton's band**. But behold, they were **more numerous among the more wicked part of the Lamanites**. And **they were called Gadianton's robbers and murderers.**

19 And **it was they who did murder the chief judge Cezoram, and his son**, while in the judgment-seat; and behold, they were not found.

The Lamanites were wise enough to see the dangers of the Gadianton robbers and to find ways to stop their growth among them.

20 And now it came to pass that **when the Lamanites found that there were robbers among them**

they were exceedingly sorrowful; and **they did use every means in their power to destroy them off the face of the earth.**

Perhaps you have been disturbed by some of the trends you have observed in politics today. In many cases, the same thing is happening today as happened among the Nephites of this period. Rather than voting corrupt and immoral people out of political office, these Nephites intentionally voted them in. Since they, themselves, had chosen wickedness and corruption in their personal lives, they wanted government officials in office who had the same values and morals as they did. That made them more comfortable in their own wickedness.

Mormon will give us a clear and important lesson about this matter in the next several verses. Among other things, you will see that Satan is "the great counterfeiter." (A "counterfeiter" is someone who makes fake copies of the real thing, like counterfeit money. Or, one who pretends to be someone else, or pretends to be teaching truth when it is not.) In other words, Satan has counterfeit covenants, oaths, signs, words, etc., which make an evil mockery of the covenants, oaths, signs, etc., that rightfully belong to the gospel of Christ.

21 But behold, Satan did stir up the hearts of **the more part** [*majority*] **of the Nephites**, insomuch that they **did unite with those bands of robbers** [*the Gadianton robbers*], **and did enter into their covenants** and their **oaths**, that they would protect and preserve one another in whatsoever difficult circumstances they should be placed, that they should not suffer [*would not be punished; a great deception sponsored by Satan*] for their murders, and their plunderings, and their stealings.

22 And it came to pass that **they did have their signs**, yea, their **secret signs**, and their **secret words**; and this **that they might distinguish** [*be able to recognize*] **a brother who had entered into the covenant**, that whatsoever wickedness his brother should do he should not be injured by his brother, nor by those who did belong to his band, who had taken this covenant.

23 And **thus they might murder, and plunder** [*destroy other peoples' peace, security, livelihood, etc.], and steal, and commit whoredoms [sexual immorality*] and **all manner of wickedness, contrary to** [*against*] **the laws of their country and also the laws of their God.**

24 And **whosoever of those who belonged to their band** [*the Gadianton robbers*] **should reveal unto the world of their wickedness and their abominations** [*who told people who were not part of their secret group*]**, should be tried** [*brought to trial*], not according to the laws of their country, but **according to the laws of their wickedness,** which had been given by Gadianton and Kishkumen.

25 Now behold, **it is these secret oaths and covenants which Alma commanded his son should not go forth unto the world,** lest they

should be a means of bringing down the people unto destruction.

Next, Mormon points out the source of these counterfeits which Gadianton had started secretly spreading among the people. In so doing, he will warn us against the devil's ways.

26 Now behold, those secret oaths and covenants did not come forth unto Gadianton from the records which were delivered unto Helaman; but behold, **they were put into the heart of Gadianton by that same being** [*Satan*] **who did entice** [*tempt*] **our first parents** [*Adam and Eve*] **to partake of the forbidden fruit**—

Just a quick note to remind you that the fall of Adam and Eve (our "first parents") was good. They "fell forward" so to speak. It had to be, and they had to have ownership of what happened to them. So it is with us in our choices. We must have significant choices, or our agency would be meaningless. Agency provides ownership of consequences. Ownership provides good reason to progress and grow and develop.

Satan's motive was to destroy the work and plan of God by tempting Adam and Eve to partake of the forbidden fruit; but, of course, he did not succeed. It was all part of God's plan. There was no "plan B," in case Adam and Eve did not partake (see 2 Nephi 2:24). Brigham Young explains this as follows:

"The Lord knew they would do this, and he had designed that they should" (*Discourses of Brigham Young*, Deseret Book, 1977, 103. See also *Institute of Religion Student Manual, Religion 430–431*, 2000 edition, 21).

We will now continue with Mormon's warnings and explanations regarding Satan.

27 **Yea, that same being** [*Satan*] **who did plot with Cain**, that if he would murder his brother Abel it should not be known unto the world [*the beginning of secret combinations*]. And **he did plot with Cain and his followers from that time forth**.

Next, the Book of Mormon supports the Bible in its account of the Tower of Babel. There are some important messages here for us; perhaps side issues, but nevertheless important ones. For instance, there is no other way to "get to heaven" other than through the gospel and Atonement of Christ. These people were convinced by Satan that they could get to heaven on their own, if they could build a tower high enough. Another message is simply how foolish and blind people can get when they allow themselves to be sufficiently deceived by the devil. To put so much time and effort into wicked pursuits and projects defies wisdom, common sense, and rational thinking.

28 And also it is **that same being** [*the devil*] who **put it into the hearts of the people to build a tower sufficiently high that they might get to heaven**. And it was that same being who led on the people who came from that tower into this land; who **spread the works of darkness and abominations** [*terrible wickedness*] **over all the face of the land**, until he dragged the people [*the Jaredites*] down to an entire destruction, and to an everlasting hell.

29 Yea, it is **that same being** [*the devil*] who **put it into the heart of Gadianton to still carry on the work of darkness, and of secret murder**; and he has brought it forth from the beginning of man even down to this time.

Next, Mormon summarizes who Satan is and what his plans are.

30 And behold, **it is he** [*Satan*] **who is the author** [*the origin*] **of all sin**. And behold, **he doth carry on his works of darkness and secret murder, and doth hand down their plots, and their oaths, and their covenants, and their plans of awful wickedness, from generation to generation according as he can get hold upon the hearts of the children of men**.

Having given us a vital lesson and warning about Satan, Mormon now applies that lesson to the Nephites. The word "hearts," as used next in verse 31, means the "center of feelings and desires." In other words, these Nephites wanted to be evil. They enjoyed wickedness and desired it.

31 And now behold, he [*Satan*] had got great hold upon the **hearts** of the Nephites; yea, insomuch that [*so that*] **they had become exceedingly wicked**; yea, the more part [*majority*] of them **had turned out of the way of righteousness, and did trample under their feet the commandments of God**, and **did turn unto their own ways** [*they made their own rules*], and did build up unto themselves idols of their gold and their silver [*they created and gathered things that replaced God in their lives*].

Mormon expresses concern that it did not take very long for the people to go from peace and righteousness (verses 7–14) back to wickedness.

32 And it came to pass that **all these iniquities** [*evils and wickednesses*] **did come unto them in the space of not many years**, insomuch that a more part of it had come unto them in the **sixty and seventh year** of the reign of the judges over the people of Nephi.

33 And **they did grow in their iniquities** [*became more and more wicked*] in the **sixty and eighth** year also, to the great sorrow and lamentation [*mourning*] of the righteous.

Next, we see some "thus we sees," which alert us that Mormon is now summarizing what he hopes we will learn from what he has shown us in this chapter.

34 And **thus we see** that the Nephites did begin to dwindle [*fall away*] in unbelief, and grow in wickedness and abominations, while the Lamanites began to grow exceedingly in the knowledge of their God; yea, they did begin to keep his statutes [*laws*] and commandments, and to walk in truth and uprightness before him.

35 And **thus we see** that the Spirit of the Lord began to withdraw from the Nephites, because of the wickedness and the hardness of their hearts.

36 And **thus we see** that the Lord began to pour out his Spirit upon the

Lamanites, because of their easiness and willingness to believe in his words.

Next, we see the Lamanites wisely and properly work to eliminate the main source of evil and wickedness among their people. Note that preaching "the word of God" is a very effective "weapon" in this war.

37 And it came to pass that **the Lamanites did hunt the band of robbers of Gadianton**; and they **did preach the word of God among the more wicked part of them**, insomuch [*with the result*] that this band of robbers was utterly destroyed from among the Lamanites.

As stated previously, personally wicked people cannot stand righteous laws and leaders in government. Therefore, they vote them out of office and replace them with leaders whose lives reflect the same sin and "anything goes" mentality of the majority of voters. Laws are then made that make personal wickedness "legal." Many citizens no longer ask, "What do the scriptures say?" Or "What does God say?" Rather, they say, "Is it legal?" Thus, corrupt laws corrupt people further. It is a downward spiral. These Nephites plunge headlong into it.

38 And it came to pass on the other hand, that **the Nephites did build them up** [*the teachings and values of the Gadianton robbers*] **and support them**, beginning at the more wicked part of them, until they had overspread all the land of the Nephites, and had seduced [*deceived; caused to commit sin*] the more part of the righteous **until they had come down to believe in their works** and partake of their spoils, and to join with them in their secret murders and combinations.

As pointed out by Mormon in verse 38, above, one of Satan's clear goals is to get people to truly believe that there is nothing wrong with sin and wickedness.

39 And **thus they** [*the wicked*] **did obtain the sole management of the government** [*the wicked were in complete control of the Nephite government*], insomuch that **they did trample under their feet and smite and rend and turn their backs upon the poor and the meek, and the humble followers of God**.

40 And **thus we see** that they were in an awful state [*condition*], and ripening for [*getting ready for*] an everlasting destruction.

41 And it came to pass that **thus ended the sixty and eighth year** of the reign of the judges over the people of Nephi.

HELAMAN 7

As you can see, things are getting really bad now, with secret combinations, in other words, very wicked groups of people called Gadianton robbers, taking over in many parts of the country.

Meanwhile, about five to six years earlier, in the sixty-third year of the reign of the judges, Nephi and his brother Lehi went north to preach to the people there (Helaman 6:6). Having had so much success on previous missions, they must have looked forward with great anticipation to the sweet privilege of bringing many more people unto Christ. Such was not to be the case.

The people in the north rejected the gospel and, after about six years of unsuccessful effort, Nephi came back home to the land of Zarahemla, thoroughly discouraged (verse 3). Not only had he been rejected in the north, but while he was gone, the Gadianton robbers had taken over the government of his land. No wonder he was discouraged! Perhaps there is an important message for us in this, namely that righteous people can become discouraged too.

Nephi wants some peace and privacy and time to meditate and pray and seek inspiration and comfort from God. But, as you will see in this chapter, rude and insensitive people will violate Nephi's privacy and gossip about him. Consequently, we will also see that there is a time and place for everything, including straight talk to wicked people.

1 BEHOLD, now it came to pass in the **sixty and ninth year** of the reign of the judges over the people of the Nephites, that **Nephi**, the son of Helaman, **returned to the land of Zarahemla from the land northward**.

2 For **he had been forth among the people who were in the land northward and did preach the word of God unto them**, and did prophesy many things unto them;

3 And **they did reject all his words**, insomuch that he could not stay among them, but returned again unto the land of his nativity [*the land of his birth*].

There are many parallels between what happened to the Nephite government and what is happening to many governments around the world today. The warnings for us, in the next few verses, are clear. They help us be wise as far as what needs to be with our own government and to do whatever we can to help.

4 And **seeing the people in a state of such awful wickedness, and those Gadianton robbers filling the judgment-seats**—having usurped [*grabbed*] the power and authority of the land; **laying aside the commandments of God**, and not in the least aright before him [*doing the things that God would approve of*]; **doing no justice** unto the children of men;

5 **Condemning the righteous** because of their righteousness; **letting the guilty and the wicked go unpunished** because of their money; and moreover **to be held in office at the head of government** [*in high government offices*], to **rule and do according to their wills** [*whatever they want to*], **that they might get gain and glory of the world**, and, moreover, **that they might the more easily commit adultery, and steal, and kill, and do according to their own wills**—

6 Now this great iniquity had come upon the Nephites, in the space of not many years; and **when Nephi saw it, his heart was swollen with sorrow**

within his breast; and he did exclaim in the agony of his soul:

Next, we get a personal glimpse into the soul of a truly great man as he yearns for "the good old days" of the past. It is a tender insight.

7 **Oh, that I could have had my days** [*lived*] **in the days when my father** [*ancestor*] **Nephi first came out of the land of Jerusalem**, that I could have joyed with him in the promised land; then were his people easy to be entreated [*easy to work with*], firm to keep the commandments of God, and slow to be led to do iniquity; and they were quick to hearken unto [*listen and obey*] the words of the Lord—

8 Yea, **if my days could have been in those days, then would my soul have had joy** in the righteousness of my brethren.

9 But behold, I am consigned [*resigned to the fact*] that **these are my days** [*I have to live now*], and that **my soul shall be filled with sorrow because of this the wickedness of my brethren**.

Apparently, Nephi had a tower in his yard where he could go to be alone to pray and to meditate on occasions. Whether having such a tower was a common thing in Nephi's culture, we don't know, but it was obviously a special place for Nephi, and he had gone there this day to pray and be alone with God.

10 And behold, now it came to pass that it was **upon a tower, which was in the garden of Nephi**, which was **by the highway which led to the chief market**, which was in the city of Zarahemla; therefore, **Nephi had bowed himself upon the tower** which was in his garden, which tower was also near unto the garden gate by which led the highway.

Perhaps you've noticed that wickedness often makes people forget manners and courtesy toward others. If the people in verse 11, next, had been spiritually sensitive or even polite, they would likely have quietly gone their ways and perhaps even invited others to go to market another way in order to preserve Nephi's privacy. They didn't.

11 And it came to pass that there were **certain men passing by** and **saw Nephi as he was pouring out his soul** [*praying*] **unto God upon the tower**; and **they ran and told the people what they had seen** [*they gossiped*], and the **people came together in multitudes** [*big crowds*] that they might know the cause of so great mourning for the wickedness of the people.

12 And now, **when Nephi arose he beheld** [*saw*] **the multitudes** of people who had gathered together.

We can easily understand why Nephi felt the way he did when he noticed that people had gathered and were staring at him. Next, we will see an example of what is termed "righteous indignation," or, in other words, righteous anger. Nephi will ask several questions in rapid-fire succession and answer them as he goes.

13 And it came to pass that **he** opened his mouth and **said unto them**: Behold, **why have ye gathered yourselves together? That I may tell you of your iniquities** [*wickedness*]?

14 Yea, **because I have got upon my tower that I might pour out my soul** [*pray*] **unto my God, because of the exceeding sorrow of my heart, which is because of your iniquities!**

15 And **because of my mourning and lamentation** [*sorrow for your sins*] **ye have gathered yourselves together, and do marvel** [*you are surprised and are wondering what is going on*]; yea, and **ye have great need to marvel; yea, ye ought to marvel because ye are given away that the devil has got so great hold upon your hearts.**

16 Yea, **how could you have given way to the enticing** [*tempting*] **of him** [*the devil*] **who is seeking to hurl** [*throw*] **away your souls down to everlasting misery and endless wo** [*hell*]? [*How could you be so blind as to what Satan has in mind for you?*]

As Nephi continues, he adds merciful reminders that these people can still repent. He strongly counsels them to do so.

17 **O repent ye, repent ye! Why will ye die** [*spiritually as well as physically when your nation is weakened by wickedness*]? **Turn ye, turn ye unto the Lord your God** [*repent!*]. **Why has he forsaken you** [*why is God not blessing and protecting you anymore*]?

18 It is **because you have hardened your hearts**; yea, **ye will not hearken unto the voice of the good shepherd** [*the Savior*]; yea, **ye have provoked him to anger against you**.

Sometimes, when people are far gone spiritually, it requires rather blunt warnings in order to have any chance of getting them back. We see such a warning in verse 19, next.

19 And behold, instead of gathering you, **except** [*unless*] **ye will repent, behold, he shall scatter you forth that ye shall become meat for dogs and wild beasts.**

Next, Nephi points out how people can turn from righteousness to extreme wickedness in such a short time.

20 O, **how could you have forgotten your God in the very day that he has delivered you** [*such a short time after he saved you from your enemies, including sin*]?

21 But behold, **it is to get gain** [*to get wealth and power*], **to be praised of men**, yea, and **that ye might get gold and silver**. And **ye have set your hearts upon the riches and the vain** [*worthless*] **things of this world, for the which ye do murder, and plunder, and steal, and bear false witness against your neighbor, and do all manner of iniquity**.

22 And **for this cause** [*this is why*] **wo** [*great troubles*] **shall come unto you**

except ye shall repent. For **if ye will not repent, behold, this great city, and also all those great cities which are round about**, which are in the land of our possession, **shall be taken away that ye shall have no place in them**; for behold, **the Lord will not grant unto you strength**, as he has hitherto [*up to now*] done, **to withstand** [*hold out*] **against your enemies.**

23 For behold, **thus saith the Lord: I will not show unto the wicked of my strength**, to one more than the other, **save** [*except*] **it be unto those who repent of their sins, and hearken unto my words.** Now therefore, I would that ye should behold, my brethren, that **it shall be better for the Lamanites than for you except ye shall repent.**

Next, we are reminded of the added accountability of those who know the truth and still rebel against it. You may wish to cross-reference verse 24, below, with Doctrine and Covenants 82:10.

24 For behold, **they are more righteous than you, for they have not sinned against that great knowledge which ye have received**; therefore the Lord will be merciful unto them; yea, he will lengthen out their days and increase their seed [*posterity, children, grandchildren, etc.*], even when **thou shalt be utterly destroyed except thou shalt repent.**

25 Yea, **wo** [*great trouble and misery*] **be unto you because of that great abomination which has come among you** [*you have joined forces with evil; see Helaman 6:21*]; and ye have united yourselves unto it, yea, to **that secret band which was established by Gadianton!**

26 Yea, **wo shall come unto you because of** that **pride** which ye have suffered [*allowed*] to enter your hearts, **which has lifted you up beyond that which is good because of your exceedingly great riches!**

27 Yea, **wo be unto you because of your wickedness and abominations** [*extreme forms of wickedness*]!

28 And **except** [*unless*] **ye repent ye shall perish** [*die*]; yea, even your lands shall be taken from you, and ye shall be destroyed from off the face of the earth [*symbolic of what will happen to the wicked at the Second Coming of Christ*].

Perhaps these people think that Nephi is saying these things because they have violated his privacy and he is irritated at them. In verse 29, next, he assures them that they need to pay close attention to what he has said, because it comes from the Lord.

29 Behold now, **I do not say that these things shall be, of myself**, because it is not of myself that I know these things; but behold, **I know that these things are true because the Lord God has made them known unto me, therefore I testify that they shall be.**

HELAMAN 8

Remember, Mormon was the great Book of Mormon prophet who, under inspiration from God, selected from all the Nephite records which things to include on the stack of gold plates that Moroni gave to Joseph Smith to translate. He was inspired to include things that would help us with specific issues we would face in our day. In these chapters especially we are given an inspired course in political science. Mormon is showing us what works to preserve freedom and agency through good government and what types of things work to destroy them.

Generally speaking, the wicked cannot stand the righteous. Their normal approach is to ignore them or attempt to do away with them, thinking it will solve their problem. It won't, but wisdom is not a strength of the wicked.

As we begin chapter 8, we hear the angry cries of the corrupt and wicked judges who claim that Nephi has violated their government by the statements he made about the wickedness of the people and their wicked leaders who have joined the Gadianton robbers. This can easily remind us of similar cries among those today who claim that any mention of God, religion, prophecy, scripture, or use of the terms "good" and "evil," "right" and "wrong," etc., is offensive to the laws and freedoms of the land.

1 AND now it came to pass that **when Nephi had said these words,** behold, **there were men who were judges, who also belonged to the secret band of Gadianton**, and **they were angry, and they cried out against him, saying unto the people: Why do ye not seize upon** [*grab; arrest*] **this man** and bring him forth, **that he may be condemned** [*punished by our laws*] **according to the crime which he has done?**

Perhaps their laws had now been changed to make it a crime to speak in public about the government and government leaders as Nephi had done.

2 **Why seest thou this man, and hearest him revile** [*speak disrespectfully*] **against this people and against our law**?

3 For behold, **Nephi had spoken unto them concerning the corruptness** [*wickedness*] **of their law; yea, many things did Nephi speak which cannot be written; and nothing did he speak which was contrary to the commandments of God**.

Next, we are told the real reason these political leaders were angry.

4 And **those judges were angry with him because he spake plainly unto them concerning their secret works of darkness**; nevertheless, they durst not [*didn't dare*] lay their own hands upon him [*arrest him themselves*], for they feared the people lest they should cry out against them.

As with the leaders of the Jews who stirred up the people against Jesus, so also with these leaders of the Nephites. They wanted to be rid of Nephi, but they wanted to make it look legal, or at least make it look like the will of the people.

5 **Therefore they did cry unto the people, saying: Why do you suffer** [*allow*] **this man to revile against us?** For behold he doth condemn all this people, even unto destruction; yea, and also that these our great cities shall be taken from us, that we shall have no place in them.

As you can plainly see, these wicked government leaders of the Nephite nation are following a classic pattern used by the devil to destroy the wicked. They believe that they are sufficiently powerful to defend against any outside enemies, when in fact, their most dangerous enemy is within. Satan is a master at decoying them to look elsewhere for danger while he carefully weakens and destroys them from the inside out.

6 And now we know that **this is impossible**, for behold, **we are powerful, and our cities great, therefore our enemies can have no power over us**.

Next, while some express anger against Nephi, others are beginning to believe him.

7 And it came to pass that **thus they did stir up the people to anger against Nephi**, and raised contentions [*fighting and arguing*] among them; for **there were some who did cry out: Let this man alone, for he is a good man, and those things which he saith will surely come to pass except we repent**;

8 Yea, behold, **all the judgments** [*punishments from God*] **will come upon us which he has testified unto us**; for we know that he has testified aright [*correctly*] unto us concerning our iniquities. And behold they are many, and he knoweth as well all things which shall befall us as he knoweth of our iniquities; [*In other words, he is a prophet, and we had better listen to him!*]

9 Yea, and behold, **if he had not been a prophet he could not have testified concerning those things** [*the secret wicked things that were going on*].

Next, those who wanted to see Nephi destroyed so he could no longer expose their wicked deeds are forced to back off.

10 And it came to pass that **those people who sought** [*wanted*] **to destroy Nephi were compelled** [*forced*] **because of their fear, that they did not lay their hands on him**; therefore **he began again to speak unto them**, seeing that he had gained favor in the eyes of some, insomuch that the remainder of them did fear.

As Nephi continues, he will remind them of past prophets who exposed wickedness among the people, warned them about coming destruction, and encouraged those who would listen to repent. He will point out that it only takes one inspired prophet to declare the truth, no matter how many people may be against him. He is leading up to the point that no matter how many Nephites oppose him, Nephi is still speaking the truth as a prophet of God. Through inspiration from God, he knows secret things that are going on. He will begin his review with Moses and his prophecies of Christ.

11 **Therefore he was constrained** [*inspired and obligated by the Spirit of the Lord*] **to speak more unto them** saying: Behold, my brethren, **have ye not read that God gave power unto one man**, even **Moses**, to smite upon the waters of the Red Sea, and they parted hither and thither [*this way and that*], insomuch that the Israelites, who were our fathers [*ancestors*], came through upon dry ground [*this confirms the Bible account that many Bible scholars and critics have tried to explain away*], and the waters closed upon the armies of the Egyptians and swallowed them up?

12 And now behold, **if God gave unto this man such power, then why should ye dispute** [*argue and debate*] **among yourselves, and say that he hath given unto me no** power whereby I may know concerning the judgments that shall come upon you except ye repent?

Many throughout the ages have claimed to believe past prophets of God but have refused to believe the ones in their own day. It is a much-used pattern of deception that is successfully practiced by the devil. These Nephites have fallen into the same trap. Next, Nephi will point out that those who reject current prophets are actually rejecting past prophets.

13 But, behold, **ye not only deny** [*reject*] **my words, but ye also deny all the words which have been spoken by our fathers** [*past prophets*], and **also the words** which were **spoken by** this man, **Moses**, who had such great power given unto him, yea, the words which he hath spoken concerning the coming of the Messiah [*Christ*].

Next, Nephi will explain some of the symbolism involved when Moses made the brass serpent for the children of Israel who had been bitten by fiery (poisonous) serpents because of their rebellion in the wilderness (Numbers 21:4–9). First, we will read Nephi's explanation, which will help us understand that the brass serpent was a "type" of Christ; or, in other words, a symbol of the Savior's Crucifixion and Atonement. Then we will turn to the Bible to read the actual account and point out the symbolism as we go.

14 Yea, did he [*Moses*] not bear record [*testify and prophesy*] that the Son of God [*Christ*] should [*would*] come? And **as he** [*Moses*] **lifted up the brazen serpent** [*the brass serpent the Lord had commanded him to make and lift up before the people on a pole*] in the wilderness, **even so shall he** [*Christ*] **be lifted up** [*on the cross*] who should come [*will come*].

15 And **as many as should look upon that serpent** [*the brass serpent made by Moses*] **should live** [*would be healed from the poisonous snake bites*], **even so as many as should look upon the Son of God with faith, having a contrite** [*humbly desiring correction as needed*] **spirit, might live** [*spiritually*], **even unto that life which is eternal** [*exaltation*].

As mentioned previously, we will now quote Numbers 21:5–9 in the Bible, pointing out possible

Atonement symbolism in the account of the brass serpent:

5 And the people spake against God, and against Moses, Wherefore [*why*] have ye brought us up out of Egypt [*symbolic of worldly wickedness; Babylon*] to die in the wilderness? for there is no bread [*symbolic of Christ; the "Bread of life," being absent in the lives of the wicked*], neither is there any water [*symbolic of "living water" or the gospel of Christ*]; and our soul loatheth [*can't stand*] this light bread [*manna, which came down as a gift from heaven; symbolizing that the wicked can't stand things that come from heaven*].

6 And the LORD sent fiery [*poisonous*] serpents [*snakes*] [*symbolizing the punishments of God upon the wicked*] among the people, and they bit the people; and much people of Israel died [*can be symbolic of spiritual death*].

7 ¶ Therefore the people came to Moses, and said, We have sinned [*they are now repenting*], for we have spoken against the LORD, and against thee; pray unto the LORD, that he take away the serpents [*perhaps symbolic of Satan's influence*] from us. And Moses prayed for the people.

8 And the LORD said unto Moses, Make thee a fiery serpent, and set it upon a pole [*symbolic of the cross; the Atonement of Christ*]: and it shall come to pass, that **every one that is bitten** [*symbolic of needing to be healed from sin*], **when he looketh upon it, shall live** [*symbolic of looking to Christ and following Him to eternal life*].

9 And Moses made a serpent of brass [*symbolic of Christ*], and put it upon a pole [*symbolic of the cross*], and it came to pass, that if a serpent [*can be symbolic of Satan, sin, wickedness, etc.*] had bitten any man, when he beheld [*saw*] the serpent of brass [*looked to Christ*], he lived [*gained salvation*].

We will now continue with Nephi's teaching. Next, he will point out that Moses was not the only prophet who testified of Christ, whom many of these Nephites and Gadianton robbers are rejecting.

16 And now behold, **Moses did not only testify of these things, but also all the holy prophets, from his days even to the days of Abraham.**

17 Yea, and behold, **Abraham saw of his coming** [*saw the coming of Christ*], and was filled with gladness and did rejoice [*see John 8:56*].

18 Yea, and behold I say unto you, that **Abraham not only knew of these things** [*Abraham was not the only ancient prophet who knew that Christ would come*], **but there were many before the days of Abraham who were called by the order of God; yea, even after the order of his Son** [*in other words, there were many before Abraham who held the Melchizedek Priesthood*]; and this **that it should be shown unto the people, a great many thousand years before his coming, that even redemption should come unto them.**

Next, Nephi will mention three prophets who are not mentioned in the Bible; namely, Zenos, Zenock, and Ezias, who lived after Abraham and who also testified of the coming of Christ. These prophets were obviously mentioned in the Brass Plates of Laban, which basically contained the Old Testament up to about 600 BC.

Zenos is mentioned twelve times in the Book of Mormon (see Index in the Book of Mormon under "Zenos"). Zenock is referred to five times (see Index under "Zenock"). Ezias is only mentioned here in Helaman, chapter eight. Along with these Old Testament prophets, Nephi also mentions Isaiah and Jeremiah, who also testified of Christ.

Nephi is "surrounding himself," so to speak, with others who have testified of Christ as he tries to help these Nephites realize that the Savior will come. In fact, Jesus will be born to Mary in Bethlehem in a little over twenty years from this time.

19 And now I would [*I desire*] that ye should know, that **even since the days of Abraham there have been many prophets that have testified these things**; yea, behold, the prophet **Zenos** did testify boldly; for the which he was slain [*Zenos was killed because he testified of Christ*].

20 And behold, also **Zenock**, and also **Ezias**, and also **Isaiah**, and **Jeremiah**, (Jeremiah being that same prophet who testified of the destruction of Jerusalem) and now we know that Jerusalem was destroyed according to the words of Jeremiah. O then why not the Son of God come, according to his prophecy?

In other words, since Jeremiah was right about the destruction of Jerusalem, why wouldn't he be right about the coming of Christ?

Perhaps you can feel the intensity increasing in Nephi's words as he adds his powerful testimony to that of past prophets. He is continuing to bear testimony of the much available evidence that prophecy is indeed fulfilled.

First, he reminds them of the destruction of Jerusalem, which was prophesied by Jeremiah and others and fulfilled when King Zedekiah was captured and forced to watch the conquerors kill his sons (except for Mulek). King Zedekiah's eyes were then put out and he was taken as a trophy of war. (See Jeremiah 39:6–7.) Nephi states the fact that descendants of the king, the Mulekites, are even at that time living among them and are solid evidence that Jerusalem was destroyed as prophesied.

21 And now **will you dispute that Jerusalem was destroyed**? **Will ye say that the sons of Zedekiah were not slain, all except it were Mulek?** Yea, and **do ye not behold** [*can't you see*] **that the seed** [*descendants*] **of Zedekiah are with us**, and they were driven out of the land of Jerusalem? But behold, this is not all [*there is much more evidence than this of the fulfillment of prophecy*]—

As Nephi continues, he points out that it is not unusual for the wicked to try to get rid of prophets of God just as these Gadianton robbers and others are trying to do away with him.

22 **Our father** [*ancestor*] **Lehi was driven out of Jerusalem because he testified of these things. Nephi also testified of these things**, and also **almost all of our fathers, even down to this time; yea, they have testified of the coming of Christ**, and have looked forward, and have rejoiced in his day which is to come.

23 And behold, **he** [*Christ*] **is God** [*the God of the Old Testament under Heavenly Father's direction], and he is with them [in paradise, where these prophets went after they died; see Alma 40:12*], and **he did manifest** [*show*] **himself unto them, that they were redeemed by him**; and they gave unto him glory, because of that which is to come. [*Among other things, Christ's mortal mission that is about to begin and the Atonement He will soon perform.*]

24 And now, **seeing** [*since*] **ye know these things and cannot deny them except ye shall lie, therefore** in this **ye have sinned**, for **ye have rejected all these things, notwithstanding** [*in spite of*] **so many evidences which ye have received**; yea, even ye have received all things, both things in heaven, and **all things** which are in the earth, as a **witness that they are true**.

The last lines in verse 24, above, go along with Moses 6:63 in the Pearl of Great Price, which says that all things bear witness of Christ. A major message here is that we are continually surrounded by lots of evidence that God exists. Nephi is basically pointing out that only the spiritually blind and the intentionally rebellious could possibly miss or ignore this fact. We will quote this verse now from Moses:

63 And behold, all things have their likeness, and **all things are created and made to bear record of me**, both things which are temporal [*physical things; having to do with the physical earth*], and things which are spiritual; things which are in the heavens above, and things which are on the earth, and things which are in the earth, and things which are under the earth, both above and beneath: **all things bear record of me**.

Nephi continues with bold testimony to these people who have interrupted his private prayer time as to what they are doing to themselves.

25 But behold, **ye have rejected the truth, and rebelled against your holy God**; and even at this time, instead of laying up for yourselves treasures in heaven, where nothing doth corrupt [*spoil and lose its value*], and where nothing can come which is unclean, **ye are heaping up for yourselves wrath against** [*severe punishment for*] **the day of judgment**.

26 Yea, even at this time ye are ripening [*you are getting close to being completely wicked*], because of your **murders** and your **fornication** [*sexual sin*] and **wickedness**, for everlasting destruction; yea, **and except ye repent it will come unto you soon**.

It is important that we not miss the invitation that is still extended to these people, even though they are so wicked. It is found at the end of verse 26, above, when Nephi said "except ye repent." In other words, even such people as these can repent, if they will come to Christ.

Isaiah 1:18 in the Bible is a powerful and clear reminder of this wonderful and comforting basic teaching of the gospel. Before we read this verse in Isaiah, we will point out that in his day, there were few "colorfast" dyes. In other words, most dyes in fabric would bleed onto other items of clothing, etc., when wet. Scarlet and crimson were colorfast dyes. The verse reads as follows:

18 Come now, and let us reason together [*let's think this through together*], saith the LORD: **though your sins be as scarlet** [*even though you think you have "colorfast" sins*], **they shall be as white as snow** [*My Atonement can cleanse them completely*]; though they be red like crimson, they shall be as wool [*which has been thoroughly cleansed by fuller's soap; also symbolizing that Christ's Atonement can provide warmth and comfort to you, and you will feel safe, protected, and at home in His presence*].

One of Nephi's major purposes in this chapter has been to show that the Lord does inspire His prophets, and they know things that others don't know. Prophets can inform others when their safety is threatened, or warn them about coming danger or destruction. Next, Nephi is blessed with this power as he tells these people that their chief judge has just been murdered by his own brother.

27 Yea, behold it [*destruction, verse 26*] is now even at your doors; yea, **go ye in unto the judgment-seat, and search; and behold, your judge is murdered, and he lieth in his blood; and he hath been murdered by his brother**, who seeketh to sit in the judgment-seat [*who wants to be the chief judge*].

Finally, Nephi tells these people that Satan and Gadianton are the founders of the secret combination that is ruining their country. He also reminds them what Satan's ultimate goal is.

28 And **behold** [*listen carefully*], **they both** [*the murdered chief judge and his brother*] **belong to your secret band** [*secret combination*], whose author [*founder*] is Gadianton and the evil one [*Satan*] **who seeketh to destroy the souls of men.**

HELAMAN 9

Nephi, as a true prophet of God, has now told these wicked men (see chapter 8, verse 25) that their chief judge, who is basically like the president of our country, has been murdered by his own brother.

Five men will run to the judgment-seat (government headquarters) to see if Nephi's words are true. They talk as they run, saying that if it is true, they will become believers in God and the gospel. They will find him dead like Nephi said. But they will be accused by the people of being the ones who murdered the chief judge. You will see much speculation, jumping to conclusions, and misinformation that will quickly cloud the simple fact that Nephi is a prophet of God. Satan uses the same methods today to confuse the simple fact that the gospel is true and that God exists.

1 BEHOLD, now it came to pass that **when Nephi had spoken these words, certain men** who were among them **ran to the judgment-seat**; yea, even **there were five** who went, and **they said among themselves, as they went**:

2 Behold, **now we will know of a surety** [*know for sure*] **whether** [*if*] **this**

man be a prophet and God hath commanded him to prophesy such marvelous things unto us. Behold, we do not believe that he hath; yea, **we do not believe that he is a prophet**; nevertheless, **if this thing which he has said concerning the chief judge be true, that he be dead, then will we believe that the other words which he has spoken are true**.

3 And it came to pass that they ran in their might, and came in unto the judgment-seat; and behold, the **chief judge had fallen to the earth, and did lie in his blood**.

4 And now behold, **when they saw this they were astonished exceedingly** [*very surprised*], **insomuch** [*so much so*] **that they fell to the earth**; for they had not believed the words which Nephi had spoken concerning the chief judge.

5 **But now, when they saw they believed**, and **fear came upon them** lest [*for fear that*] all the judgments [*punishments from God*] which Nephi had spoken should [*would*] come upon the people; **therefore they did quake** [*tremble and shake*], **and had fallen to the earth**.

6 Now, immediately when **the judge** had been murdered—he being **stabbed by his brother by a garb** [*cloak*] **of secrecy** [*a secret agreement*], and he fled, and **the servants ran and told the people**, raising the cry of murder among them;

7 And behold **the people did gather** themselves together **unto the place of the judgment-seat**—and behold, to their astonishment **they saw those five men** who had fallen to the earth.

8 And now behold, **the people knew nothing concerning the multitude who had gathered together at the garden of Nephi**; [*in other words, these people who had rushed to government headquarters when they heard that their president or chief judge had been murdered knew nothing of what Nephi had told those who had gathered in curiosity as he was praying in his garden; see Helaman 7:11*] **therefore they said among themselves: These men are they who have murdered the judge**, and God has smitten them that they could not flee from us.

9 And it came to pass that they laid hold on them [*they arrested them*], and bound them and cast them into prison. And **there was a proclamation sent abroad that the judge was slain, and that the murderers had been taken and were cast into prison**.

10 And it came to pass that **on the morrow** [*the next day*] **the people did assemble themselves together** to mourn and to fast, at the burial of the great chief judge who had been slain.

In the next several verses, we will see that the wicked will believe almost anything in order to avoid facing the truth that God exists and that He does have prophets on earth. First, some of the corrupt government officials who heard what Nephi said from his garden tower (chapter 7) and tried to incite the people to grab Nephi (chapter 8, verses 1–6) now wonder where the five men are who were sent to check out Nephi's statement that their chief judge was dead.

11 And thus also **those judges who were at the garden of Nephi, and heard his words, were also gathered together at the burial**.

12 And it came to pass that **they inquired** [*asked*] among the people, saying: **Where are the five** who were sent to inquire concerning the chief judge whether [*to see if*] he was dead? And they answered and said: **Concerning this five** whom ye say ye have sent, **we know not**; but **there are five who are the murderers**, whom **we have cast into prison**.

13 And it came to pass that the judges desired that they should be brought; and **they were brought**, and behold they were the five who were sent; and behold **the judges inquired** of them to know concerning the matter, and **they told them all that they had done**, saying:

What these five men tell their government officials is not what they want to hear.

14 We ran and came to the place of the judgment-seat, and when **we saw all things even as Nephi had testified** [*everything was just as Nephi said it would be*], we were astonished insomuch that **we fell to the earth**; and **when we were recovered from our astonishment, behold they cast us into prison**.

15 Now, **as for the murder of this man, we know not who has done it**; and only **this much we know, we ran and came according as ye desired**, and behold **he was dead, according to the words of Nephi**.

Notice how quickly these wicked judges twist the facts in an attempt to keep the people from believing that Nephi is a true prophet, which would ruin their power over them. They claim that the entire thing is an elaborate plot set up by Nephi and another man to fool the people into thinking that he is a prophet so he can gain power and control over them himself.

16 And now it came to pass that **the judges** did expound [*explain*] the matter unto the people, and **did cry out against Nephi**, saying: Behold, **we know that this Nephi must have agreed with some one to slay** [*kill*] **the judge, and then he might declare it unto us** [*tell us what had happened*], **that he might convert us unto his faith** [*his church, his gospel*], **that he might raise himself to be** [*make it look like he is*] **a great man, chosen of God, and a prophet**.

17 And now behold, **we will detect this man** [*we will find out who this other man is who collaborated with Nephi to murder the chief judge and make Nephi look like a prophet*], and **he shall confess his fault and make known unto us the true murderer of this judge**.

Much to the disappointment of these judges who were trying to make it look like Nephi set the whole thing up, the five men who were set free came to his defense.

18 And it came to pass that **the five were liberated** [*set free*] **on the day of the burial**. Nevertheless, **they did rebuke** [*scold*] **the judges in the words which they had spoken against Nephi**, and did contend [*argue; debate the matter*] with them one by one, insomuch that [*to the extent that*] they did confound them [*they confused the judges*].

19 Nevertheless, **they** [*the judges*] **caused that Nephi should be taken** [*arrested*] and bound [*tied up*] and brought before the multitude [*crowd*], and they **began to question him** in divers [*various*] ways **that they might cross him** [*trick him into saying things that would prove that he was guilty*], **that they might accuse him to death** [*find him worthy of the death penalty; they wanted to make his death appear legal*]—

It is often the case that wicked people assume that all people think basically the same way they do. Since they will accept bribes (being paid money for lying) themselves, these judges assume that everyone, including Nephi, will accept bribes if offered enough money.

20 Saying unto him: **Thou art confederate** [*you have a partner in this crime*]; **who is this man that hath done this murder**? Now tell us, and acknowledge thy fault; saying, **Behold here is money** [*a bribe*]; and also **we will grant unto thee thy life if thou wilt tell us**, and acknowledge the agreement which thou hast made with him.

No doubt, Nephi's strong reply caught these men off guard.

21 But Nephi said unto them: **O ye fools, ye uncircumcised of heart** [*wicked; hearts are, figuratively, far away from God*], **ye blind** [*spiritually blind and totally lacking in wisdom and common sense*], and **ye stiffnecked** [*not humble; full of pride and arrogance*] people, **do ye know how long the Lord your God will suffer** [*permit*] **you that ye shall go on in this your way of sin?**

22 O **ye ought to begin to howl and mourn** [*you might as well start howling and weeping now*], because of the great destruction which at this time doth await you, **except** [*unless*] **ye shall repent** [*you can still repent*].

Nephi now tells these men that the real reason they are trying to falsely accuse him is that they do not want to believe that God inspired him to know that the chief judge had just been murdered and that his brother was the murderer. If they believe that God inspired him on this matter, they would have to believe that what he has said about their wickedness is also true. They don't want to believe it.

23 Behold **ye say** that I have agreed with a man that he should murder Seezoram, our chief judge. But behold, **I say** unto you, that this is because **I have testified unto you that ye might know concerning this thing**; yea, even **for a witness unto you, that I did know of the wickedness and abominations which are among you**.

24 And because I have done this, **ye say** that **I have agreed with a man that he should do this thing**; yea, because I showed unto you this sign ye are angry with me, and seek to destroy my life.

As the intensity of this situation continues to increase, Nephi tells these men that he has yet another sign to show them. He tells them in great prophetic detail what will happen when they face the murderer of the chief judge with what Nephi has told them.

25 And now behold, **I will show unto you another sign**, and see if ye will in this thing seek to destroy me.

26 Behold I say unto you: **Go to the house of Seantum, who is the brother of Seezoram** [*the murdered chief judge*]**, and say unto him—**

27 **Has Nephi**, the pretended prophet, who doth prophesy so much evil concerning this people, **agreed with thee, in the which ye have murdered Seezoram, who is your brother?**

28 And behold, **he shall say unto you, Nay**.

29 And **ye shall say unto him: Have ye murdered your brother?**

30 And **he shall stand with fear, and wist not what to say** [*he won't know what to say*]. And behold, **he shall deny** unto you; and **he shall make** [*act, pretend*] **as if he were astonished**; nevertheless, **he shall declare unto you** [*say*] **that he is innocent** [*that he didn't do it*].

31 But behold, **ye shall examine him**, and **ye shall find blood upon the skirts** [*bottom borders*] **of his cloak**.

32 And when ye have seen this, **ye shall say: From whence** [*where*] **cometh this blood?** Do we not know that it is the blood of your brother?

33 And **then shall he tremble, and shall look pale**, even as if death had come upon him.

34 And **then shall ye say**: Because of this fear and this paleness which has come upon your face, behold, **we know that thou art guilty**.

35 And **then shall greater fear come upon him; and then shall he confess** unto you, and deny no more that he has done this murder.

36 And **then shall he say** unto you, that I, Nephi, know nothing concerning the matter save it were given unto me by the power of God. And **then shall ye know** that I am an honest man, and that I am sent unto you from God.

37 And it came to pass that **they went and did, even according as Nephi had said unto them. And behold, the words which he had said were true**; for according to the words he did deny; and also according to the words he did confess.

38 And **he was brought to prove that he himself was the very murderer, insomuch that the five were set at liberty** [*set free*]**, and also was Nephi**.

At this point, we would hope that all these people would humble themselves and believe the obvious, namely, that Nephi truly is a prophet of God. The evidence is undeniable to anyone who is thinking. But, as you have no doubt noticed, one of Satan's cunning and subtle goals is to gradually draw a curtain of haze over the ability of people to think with wisdom and common sense. He does this through pride, self-indulgence, sin, poor priorities, etc. Many of these Nephites have fallen victim to these temptations of the devil to the extent that they immediately begin to argue with each other as to who Nephi really is rather than humbly turning to him and asking him to tell them. Their sad behavior is a strong reminder that wickedness does not promote rational thought.

39 And there were **some of the Nephites** who **believed on the words of Nephi**; and there were **some** also, who **believed because of the testimony of the five**, for they had been converted while they were in prison.

40 And now there were **some** among the people, who **said that Nephi was a prophet**.

41 And there were **others** who **said**: Behold, **he is a god**, for except [*unless*] he was a god he could not know of all things. For behold, he has told us the thoughts of our hearts, and also has told us things; and even he has brought unto our knowledge the true murderer of our chief judge.

HELAMAN 10

These people have become so wicked that they completely miss the point as to what Nephi has done in prophesying what has happened to their chief judge. It is very strong evidence that he actually is a true prophet of God. As you will see, though, in the first verse of this chapter, these people will continue arguing about who Nephi really is until they divide up and go their ways, leaving Nephi completely alone, rather than asking him to teach them as a prophet from God. This is very hard on him.

1 AND it came to pass that **there arose a division among the people, insomuch that they divided hither and thither** [*this way and that*] **and went their ways, leaving Nephi alone**, as he was standing in the midst of them.

In this chapter, Nephi will be given the power of God. Perhaps you have wondered how you would handle this power if you were given it. At first thought, some people think they would do things differently if they were God. They find themselves wondering why He doesn't step in and stop famine, disease, war, severe abuse, torture, etc., especially when it comes to innocent victims, particularly children.

As we continue studying this chapter and chapter 11, we will be given a short course in some aspects of why God allows such things to happen. It centers around the sacredness of agency, given to us by our Father in Heaven. He will not take it from us nor violate it. Satan seeks to take it away. (See Moses 4:3.)

We are the only ones who can give it away or lose it. (See Alma 34:35.) Through Nephi's eyes and heart, we will see, for instance, why God sometimes sends famine in order to stop war and bloodshed.

Remember from the end of chapter 9 and the first verse in this chapter that Nephi has been left completely alone, while people who should have been seeking his counsel and teachings walk away, still arguing as to who he really is. They are relying on the wisdom of men to understand the things of God. It doesn't work.

2 And it came to pass that **Nephi went his way towards his own house**, pondering upon the things which the Lord had shown unto him.

3 And it came to pass as he was thus pondering—being **much cast down** [*dejected and discouraged*] **because of the wickedness of the people of the Nephites**, their secret works of darkness, and their murderings, and their plunderings [*destroying things, hurting people, and taking their stuff*], and all manner of iniquities [*all kinds of wickedness*]—and it came to pass **as he was thus pondering** [*thinking deeply*] **in his heart, behold, a voice came unto him saying**:

As the Lord speaks to Nephi in verse 4, next, we will be shown six things that lead toward exaltation, which is the highest degree of glory in the celestial kingdom. They will be numbered and bolded/italicized, with notes to explain as we study the verse.

4 **Blessed art thou, Nephi**, for **those things which thou hast done** [*1. Actions must accompany belief*]; for I have beheld how thou hast with ***unwearyingness*** [*2. We must be consistently faithful*] declared the word, which I have given unto thee, unto this people. And ***thou hast not feared them*** [*3. We must be more concerned about what God thinks than what people think*], and ***hast not sought thine own life*** [*4. We must not make our own pleasure and desires top priority*], but ***hast sought my will*** [*5. We must subject our will to God's will*], ***and to keep my commandments*** [*6. We must strive to keep His commandments*].

Next, Nephi is told that he will ultimately receive exaltation, or, in other words, he has his "calling and election" made sure. Then he is told he will receive God's power to use right now on earth to try to get these wicked people to repent.

5 And now, because thou hast done this with such unwearyingness, behold, **I will bless thee forever**; and **I will make thee mighty in word and in deed, in faith and in works**; yea, even that **all things shall be done unto thee according to thy word** [*whatever you say will happen, just as is the case with God*], for thou shalt not ask that which is contrary to my will [*God can trust Nephi completely*].

6 Behold, thou art Nephi, and I am God [*You will be as I am in your dealings with these people*]. Behold, I declare it unto thee in the presence of mine angels, that **ye shall have power over this people**, and **shall smite** the earth

with famine, and with **pestilence** [*you can cause plagues, diseases, disasters, etc.*], and **destruction**, according to the wickedness of this people.

Did you notice the formula at the end of verse 6, above? In effect, the Lord tells Nephi that the famine, pestilence, and destruction He sends upon the rebellious will need to be equal to the degree of wickedness of those people, just like God does it.

We must be a bit cautious about applying this formula to all situations in which things don't go well. Obviously, the righteous grow in many needed ways as they overcome adversity. Therefore, we must apply the above formula in the context of wickedness in society wherein the Lord is trying to humble His children in order to get them to repent so He can save them.

As we continue, the Lord explains more about this power of God that He is giving Nephi.

7 Behold, **I give unto you power**, that **whatsoever ye shall seal on earth shall be sealed in heaven**; and **whatsoever ye shall loose on earth shall be loosed in heaven**; and thus shall ye have power among this people.

8 And thus, **if ye shall say unto this temple** it shall be **rent in twain** [*be torn in two*], **it shall be done.**

9 And **if ye shall say unto this mountain, Be thou cast down and become smooth, it shall be done**.

10 And behold, **if ye shall say that God shall smite** [*punish*] **this people, it shall come to pass.**

Next, God commands Nephi to do what God always does before destroying a society; namely, teach them the gospel and invite them to repent and return to Him.

11 And now behold, **I command you**, that ye shall **go and declare unto this people**, that **thus saith the Lord God**, who is the Almighty: **Except ye repent ye shall be smitten, even unto destruction.**

Next, Nephi obeys God and immediately begins again to teach the gospel and warn of coming destruction if the people don't repent. We see once more the wonderful power of the Atonement to cleanse and heal in the fact that these wicked people are again invited to repent, even after failing to respond to the obvious evidence they had received that Nephi is a prophet, when he told them that the chief judge had been murdered by his own brother.

12 And behold, now it came to pass that when the Lord had spoken these words unto **Nephi**, he **did stop and did not go unto his own house, but did return unto the multitudes who were scattered about upon the face of the land, and began to declare** [*teach and explain*] **unto them the word of the Lord which had been spoken unto him, concerning their destruction if they did not repent.**

13 Now behold, notwithstanding [*in spite of*] that great miracle which Nephi had done in telling them concerning the death of the chief judge, **they did harden their hearts** [*they did not humble themselves*] **and did not hearken unto** [*did not listen to and obey*] **the words of the Lord.**

14 **Therefore Nephi did declare unto them the word of the Lord, saying: Except ye repent, thus saith the Lord, ye shall be smitten even unto destruction.**

15 And it came to pass that when Nephi had declared unto them the word, behold, **they did still harden their hearts and would not hearken unto his words**; therefore **they did revile against him** [*they mocked and ridiculed him, just like people did to Jesus*], and **did seek to lay their hands upon him** [*arrest him, just like they did Jesus*] **that they might cast him into prison**.

Next, another obvious miracle takes place before their eyes, but they still don't see the truth.

16 But behold, the power of God was with him, and **they could not take him to cast him into prison**, for **he was taken by the Spirit and conveyed away** [*taken away*] **out of the midst of them.**

17 And it came to pass that thus **he did go forth in the Spirit, from multitude to multitude, declaring the word of God**, even until he had declared it unto them all, or sent it forth among all the people.

In other words, everyone has now been given an opportunity to repent and have been warned of spiritual and physical destruction if they don't. This is similar to the last days before the Second Coming of the Savior. The gospel will be "preached in all the world . . . and then shall the end come" (Matthew 24:14).

18 And it came to pass that **they would not hearken unto his words** [*similar to the last days, when things will continue to get worse until the Lord has finished His work leading up to the Second Coming of the Savior and the Millennium; see D&C 84:97–98*]; and **there began to be contentions, insomuch that they were divided against themselves and began to slay** [*kill*] **one another** with the sword [*many wars, similar to the last days*].

19 And thus ended **the seventy and first year** of the reign of the judges over the people of Nephi [*20–21 years before the birth of Christ to Mary in Bethlehem*].

HELAMAN 11

The years will go by fast in this chapter. By the time it ends, it will be just six years before the birth of the Savior. Remember, Nephi has been given the power of God (Helaman 10:6–10) to use as he sees fit to try to get these wicked people to repent and, thus, save souls. As we continue, we will see him use the power of famine to stop war and bloodshed. We will watch the humbled people repent. And, as the chapter continues, we will see the "cycle of apostasy" again as the people go from humility to repentance, to being blessed to peace to prosperity, to a few disagreements to some apostasy, to widespread pride and wickedness, and finally to a condition of becoming ready for the Lord to destroy them.

While it becomes discouraging to see this "cycle of apostasy" so many times in the Book of Mormon, it is to our advantage to consider it a warning to all of us that unless we intentionally and constantly remain humble and keep our covenants and commitments to the Lord, this same cycle of apostasy can take place at an alarming rate in our own personal lives.

1 AND now it came to pass in **the seventy and second year** of the reign of the judges [*20 BC*] that the **contentions did increase**, insomuch that there were **wars throughout all the land** among all the people of Nephi.

2 And **it was this secret band of robbers** [*the Gadianton robbers*] **who did carry on this work of destruction and wickedness**. And this war did last all that year; and in **the seventy and third year** it did also last.

It has been about two years now since Nephi was given the power of God, but he has not yet used it to smite the people in order to humble them and get them to repent. This is a reminder to us of how patient God is and how careful He is to not smite us until it is absolutely necessary.

Next, though, Nephi will request that there be a famine. In these next verses, we will be taught the purpose of famines when the majority of people are wicked.

3 And it came to pass that in this year **Nephi did cry unto the Lord, saying:**

4 O Lord, **do not suffer** [*do not allow*] **that this people shall be destroyed by the sword** [*by wars*]; **but O Lord, rather let there be a famine in the land, to stir them up in remembrance of the Lord their God, and perhaps they will repent and turn unto thee.**

Did you notice the word, "perhaps," at the end of verse 4, above? It is an important reminder that even in the case of severe famines, diseases, plagues, etc., agency is still preserved. Even though they have severely limited their agency through wickedness, such people still have the God-given agency to choose to repent or to become harder, even to the point of cursing God as they die, which some people have done (see D&C 45:32).

Some people think that agency is taken away when the only options left are to repent or be destroyed. Such is not the case. Wickedness reduces the options available. Righteousness increases one's options. It is possible for the wicked to give up more and more of their agency, until in the end, they have none because they have given it all to Satan (Alma 34:35). On the other hand, the righteous gain more and more knowledge, light, and intelligence. Light and knowledge increase options. Thus, the righteous progress until finally they "shall comprehend even God" (D&C 88:49). Ultimately, they become gods (D&C 76:58) and "see as they are seen (by God), and know as they are known (by God; see D&C 76:94)." Gods are the freest individuals in the universe. They have all the agency options still. Plus, they have perfect righteousness so that they would never exercise their agency in inappropriate ways. Thus, they remain gods forever.

Now, back to Nephi and his exercising of the power of a god. Watch what happens as a result of the famine, meaning lack of food, rain, and so forth.

5 **And so it was done, according to the words of Nephi** [*just like things are done, according to the word of God*]. And **there was a great famine** upon the land, among all the people of Nephi. And thus in **the seventy and fourth year** the famine did continue, and **the work of destruction did cease by the sword** but became sore [*severe, very bad*] by famine [*many were destroyed by the famine*].

6 And this work of destruction did also continue in **the seventy and fifth year**. For **the earth was smitten that it was dry, and did not yield forth grain** in the season of grain [*they could not grow grain*]; and the whole earth was smitten, **even among the Lamanites** as well as among the Nephites, so that they were smitten that **they did perish** [*they died*] **by thousands in the more wicked parts of the land.**

7 And it came to pass that the people saw that they were about to perish by famine, and **they began to remember the Lord their God; and** they began to remember **the words of Nephi.**

The people are beginning to show true repentance. You may ask, "What would have happened if Nephi had stopped the famine too soon? What if he had stopped it before anyone actually died as a result of the famine? What if he had just let these wicked people get really hungry?" Obviously, the famine would not have done its job.

Next time someone asks why the Lord doesn't stop the famines, earthquakes, natural disasters, and disease, etc., in the world today, you might simply reply, "Because if He did, they wouldn't repent like He wants them to."

8 And **the people began to plead with their chief judges and their leaders**, that they would **say unto Nephi**: Behold, we know that **thou art a man of God**, and **therefore cry unto the Lord our God** [*notice that they didn't say "your God," but rather "our God;" their hearts have softened*] **that he turn away from us this famine**, lest all the words which thou hast spoken concerning our destruction be fulfilled. [*They now believe Nephi's prophecies.*]

9 And it came to pass that **the judges did say unto Nephi, according to the words which had been desired**. And it came to pass that **when Nephi saw that the people had repented** and did humble themselves in sackcloth [*clothing made from coarse fabric, showing humility, mourning, repentance, etc., in Nephi's country*], he cried again unto the Lord, saying:

It is important to realize that the people had shown their repentance already by their actions, including cleaning out their corrupt government leaders, according to verse 10, next. Such action gave them confidence to approach Nephi in the same way that changing our lives for the better can give us confidence to approach God in prayer.

Next, even though Nephi had been given the power of a god, he has remained humble and now approaches God in powerful, humble prayer. From his example, we can learn much about how to make our own prayers more effective. Notice how specific he is.

10 **O Lord, behold** [*see that*] **this people repenteth**; and **they have swept away the band of Gadianton from amongst them insomuch that they have become extinct** [*ceased to exist*], and they have concealed their secret plans in the earth.

11 **Now, O Lord, because of this their humility wilt thou turn away thine anger**, and **let thine anger be appeased** [*satisfied*] **in the destruction of those wicked men whom thou hast already destroyed**.

12 **O Lord, wilt** thou turn away thine anger, yea, thy fierce anger, and **cause that this famine may cease** [*stop*] **in this land.**

13 O Lord, **wilt thou hearken unto me, and cause that it may be done according to my words, and send forth rain** upon the face of the earth, that she may bring forth her fruit, and her grain in the season of grain.

14 O Lord, **thou didst hearken unto my words when I said, Let there be a famine**, that the pestilence of the sword might cease; and **I know that thou wilt, even at this time, hearken unto my words**, for thou saidst that: If this people repent I will spare them.

15 Yea, O Lord, and **thou seest that they have repented, because of the famine and the pestilence** [*all kinds of troubles, diseases, etc.*] **and destruction** which has come unto them.

16 And now, O Lord, wilt thou turn away thine anger, and try [*test*] again if they will serve thee? [*Please test them again; give them another chance.*] And **if so, O Lord, thou canst bless them** [*Nephi has the charity of a god. He wants his people to be blessed and happy.*] according to thy words which thou hast said.

17 And it came to pass that in **the seventy and sixth year** [*it has been between four and five years since Nephi was given the power of God*] **the Lord did turn away his anger** from the people, **and caused that rain should fall upon the earth**, insomuch that **it did bring forth her fruit** in the season of her fruit. And it came to pass that **it did bring forth her grain** in the season of her grain.

18 And behold, **the people did rejoice and glorify God** [*one meaning of "glorify God" is to bring Him happiness and joy by living the gospel so we can return to live with Him eternally; see Moses 1:39*], and **the whole face of the land was filled with rejoicing; and they did no more seek to destroy Nephi, but they did esteem** [*consider, look upon*] **him as a great prophet**, and a man

of God, having great power and authority given unto him from God.

19 And behold, **Lehi, his brother** [*Helaman 5:4*], **was not a whit** [*not a bit*] **behind him as to things pertaining to righteousness.**

20 And thus it did come to pass that **the people of Nephi began to prosper again** in the land, and began to build up their waste places [*the places that had been ruined by the wars and famines*], and began to multiply and spread [*began to increase in population because they were not being killed off anymore*], even until they did cover the whole face of the land, both on the northward and on the southward, from the sea west to the sea east.

Perhaps you are like me. By this point in the Book of Mormon, as soon as I hear the word "prosper," I immediately begin to brace myself for the "cycle of apostasy." I keep hoping that a group of people will come along who don't go through this cycle of prosperity, pride, and destruction again and again. Unfortunately, this group will. For the remainder of this chapter, this cycle will be pointed out in ***bold italics***.

21 And it came to pass that **the seventy and sixth year** did end in ***peace***. And the seventy and seventh year began in ***peace***; and the church did spread throughout the face of all the land; and the more part [*majority*] of the people, both the Nephites and the Lamanites, did belong to the church; and they did have exceedingly ***great peace*** in the land; and thus ended the seventy and seventh year.

22 And also they had ***peace*** in **the seventy and eighth year**, save it were ***a few contentions*** concerning the points of doctrine which had been laid down by the prophets.

The "points of doctrine" (verse 6, above), of the true gospel of Christ, set the true Church apart from all other religions. Ours is "the church that answers questions."

In the early days of the Restoration through the Prophet Joseph Smith, the Lord told the Saints that he would restore "the true points of my doctrine" (D&C 10:62), which had been lost to the world with the loss of many "plain and precious things" (1 Nephi 13:29). Satan does his best to make religion vague, indefinite, mysterious, and distant, but the Lord wants His people to have much by way of facts and doctrinal details upon which to base wise and informed decisions.

Faith leads to obedience. Obedience leads to additional revelation and knowledge of doctrine (see Moses 5:5–11). Knowledge of true doctrine leads to perspective and purpose. Perspective and purpose lead to humility, spiritual strength, and reliance upon God. Consistent reliance upon God leads to exaltation.

Thus, there is great power in these "points of doctrine," this wonderful gospel knowledge of the teachings in the plan of salvation. In fact, the Lord said, "It is impossible for a man to be saved in ignorance." (See D&C 131:6.) In this context, "ignorance" refers to gospel knowledge. As members of the Lord's true Church, we are blessed with a great number of "points of doctrine" of the plan of salvation, which doctrines and facts stretch all the way from our premortal life with our Heavenly Parents to the opportunity for exaltation in the highest degree of glory in the celestial kingdom. Thus, we have a finely-tuned sense of purpose for every stage of progression along the way.

23 And in **the seventy and ninth year** there began to be ***much strife***. But it came to pass that Nephi and Lehi, and many of their brethren who knew concerning **the true points of doctrine**, having many revelations daily, therefore they did preach unto the people, insomuch that they did put an end to their strife in that same year.

24 And it came to pass that in the eightieth year of the reign of the judges over the people of Nephi, there were a certain number of the ***dissenters*** [*apostates*] from the people of Nephi, who had some years before gone over unto the Lamanites, and taken upon themselves the name of Lamanites, and also a certain number who were real descendants of the Lamanites, being ***stirred up to anger*** by them, or by those dissenters, therefore they commenced a ***war*** with their brethren.

25 And they did commit ***murder*** and ***plunder***; and then they would retreat back into the mountains, and into the wilderness and secret places, hiding themselves that they could not be discovered [*typical behavior of terrorists*], receiving ***daily an addition to their numbers***, inasmuch as there were ***dissenters*** that went forth unto them.

26 And thus in time, yea, even in the space of not many years, they became an exceedingly great band of robbers; and they did ***search out all the secret plans of Gadianton*** [*they studied wickedness and how Satan operates, so they could make their terrorism more productive*]; and thus they became robbers of Gadianton.

27 Now behold, **these robbers did make great havoc** [*destruction*], yea, even great destruction among the people of Nephi, and also among the people of the Lamanites.

28 And it came to pass that **it was expedient** [*necessary*] **that there should be a stop put to this work of destruction; therefore they sent an army of strong men into the wilderness and upon the mountains to search out this band of robbers, and to destroy them.**

The situation among these people was very similar to the situation in the world today in terms of secret combinations of terrorists, which seem to defy all attempts to render them ineffective. Again, we can see the relevance of this part of the Book of Mormon to our day.

29 But behold, it came to pass that in that same year **they were driven back** even into their own lands. And thus ended **the eightieth year** of the reign of the judges over the people of Nephi.

30 And it came to pass in the commencement of **the eighty and first year they did go forth again against this band of robbers, and**

did destroy many; and they were also visited with much destruction.

31 And **they were again obliged** [*forced*] **to return** out of the wilderness and out of the mountains **unto their own lands**, because of the exceeding greatness of the numbers of those robbers who infested the mountains and the wilderness. [*Their best efforts were not sufficient to win their war against these robbers whose basic goals were robbing, plundering, and terrorism designed to bring them unrighteous power over the daily lives of people.*]

Again, in verse 32, next, we see definite parallels between the problems these people had with the Gadianton robbers and the trouble we have with terrorists in the world today.

32 And it came to pass **that thus ended this year. And the robbers did still increase and wax** [*grow*] **strong**, insomuch that **they did defy the whole armies of the Nephites, and also of the Lamanites**; and **they did cause great fear to come unto the people upon all the face of the land.**

33 Yea, for they did visit many parts of the land, and did do ***great destruction*** unto them; yea, did kill many, and did carry away others captive into the wilderness, yea, and more especially their women and their children.

Next, Mormon reminds us that these tragic troubles were the direct result of widespread wickedness.

34 Now this ***great evil***, which came unto the people ***because of their iniquity, did stir them up again in remembrance of the Lord*** their God.

35 And thus ended **the eighty and first year** of the reign of the judges.

36 And in **the eighty and second** year they ***began again to forget the Lord*** their God. And in the eighty and third year they ***began to wax strong in iniquity***. And in **the eighty and fourth year** they did not mend their ways [*did not repent*].

37 And it came to pass in **the eighty and fifth year** they did wax stronger and stronger in their ***pride***, and in their ***wickedness***; and thus they were ***ripening again for destruction***.

38 And thus ended **the eighty and fifth year**. [*It has now been about ten years since the peace in verse 21. It is now about six years before the birth of Christ and only about forty years before the destruction of the wicked in America just before the coming of the Resurrected Lord to the Nephites.*]

HELAMAN 12

Chapter 12 is a "thus we see" chapter in which Mormon explains the cycle of apostasy to us. He also teaches us about the power of God and how foolish it is to leave Him out of our lives. He even gives us a brief course in astronomy as he explains that it is the earth that rotates, rather than the sun's going around the earth, as many believed in ancient times.

Remember that whenever we see "and thus we see" or a variation of it, it alerts us that Mormon is now going to take time to tell us what he hopes we will learn from what he has just presented to us. The cycle of apostasy he discusses is identified with ***bold italics***.

1 **AND thus we can behold** [*And thus we see*] **how false, and also the unsteadiness of the hearts of the children of men**; yea, **we can see** that the Lord in his great infinite goodness doth bless and ***prosper*** those who put their trust in him.

> Mormon warns us that prosperity can be dangerous. It doesn't have to be. Remember the 200 years of peace among the people in Third Nephi after the Savior's appearance to them, and the 225 years of wealth, prosperity, righteousness, and peace in Ether 9:15–25. Remember also what Jacob said about wealth in Jacob 2:18–19.

2 Yea, and **we may see** [*thus we see*] **at the very time when he doth *prosper* his people**, yea, in the increase of their fields, their flocks and their herds, and in gold, and in silver, and in all manner of precious things of every kind and art; sparing their lives, and delivering them out of the hands of their enemies; softening the hearts of their enemies that they should not declare wars against them; yea, and in fine [*in summary; in short*], doing all things for the welfare and happiness of his people; yea, **then is the time that they do *harden their hearts***, and do ***forget the Lord*** their God, and do trample under their feet the Holy One [*make a mockery of Christ and His teachings*]—yea, and this ***because of their ease, and their exceedingly great prosperity***.

3 And **thus we see** that **excep**t [*unless*] **the Lord doth chasten** [*discipline*] **his people with** many ***afflictions***, yea, except he doth visit them with ***death*** and with ***terror***, and with ***famine*** and with all manner of ***pestilence***, **they will not remember him**.

4 O how ***foolish***, and how ***vain***, and how ***evil***, and ***devilish***, and how ***quick to do iniquity***, and how ***slow to do good***, are the children of men; yea, how ***quick to hearken unto the words of the evil one*** [*the devil*], and to ***set their hearts upon the vain things of the world***!

5 Yea, how quick to be lifted up in ***pride***; yea, how quick to ***boast***, and do ***all manner of that which is iniquity***; and how ***slow are they to remember the Lord their God, and to give ear unto his counsels***, yea, how ***slow to walk in wisdom's paths***!

6 Behold, ***they do not desire that the Lord their God, who hath created them, should rule and reign over them***; notwithstanding [*in spite of*] his great goodness and his mercy towards them, ***they do set at naught his counsels*** [*ignore His gospel*], and ***they will not that he should be their guide*** [*they do not want His guidance*].

> Next, Mormon gives a course in perspective. We must be careful to keep his words here in context. We know from scriptures, such as Doctrine and Covenants 18:10, that "the worth of souls is great in the sight of God."

One aspect of what Mormon is showing us is that even particles of dust obey God, whereas people often don't. Thus, in effect, people are "dumber than dust" when it comes to obeying God. They are less wise than dust!

Another aspect is that, compared to God and His power, the power and strength of mankind are nothing. Moses discovered this when he was shown "the world and the ends thereof, and all the children of men which are, and which were created" and concluded, "I [*now*] know that man is nothing, which thing I never had supposed." See Moses 1:8–10.

7 O **how great is the nothingness of the children of men; yea, even they are less than the dust of the earth**.

8 For behold, **the dust of the earth moveth hither and thither**[*here and there*], to the dividing asunder, **at the command of our great and everlasting God**.

9 Yea, behold **at his voice** [*at His command*] **do the hills and the mountains tremble and quake**.

10 And **by the power of his voice they are broken up, and become smooth**, yea, even like unto a valley.

11 Yea, **by the power of his** voice doth the whole earth shake;

12 Yea, **by the power of his voice, do the foundations rock**, even to the very center.

13 Yea, and **if he say unto the earth—Move—it is moved**.

14 Yea, **if he say unto the earth—Thou shalt go back** [*turn backward*], that it lengthen out the day for many hours—it is done;

As mentioned in the note at the beginning of this chapter, Mormon understood some facts about our solar system, particularly that the earth rotates and that is what makes the sun look like it is going around the earth. Abraham, in the Pearl of Great Price, had been taught much about astronomy by the Lord (see Abraham 3, plus Facsimile No. 2, in the Book of Abraham). We know from the last line of the "Explanation" accompanying Facsimile No. 3, in the Book of Abraham, that Abraham taught astronomy while he was in Egypt. Therefore, this knowledge of planets and stars must have been widespread among the ancients.

Thus we understand that when people apostatize from the true gospel, much more than gospel knowledge is lost. For instance, knowledge of health rules and sanitation procedures is lost. Such knowledge was given by revelation from God, thousands of years before germs were discovered in the AD 1800s. An example of this is found in the Old Testament in Deuteronomy 23:13:

13 And thou shalt have a paddle [*a shovel*] upon thy weapon [*which fits over the end of your spear or whatever*]; and it shall be, when thou wilt ease thyself abroad [*when you go to the bathroom, which should be done out away from camp*], thou shalt dig therewith [*with the paddle*], and shalt turn back and cover that which cometh from thee [*your body waste*]:

This commandment, if followed, would obviously reduce disease among people who live in large groups close to each other.

When revealed truths about the earth, the planets, the sun, etc., are lost through apostasy, people tend to revert to false notions and superstitions, including the ideas among some that the earth is flat, that the sun is a small orb that rotates around the earth, that the earth is the center of the observable universe, etc. Such thinking often becomes religion, and, in fact, made it heresy (subject to severe punishment for speaking disrespectfully of God or His creations) for some ancient astronomers to claim otherwise based on their observations through telescopes.

Next, Mormon gives a very brief lesson about the relationship between the earth and sun. His explanation starts in verse 14, above, and continues into verse 15. He could easily be referring to events in the Old Testament (which was available to Mormon on the Brass Plates of Laban) where the sun stood still (Joshua 10:12–13), and where the sun went back ten degrees according to the sun dial (Isaiah 38:7–8 and 2 Kings 20:8–11).

15 And thus, according to his word **the earth goeth back**, and **it appeareth unto man that the sun standeth still**; yea, and behold, this is so; for surely **it is the earth that moveth and not the sun**.

16 And behold, also, **if he say unto the waters of the great deep—Be thou dried up—it is done**.

Example: the parting of the Red Sea, through which the children of Israel went on dry ground. (See Exodus 14:22.) This can also refer to the creation of the earth during which God commanded the waters to gather into their place so that dry land could appear. (See Genesis 1:9.)

17 Behold, **if he say unto this mountain—Be thou raised up, and come over and fall upon that city** [*Example: 3 Nephi 8:10; 9:8*], that it be buried up—behold **it is done**.

18 And behold, **if a man hide up a treasure in the earth**, and the Lord shall say—Let it be accursed, because of the iniquity [*sins and wickedness*] of him who hath hid it up—behold, it shall be accursed.

19 And **if the Lord shall say—Be thou accursed, that no man shall find thee** from this time henceforth and forever—behold, no man getteth it henceforth and forever.

Next, Mormon makes a transition from the fact that the elements are subject to God and obey His commands to the fact that people are also subject to God, and what He says will happen whether they decide to obey or not. He focuses especially on Final Judgment and the condition and position of each individual in eternity.

20 And behold, **if the Lord shall say** unto a man—Because of thine iniquities [*because of your wickedness*], thou shalt be accursed [*stopped from eternal progression*] forever—it shall be done.

In the note in verse 20, above, we used the phrase "eternal progression." Some members of the Church confuse this type of progression with other kinds of limited progression, such as that found in the telestial glory. "Eternal progression" refers only to the highest degree of glory in the celestial kingdom; or, in other words, to exaltation for those who ultimately become gods. No others in the celestial kingdom or in any other degree of glory, especially those in outer darkness, will have the gift of eternal progression. Thus, they will never get to the point of becoming gods. (See D&C 29:29; 76:112.)

21 And **if the Lord shall say—Because of thine iniquities thou shalt be cut off from my presence**—he will cause that **it shall be so.**

22 And wo [*deep trouble*] unto him to whom he shall say this, for it shall be unto him that will do iniquity, and **he cannot be saved** [*after Final Judgment*]; therefore, **for this cause, that men might be saved, hath repentance been declared.**

At the end of verse 22, above, and into the next verses, below, Mormon still reminds us that the Atonement of Christ is still available if people will repent.

23 Therefore, **blessed are they who will repent and hearken unto the voice of the Lord their God; for these are they that shall be saved.**

24 And **may God grant, in his great fulness** [*possibly meaning His all-inclusive plan, which will ultimately give everyone a completely fair opportunity to accept or reject the gospel of Christ before Final Judgment*], **that men might be brought unto repentance and good works, that they might be restored** [*through the Atonement*] unto grace for grace [*possibly meaning restored to the privilege of eternal progression*], according to their works.

25 And **I would** [*wish*] **that all men might be saved. But we read** [*in the scriptures*] **that in the great and last day** [*on Final Judgment Day*] **there are some who shall be cast out, yea, who shall be cast off from the presence of the Lord;**

26 Yea, **who shall be consigned** [*sent*] **to a state of endless misery,** fulfilling the words which say: **They that have done good shall have everlasting life** [*eternal exaltation*]; and **they that have done evil** [*and haven't repented*] **shall have everlasting damnation** [*stopped from the privilege of eternal progression—forever*]. And thus it is. Amen.

I recently heard once again the theory that everyone, including sons of perdition, will ultimately be saved in celestial exaltation. According to Mormon, above (verses 25–26), this is false doctrine. In fact, it is a very damaging false teaching, because anyone who believes it might decide that he or she will "party" now and repent later, thinking that the chance to repent will be given again sometime in the eternities.

People who believe and teach this false doctrine generally base it upon the incorrect belief that "eternal progress" refers to everyone after Final judgment. With this belief as a crumbling foundation on which to build their false theory, they carefully pick and choose a few verses, take them out of the larger context of the scriptures, and use them to support their opinion. Some who don't understand what Mormon emphasized, above, can easily be persuaded to believe such falsehood.

Such an incorrect belief can easily take away from the urgency of the scripture that warns us that now "is the time for men to prepare to meet God" (Alma 34:32–33).

HELAMAN 13

Perhaps you have heard of Samuel the Lamanite. He is one of the favorite Book of Mormon characters for many members of the Church. In chapters 13–16, we are introduced to him and will also say goodbye to him. He is one of the great prophets of the Book of Mormon who comes on the scene to give his message and then leaves, never to be heard from again. It will be a pleasure to meet him in the next life.

As we begin chapter 13, it is six years before the birth of Christ to Mary in Bethlehem. The Lamanites have become a righteous people in America, but the Nephites continue in wickedness. Samuel is sent to the Nephites in the land of Zarahemla to preach repentance to them. Since they refuse to listen to him, he will stand on a city wall and preach and prophesy to them.

We will be taught many things by Samuel about the way the minds of the wicked operate. If we pay close attention, we will be helped greatly in avoiding such thought processes and resulting behaviors ourselves. Along the way, the invitation to repent and return to the covenant path of true happiness will be extended to the wicked Nephites several times.

1 AND now it came to pass in **the eighty and sixth year** [*6 BC*], **the Nephites did still remain in wickedness**, yea, in great wickedness, while **the Lamanites did observe strictly to keep the commandments of God**, according to the law of Moses [*the laws and commandment given in the Old Testament by Moses to get the people ready for Jesus and the higher laws He gave*].

2 And it came to pass that in this year there was one **Samuel, a Lamanite, came into the land of Zarahemla, and began to preach unto the people**. And it came to pass that he did preach, many days, repentance unto the people, and **they did cast him out**, and he was about to return to his own land.

3 **But behold, the voice of the Lord came unto him, that he should return again**, and prophesy unto the people whatsoever things should come into his heart [*whatever the Lord inspired him to say*].

4 And it came to pass that **they would not suffer** [*allow*] **that he should enter into the city; therefore he went and got upon the wall** thereof, and stretched forth his hand and cried with a loud voice, and prophesied unto the people whatsoever things the Lord put into his heart.

In the next several verses, we will be reminded that the Lord knows the future. He inspires Samuel to prophesy with much detail about it.

5 And **he said** unto them: Behold, **I, Samuel, a Lamanite, do speak the words of the Lord which he doth put into my heart**; and behold he hath put it into my heart to say unto this people that **the sword of justice** [*the punishment of the Lord*] **hangeth over this people**; and **four hundred years pass not away save the sword of justice falleth upon this people** [*in about 400 years, the Nephites will be destroyed*].

The Nephites were completely destroyed as a people by about AD 400, mostly by wars (see Mormon 6), but also by absorption into the worldly culture of the Lamanites.

6 Yea, heavy destruction awaiteth this people, and it surely cometh unto this people, and **nothing can save this people save it be repentance and faith on the Lord Jesus Christ,** who surely shall come into the world, and shall suffer many things and shall be slain for his people.

7 And behold, **an angel of the Lord hath declared it unto me**, and he did bring glad tidings [*about the soon-to-be birth of Jesus*] to my soul. And behold, I was sent unto you to declare it unto you also, that ye might have glad tidings; but behold ye would not receive me.

Next, Samuel tells us what happens to people when they reject the gospel. These things are required because of the Lord's respect for our agency.

8 Therefore, thus saith the Lord: Because of the hardness of the hearts [*lack of humility and spiritual insensitivity*] of the people of the Nephites, **except** [*unless*] **they repent I will take away my word** [*gospel*] **from them**, and **I will withdraw my Spirit from them**, and **I will suffer them no longer** [*I can no longer exercise patience toward them, after the four hundred years is over*], and **I will turn the hearts of their brethren** [*the Lamanites*] **against them**.

9 And **four hundred years shall not pass away before** I will cause that **they shall be smitten**; yea, I will visit [*punish*] them **with the sword** [*wars*] and with **famine** and with **pestilence** [*all types of troubles, including plagues, diseases, natural disasters, famine, etc.*].

10 Yea, **I will visit** [*punish*] **them in my fierce anger** [*another name for the law of justice*], and there shall be those of the fourth generation [*about AD 400*] who shall live, of your enemies, to behold your **utter destruction**; and this shall surely come **except ye repent**, saith the Lord; and those of the fourth generation shall visit [*participate in*] your destruction.

Next, in verse 11, Samuel summarizes what he has just taught these Nephites, emphasizing the positive.

11 But **if ye will repent and return unto the Lord your God I will turn away mine anger** [*in other words, the law of mercy will be put in place rather than the*

law of justice], saith the Lord; yea, thus saith the Lord, **blessed are they who will repent and turn unto me, but wo** [*big trouble*] **unto him that repenteth not.**

Because the law of justice will have to take over, which means you will have to pay for your own sins, which will be miserable beyond your ability to comprehend. (See D&C 19:17.)

Next, Samuel teaches that a few righteous people in a wicked city can prevent its complete destruction.

12 Yea, **wo unto this great city of Zarahemla**; for behold, **it is because of those who are righteous that it is saved**; yea, wo unto this great city, for I perceive, saith the Lord, that there are many, yea, even the more part [*the majority*] of this great city, that will harden their hearts against me, saith the Lord.

13 But **blessed are they who will repent, for them will I spare**. But behold, **if it were not for the righteous who are in this great city, behold, I would cause that fire should come down out of heaven and destroy it.**

You may recall that the wicked city of Ammonihah was completely and utterly destroyed after they ran the righteous men out of the city and burned their women and children. See Alma 14:7–8 and 16:9–10.

Next, Samuel will warn these Nephites about the dangers to them if they run the righteous people out from among them.

14 But behold, **it is for the righteous' sake that it is spared**. But behold, the time cometh, saith the Lord, that **when ye shall cast out the righteous from among you, then shall ye be ripe for destruction**; yea, wo be unto this great city, because of the wickedness and abominations which are in her.

15 Yea, and **wo be unto the city of Gideon**, for the wickedness and abominations [*extreme forms of evil and wickedness*] which are in her.

16 Yea, and **wo be unto all the cities which are in the land round about, which are possessed by the Nephites**, because of the wickedness and abominations which are in them.

Next, Samuel talks about the materialistic (focusing on money and material things) mentality of most wicked people and the "curse" of not being able to keep their wealth, which has become a top priority in their misguided lives.

17 And behold, **a curse shall come upon the land**, saith the Lord of Hosts, because of the people's sake [*because of the wickedness among the Nephites*] who are upon the land, yea, because of their wickedness and their abominations [*extra wicked sins*].

18 And it shall come to pass, saith the Lord of Hosts [*another name for Jehovah, the premortal Jesus, who is the God of the Old Testament under Heavenly Father's direction; the Lord of the armies of Israel and the armies of heaven; see Bible Dictionary, under "Sabaoth"*], yea, our great and true God, **that whoso shall hide up treasures**

in the earth shall find them again no more, because of the great curse of the land, save [*unless*] he be a righteous man and shall hide it up unto the Lord [*and he has consecrated everything he has to the Lord*].

These verses contain an important reminder to us about priorities as far as money, wealth, and material possessions are concerned. Jacob 2:18–19 confirms that wealth is not anti-God if we have our priorities straight. The Lord is inspiring Samuel here to give the same message. If people will consecrate, or, in other words, dedicate all they have to the Lord by helping others, and keep wealth and material means in proper perspective in their lives, it enables the Lord to bless them and help them preserve their wealth whether it is great or just adequate.

The "curse" that we see in these verses can refer to the loss of spirituality, charity, etc., which always accompanies greed and meanness, as well as the literal loss of wealth and material things that have become, in effect, idols that have replaced God in these people's lives.

19 For **I will** [*desire*], saith the Lord, **that they shall hide up their treasures unto me** [*gain wealth in order to do good for others*]; and **cursed be they who hide not up their treasures unto me**; for none hideth up their treasures unto me save it be the righteous; and he that hideth not up his treasures unto me, cursed is he, and also the treasure, and none shall redeem it [*be able to hold on to it*] because of the curse of the land.

20 And the day shall come that they shall hide up their treasures, **because they have set their hearts upon riches**; and because they have set their hearts upon their riches, and will hide up their treasures when they shall flee before their enemies; because they will not hide them up unto me, cursed be they and also their treasures; and in that day shall they [*the Nephites*] be smitten, saith the Lord.

21 Behold ye, the people of this great city, and hearken unto my words; yea, hearken unto the words which the Lord saith; for behold, he saith that **ye are cursed because of your riches**, and **also are your riches cursed** [*you will lose them*] **because ye have set your hearts upon them**, and have not hearkened unto the words of him [*God*] who gave them unto you.

Next, Samuel teaches a lesson in cause and effect.

22 **Ye do not remember the Lord** your God in the things with which he hath blessed you, **but ye do always remember your riches** [*your wealth*], not to thank the Lord your God for them; yea, **your hearts are not drawn out unto the Lord** [*your hearts don't have gratitude to God*], **but they do swell with great** [*but your hearts do have*] **pride**, unto **boasting**, and unto **great swelling, envyings, strifes, malice, persecutions**, and **murders**, and **all manner of iniquities** [*sins and wickedness*].

23 **For this cause hath** [*this is why*] **the Lord God caused that a curse should come upon the land**, and

also upon your riches, and this **because of your iniquities**.

As Samuel continues his sermon on cause and effect and how the minds of the wicked work, he now points out that as pride and materialism take over the mentality of people, their minds eventually turn to the irritation caused to them by the prophets of God. Having deteriorated so far, they no longer have any hesitation about getting rid of the servants of the Lord from among them.

24 Yea, **wo** [*great trouble is coming*] **unto this people**, because of this time which has arrived, that **ye do cast out the prophets**, and do mock them, and cast stones at them, and do slay them, and do all manner of iniquity unto them, even as they did of old time [*just like the wicked did in times past*].

Throughout history, people have had a tendency to honor ancient prophets but to not follow and obey the current ones. This is one of Satan's prized deceptions. Convinced that they are righteous because they have been deceived into thinking they are, they respect the prophets of old but become blind to the fact that the current ones are delivering the same message. Next, Samuel addresses this issue. He is a great teacher!

25 And now when ye talk [*among yourselves*], **ye say: If our days had been in the days of our fathers** [*ancestors*] of old, **we would not have slain the prophets**; **we would not have stoned them, and cast them out**.

26 Behold **ye are worse than they**; for as the Lord liveth, **if a prophet come among you and declareth** [*teaches and explains*] **unto you the word of the Lord, which testifieth of your sins and iniquities, ye are angry with him**, and **cast him out** and **seek all manner of ways to destroy him**; yea, **you will say that he is a false prophet**, and that he is a sinner, and of the devil [*wicked men among the Jews said the same thing about Christ; see John 10:20*], **because he testifieth** [*tells you*] **that your deeds are evil**.

Next, having boldly exposed their thinking and actions toward true prophets, Samuel tells these Nephites how foolish and gullible they are when it comes to false prophets.

27 But behold, **if a man shall come among you and shall say: Do this, and there is no iniquity** [*if he says that evil is not evil*]; **do that and ye shall not suffer**; yea, he will say: Walk after the pride of your own hearts; yea, walk after the pride of your eyes, and **do whatsoever your heart desireth**—and **if a man shall come among you and say this, ye will receive him, and say that he is a prophet**.

In other words, if someone calls "evil good, and good evil" (Isaiah 5:20), you accept him as a prophet.

28 Yea, **ye will lift him up** [*you honor and praise him*], and ye will **give unto him of your substance**; ye will give unto him of **your gold**, and of **your silver**, and ye will **clothe him with costly apparel** [*clothing*]; and **because he speaketh flattering words unto**

you, and he saith that all is well, then ye will not find fault with him [*like you do with true prophets*].

Much of our modern society is in exactly the same mode as described in verses 27 and 28, above. For example, many organized religions have departed from the Bible and teach salvation by grace alone rather than by grace and works. Many now say premarital sex is permitted (as long as those involved are in love), along with homosexuality, same sex marriage, improper activities on the Sabbath, gambling, and a host of other things pleasing to those who want to be saved in their sins rather than from their sins (Alma 11:34–37).

29 **O ye wicked and ye perverse generation** [*group of people living at the same time*]; **ye hardened** [*hard-hearted; insensitive to the Spirit*] and ye **stiffnecked** [*prideful; not humble*] people, how long will ye suppose that the Lord will suffer you [*allow you to keep going like this*]? Yea, how long will ye suffer yourselves [*allow yourselves*] to be led by foolish and blind guides? Yea, **how long will ye choose darkness rather than light**?

30 Yea, behold, the anger of the Lord is already kindled [*started*] against you; behold, **he hath cursed the land because of your iniquity**.

What Samuel teaches next is part of the "cycle of apostasy." It is the devastation and destruction portion of the cycle in which people's wicked and foolish lifestyles are destroyed. This part of the cycle is designed to humble and soften hearts to the point that people humble themselves and use their agency to call upon God for help, which is then appreciated and treasured. People who learn their lessons from this part of the cycle find that spirituality enters their souls and blessings and eventual prosperity follow. Those who refuse to learn from this phase of the cycle go on to destruction. This will be the case with the Nephites about AD 400.

As Samuel continues with this part of the cycle of apostasy, he will tell them that it is too late for most of them. This lets us know that they are so far gone that they have no desire at all to use their agency to choose to repent when devastation and destruction come upon them. While they might "weep and howl" (verse 32), trying to get the Lord to rescue them, it would be desperation rather than sincere repentance. And as soon as they were out of physical danger and misery, they would immediately go back to their wickedness. This was the case with Korihor (Alma 30:55). Most of these people have allowed themselves to actually get beyond the point where they would ever sincerely repent and have a change of heart.

This is a serious warning to us that people can become so wicked that the desire to repent no longer enters their hearts, no matter what the circumstances. Like Laman and Lemuel, they get to the point that they are "past feeling" (1 Nephi 17:45).

However, don't miss the last four words of this chapter, in which the Lord, through Samuel, invites even these Nephites to "repent and be saved."

31 And behold, **the time cometh that he curseth your riches, that**

they become slippery, that ye cannot hold them; and **in the days of your poverty** [*when poverty comes upon you*] ye cannot retain them.

32 And **in the days of your poverty ye shall cry unto the Lord**; and **in vain** [*it won't work*] **shall ye cry**, for your desolation is already come upon you, and **your destruction is made sure**; and then shall ye weep and howl in that day, saith the Lord of Hosts. And then shall ye lament [*mourn*], and say:

33 **O that I had repented**, and had **not killed the prophets**, and stoned them, and cast them out. Yea, in that day ye shall say: **O that we had remembered the Lord our God** in the day that he gave us our riches, and then they would not have become slippery that we should lose them; for behold, our riches are gone from us.

34 Behold, **we lay a tool here and on the morrow it is gone**; and behold, our swords are taken from us in the day we have sought them for battle.

35 Yea, **we have hid up our treasures and they have slipped away from us**, because of the curse of the land.

36 **O that we had repented** in the day that the word of the Lord came unto us; for behold the land is cursed, **and all things are become slippery, and we cannot hold them**.

37 Behold, **we are surrounded by demons**, yea, **we are encircled about by the angels of him** [*the devil*] **who hath sought to destroy our souls**. Behold, **our iniquities are great** [*we are very wicked*]. O Lord, canst thou not turn away thine anger from us? And this shall be your language in those days [*this is what you will say when destruction comes upon you*].

38 But behold, **your days of probation are past; ye have procrastinated** [*put off*] **the day of your salvation** [*your opportunities to live the gospel*] **until it is everlastingly too late**, and your destruction is made sure; yea, for ye have sought all the days of your lives for that which ye could not obtain; and **ye have sought** [*looked*] **for happiness in doing iniquity**[*being wicked*], **which thing is contrary to the nature of that righteousness which is in our great and Eternal Head** [*wickedness is the exact opposite of the nature of God*].

39 O ye people of the land, that ye would hear my words! And I pray that the anger of the Lord be turned away from you, and that ye would **repent and be saved**.

HELAMAN 14

In this chapter, Samuel will give the sign of the Savior's birth, including a "day and a night and a day" without darkness (see verse 4). When they see this, they will know that Jesus has just been born to Mary in Bethlehem. He tells them that this sign will be given in five years (verse 2). He will also give the sign of the Savior's death, which was to be three days of darkness (see verses 14 and 20).

These two signs are highly symbolic. When we invite Christ into our lives, "light" enters our souls. When we remove the Savior and His gospel from our lives, we find ourselves in spiritual "darkness."

This entire chapter, as well as chapter 15 that follows, are an effort by a kind and loving God to reclaim these wicked Nephites who have rejected every effort to save them so far. This is a follow-up on the last four words of chapter 13, which again invite these people to repent.

1 AND now it came to pass that **Samuel, the Lamanite, did prophesy a great many more things which cannot be written**.

2 And behold, **he said unto them: Behold, I give unto you a sign**; for **five years more** cometh, and behold, **then cometh the Son of God to redeem all those who shall believe on his name** [*Christ will be born in five years*].

> Next, Samuel gives details of the sign of Christ's birth in Bethlehem to Mary. Thus, in spite of their being on the other side of the world and without "modern communication," the most "modern" and "ancient" of all communication will be used to tell them of the birth of the Christ Child; namely, communication from God.

3 And behold, **this will I give unto you for a sign at the time of his coming**; for behold, there shall be **great lights in heaven**, insomuch that **in the night before he cometh there shall be no darkness**, insomuch that it shall appear unto man as if it was day.

4 Therefore, **there shall be one day and a night and a day, as if it were one day** and there were no night; and this shall be unto you for a sign; for **ye shall know of the rising of the sun and also of its setting**; therefore they shall know of a surety [*there will be no room for doubt*] that there shall be two days and a night; nevertheless **the night shall not be darkened**; and **it shall be the night before he is born**.

> The day and the night and again day, with no darkness, was not the only sign given among these people on the Western Hemisphere. In verses 5 and 6, next, Samuel tells of additional signs.

5 And behold, there shall **a new star** arise, such an one as ye never have beheld; and this also shall be a sign unto you.

6 And behold this is not all, there shall be **many signs and wonders in heaven**.

> Just as there were many "signs and wonders" that signaled the Nephites that the First Coming of Christ was getting close, so also there are many signs and wonders occurring now in the last days, indicating that His Second Coming is getting close. These signs are referred to as "the signs of the times."

7 And it shall come to pass that ye [*Nephites*] **shall all be amazed, and wonder**, insomuch that ye shall fall to the earth.

8 And it shall come to pass that **whosoever shall believe on the Son of God, the same shall have everlasting life**.

Just a quick doctrinal reminder. The phrase "everlasting life," in verse 8 above, does not refer to living forever. The term for that is "immortality." "Everlasting life" means the kind of life God has; or, in other words, exaltation or eternal life. See Moses 1:39, wherein the terms "immortality" and "eternal life" obviously refer to two different conditions.

9 And behold, **thus hath the Lord commanded me, by his angel**, that I should come and tell this thing unto you; yea, he hath commanded **that I should prophesy these things unto you**; yea, he hath said unto me: Cry unto this people, **repent** and **prepare the way of the Lord**.

There are many lessons that could be taught using the phrase "prepare the way of the Lord" in verse 9, above. We will take time for just one. This phrase can mean "Prepare a pathway for the Lord into your heart."

Next, Samuel continues pointing out how the minds of wicked people work in order to avoid truth and light from God. Among other things, prejudice, irritation, and anger can stand in the way of everlasting life.

10 And now, **because I am a Lamanite, and have spoken unto you the words which the Lord hath commanded me**, and **because it was hard against you, ye are angry with me** and do seek to destroy me, and have cast me out from among you.

Samuel will not stop or give up, until his message is delivered.

11 And **ye shall hear my words**, for, for this intent [*purpose*] have I come up upon the walls of this city, **that ye might hear and know of the judgments** [*punishments during mortality as well as judgment on Judgment Day*] **of God which do await you** because of your iniquities, and **also that ye might know the conditions of repentance** [*and also I want to explain to you how you can still repent*];

12 And **also that ye might know of the coming of Jesus Christ**, the Son of God [*Heavenly Father's Son*], the Father [*the Creator*] of heaven and of earth, the Creator of all things from the beginning; **and that ye might know of the signs of his coming**, to the intent that ye might believe on his name. [*I must teach you who Christ is so that you have the ability to realize how important He is for you.*]

13 And **if ye believe on his name ye will repent of all your sins**, that thereby ye may have a remission of them [*so that you can be forgiven of them*] through his merits [*through what Christ did for you*].

Next, Samuel the Lamanite prophesies and gives these people a sign of the death of Jesus so that these Nephites will know when He has been crucified in Jerusalem. Then he explains why it is necessary for the Savior to give His life. He tells them that Christ has to complete His mission so that all of us can be resurrected and so that we will be enabled to overcome spiritual death through repentance.

14 And behold, again, **another sign I give unto you, yea** [*namely*], **a sign of his death**.

15 For behold, **he surely must die that salvation may come**; yea, it behooveth him [*He is obligated to do this by His premortal covenant to become our Redeemer*] and becometh expedient [*necessary*] that he dieth, **to bring to pass the resurrection of the dead**, that thereby men may be brought into the presence of the Lord [*accountability*].

Remember that Samuel is speaking here of Christ's death and Resurrection, plus two kinds of death for us: namely, physical (the death of the body) and spiritual (being cut off from the literal presence of God). It is important to keep these two different definitions of death straight in our minds as we read Samuel's words. You may wish to put notes in your scriptures on these.

16 Yea, behold, **this death** [*Christ's death*] **bringeth to pass the resurrection**, and redeemeth [*saves*] all mankind from **the first death—that spiritual death**; for all mankind, **by the fall of Adam being cut off from the presence of the Lord**, are considered as **dead, both as to things temporal** [*physical death*] **and to things spiritual** [*spiritual death*].

Spiritual death (above) refers to Adam and Eve when they were cast out from the Garden of Eden. By partaking of the forbidden fruit, they were cast out of the literal presence of the Father and Son, thus being cut off from direct, face-to-face communication with Them. This is one definition of spiritual death.

Next, Samuel speaks of how Christ overcame physical death for all who have been born and for all who will be born into a physical body.

17 But behold, **the resurrection of Christ redeemeth mankind**, yea, even **all mankind** [*overcomes physical death for all mortals; see 2 Nephi 9:22*], and bringeth them back into the presence of the Lord [*all are ultimately resurrected and brought to face Final Judgment*].

As Samuel continues, he speaks next of Christ's opening the door for us to overcome the "spiritual death" brought upon Adam and Eve and, consequently, upon all of us because of Adam's fall. In other words, Christ makes it possible for us to repent, be forgiven, and return to the literal presence of the Father and live with Him and Jesus forever in the celestial kingdom. This, then, overcomes the "first death" or "spiritual death" (verse 16, above).

18 Yea, and **it** [*Christ's Atonement, death, and Resurrection*] **bringeth to pass the condition of repentance** [*makes repentance available*], that **whosoever repenteth** the same **is not hewn down and cast into the fire** [*comes under the law of mercy; in other words, will be forgiven of sins and does not suffer the type of punishment Christ suffered for our sins (D&C 19:15–19) and is not subject to permanent separation (spiritual death) from God*]; but **whosoever repenteth not** is hewn down and cast into the fire [*comes under the law of justice and will be punished for their own sins*]; and there cometh upon them **again a spiritual death**, yea, **a second death**, for **they are cut off again** as to things pertaining to righteousness.

Samuel is being specific, technical, and context sensitive in his use of terms. In verse 18, above, we see the terms "again," "spiritual death" and "second death." He used the phrase "spiritual death" to mean the "first death" in the context of Adam and Eve being cast out of the direct, literal presence of God in verse 16. In verse 18, he again uses the term "spiritual death," but this time it refers to a second "spiritual death" in the context of failure to repent and prepare to have a pleasant Final Judgment. He calls this second spiritual death "a second death." In verse 19, next, he refers to it as "this second death." In our gospel discussions, we commonly refer to it as "the second death," meaning failure to become worthy and capable of returning to live with God forever.

19 Therefore **repent ye, repent ye**, lest by knowing these things and not doing them ye shall suffer [*allow*] yourselves to come under condemnation [*stopped from eternal progression forever*], and ye are brought down unto **this second death** [*placed outside the direct presence of God forever*].

In summary, in the context of Samuel's address, we have the following definitions of death:

1. "This death" (verse 16): The Savior's death, which brought about resurrection for us all.
2. "The first death—that spiritual death" (verse 16): The first death or spiritual death, which occurred at the fall of Adam, wherein Adam and Eve were cast out from the direct, physical presence of God in the Garden of Eden.
3. "Temporal [*death*]" (verse 16): The death of the physical body.
4. "Second death" (verses 18–19): The second "spiritual death," being permanently banished at the Final Judgment from living in the direct physical presence of God. This "second death" is the direct result of our refusing to repent and become worthy and capable of living with the Father and the Son in celestial glory forever.

Samuel will now provide more detail regarding the signs to be given to these people at the time of the Savior's Crucifixion.

20 But behold, as I said unto you concerning another sign, a sign of his death, behold, in that day that he shall suffer death **the sun shall be darkened and refuse to give his light unto you; and also the moon and the stars; and there shall be no light upon the face of this land, even from the time that he shall suffer death, for the space of three days**, to the time that he shall rise again from the dead [*when He is resurrected*].

21 Yea, **at the time that he shall yield up the ghost** [*when He dies on the cross*] there shall be **thunderings and lightnings** for the space of many hours, and **the earth shall shake and tremble**; and **the rocks** which are upon the face of this earth, which are both above the earth and beneath, which ye know at this time are solid, or the more part of it is one solid mass, **shall be broken up**;

22 Yea, **they shall be rent in twain** [*torn apart*], and shall ever after be found in seams and in cracks, and in broken fragments upon the face of the whole earth, yea, both above the earth and beneath.

23 And behold, **there shall be great tempests**, and there shall be **many mountains laid low**, like unto a valley, and **there shall be many places which are now called valleys which shall become mountains**, whose height is great.

24 And **many highways shall be broken up**, and **many cities shall become desolate** [*empty, no people will live in them*].

25 And **many graves shall be opened**, and shall yield up many of their dead [*they will be resurrected*]; and **many saints shall appear unto many**.

The resurrections spoken of in verse 25, above, are resurrections of celestial-quality people only, or, in other words, "Saints" (verse 25). No terrestrial-quality people will be resurrected until the Second Coming of Christ. (They will be resurrected during the first part of the Millennium, after the resurrection of celestials. See D&C 88:97–99.) No telestial-quality people will be resurrected at all until the end of the Millennium. (See D&C 88:100–101.)

26 And behold, thus hath the angel spoken unto me; for he said unto me that **there should be** [*will be*] **thunderings and lightnings for the space of many hours**.

27 And he said unto me that while the thunder and the lightning lasted, and the tempest, that these things should be, and that **darkness should cover the face of the whole earth for the space of three days**.

28 And the angel said unto me that **many shall see greater things than these**, to the intent [*so*] that they might believe that these signs and these wonders should come to pass upon all the face of this land, **to the intent that there should be no cause for unbelief** [*no excuse for not believing*] **among the children of men** [*among the people*]—

29 And this to the intent **that whosoever will believe might be saved**, and that **whosoever will not believe, a righteous** [*a fair and just*] **judgment might come upon them**; and also **if they are condemned** [*punished by God*] **they bring upon themselves their own condemnation**.

Individuals truly are "free to choose" (2 Nephi 2:27).

One of the major messages of Samuel is that moral agency is held sacred by the Lord. He will not violate it. Thus, as Samuel concludes this part of his speech, he emphasizes the privilege of choosing as well as the unavoidable accountability we have for the choices we make. He teaches that we are indeed the ones who determine our eternal destiny.

30 And now **remember, remember**, my brethren [*Samuel loves these people who have treated him so harshly*], **that whosoever perisheth, perisheth unto**

himself [*brings it upon himself*]; and whosoever doeth iniquity [*commits sin*], doeth it unto himself [*hurts himself*]; for behold, **ye are free; ye are permitted to act for yourselves**; for behold, **God hath given unto you a knowledge** [*so you have the ability to use your agency*] **and he hath made you free** [*has given us the moral agency to choose for ourselves*].

31 **He hath given unto you that ye might know good from evil**, and **he hath given unto you that ye might choose life or death**; and **ye can do good and be restored unto that which is good**, or have that which is good restored unto you [*you can have your personal righteousness reflect back upon you on the Final Judgment Day*]; **or ye can do evil, and have that which is evil restored unto you** [*or you can have your wickedness reflect on you at the Final Judgment*].

This is discussed by Alma as he counsels his son, Corianton, in Alma 41. Another way to put it might be that you can use your God-given agency to overcome "spiritual death" through the Atonement of Christ, or you can use your agency to choose the "second death."

HELAMAN 15

Samuel is still standing high up on the wall delivering his inspired message. He now gives the final part of his message from God to the Nephites. He has Christlike love for these wicked people, as you will see again in verse one. This love requires that he leave a very clear message with these Nephites so they will have a definite understanding of the consequences, meaning the results, of their choices (or for the misuse of their agency).

1 AND now, **my beloved brethren**, behold, **I declare** [*teach and explain*] **unto you that except** [*unless*] **ye shall repent your houses shall be left unto you desolate** [*empty, uninhabited*].

2 Yea, **except ye repent, your women shall have great cause to mourn** in the day that they shall give suck [*are nursing babies; raising small children*]; for **ye shall attempt to flee and there shall be no place for refuge** [*for you to go to get away*]; yea, and wo unto them which are with child [*pregnant*], for they shall be heavy and cannot flee; therefore, they shall be trodden down and shall be left to perish.

3 Yea, **wo unto this people who are called the people of Nephi except they shall repent**, when they shall see all these signs and wonders which shall be showed unto them; for behold, **they have been a chosen people of the Lord**; yea, **the people of Nephi hath he** [*the Lord*] **loved** [*has been enabled to bless*], and also hath he chastened [*disciplined*] them; yea, **in the days of their iniquities hath he chastened** [*punished*] **them because he loveth them**.

4 But behold **my brethren, the Lamanites hath he hated** [*has not been able to bless as much*] **because their deeds have been evil continually**, and this because of the iniquity of

the tradition of their fathers. But behold, salvation hath come unto them through the preaching of the Nephites; and for this intent hath the Lord prolonged their days. [*This is why the Lord did not destroy them earlier when they were so wicked.*]

As you noticed in verses 3 and 4, above, we defined the words "loved" (verse 3) and "hated" (verse 4) differently than the usual definitions. These context-sensitive definitions are important; otherwise, through the misinterpretation of these two words, readers can come to believe that God hates some people. In the February 2003 *Ensign*, pages 20–25, Elder Russell M. Nelson, of the Quorum of the Twelve Apostles, defined the word "hate" in this type of scriptural context as to "bless less." With this definition as a foundation, we defined "loved" as meaning "has been enabled to bless more" (verse 3), and "hated" as "has not been able to bless as much" (verse 4). This is an example of how important it is to have modern prophets to help us understand the scriptures correctly, which, in turn, enables us to understand God correctly.

Verse 5, next, reminds us that, at this point in the Book of Mormon, most of the Lamanites are righteous.

5 And **I would that ye should behold** [*I want you to see*] **that the more part of them** [*that the majority of the Lamanites*] are in the path of their duty [*are living the gospel, are on the covenant path*], and **they do walk circumspectly** [*righteously, with honor, dignity, and integrity*] **before God**, and they do observe to **keep his commandments and his statutes** [*laws*] **and his judgments** [*rules*] according to the law of Moses.

Just a reminder: The Law of Moses, referred to in verse 5, above, refers to the commandments, rituals, and ordinances that the Lord gave the children of Israel through Moses in the Old Testament. It was a preparatory set of rules and commandments designed by the Lord to lift them from the degradation and wickedness they had learned as slaves in Egypt to a point where they could accept and live the higher laws of the Savior's gospel. The Law of Moses was designed to teach obedience and to point the people's minds to the Savior, the "Lamb of God," who was to be sacrificed for the sins of the world.

According to the Apostle Paul, it was "a schoolmaster to bring us unto Christ, that we might be justified [*brought into harmony with God*] by faith." (See Galatians 3:24.)

The Law of Moses is basically contained in the Bible in the books of Exodus, Leviticus, Numbers, and Deuteronomy.

6 Yea, I say unto you, that **the more part of them** [*the Lamanites*] **are doing this** [*keeping the Law of Moses faithfully and looking forward to Christ and His ministry*], and they are striving with unwearied diligence [*constantly trying*] that they may bring the remainder of their brethren to the knowledge of the truth; therefore there are many who do add to their numbers daily [*they have many converts to the Church daily*].

As Samuel continues, he will teach the importance of faith and repentance in leading to a change of heart. "Change of heart" means that he or she has become a different person because of the gospel of Christ. For this reason, we do not correctly refer to sinners who have repented as "repentant sinners." Rather, we say they are "born again" and have become "new creatures" (2 Corinthians 5:17). They "walk in newness of life" (Romans 6:4).

7 And behold, **ye** [*Nephites*] **do know of yourselves,** for ye have witnessed [*seen*] it, that **as many of them as are brought to the knowledge of the truth**, and **to know of the wicked and abominable traditions of their fathers**, and are led **to believe the holy scriptures**, yea, the prophecies of the holy prophets, which are written, **which leadeth them to faith** on the Lord, and **unto repentance**, which faith and repentance bringeth **a change of heart** unto them—

8 Therefore, **as many as have come to this, ye know of yourselves are firm and steadfast** [*solid*] **in the faith** [*gospel*]**, and in the thing wherewith they have been made free**.

The gospel brings the highest freedom of all to those who live it faithfully.

As Samuel continues teaching these Nephites, he reminds them of the commitment level required to have this "change of heart" (verse 8, above), using the people of Ammon (the Lamanites [*Anti-Nephi-Lehies*] who were converted by the four sons of Mosiah and their companions) as an example.

You may recall that these faithful converts had truly experienced a change of heart to the extent that they refused to take up weapons to defend themselves. They feared that killing their enemies might throw them back into their old ways of enjoying the misery of others. Consequently, they buried their weapons of war. Later, 1005 of them were killed without resisting. (See Alma 24:15–26.)

9 And **ye know also that they have buried their weapons of war**, and **they fear to take them up lest by any means they should sin**; yea, ye can see that **they fear to sin**—for behold they will suffer themselves that they be trodden down and slain by their enemies, and will not lift their swords against them, and this **because of their faith in Christ**.

Next, Samuel points out that once the Lamanites have the light of the gospel and gain a testimony, resulting in this "change of heart," they are among the most faithful of Saints. The only thing that stops them from believing is that they have not yet had a fair chance to hear the gospel under circumstances in which they can truly understand it. Therefore, the Lord will see to it that they are not destroyed so they can have this chance.

This is an important principle. Between this mortal life and the Final Judgment Day, everyone will be given a completely fair chance to understand and then accept—or reject—the gospel of Christ. Whether in this life, the spirit world, or the Millennium, all will have a perfect opportunity. Like these Lamanites spoken of by Samuel, many, many others, when taught so that they truly understand the gospel, will accept and remain faithful forever. Thus, Doctrine and Covenants 76:67 teaches that those who gain exaltation will be "innumerable," as does Revelation 7:9, in other words, so many that you couldn't even begin to count them.

Samuel will give a great prophecy about the bright future of the Lamanites. We are living in a day when this prophecy is being fulfilled.

10 And now, **because of their steadfastness** when they do believe in that thing which they do believe, for because of their firmness **when they are once enlightened**, behold, **the Lord shall bless them and prolong their days**, notwithstanding their iniquity [*even though the Lamanites have times of great wickedness and unbelief*]—

11 Yea, even if they should dwindle in unbelief **the Lord shall prolong their days, until the time shall come** which hath been spoken of by our fathers, and also by the prophet Zenos, and many other prophets, **concerning the restoration of our brethren, the Lamanites, again to the knowledge of the truth**—

Samuel prophesies that in the last days, the Lamanites will be brought back to the Lord. You may wish to read Doctrine and Covenants 49:24 in conjunction with this promise. In his prophecy, Samuel details some of the troubles that will come upon the Lamanites in the meantime.

12 Yea, I say unto you, that **in the latter times** [*the last days, before the Second Coming*] **the promises of the Lord have been extended to our brethren, the Lamanites**; and **notwithstanding** [*in spite of*] **the many afflictions which they shall have, and notwithstanding they shall be driven to and fro upon the face of the earth**, and be **hunted**, and shall be **smitten** and **scattered** abroad, having **no place for refuge, the Lord shall be merciful unto them.**

13 And **this is according to the prophecy**, that **they shall again be brought to the true knowledge, which is the knowledge of their Redeemer, and their great and true shepherd, and be numbered among his sheep**.

14 Therefore I say unto you [*this is why I've been telling you*], **it shall be better for them than for you except ye repent**.

15 For behold, **had the mighty works been shown unto them which have been shown unto you**, yea, unto them who have dwindled in unbelief because of the traditions of their fathers, ye can see of yourselves that **they never would again have dwindled in unbelief**.

People sometimes wonder why the Lord doesn't just arrange to have everyone in every generation, all at the same time, have their "perfect chance" to understand and accept or reject the gospel. That way, there would always be a large number of righteous people on earth at any given time.

In light of what Samuel has been teaching us in the above verses, perhaps one of the reasons is that we must all learn to be patient with people who don't think as we do. This is a most important aspect of our training to become gods. Gods have to be patient, or they would end up destroying most of their people prematurely before they had a fair chance to exercise their agency wisely by living the gospel.

At any rate, whatever the reason, it is obvious that God's timetable is often different than ours. In intermixing us with others who come unto Christ at differing times—some in this life, some in the spirit world, and some never—we are given an advanced course in character development. Keeping in mind that we are indeed in training to become gods is a vital perspective that can provide us with many answers.

16 **Therefore, saith the Lord: I will not utterly destroy them**, but I will cause that **in the day of my wisdom** [*according to My timetable*] **they shall return again unto me**, saith the Lord.

17 And **now behold, saith the Lord, concerning the people of the Nephites** [*many of whom have apparently had their fair chance*]: **If they will not repent**, and observe to do my will, **I will utterly destroy them**, saith the Lord, **because of their unbelief notwithstanding** [*in spite of*] **the many mighty works which I have done among them**; and as surely as the Lord liveth shall these things be, saith the Lord.

HELAMAN 16

This is the last chapter about Samuel the Lamanite. He will finish his message to these wicked Nephites and then leave. Some will believe him, but most will not.

By the end of this chapter, we will be down to one year before the birth of Christ in Bethlehem. This chapter contains one of the favorite scenes in artwork by members of the Church, namely, Samuel, the Lamanite, standing on the wall, with arrows and stones from the angry Nephites missing him. It is a magnificent scene depicting the power and majesty of a humble servant of God who completed his mission to these Nephites with God's protection so he could finish his message to them.

Many Nephites will be converted by Samuel's inspired and prophetic message and will find Nephi and ask him to baptize them. But the majority will not be converted. As is typical of the wicked, they will keep the truth from penetrating their hearts by becoming angry. They will use this anger as momentum in seeking to destroy Samuel.

1 AND now, it came to pass that **there were many who heard the words of Samuel, the Lamanite, which he spake upon the walls of the city**. And **as many as believed on his word went forth and sought** [*looked*] **for Nephi; and when they had come forth and found him they confessed unto him their sins and denied not** [*did not try to hide*

their sins from him], **desiring that they might be baptized unto the Lord.**

2 But as **many** as there were **who did not believe in the words of Samuel were angry with him**; and **they cast** [*threw*] **stones at him upon the wall**, and **also many shot arrows at him** as he stood upon the wall; **but the Spirit of the Lord was with him, insomuch that** [*so that*] **they could not hit him with their stones neither with their arrows.**

Many more were converted at this point.

3 Now **when they saw that they could not hit him, there were many more who did believe** on his words, insomuch that **they went away unto Nephi to be baptized.**

4 For behold, **Nephi was baptizing**, and **prophesying**, and **preaching, crying** [*teaching*] **repentance** unto the people, **showing signs and wonders, working miracles** among the people, **that they might know that the Christ must** [*would*] **shortly come—**

5 **Telling them of things which must shortly come** [*soon take place*], **that they might know and remember at the time of their coming** [*when these prophecies were fulfilled, in other words, when they took place*] **that they had been made known unto them beforehand** [*before they took place*], to the intent that they might believe; therefore as many as believed on the words of Samuel went forth unto him [*Nephi*] to be baptized, for **they came repenting and confessing their sins.**

A simple message from verses 4 and 5, above, is that for those who, in the timetable of the Lord, have the gospel available to them, there is plenty of evidence that it is true.

Verse 6 reminds us again that being wicked makes people so they can't think very well.

6 **But the more part** [*the majority*] **of them did not believe in the words of Samuel**; therefore **when they saw that they could not hit him with their stones and their arrows, they cried** [*shouted*] **unto their captains, saying: Take this fellow and bind him** [*tie him up*], **for behold he hath a devil**; and because of the power of the devil which is in him we cannot hit him with our stones and our arrows; therefore take him and bind him, and away with him.

7 And **as they went forth to lay their hands on him** [*to catch him*], behold, **he did cast himself down from the wall, and did flee** [*run quickly*] **out of their lands, yea, even unto his own country, and began to preach and to prophesy among his own people.**

8 And behold, **he was never heard of more among the Nephites**; and thus were the affairs of the people.

9 And thus ended **the eighty and sixth year** of the reign of the judges [*6 BC*] over the people of Nephi.

10 And thus ended also **the eighty**

and seventh year of the reign of the judges, **the more part** [*majority*] **of the people remaining in their pride and wickedness**, and the lesser part [*the minority*] walking more **circumspectly** [*righteously*] before God.

11 And these were the conditions also, in **the eighty and eighth year** of the reign of the judges.

12 And there was but little alteration [*change*] in the affairs of the people, save [*except*] it were **the people began to be more hardened in iniquity** [*became more and more wicked*], **and do more and more of that which was contrary to** [*against*] **the commandments of God**, in **the eighty and ninth year** of the reign of the judges.

13 But it came to pass in **the ninetieth year of the reign of the judges** [*2 BC; in other words, two years before the birth of Jesus*], there were **great signs given unto the people, and wonders**; and **the words of the prophets began to be fulfilled**.

14 And **angels did appear unto men**, wise men, and did declare unto them glad tidings of great joy; thus **in this year the scriptures began to be fulfilled**.

Another sign of the times, which fit their day and also fits our day, is that more and more people explain away the obvious signs of the times (things that happen that show us that the coming of Christ is getting quite close) rather than accepting them as the marvelous proofs they are that God exists and the scriptures are true.

15 Nevertheless, **the people began to harden their hearts** [*against God and spiritual things*], all save [*except*] it were the most believing part of them, both of the Nephites and also of the Lamanites, and **began to depend upon their own strength and upon their own wisdom, saying**:

16 **Some things they may have guessed right, among so many** [*the "so-called" prophets may have gotten lucky on some things*]; but behold, **we know that all these great and marvelous works cannot come to pass**, of which has been spoken.

One of the saddest comparisons between their day and our day is that in both cases, among the Nephites and in our day, people find ways of disbelieving that there is a Christ.

17 And **they began to reason and to contend** among themselves, **saying**:

18 That **it is not reasonable that such a being as a Christ shall come; if so**, and he be the Son of God, the Father of heaven and of earth, as it has been spoken, **why will he not show himself unto us as well as unto them who shall be at Jerusalem**?

19 Yea, **why will he not show himself in this land as well as in the land of Jerusalem**?

Yet another parallel between our day and theirs is that people rationalize away truth, calling light darkness, and darkness light; evil good, and good evil (Isaiah 5:20). They claim that the real motive of prophets and Church leaders is to keep people in their power.

20 But behold, **we know that this** [*the coming of Christ*] **is a wicked tradition**, which has been handed down unto us by our fathers [*ancestors*], to cause us that we should believe in some great and marvelous thing which should come to pass, but not among us, but in a land which is far distant, a land which we know not; **therefore they can keep us in ignorance, for we cannot witness with our own eyes that they are true** [*in other words, what we can't see we can't possibly be expected to believe*].

21 And **they will, by the cunning and the mysterious arts of the evil one** [*the devil*], **work some great mystery which we cannot understand, which will keep us down to be servants to their words, and also servants unto them**, for we depend upon them to teach us the word; and **thus will they keep us in ignorance** if we will yield ourselves unto them, all the days of our lives.

Next, Mormon, whose abridgment we are reading, sheds the light of truth on what was in the hearts of those who refused Samuel's message. He also explains some of Satan's ways of tempting us and confusing us about the truth.

22 And **many more things did the people imagine up in their hearts**, which were **foolish and vain**; and they were much disturbed, for **Satan did stir them up** to do iniquity continually; yea, **he did go about spreading rumors and contentions** upon all the face of the land, **that he might harden the hearts of the people against that which was good and against that which should come** [*in other words, against Christ*].

23 And notwithstanding [*in spite of*] the signs and the wonders which were wrought [*performed*] among the people of the Lord, and the many miracles which they did [*in other words, in spite of the obvious evidence supporting the words of the prophets and the scriptures*], **Satan did get great hold upon the hearts** of the people upon all the face of the land.

Satan is a master of putting feelings into people's hearts (Helaman 6:28–29) through which he deceives and controls them.

24 And thus ended **the ninetieth year** of the reign of the judges [*1 BC*] over the people of Nephi.

25 And **thus ended the book of Helaman**, according to the record of Helaman and his sons.

THIRD NEPHI
THE BOOK OF NEPHI

Third Nephi can be one of the most inspiring and helpful books of the Book of Mormon for you to read because it lets you feel extra close to the Savior, with the help of the Holy Ghost. Third Nephi is the focal point of the Book of Mormon. Everything has been leading up to it. On average, Christ is mentioned every 1.7 verses throughout the Book of Mormon. And now, in Third Nephi, we will have the privilege of experiencing the visit of the resurrected Lord to the people in the Americas. We will watch His tenderness toward them, feel with them the prints of the nails in His hands and feet, listen carefully as He teaches them, rejoice as He teaches us the doctrines of salvation, and wish with them that He could stay longer when He leaves.

Third Nephi is the record of Nephi, who is Alma the Elder's great-great-great-grandson. Alma was converted by Abinadi's preaching in wicked King Noah's court (Mosiah 17:2). By way of quick review, we will list these prophets from Alma the Elder to Nephi: Alma the Elder, Alma the Younger, Helaman, Helaman, Nephi, and Nephi.

THIRD NEPHI 1

In chapter one, you will see the fulfillment of the signs prophesied by Samuel the Lamanite, showing the people in the Americas that the Savior has been born to Mary in Bethlehem. Just before they are fulfilled, it will seem to many in America that the five years spoken of by Samuel (Helaman 14:2–3) have come and gone without the signs being given. Thus, the enemies of the Saints will rejoice, and even some faithful Saints will become worried (3 Nephi 1:7).

There could be a possible similarity between this and the Saints in the last days as enemies of righteousness mock their belief in the Second Coming of Christ. However, just as the "day and a night and a day" with no darkness came to pass in the days of Nephi, so also will the Savior's Second Coming take place to the surprise and fear of the wicked and with similar rejoicing of the faithful.

As we begin this chapter, it has been six hundred years since Lehi left Jerusalem. First, we will say goodbye to Nephi, son of Helaman II, who, with his brother, Lehi, dedicated his life to preaching the gospel. This was the Nephi that the Lord gave His power to so he could command famines, etc., and be obeyed just as God is (Helaman 10:5–10). After Nephi departs, Mormon will begin using the records kept by Nephi's son, Nephi, (3 Nephi 1:3) for his abridgment or summary of the events presented in Third Nephi.

1 NOW it came to pass that **the ninety and first year** had passed away and **it was six hundred years from the time that Lehi left**

Jerusalem; and it was in the year that Lachoneus was the chief judge and the governor over the land.

2 And **Nephi, the son of Helaman, had departed out of the land of Zarahemla, giving charge** [*the responsibility*] **unto his son Nephi, who was his eldest son, concerning the plates of brass, and all the records which had been kept, and all those things which had been kept sacred from the departure of Lehi out of Jerusalem**.

We understand from Mosiah 1:16 that "all the records" and "all those things which had been kept sacred from the departure of Lehi out of Jerusalem," mentioned in verse 2, above, would include the plates of Nephi, the sword of Laban, and the Liahona.

3 Then he [*Nephi*] departed out of the land, and whither [*where*] he went, no man knoweth; and **his son Nephi did keep the records in his stead** [*in his place*], yea, the record of this people.

4 And it came to pass that **in the commencement** [*beginning*] **of the ninety and second year**, behold, **the prophecies of the prophets began to be fulfilled more fully**; for there began to be **greater signs and greater miracles** wrought [*done*] among the people.

Just as there were "greater signs and greater miracles" among these people as the birth of Christ drew closer, so also there are more signs of the times being fulfilled as we get closer to the Savior's Second Coming.

Next, some people among the Nephites claim that the time is past for the signs of Christ's birth to be fulfilled as prophesied by Samuel the Lamanite. They take delight in tormenting the faithful members of the Church and attempting to destroy their faith.

5 But **there were some who began to say that the time was past for the words to be fulfilled, which were spoken by Samuel, the Lamanite**.

6 And they began to rejoice over their brethren [*they began to be happy that faithful members of the Church were worried*], **saying**: Behold **the time is past** [*the time is up*], and **the words of Samuel are not fulfilled; therefore, your joy and your faith concerning this thing** [*the birth of Christ*] **hath been vain** [*useless*].

7 And it came to pass that **they did make a great uproar** [*a lot of noise and talking about it*] **throughout the land; and the people who believed** [*in Samuel's prophecies*] **began to be very sorrowful**, lest by any means those things which had been spoken might not come to pass.

The worry and sorrow of these Saints who were concerned that the prophesied sign of the birth of the Savior might not come to pass can remind us of our day and the disappointment and worry of some Christians, who, in their understanding of the scriptures, thought the Second Coming of Christ would take place by the end of the year AD 1999, or at least by the end of the year AD 2000. In the case of our day, Doctrine and Covenants 77:12–13 clearly states that the Second Coming will not be at the end of the sixth one-thousand-year period from the time of the fall of Adam. Rather, His Coming will be sometime in the beginning of the seventh one-thousand-year period. Many signs of the times will take place in the beginning of the seventh one-thousand-year period before He comes. (See the headings for the book of Revelation in the Bible, chapters 8 and 9.)

In the case of the faithful Saints at the time of Nephi, who were ridiculed by enemies who claimed that the time for the "day and a night and a day" without darkness was past, they continued faithful in spite of opposition.

8 But behold, **they did watch steadfastly** [*with solid focus and faith*] **for that day and that night and that day** which should be as one day as if there were no night, **that they might know that their faith had not been vain** [*useless*].

Faith is one of the gifts of the Spirit. (See 1 Corinthians 12:9.) Some people are blessed with such great faith that they never have the slightest doubt about the gospel no matter what happens. Others, who are equally faithful and steadfast in living the gospel, seem to have to struggle somewhat to keep their faith up in times of disappointment and opposition.

A helpful aspect of the Book of Mormon is that it demonstrates how varying personality types can be successful in living the gospel and keeping covenants. From verses 7 and 8, above, we see that some faithful members worried "lest by any means those things which had been spoken [*about the signs to accompany the birth of Christ*] might not come to pass." However, we also see that they remained faithful, that "they did watch steadfastly for that day and that night and that day which should be as one day."

Thus, we understand that those whose testimonies are strong but who have to exercise extra restraints on themselves to remain faithful when things do not go according to their understanding of the Lord's plans can also be counted among the worthy.

Next, Mormon tells us that things among the people in Third Nephi had come to the point where the wicked had set a deadline to execute all who believed in the signs spoken of by Samuel, the Lamanite, if his prophecy had not come to pass by then. One might wonder why non-believers would make such a big issue out of the beliefs of these Saints. Clear thinking would tell us that they should simply feel sorry for those who are gullible enough, from their point of view, to believe in prophets and in a god of some sort and who thus can't be comfortable in "eating, drinking, and being merry." But wickedness interferes with people's ability to think clearly.

Perhaps part of the answer as to why the wicked can't seem to leave the righteous alone lies in the fact that Satan doesn't leave such people alone. Therefore, those who follow the devil's ways can't leave good people alone either. The devil is their master, and they are usually unaware of it.

9 Now it came to pass that **there was a day set apart** [*there was a date set*] **by the unbelievers, that all those who believed in those traditions** [*who believed in the gospel of Christ and His birth coming very soon, including the day, night, and day prophecy of Samuel the Lamanite*] **should be put to death except** [*unless*] **the sign should come to pass,** which had been given by Samuel the prophet.

Next, we will witness one of the most touching and beautiful scenes in the Book of Mormon. The voice of the Lord comes to Nephi, telling him that He will be born the next day.

We understand that at this point in time, Mary is in labor, and Joseph is worried that they can't find a comfortable place to stay in Bethlehem.

Furthermore, we can't help but wonder what feelings filled the Savior's heart several months earlier when His mother, Mary, was "found with child" (Matthew 1:18). The Lord knew that finally, after having created "worlds without number" (Moses 1:33), many of which had already finished up or "passed away" (Moses 1:35) with innumerable spirit brothers and sisters of His being born there and receiving the opportunity to work out their salvation through His gospel and role as Redeemer (D&C 76:24), He would have His own turn to be born, and it would be at the time specified to Nephi as he humbly prayed about the coming execution of his people by the wicked.

10 Now it came to pass that when **Nephi, the son of Nephi, saw this wickedness of his people, his heart was exceedingly** [*very*] **sorrowful**.

11 And it came to pass that **he went out and bowed himself down upon the earth, and cried** [*prayed*] **mightily to his God in behalf of** [*for*] **his people, yea, those who were about to be destroyed** because of their faith in the tradition of their fathers [*because they believed in the same gospel and God that their righteous ancestors believed in*].

12 And it came to pass that **he cried mightily unto the Lord all that day**; and behold, **the voice of the Lord came unto him, saying**:

13 Lift up your head and **be of good cheer** [*cheer up, be happy*]; for behold, the time is at hand, and **on this night shall the sign be given**, and **on the morrow** [*tomorrow*] **come I into the world** [*tomorrow, I will be born*], to show unto the world that I will fulfil all that which I have caused to be spoken by the mouth of my holy prophets.

Next, in verse 14, the Savior summarizes the purposes of His mortal ministry into two major points as follows:

1. I come unto my own, to fulfil all things which I have made known unto the children of men from the foundation of the world.
2. [*I come*] to do the will, both of the Father and of the Son.

The Lord then tells Nephi that this is the night that will not grow dark when the sun goes down.

14 Behold, **I come unto my own** [*to the covenant people, Israel, especially the Jews; see Acts 3:13–18; 2 Nephi 10:3; John 1:11; 3 Nephi 9:16*], **to fulfil all things which**

I have made known [*everything I have had taught and prophesied*] unto the children of men [*people*] from the foundation of the world [*since the beginning of the world*], **and to do the will, both of the Father and of the Son**—of the Father because of me, and of the Son because of my flesh. And behold, **the time is at hand, and this night shall the sign be given**.

Let's take a moment to define the terms "Father" and "Son" as used in verse 14, above, and elsewhere in this type of context (setting and background) in the scriptures. Literally, the "Father" is Elohim, our Heavenly Father. Christ is the "Father" in many ways. For instance, He is the "Father" or "Creator" of the world. He is also the "Father" because He is the "Father" or the "Author" of our salvation. He is the "Father" of our happiness. He is the "Father" of our forgiveness for sins. He is the "Father" of our spiritual rebirth. Through Him, we are spiritually "born again."

In a similar sense, George Washington is the "father" of our country. Henry Ford is the "father" of the production line assembly process. Thomas Edison is the "father" of the incandescent light bulb.

When verse 14 says, "The Father because of me," it means, in effect, that Jesus is just like the Father and thinks and acts just like Him because of the attributes that He inherited from His Father, Elohim. The phrase "the Son because of my flesh" means that Jesus is literally the mortal Son of God the Father, born to Mary.

As we continue, the signs of Christ's birth are given. People who had planned the death of the believers are shocked. Watch how they react.

15 And it came to pass that the words which came unto Nephi were fulfilled, according as they had been spoken; for behold, **at the going down of the sun there was no darkness; and the people began to be astonished** [*very surprised*] **because there was no darkness** when the night came.

16 And there were **many, who had not believed the words of the prophets,** who **fell to the earth and became as if they were dead**, for they knew that the great plan of destruction which they had laid for those who believed in the words of the prophets had been frustrated [*turned out to be wrong*]; for the sign which had been given was already at hand [*was already happening*].

17 And **they began to know that the Son of God must shortly appear**; yea, **in fine** [*in summary*], **all the people** upon the face of the whole earth [*this part of the Americas*] from the west to the east, both in the land north and in the land south, were so exceedingly astonished that they **fell to the earth**.

18 **For they knew that the prophets had testified of these things for many years**, and that the sign which had been given was already at hand; and **they began to fear** because of their iniquity [*wickedness, sins*] and their unbelief.

19 And it came to pass that **there was no darkness in all that night, but it was as light as though it was mid-day**. And it came to pass that the sun did rise in the morning again, according to its proper order; and **they knew that it was the day that the Lord should be born**, because of the sign which had been given.

As mentioned previously, there is beautiful symbolism in the light that came upon these Book of Mormon people at the time of the Savior's birth. It is that when we allow the light of the Savior's gospel and His Atonement to enter into our life, our soul is filled with spiritual light and knowledge.

20 And **it had come to pass, yea, all things** [*it was all fulfilled*], every whit [*every bit*], **according to the words of the prophets**.

21 And it came to pass also that **a new star did appear**, according to the word [*just as the prophets said it would*].

Many changed their minds and believed, based on the signs given, and were baptized, bringing peace to the land.

However, Mormon has an immediate warning for us in verse 22, next; namely, that even at a point when strong testimony has been given as to the truthfulness of the gospel, Satan cunningly plants ideas in people's minds that can lead to future doubts and apostasy, sometimes far down the road. Certainly, one lesson for us in this is that we can't merely ride along through life basing our commitment to God on past testimony alone. We must continue living faithfully so that ongoing testimony is born to us by the Holy Ghost.

22 And it came to pass that **from this time forth there began to be lyings sent forth among the people, by Satan, to harden their hearts** [*resist spirituality and righteous things*], **to the intent that they might not believe in those signs and wonders which they had seen**; but notwithstanding [*in spite of*] these lyings and deceivings the more part [*majority*] of the people did believe, and were converted unto the Lord.

23 And it came to pass that **Nephi went forth** among the people, and also many others, **baptizing unto repentance**, in the which **there was a great remission** [*forgiveness*] **of sins**. And **thus the people began again to have peace in the land**.

A simple, important message reoccurs throughout the Book of Mormon: remission of sins, in other words, forgiveness of sins through the Atonement of Christ, leads to peace, both on an individual level as well as in entire societies.

24 And **there were no contentions** [*fighting and quarreling*], **save** [*except*] **it were a few** that began to preach, endeavoring [*attempting*] to prove by the scriptures that it was no more expedient [*necessary*] to observe [*obey*] the law of Moses [*the rules, laws, and commandments Moses gave to the children of Israel in the Old Testament*]. Now in this thing they did err [*they were making a mistake*], having not understood the scriptures.

25 **But** it came to pass that **they soon became converted, and were convinced of the error which they were in**, for it was made known unto them that the law [*of Moses*] was not yet fulfilled, and that it must be fulfilled in every whit [*bit*]; yea, the word came unto them that it must be fulfilled; yea, that one jot or tittle [*not even the tiniest bit*] should not pass away till it should all be fulfilled; therefore in this same year were they brought to a knowledge of their error and did confess their faults.

26 And thus **the ninety and second year** [*AD 1; in other words, one year after Christ was born*] **did pass away, bringing glad tidings unto the people** because of the signs which did come to pass, according to the words of the prophecy of all the holy prophets.

In the next verse, we will be told of Gadianton robbers, who continue to commit many crimes and murders. One wonders how these individuals could go on committing crimes in spite of personally seeing the day, night, and day without darkness. In the first three verses of chapter 2, Mormon will explain how this can be.

27 And it came to pass that **the ninety and third year did also pass away in peace, save** [*except*] it were **for the Gadianton robbers**, who dwelt upon the mountains, **who did infest the land**; for so strong were their holds and their secret places that **the people could not overpower them**; therefore **they did commit many murders, and did do much slaughter among the people**.

28 And it came to pass that **in the ninety and fourth year they began to increase** in a great degree, because there were many dissenters [*apostates*] of the Nephites who did flee unto them, **which did cause much sorrow unto those Nephites who did remain in the land**.

It brings sorrow and trouble when children do not follow the righteous traditions of their parents and relatives. Mormon points this out in verse 29, next. The Zoramites, mentioned here, were apostate Nephites. (See Alma 30:59.) It is also a disappointment to see the Lamanites, who were so faithful a few years earlier, falling away into apostasy (verses 29 and 30).

29 And there was also a cause of much sorrow among **the Lamanites**; for behold, they **had many children who did grow up** and began to wax strong in years [*began to grow older*], that **they became for themselves** [*they made their own rules, which led away from the gospel*], and **were led away by some who were Zoramites**, **by their lyings** and their **flattering words**, to **join** those **Gadianton robbers**.

30 And **thus were the Lamanites afflicted also**, and **began to decrease as to their faith and righteousness**, because of the wickedness of the rising generation [*their children who were growing up*].

THIRD NEPHI 2

In chapter 2, we will cover about eleven years after the sign (a day and a night and a day with no darkness) was given to the Nephites of the birth of Christ, in other words, from AD 5 to AD 16. Perhaps you will recall that one of the most important means of keeping your personal testimony of the truthfulness of the gospel is to remember past blessings from God (see Alma 5:6). On the other hand, one of the ways to lose a testimony is to forget or ignore previous blessings and spiritual experiences. Verse 1, next, points this out. We will use **bold** to emphasize this and several other points associated with loss of personal spirituality and loyalty to God.

1 AND it came to pass that thus passed away **the ninety and fifth year** also, and **the people began to forget those signs and wonders which they had heard**, and began to be **less and less astonished at a sign or a wonder from heaven** [*less and less influenced by obvious evidence around them of God's existence*], insomuch [*such that*] that they began to be **hard in their hearts** [*insensitive to spiritual things*], and **blind in their minds** [*including lack of wisdom; lack of ability to see future consequences of present choices*], and **began to disbelieve all which they had heard and seen**—

Next, in verse 2, we catch a glimpse of one reason why people quit paying attention to obvious testimony-building experiences. Remember that among the things they are explaining away are the day, night, and day without darkness, plus the new star that appeared. We are again reminded that personal wickedness leads away from the ability to think rationally, in other words, clearly and wisely.

2 **Imagining up some vain** [*foolish*] **thing in their hearts, that it was wrought** [*that the signs and wonders they had seen with their own eyes were done*] **by men and by the power of the devil**, to lead away and deceive [*fool*] the hearts of the people; **and thus did Satan get possession of the hearts of the people again**, insomuch [*so that*] that **he did blind their eyes and lead them away to believe that the doctrine of Christ was a foolish and a vain** [*not worthwhile*] **thing**.

In these verses and others in the Book of Mormon, we see a simple sequence employed by the devil to deceive people. First, the people saw the actual signs from God, bearing clear and obvious witness to them of the Savior's birth in Bethlehem. Second, while still acknowledging and admiting that they saw something, they explain it in ways that put God out of the picture. Third, they get to the point where they no longer even believe that they saw something unusual.

Next, we are reminded that one tool Satan uses is to convince people who believe in God that miracles, signs, and wonders have stopped (see Mormon 9:10). This has been a common teaching of many Christian churches today and was taught under Satan's direction anciently, as explained in verse 3.

3 And it came to pass that **the people began to wax** [*grow*] **strong in**

wickedness and abominations [*extra-wicked sins*]; and **they did not believe that there should be any more signs or wonders given**; and Satan did go about, leading away the hearts of the people, tempting them and causing them that they should do great wickedness in the land.

4 And thus did pass away **the ninety and sixth year**; and also **the ninety and seventh year**; and also **the ninety and eighth year**; and also **the ninety and ninth year** [*about AD 9*];

5 And also **an hundred years had passed away since the days of Mosiah** [*King Mosiah II, who set up the Nephite democracy; see Mosiah 29*], who was king over the people of the Nephites.

6 And **six hundred and nine years had passed away since Lehi left Jerusalem.**

7 And **nine years had passed away from the time when the sign was given**, which was spoken of by the prophets, **that Christ should come into the world** [*was born in Bethlehem*].

Next, we are told that the Nephites began a new calendar system following the signs accompanying Christ's birth. Up to now, they had been using two calendar systems as follows:

1. Their first calendar was based upon how many years it had been since Lehi left Jerusalem in 600 BC.

2. Their second method of keeping track of time began with the reign of the judges and was based on how many years it had been since the beginning of the reign of the judges in 92 BC. (See Mosiah 29.)

With the signs that accompanied the birth of Jesus, they began a third calendar system, counting the years from that event. Thus, at this point in the Book of Mormon, using all three calendar systems, we are 609 years from the time Lehi left Jerusalem, 100 years from the beginning of the reign of the judges, and 9 years after the birth of Christ, or AD 9 in our modern calendar system.

By the way, AD stands for "Anno Domini," which means "in the year of our Lord;" or, in other words, since the birth of Christ.

8 Now **the Nephites began to reckon** [*keep track of*] **their time from this period when the sign was given, or from the coming of Christ**; therefore, nine years had passed away [*according to the new Nephite calendaring system*].

9 And **Nephi** [*who left the land of Zarahemla in 3 Nephi 1:2–3 and was never seen again*], **who was the father of Nephi**, who had the charge of the records, **did not return to the land of Zarahemla, and could nowhere be found in all the land**.

10 And it came to pass that **the people did still remain in wickedness**, notwithstanding [*in spite of*] the much preaching and prophesying which was sent among them; and **thus passed away the tenth year** also; and **the eleventh year also** passed away in iniquity.

As mentioned previously, the "signs of the times" among the Nephites as they drew closer to the destruction of the wicked (3 Nephi 8) and the appearance of the resurrected Christ to them, are similar to the signs of the times in our last days before the Second Coming. One of these signs is "wars and rumors of wars" (Matthew 24:6). Another is widespread wickedness and corruption, in other words, dishonest behavior, bribery, not following the rules, etc.

11 And it came to pass in **the thirteenth year** there began to be **wars and contentions** [*fighting and arguing*] **throughout all the land**; for the **Gadianton robbers had become** so **numerous**, and did slay so many of the people, and did lay waste [*destroy*] so many cities, and did spread so much death and carnage [*injuring, hurting, slaughter*] throughout the land, that it became expedient [*necessary*] that all the people, both the Nephites and the Lamanites, should take up arms [*weapons*] against them.

Another sign of the times for us in our day is that people will have to decide either to be on the side of right or on the side of wrong. There will not be much "grey area." See Doctrine and Covenants 1:35–36, where we are told that in the last days peace will be taken from the earth and "the devil shall have power over his own dominion. And also the Lord shall have power over his Saints." This same condition developed among the Nephites about nineteen years before the Savior's appearance to them after He had been crucified, as described in the following verses.

12 Therefore, **all the Lamanites who had become converted unto the Lord did unite with their brethren, the Nephites**, and were compelled, for the safety of their lives and their women and their children, **to take up arms against those Gadianton robbers**, yea, and also **to maintain their rights**, and the privileges of **their church** and of their **worship**, and their **freedom** and their **liberty**.

13 And it came to pass that before this **thirteenth yea**r had passed away **the Nephites were threatened with utter destruction because of this war**, which had become exceedingly sore [*bad*].

In the next verses, the "curse" that had come upon the Lamanites is mentioned. We will take time here to remind you that the curse was the withdrawal of the Spirit of the Lord. This was taught by Apostle Joseph Fielding Smith as follows (bold added for teaching purposes):

"The dark skin was placed upon the Lamanites so that they could be distinguished from the Nephites and to keep the two peoples from mixing. The dark skin was the sign of the curse. The curse was the withdrawal of the Spirit of the Lord and the Lamanites becoming a 'loathsome and filthy people, full of idleness and all manner of abominations' (I Nephi 12:23). The Lord commanded the Nephites not to intermarry with them, for if they did they would partake of the curse" (Joseph Fielding Smith, *Answers to Gospel Questions*, 5 vols. [Salt Lake City: Deseret Book, 1957–66], 3:122).

14 And it came to pass that **those Lamanites who had united with the Nephites were numbered among the Nephites** [*considered to be Nephites*];

15 And **their curse was taken from them** [*in other words, the Spirit of the Lord was able to be upon them because of their righteousness*], and **their skin became white like unto the Nephites**;

16 And **their young men and their daughters became exceedingly fair** [*handsome and beautiful*], and **they were numbered** [*counted*] **among the** Nephites, **and were called Nephites.** And thus ended **the thirteenth year.**

As indicated in verse 16, above, at this point in the Book of Mormon, the term "Nephites" basically refers to all those who desire to live the gospel regardless of whether they are bloodline Nephites or Lamanites.

17 And it came to pass in the commencement [*beginning*] of the fourteenth year, **the war between the robbers and the people of Nephi did continue and did become exceedingly sore** [*very severe*]; nevertheless, **the people of Nephi did gain some advantage of the robbers**, insomuch [*to the extent*] **that they did drive them back out of their lands** into the mountains and into their secret places.

In verse 18, next, we are once again reminded of a major message of the Book of Mormon; namely, that the real danger to an individual or to a nation comes from within. When personal righteousness prevails or is mostly the case, eternal blessings are not threatened. When corruption enters personal lives, the individuals, and eventually the nation, are at risk.

18 And thus ended **the fourteenth year.** And in **the fifteenth year** [*AD 15; about nineteen years before the resurrected Savior will come to the Nephites*] they [*the Gadianton robbers*] did come forth against the people of Nephi; and **because of the wickedness of the people of Nephi, and their many contentions and dissensions** [*fighting and arguing among themselves*], **the Gadianton robbers did gain many advantages over them.**

19 And thus ended **the fifteenth year**, and thus were the people in a state of many afflictions; and **the sword of destruction did hang over them** [*similar to the world in the last days before the Savior's Second Coming*], insomuch that they were about to be smitten down by it, and **this because of their iniquity** [*wickedness*].

THIRD NEPHI 3

One of Satan's very effective ways of fooling people seems to be to get his wicked followers to believe that what they are doing is right and that those who follow God's teachings are doing wrong, or at least, what they are doing is foolish. In fact, Korihor, the antichrist, got to the point where he believed that the words he taught, which came from the devil, were true (see Alma 30:53).

In this chapter, we meet another wicked leader, Giddianhi, who has been likewise deceived by the devil to the point that he claims with great flowing words that the cause of the Gadianton robbers is just and right and that the Nephites are in the wrong. We see much of this today as Satan gains converts through cunning deception. Isaiah prophesied that we would see much of calling "evil good and good evil" (Isaiah 5:20).

In this case, Lucifer has succeeded in deceiving (in other words, fooling) Giddianhi into believing that what he is doing is right, not wrong. In fact, Giddianhi seems to feel that he is a kind and generous soul and is treating Lachoneus, the righteous leader of the Nephites, with respect. Note also that Giddianhi has obviously had a lot of experience and success in using flattery, which is another form of deception.

1 AND now it came to pass that in **the sixteenth year** from the coming of Christ [*AD 16*], **Lachoneus, the governor of the land** [*the righteous leader of the Nephites*], **received an epistle** [*a letter*] **from the leader and the governor** [*Giddianhi*] **of this band of robbers**; and these were the words which were written, **saying**:

2 **Lachoneus, most noble and chief governor of the land**, behold, **I write this epistle unto you, and do give unto you exceedingly great praise because of your firmness, and also the firmness of your people, in maintaining that which ye suppose to be your right and liberty**; yea, **ye do stand well**, as if ye were supported by the hand of a god, in the defence of your liberty, and your property, and your country, or that which ye do call so [*in other words, the country that you claim to be yours is actually ours*].

3 And **it seemeth a pity unto me, most noble Lachoneus, that ye should be so foolish and vain as to suppose that ye can stand against so many brave men** who **are at my command**, who do now at this time stand in their arms [*have their weapons ready*], and do await with great anxiety for the word—Go down upon the Nephites and destroy them.

4 And I, knowing of their unconquerable spirit [*their great courage*], having proved them in the field of battle, and **knowing of their everlasting hatred towards you because of the many wrongs which ye have done unto them**, therefore if they should come down against you they would visit you with utter destruction.

5 **Therefore I have written this epistle**, sealing it with mine own hand, **feeling for your welfare** [*I really care about you*], **because of your firmness in that which ye believe to be right**, and **your noble spirit in the field of battle**.

One characteristic of those who have been deceived is that they believe others cannot see through their attempts at deceiving them. In verses 6 and 7, plus the first part of verse 8, next, Giddianhi makes a ridiculous offer, which he apparently thinks will sound good to Lachoneus.

6 Therefore I write unto you, desiring that ye would **yield up** [*surrender*] **unto this my people** [*the Gadianton robbers*], **your cities**, your **lands**, and your **possessions**, rather than that they should visit you with the sword and that destruction should come upon you.

7 Or in other words, yield yourselves up unto us [*surrender to us*], and **unite with us** and **become acquainted with our secret works**, and **become our brethren** [*brothers*] that ye may **be like unto us—not our slaves, but our brethren and partners of all our substance**.

Giddianhi's promise to the Nephites that they can be "partners of all our substance" (verse 2, above) presents a problem. His people survive by robbing and plundering the Nephites. Just where does he propose to get "all our substance" from now on if he keeps his word to them?

8 And behold, **I swear unto you** [*I promise*], **if ye will do this, with an oath** [*a very strong promise*], **ye shall not be destroyed**; but if ye will not do this, I swear unto you with an oath, that on the morrow month [*next month*] I will command that my armies shall come down against you, and they shall not stay their hand [*they will not hold back*] and shall spare not, but shall slay you, and shall let fall the sword upon you even until ye shall become extinct.

9 And behold, I am Giddianhi; and **I am the governor of this the secret society of Gadianton** [*secret combination of Gadianton robbers*]; which society and **the works thereof I know to be good**; and they are of ancient date [*they are very old*] and they have been handed down unto us.

The idea in the last part of verse 9, above, that something is "good" because it is "of ancient date," meaning goes way back in history, seems to play prominently in the minds of many people. For instance, many believe the words of ancient prophets but reject even the idea of having modern prophets. The Jews rejected Christ because His teachings appeared to them to go against the teachings of Abraham, Moses, and other ancient prophets. Satan seems to use the notion that "ancient" means "good," quite often in his winning and retaining of followers.

10 And I write this epistle [*letter*] unto you, Lachoneus, and **I hope that ye will deliver up** [*surrender*] **your lands and your possessions**, without the shedding of blood [*so we don't have to kill any of you*], **that this my people may recover** [*get back*] **their rights and government, who have dissented away** [*apostatized*] **from you because of your wickedness in retaining from them their rights of government**, and except ye do this, **I will avenge their wrongs** [*in other words, I will bring justice to you because of the wrongs you have done to my righteous people*]. I am Giddianhi.

Next, we will see how Lachoneus, a righteous leader of a democracy, deals with the threats and demands of a terrorist like Giddianhi, whose ultimate goal is to exercise power and unrighteous dominion over others.

11 And now it came to pass **when Lachoneus received this epistle** [*letter*] **he was exceedingly astonished** [*very, very surprised*], because of the boldness of Giddianhi demanding the possession of the land of the Nephites, and also of **threatening the people and avenging the wrongs** [*getting revenge*] **of those that had received no wrong**, save it were **they had wronged themselves** by dissenting [*apostatizing*] unto those wicked and abominable robbers.

12 Now behold, this **Lachoneus**, the governor, **was a just man** [*a righteous man, who lived the gospel with honor and exactness*], **and could not be frightened by the demands and the threatenings of a robber**; therefore **he did not hearken to the epistle of Giddianhi**, the governor of the robbers, but **he did cause that his people should cry** [*pray*] **unto the Lord for strength against the time that the robbers should come down against them**.

Remember that Giddianhi had invited the Nephites to surrender and to join with his band of robbers and share their "substance" (verse 8). Watch what happens now as the Nephites gather all of their "substance" and put it out of reach of these robbers.

13 Yea, **he sent a proclamation** among all the people, that they should **gather together their women, and their children, their flocks** [*animals*] **and their herds, and all their substance**, save [*except*] it were their land, **unto one place**.

14 And **he caused that fortifications should be built** round about them, and the strength thereof should be exceedingly great. **And he caused that armies,** both of the Nephites and of the Lamanites, or of all them who were numbered among the Nephites, **should be placed as guards round about to watch them, and to guard them from the robbers day and night**.

As a righteous leader, Lachoneus preaches repentance to his people. They listen and repent as needed.

15 Yea, **he said unto them**: As the Lord liveth, **except** [*unless*] **ye repent of all your iniquities, and cry unto the Lord, ye will in no wise** [*no way*] **be delivered out of the hands of those Gadianton robbers**.

16 And so great and marvelous were the words and prophecies of Lachoneus that they did cause fear to come upon all the people; and **they did exert themselves in their might** [*they tried very hard*] **to do according to the words of Lachoneus**.

17 And it came to pass that **Lachoneus did appoint chief captains over all the armies of the Nephites**, to command them at the time that the robbers should come down out of the wilderness against them.

Next, we will meet one of the great, righteous military commanders of the Nephites. His name is Gidgiddoni. You will see that he is a very good man.

18 Now the chiefest among all the chief captains and **the great commander of all the armies of the Nephites** was appointed, and his name **was Gidgiddoni**.

19 Now **it was the custom among all the Nephites to appoint for their chief captains**, (save it were in their times of wickedness) **some one that had the spirit of revelation and also prophecy**; therefore, this Gidgiddoni was **a great prophet among them**, as also was the chief judge.

Next, the Nephites will request permission to attack the Gadianton robbers in their strongholds. Captain Moroni had rooted out the king-men (Alma 51, especially verses 17–18) in this manner, but the Lord will not allow these Nephites to do the same. This points out the importance of following the current word of the Lord, no matter what has been done under similar circumstances by men of God in the past.

20 Now **the people said unto Gidgiddoni: Pray unto the Lord, and let us go up upon the mountains and into the wilderness, that we may fall upon the robbers and destroy them in their own lands**.

21 **But Gidgiddoni saith** unto them: **The Lord forbid**; for **if we should go up against them the Lord would deliver us into their hands**; therefore we will prepare ourselves in the center of our lands, and we will gather all our armies together, and **we will not go against them, but we will wait till they shall come against us**; therefore as the Lord liveth, **if we do this he will deliver them into our hands** [*we will win*].

22 And it came to pass in **the seventeenth year**, in the latter end of the year [*well over a year has passed since Giddianhi had invited the Nephites to surrender and join him and his robbers*], the proclamation of [*orders and instruction from*] Lachoneus had gone forth throughout all the face of the land, and **they** [*the Nephites*] **had taken their horses,** and their **chariots**, and their **cattle**, and all their **flocks**, and their **herds**, and their **grain**, and **all their substance** [*stuff*], and did march forth by thousands and by tens of thousands, until they had all gone forth **to the place which had been appointed that they should gather themselves together**, to defend themselves against their enemies.

23 And **the land which was appointed was the land of Zarahemla, and the land which was between the land Zarahemla and the land Bountiful**, yea, to the line which was between the land Bountiful and the land Desolation.

24 And **there were a great many thousand people who were called Nephites**, who **did gather themselves together in this land**. Now Lachoneus did cause that they should gather themselves together in the land southward, because of the

great curse which was upon the land northward.

The "curse which was upon the land northward" (verse 24, above) appears to refer to the ruins of the Jaredite civilization, which apparently was still "covered with bones of men, and of beasts, and . . . ruins of buildings" (Mosiah 8:8; Alma 22:30–31).

25 And **they did fortify** [*strengthen*] **themselves against their enemies; and they did dwell** [*live*] **in one land, and in one body** [*group*], and they did fear [*this type of "fear" includes the aspects of respect and obedience*] the words which had been spoken by Lachoneus, insomuch that **they did repent of all their sins**; and they did **put up their prayers unto the Lord their God**, that he would deliver them in the time that their enemies should come down against them to battle.

26 And they were exceedingly sorrowful because of their enemies. And **Gidgiddoni did cause that they should make weapons of war of every kind**, and they should be strong with armor, and with shields, and with bucklers, after the manner of his instruction.

THIRD NEPHI 4

In chapters 4 through 7, we will see many things among the Nephites before the destruction of the wicked and the appearance of the resurrected Christ to them. Many of the things which happened to them are also typical of our last days before the Savior's Second Coming and the resulting destruction of the wicked. (They will be destroyed by the Savior's glory; see 2 Nephi 12:19; D&C 5:19). It is no doubt significant that such parallels or comparisons exist. They are, among other things, a pattern from which we can learn and gain stronger testimonies.

For example, in the Book of Mormon, at this point in time, there were a great number of wicked people whose entire goal in life was to rob and plunder, in other words, take things from others (3 Nephi 2:11). It is basically the same in our day.

There was great prosperity among the Nephites, and also many lawyers (3 Nephi 6:4–11). Many who had been faithful members of the Church became entangled in pride, while many remained humble and faithful (3 Nephi 6:13).

Many people divided up into ethnic groups, meaning their own groups according to their race and culture, which destroyed the central government's ability to function (3 Nephi 7:2). Church leaders continued to speak out boldly and clearly concerning the evils of the day and the availability of forgiveness through repentance (3 Nephi 7:16–17). Many citizens became angry because of the power and authority of Nephi (3 Nephi 7:17–20).

There were a great many miracles, which provided much obvious evidence that God exists and the gospel is true (3 Nephi 7:22). There were many convert baptisms (3 Nephi 7:26).

We will now study chapter 4 as we continue with the "countdown" to the coming of the Lord to the Nephites. Remember that the Nephites, under the direction of their leaders, have now gathered by tens of thousands (3 Nephi 3:22) into one location. This will prove to be a most difficult problem for the Gadianton robbers, who are used to living off of wild game, as well as stealing and robbing from the Nephites.

1 AND it came to pass that in the latter end of **the eighteenth year those** armies of **robbers** had prepared for battle, and **began to come down** and to sally forth [*come, venture out*] from the hills, and out of the mountains, and the wilderness, and their strongholds [*places where they had gathered for safety*], and their secret places, and began to take possession of the lands, both which were in the land south and which were in the land north, **and began to take possession of all the lands which had been deserted by the Nephites, and the cities which had been left desolate** [*with nobody living there*].

2 **But** behold, **there were no wild beasts nor game in those lands which had been deserted by the Nephites**, and there was no game [*no wild animals to hunt*] for the robbers save it were [*except*] in the wilderness.

3 And **the robbers could not exist save it were in the wilderness, for the want** [*because of the lack*] **of food**; for **the Nephites had left their lands desolate**, and had gathered their flocks and their herds and all their substance [*they had a seven-year supply of food and provisions; see verse 4*], and they were in one body [*group, were all together in one place*].

4 Therefore, **there was no chance for the robbers to plunder and to obtain food, save it were to come up in open battle against the Nephites**; and **the Nephites** being in one body, and having so great a number, and having **reserved for themselves provisions, and horses and cattle, and flocks of every kind, that they might subsist** [*survive*] **for the space of seven years**, in the which time they did hope to destroy the robbers from off the face of the land; and thus **the eighteenth year** did pass away.

5 And it came to pass that in **the nineteenth year Giddianhi** [*the leader of the robbers*] **found that it was expedient** [*necessary*] that he should **go up to battle against the Nephites**, for **there was no way that they could subsist save it were to plunder and rob and murder**.

6 And **they durst not** [*did not dare*] **spread themselves upon the face of the land** insomuch **that they could raise grain**, lest [*for fear that*] the Nephites should come upon them and slay them; **therefore Giddianhi gave commandment unto his armies that in this year they should go up to battle against the Nephites**.

One of the messages that has been given a number of times already in the Book of Mormon, and one that could be considered to be sensitive and not "politically correct" on our day, is that the farther people stray from God, the less modest and the more wild and bizarre their fashions, grooming, and appearances become. We saw this in Enos 1:20 and in Alma 3:5, and now we see it again in verse 7, next.

7 And it came to pass that they did come up to battle; and it was in the sixth month; and behold, great and terrible was the day that they did come up to battle; and they were girded [*dressed*] about after the manner [*according to the fashions, dress styles*] of robbers; and **they had a lamb-skin about their loins** [*their waist*], and they were **dyed in blood**, and their **heads were shorn** [*shaved*], and they had headplates upon them; and **great and terrible was the appearance of the armies of Giddianhi**, because of their armor, and because of their **being dyed in blood**.

Next, the robbers will think that their appearance has frightened the Nephites into giving up. They are mistaken.

8 And it came to pass that **the armies of the Nephites**, when they saw the appearance of the army of Giddianhi, **had all fallen to the earth**, and **did lift their cries** [*pray*] **to the Lord their God**, that he would spare them and deliver them out of the hands of their enemies.

9 And it came to pass that when **the armies of Giddianhi** saw this they began to shout with a loud voice, because of their joy, for they had **supposed that the Nephites had fallen with fear because of the terror of their armies**.

10 But in this thing they were disappointed, for **the Nephites did not fear them; but they did fear their God and did supplicate him** [*prayed to Him*] **for protection**; therefore, when the armies of Giddianhi did rush upon them they were prepared to meet them; yea, **in the strength of the Lord they did receive them**.

At the beginning of this chapter, we mentioned a number of parallels between this time among the Nephites and our last days. Next, in verse 11, we see another similarity; namely, this was the worst battle the Nephites had ever seen. So likewise, in the last days, there will be "war and rumors of wars" as never before.

11 And **the battle commenced** [*began*] in this the sixth month; and **great and terrible was the battle** thereof, yea, great and terrible was the slaughter [*killing*] thereof, insomuch that **there never was known so great a slaughter among all the people of Lehi since he left Jerusalem**.

12 And notwithstanding [*in spite of*] the threatenings and the oaths which Giddianhi had made, behold, **the Nephites did beat them**, insomuch that they did fall back from before them.

13 And it came to pass that **Gidgiddoni** [*the commander of the Nephite armies*] **commanded that his armies should pursue them as far as the borders of the wilderness**, and that

they should not spare any that should fall into their hands by the way; and **thus they did pursue them and did slay them**, to the borders of the wilderness, even until they had fulfilled the commandment of Gidgiddoni.

14 And it came to pass that **Giddianhi** [*the leader of the robbers*], who had stood and fought with boldness, was pursued as he fled; and being weary because of his much fighting he **was overtaken and slain**. And thus was the end of Giddianhi the robber.

15 And it came to pass that **the armies of the Nephites did return again to their place of security** [*in the land of Zarahemla and between there and Bountiful; see 3 Nephi 3:23*]. And it came to pass that this **nineteenth year** did pass away, and the robbers did not come again to battle; neither did they come again in the **twentieth year**.

16 And in the **twenty and first year** they did not come up to battle, but **they came up on all sides to lay siege** [*set up a line of soldiers*] round about the people of Nephi; for they did suppose that if they should cut off the people of Nephi from their lands, and should hem them in on every side, and if they should cut them off from all their outward privileges [*their ability to come and go as needed, including raising crops for food, etc.*], that they could cause them to yield themselves up [*to surrender*] according to their wishes.

17 Now **they had appointed unto themselves another leader** [*to replace Giddianhi*], **whose name was Zemnarihah**; therefore it was Zemnarihah that did cause that this siege should take place.

18 But behold, **this was an advantage to the Nephites**; for it was impossible for the robbers to lay siege sufficiently long to have any effect upon the Nephites, because of their much provision which they had laid up in store [*because of all the food and supplies they had stored up*],

As you will see, things are going from bad to worse among the Gadianton robbers.

19 And because of the scantiness of provisions among **the robbers**; for behold, they **had nothing save it were** [*except*] **meat for their subsistence** [*to keep them alive*], which meat they did obtain in the wilderness;

20 And it came to pass that **the wild game became scarce in the wilderness insomuch** [*so much so*] **that the robbers were about to perish** [*die*] **with hunger**.

21 And **the Nephites were continually marching out by day and by night, and falling upon their armies, and cutting them off by thousands and by tens of thousands**.

Next, the robbers decide to give up.

22 And thus **it became the desire of the people of Zemnarihah to withdraw from their design** [*their plans to conquer the Nephites*], because of the great destruction which came upon them by night and by day.

23 And it came to pass that **Zemnarihah did give command unto his people that they should withdraw** themselves from the siege, and march into the furthermost parts of the land northward.

24 And now, **Gidgiddoni** [*the leader of the Nephite armies*] being aware of their design, and knowing of their weakness because of the want of food, and the great slaughter which had been made among them, therefore he **did send out his armies in the night-time, and did cut off the way of their retreat**, and did place his armies in the way of their retreat.

25 And this did they do in the night-time, and got on their march beyond the robbers, so that on the morrow [*the next day*], when **the robbers** began their march, they **were met by the armies of the Nephites both in their front and in their rear**.

26 And **the robbers who were on the south were also cut off in their places of retreat**. And all these things were done by command of Gidgiddoni.

Remember that Gidgiddoni was a righteous prophet-leader of the Nephite armies (3 Nephi 3:19). This is important to keep in mind. Otherwise, a person could think that the actions of the Nephite soldiers in verse 27 were too harsh. Dangerous times often require no-nonsense action. The laws of self-defense (see D&C 98), given by the Lord to His people through their prophets, are no doubt being applied here.

27 And there were **many thousands who did yield themselves up** [*surrendered as*] **prisoners** unto the Nephites, and **the remainder of them were slain**.

28 And **their leader, Zemnarihah, was taken and hanged upon a tree**, yea, even upon the top thereof until he was dead. And when they had hanged him until he was dead they did fell [*cut*] the tree to the earth [*note their symbolism in doing this, as explained in verse 29*], and did cry with a loud voice, saying:

29 May the Lord preserve his people in righteousness and in holiness of heart, **that they may cause to be felled** [*cut down*] **to the earth all who shall seek to slay them because of power and secret combinations, even as this man hath been felled to the earth**.

30 And **they did rejoice** and cry again with one voice [*united*], saying: **May the God of Abraham, and the God of Isaac, and the God of Jacob, protect this people in righteousness, so long as they shall call on the name of their God for protection**.

31 And it came to pass that **they did break forth**, all as one, **in singing, and praising their God** for the great thing which he had done for them, in preserving them from falling into the hands of their enemies.

The word "Hosanna," as used in verse 32, next, means "Lord, save us now" or "save now." (See Bible Dictionary, under "Hosanna.")

32 Yea, they did cry: **Hosanna to the Most High God**. And they did cry: Blessed be the name of the Lord God Almighty, the Most High God.

One of the most healing attributes of all is that of gratitude to God (see D&C 59:21). When we have gratitude in our hearts for blessings we receive, we tend to be happy. We see a rich outpouring of this character trait in verse 33, next.

33 And **their hearts were swollen with joy, unto the gushing out of many tears, because of the great goodness of God in delivering them out of the hands of their enemies**; and they knew it was because of their repentance and their humility that they had been delivered from an everlasting destruction.

THIRD NEPHI 5

In this chapter, you can learn quite a bit about how to repent. Mormon first explains why the Nephites were so successful in repenting and how they rid themselves of the secret combinations that had come so close to destroying them completely as a people.

Then, Mormon will take time to introduce himself to us in brief detail.

As to why these Nephites were so successful in repenting completely, Mormon explains next that it was because they had complete faith. This is an example of why faith in Jesus Christ has to be the first principle of the gospel (see Articles of Faith, number 4). If we have faith in Christ and His Atonement, we then understand that repenting is worthwhile because, among other things, we know that we can be forgiven of our sins and can continue to progress until we achieve exaltation.

1 AND now behold, **there was not a living soul among all the people of the Nephites who did doubt in the least** [*they had complete faith*] **the words of all the holy prophets** [*the scriptures*] who had spoken; for they knew that it must needs be [*it was necessary*] that they must be fulfilled.

2 And **they knew** that it must be expedient [*it had to be*] **that Christ had come**, because of the many signs which had been given, according to the words of the prophets; and because of the things which had come to pass already **they knew that it must needs be** [*it was absolutely certain*] **that all things should come to pass according to that which had been spoken** [*which would no doubt include that the resurrected Savior would visit them soon as prophesied*].

3 **Therefore** [*this is the reason*] **they did forsake** [*stop*] **all their sins**, and their abominations [*extreme wickedness*], and their whoredoms [*sexual immorality*], and did serve God with all diligence day and night [*not "now and again" but continually*].

Next, we are reminded that a change in heart brought about by the gospel of Jesus Christ is a very effective way to cut down on prison populations. Without a true change of heart, enemies are still a serious danger to freedom and peace, and wisdom dictates that they be treated as such.

4 And now it came to pass that **when they had taken all the robbers prisoners**, insomuch that none did escape who were not slain, **they did cast their prisoners into prison, and did cause the word of God** [*the gospel*] **to be preached unto them; and as many as would repent of their sins and enter into a covenant that they would murder no more were set at liberty**.

5 But **as many as there were who did not enter into a covenant, and who did still continue to have those secret murders in their hearts**, yea, as many as were found breathing out threatenings against their brethren **were condemned and punished according to the law**.

6 And **thus** [*this is how*] **they did put an end to all those wicked, and secret, and abominable combinations**, in the which there was so much wickedness, and so many murders committed.

7 And thus had **the twenty and second year** passed away, and **the twenty and third year** also, and **the twenty and fourth**, and **the twenty and fifth**; and thus had twenty and five years passed away.

It is now just eight years before the destruction of the wicked and the coming of the resurrected Christ to the Nephites in America.

Mormon next takes time to talk to us, in our day, about the records he is in charge of and to introduce himself a bit more to us than he did in Words of Mormon 1:1–9.

8 And **there had many things transpired** [*taken place*] which, in the eyes of some, would be great and marvelous; nevertheless, **they cannot all be written in this book** [*probably referring to Mormon's abridgment of the large plates of Nephi; see Helaman 2:14; Mormon 2:17–18; Words of Mormon 1:3 and 5*]; yea, **this book cannot contain even a hundredth part of what was done among so many people in the space of twenty and five years** [*since the signs of the birth of Christ were given*];

Next, Mormon tells us that a great many records were kept by the Nephites over the centuries.

9 But behold **there are records which do contain all the proceedings of this people**; and **a shorter but true account was given by Nephi**.

10 Therefore **I have made my record** [*Mormon's abridgement or summary*] **of these things according to the record of Nephi** [*large plates of Nephi*], **which was engraven on the plates which were called the plates of Nephi**.

11 And behold, I do make the record **on plates which I have made with mine own hands**.

Just imagine how much work it would take for Mormon to make the delicately thin metal plates upon which he could carefully engrave his abridgement of the Nephite records.

From the accounts given by Joseph Smith's mother, we understand that Mormon's abridgement consisted of the small plates of Nephi and a set of gold plates that were approximately 6 inches wide, 9 inches in length, and 6 inches high, weighing approximately 60 pounds. Such a set would contain a rather large number of individual thin sheets or plates. While we don't know exactly how he made them, one possible scenario might be as follows:

1. Find a source of gold and possibly other precious metals that could be alloyed with the gold for the exact qualities needed for the plates.

2. Hunt animals for hides with which to make a bellows in order to blow a fire to heat the ore hot enough to melt the metal out of it.

3. Perhaps find iron ore to smelt metal from to make the tools required for pounding the plates to the needed thinness.

4. Obtain the necessary metal to make an engraving tool out of, which would need to hold up under extended use.

Whatever the process, we respect and admire Mormon for the tremendous effort required to make the plates himself and for the great amount of time and effort it took to engrave them for our benefit.

Next, Mormon tells us more about himself. Quoting the Prophet Joseph Smith, "The word Mormon means, literally, more good" (*History of the Church*, 5:399–400). We know from Mormon 1:15 that he was fifteen years old about AD 326 and that he was about seventy-four years old at the time of the final battles of his people, which took place about AD 385 (see Mormon 6:5).

12 And behold, **I am called Mormon**, being called after [*named after*] the land of Mormon [*Mosiah 18:4*], the land in which Alma [*Alma the Elder*] did establish the church among the people, yea, the first church which was established among them after their transgression [*in the days of wicked King Noah, who had Abinadi the prophet killed; see Mosiah, chapters 11–18*].

13 Behold, **I am a disciple of Jesus Christ**, the Son of God. I have been called of him [*by Him*] to declare his word among his people, that they might have everlasting life [*eternal life, exaltation in the highest degree of glory in the celestial kingdom*].

The next verse is a bit complex. It is hoped that the notes in brackets will help simplify it. The basic sentence in the verse will be **bold**. Read the **bold** first and then go back and read the other phrases.

14 **And it hath become expedient** [*necessary*] **that I**, according to the will of God, that [*in order that*] the prayers of those who have gone hence [*who have passed on; died*], who were the holy ones [*prophets and record keepers*], should be fulfilled according to their faith, **should make a record of these things which have been done**—

In other words, it was necessary for Mormon to make his abridgement so that the prayers of past prophets could be answered. These prophets prayed that their records might be preserved and that their descendants would have a chance to hear and accept the gospel (see Enos 1:13).

15 Yea, **a small record** [*an abridgement or "condensed version"*] **of that which hath taken place from the time that Lehi left Jerusalem, even down until the present time** [*probably referring to Mormon's day or about AD 385; see Mormon 6*].

16 **Therefore I do make my record from the accounts which have been given by those who were before me, until the commencement** [*beginning*] **of my day**;

17 And then **I do make a record** [*Mormon chapters 1 through 7*] **of the things which I have seen** with mine own eyes [*see Mormon 1:1*].

Next, Mormon bears testimony to us of the truthfulness of his record and expresses his concern about the limitations of his written language.

18 And **I know the record which I make to be a just and a true record**; nevertheless there are many things which, according to our language, we are not able to write.

19 And now **I make an end of my saying, which is of myself** [*I will finish what I wanted to tell you about me*], **and proceed to give my account of the things which have been before me** [*and then continue telling you about things that have taken place before my time*].

20 **I am Mormon, and a pure descendant of Lehi. I have reason to bless** [*praise*] **my God** and my Savior Jesus Christ, that he brought our fathers [*ancestors*] out of the land of Jerusalem, (and no one knew it save it were himself and those whom he brought out of that land) and that **he hath given me and my people so much knowledge unto the salvation of our souls** [*which will help us to be saved in the celestial kingdom*].

At the end of verse 20, above, Mormon reminds us that we must know the gospel in order to be saved. Joseph Smith taught this same vital, meaning absolutely necessary, doctrine when he said, "It is impossible for a man to be saved in ignorance" (D&C 131:6).

21 **Surely he hath blessed the house of Jacob** [*Israel; Jacob's descendants*], and hath been merciful unto the seed of Joseph [*the descendants of Joseph, who was sold into Egypt*].

Lehi's descendants are among the "seed of Joseph" referred to in verse 21, above. Joseph, who was sold into Egypt, was told that his posterity would "run over the wall" (Genesis 49:22). In other words, that his descendants would cross over the ocean. In verse 22, next, Mormon ties the descendants of Lehi into the blessings promised to Joseph's posterity.

22 And **insomuch as** [*whenever*] **the children** [*descendants*] **of Lehi have kept his commandments he hath blessed them and prospered them** according to his word [*just as He promised*].

Next, Mormon prophesies of a great conversion and gathering of the descendants of Joseph, as well as all of the tribes of Israel at some time in the future.

23 Yea, and **surely shall he again bring a remnant** [*a remaining part*] **of the seed of Joseph to the knowledge of the Lord their God**.

24 And as surely as the Lord liveth, will he **gather in from the four quarters of the earth** [*from throughout the entire world*] **all the remnant of the seed** [*descendants*] **of Jacob, who are scattered abroad upon all the face of the earth**.

Your patriarchal blessing will tell you which of the tribes of Israel is your lineage, meaning which tribe your blessings and responsibilities to spread the gospel come through.

25 And **as he hath covenanted with all the house of Jacob** [*with all of the tribes of Israel*], **even so shall the covenant wherewith he hath covenanted with the house of Jacob be fulfilled in his own due time** [*when the time is right*], unto the restoring all the house of Jacob unto the knowledge of the covenant that he hath covenanted with them.

Next, Mormon explains what will happen when people are converted and gathered in. The most important cause of this "gathering" is that people will know and understand the Savior and His gospel in their own minds and hearts.

26 And **then shall they know their Redeemer**, who is Jesus Christ, the Son of God; and **then shall they be gathered** in from the four quarters of the earth [*from all over the world*] unto their own lands, from whence they have been dispersed [*scattered*]; yea, as the Lord liveth so shall it be. Amen.

THIRD NEPHI 6

By way of quick review, in chapters three and four of Third Nephi, the Nephites had gathered together in one location by the tens of thousands, with a seven-year supply of food and supplies (3 Nephi 4:4). This was in response to the Gadianton robbers, who threatened to destroy them completely if they did not agree to surrender and join them (3 Nephi 3:6–8).

These robbers were destroyed over the next five years. Now, as we begin chapter six, the Nephites return to their former lands. They will have a time of peace and prosperity. They even give land to their former enemies (who covenant and promise to be peaceful) so they can be self-supporting and maintain their Lamanite identity if they so desire.

Sadly, we will once again see the "cycle of apostasy" follow the prosperity that came upon the Nephites and those with them. As usual, pride (verse 10) will be the root cause. Therefore, we see that we must avoid pride if we want to avoid this cycle in our own lives.

1 AND now it came to pass that the people of **the Nephites did all return to their own lands** in **the twenty and sixth year**, every man, with his family, his flocks and his herds, his horses and his cattle, and all things whatsoever did belong unto them.

2 And it came to pass that **they had not eaten up all their provisions** [*their seven year's supply; 3 Nephi 4:4*]; therefore they did take with them all that they had not devoured [*used up*], of all their grain of every kind, and their gold, and their silver, and all their precious things, and they did return to their own lands and their possessions, both on the north and on the south, both on the land northward and on the land southward.

3 And **they granted unto those robbers who had entered into a covenant to keep the peace of the land, who were desirous to remain Lamanites** [*who wanted to keep their identity as Lamanites*], **lands, according to their numbers, that they might have, with their labors, wherewith to subsist** [*the means needed to survive*] **upon**; and thus they did establish peace in all the land.

The word "prosper," in verse 4, next, is a word we have come to almost fear by this point in the Book of Mormon, because it is almost always followed by pride and wickedness. We must remember that this does not have to be the case, as we will see during the nearly two hundred years of peace following the Savior's visit to the Nephites.

4 And they began again to **prosper** and to wax [*grow*] great; and the twenty and sixth and seventh years passed away, and there was great order in the land; and **they had formed their laws according to equity** [*fairness*] **and justice**.

Perhaps you will recall that the Nephite democracy was founded upon the laws of God (Mosiah 29), and as the Nephites became wicked, they changed the laws of the land to reflect their personal wickedness (Helaman 4:21–24). Now, at the end of verse 4, above, we see them reform their laws and change them back to righteous ones. Thus, the only danger to the Nephite democracy at this time is sin and wickedness among the citizens themselves.

5 And now there was nothing in all the land to hinder [*stop*] the people from prospering continually, **except they should fall into transgression**.

Next, Mormon reminds us of the vital role of righteous elected and appointed government officials in securing true prosperity for a nation.

6 And now **it was Gidgiddoni, and the judge, Lachoneus, and those who had been appointed leaders, who had established this great peace in the land**.

7 And it came to pass that there **were many cities built anew** [*rebuilt*], and there were **many old cities repaired**.

8 And there were **many highways** cast up, and **many roads made**, which led from city to city, and from land to land, and from place to place.

9 And thus passed away **the twenty and eighth year**, and the people had continual peace.

One of the first messages the Savior taught the Nephites after He appeared to them was that "the spirit of contention is not of me" (3 Nephi 11:29). Contention, arguing and fighting among yourselves, is a powerful tool of the devil, and we see it being employed by him in verse 10, next, along with pride and materialism (focusing on money and things) as the "cycle of apostasy" begins again.

In fact, in just seven verses, Mormon will show us how Satan dismantles or takes apart a righteous society.

10 But it came to pass in **the twenty and ninth year** [*AD 29, about five years before the coming of the resurrected Christ to America*] there began to be some **disputings** among the people; and some were lifted up unto **pride** and **boastings because of their exceedingly great riches**, yea, even unto great **persecutions** [*being mean to others*];

11 For there were **many merchants** [*people who owned stores and businesses, in other words, much emphasis on material things*] in the land, and also **many lawyers** [*many of whom create contention to gain personal wealth*], and **many officers**.

This perhaps indicates that the government was growing much faster than the population, with a resulting decrease in self-reliance and an increase in dependency on government.

12 And the **people began to be distinguished by ranks, according to their riches and their chances for learning** [*people were divided into a class system, which is the opposite of living together in peace and unity*]; yea, **some were ignorant** [*not well-educated*] **because of their poverty** [*they no longer had equal opportunity education*], and **others did receive great learning because of their riches** [*wealth*].

13 **Some were lifted up in pride**, and **others were exceedingly humble**; some did **return railing for railing** [*some yelled back when yelled at, or, in other words, had an attitude of wanting revenge*], while **others would receive railing and persecution and all manner of afflictions**, and would not turn and revile again, but **were humble and penitent before God** [*concentrated on their own faults rather than on the faults of others*].

14 And thus there became a **great inequality in all the land**, insomuch [*to the extent*] that **the church began to be broken up**; yea, insomuch that in **the thirtieth year** [*about three or four years before the coming of Christ*] **the church was broken up** in all the land **save it were** [*except*] **among a few of the Lamanites who were converted unto the true faith**; and they would not depart from it, for they were firm, and steadfast, and immovable, willing with all diligence to keep the commandments of the Lord.

Next, Mormon summarizes what happened to cause such a rapid decline among these Nephites.

15 Now **the cause of this iniquity** [*sin and wickedness*] **of the people was this**—Satan had great power, unto the **stirring up of the people to do all manner of iniquity**, and to the puffing them up with **pride**, tempting them to **seek for power**, and

authority, and **riches**, and the **vain things of the world** [*prioritizing on things of no lasting or eternal value*].

16 And **thus Satan did lead away the hearts of the people to do all manner of iniquity**; **therefore they had enjoyed peace but a few years.**

As Mormon continues teaching us, he will basically point out how foolish and gullible, meaning easy to fool, people are who allow Satan to "carry them about" wherever he wants to carry them. One of Satan's greatest deceptions is to convince people that he does not exist and that they are in charge of their own lives as they submit to wickedness. Many who do believe in the devil have a strong tendency to underestimate his influence for evil in the lives of people and societies.

17 And thus, in the commencement of **the thirtieth year**—the people having been delivered up for the space of a long time to be **carried about by the temptations of the devil whithersoever he desired to carry them**, and **to do whatsoever iniquity he desired they should**—and thus in the commencement of this, the thirtieth year, **they were in a state** [*condition*] **of awful wickedness.**

Next, Mormon points out the extremely dangerous position these people had placed themselves in, because they definitely knew better. They were in intentional, open rebellion against the gospel. Thus, their accountability level was high.

18 Now **they did not sin ignorantly**, for **they knew the will of God concerning them**, for **it had been taught unto them**; therefore **they did wilfully rebel against God.**

19 And now **it was in the days of Lachoneus, the son of Lachoneus** [*the righteous leader of the Nephite democracy to whom Giddianhi had written the letter inviting the Nephites to surrender and join the Gadianton robbers; see 3 Nephi 3:2–10*], for Lachoneus did fill the seat [*led the Nephites in place*] of his father and did govern the people that year.

As the coming of Christ, with the accompanying destruction of the wicked among the Nephites, got closer and closer, more opportunities to understand and accept the gospel were provided to the people. The same thing is happening in our day as the gospel goes forth into all the world before the Second Coming of Christ.

20 And **there began to be men inspired from heaven** and **sent forth**, standing among the people **in all the land, preaching and testifying boldly of the sins and iniquities** of the people, and **testifying unto them concerning the redemption which the Lord would make for his people** [*telling them that they could still repent*], **or in other words, the resurrection of Christ; and they did testify boldly of his death and sufferings.**

Just as in our day, people among the Nephites became angry and bitterly opposed to those who preached the truth. In a pattern also repeated in our day, those who were especially angry were corrupt high government officials, prominent religious leaders, and lawyers, all of whose livelihoods and unrighteous dominions were threatened if people became righteous.

21 Now **there were many of the people who were exceedingly angry because of those who testified of these things**; and **those who were angry were chiefly the chief judges**, and they who had been **high priests** and **lawyers**; yea, all those who were lawyers were angry with those who testified of these things.

Next, Mormon tell us of murders carried out secretly by the wicked in power because they couldn't get rid of the righteous legally. You will see the reappearance of secret combinations (verses 27–30) inspired by the devil.

22 Now there was **no lawyer nor judge nor high priest** that **could have power to condemn any one to death** save [*unless*] their condemnation was signed by the governor of the land.

23 Now there were **many of those who testified of the things pertaining to Christ who testified boldly, who were taken and put to death secretly by the judges**, that the knowledge of their death came not unto the governor of the land until after their death.

24 Now behold, **this was contrary to the laws of the land**, that any man should be put to death except they had power from the governor of the land—

25 Therefore **a complaint came up unto the land of Zarahemla, to the governor of the land, against these judges** who had condemned the prophets of the Lord unto death, not according to the law.

26 Now it came to pass that **they were taken and brought up before the judge**, to be judged of the crime which they had done, according to the law which had been given by the people.

27 Now it came to pass that **those** [*corrupt*] **judges had many friends and kindreds** [*relatives*]; and the remainder, yea, even **almost all the lawyers and the high priests, did gather themselves together, and unite with the kindreds** [*relatives*] **of those judges who were to be tried according to the law.**

Next, in verses 28–30 comes the "secret combination."

28 And **they did enter into a covenant one with another**, yea, even into **that covenant which was given by them of old** [*in olden days*], which covenant was **given and administered by the devil** [*beginning with Cain; see Moses 5:29*], **to combine against all righteousness**.

29 Therefore **they did combine against the people of the Lord, and enter into a covenant to destroy them, and to deliver those who were guilty of murder from the grasp of justice**, which was about to be administered according to the law.

30 And **they did set at defiance** [*oppose; disobey*] **the law and the rights of their country**; and **they did covenant one with another to destroy the governor, and to establish a king over the land**, that the land should no more be at liberty but should be subject unto kings.

THIRD NEPHI 7

In this chapter, which takes us up to the time of the destruction of the wicked in the Americas when Jesus was crucified just outside the walls of Jerusalem, you will see all kinds of troubles that result when most people no longer live the gospel, or even believe in God. You will see a "last days" pattern of political assassination, dividing into ethnic groups and gangs, weakening of the central government, wickedness among members of the Church, growth of secret combinations, increase in righteousness among the faithful, increased miracles and powerful preaching of the gospel, and many convert baptisms. In short, about the same thing as is happening in our last days before the Savior's Second Coming.

Our main teaching approach in this chapter will be to bold the words of Mormon in the actual Book of Mormon text to point out the above-mentioned things.

1 NOW behold, **I** [*Mormon*] **will show unto you** that they did not establish a king over the land; but in this same year, yea, **the thirtieth year** [*AD 30*], **they** did destroy upon the judgment-seat, yea, **did murder the chief judge of the land**.

2 And **the people were divided one against another**; and they did **separate** one from another **into tribes**, every man according to his family and his kindred [*relatives*] and friends; and **thus they did destroy the government of the land**.

3 And **every tribe did appoint a chief or a leader** over them; and **thus they became tribes and leaders of tribes**.

4 Now behold, there was no man among them save he had much family and many kindreds and friends; therefore **their tribes became exceedingly great** [*large*].

5 Now all this was done, and there were **no wars as yet** among them; and **all this iniquity had come upon the people because they did yield themselves unto the power of Satan**.

6 And **the regulations** [*laws and rules*] **of the government were destroyed, because of the secret combination** of the friends and kindreds of those who murdered the prophets.

7 And they did cause a **great contention** [*fighting and quarreling*] in the land, insomuch [*so*] that **the more righteous part of the people had nearly all become wicked**; yea, there were but **few righteous** men among them.

As Mormon points out, next, it is surprising and even startling how quickly people can turn from righteousness to wickedness. He has taught us several times so far in the Book of Mormon that this happens when they allow pride to replace humility in their personal lives.

8 And thus **six years had not passed away since the more part of the people had turned from their righteousness, like the dog to his vomit, or like the sow** [*female pig*] **to her wallowing in the mire** [*mud*].

9 Now **this secret combination**, which had brought so great iniquity upon the people, **did gather themselves together, and did place at their head a man whom they did call Jacob**;

It is perhaps significant to note that even Satan's kingdom employs careful and strict organization in order to disorganize righteousness. Ultimately, the devil's ways promote confusion and lack of self-discipline, but he uses counterfeits or fakes of God's organization on the way to gaining converts to his evil kingdom.

10 And **they did call him their king**; therefore he became a king over this wicked band; and **he was one of the chiefest who had given his voice against the prophets who testified of Jesus**.

11 And it came to pass that **they were not so strong in number as the tribes of the people** [*Jacob's secret combination people were not in the majority*], **who were united together** save it were their leaders did establish their laws, every one according to his tribe; nevertheless they were enemies; notwithstanding they were not a righteous people, yet **they** [*the tribes and their leaders*] **were united in the hatred of those** [*Jacob's people*] **who had entered into a covenant to destroy the government**.

12 Therefore, **Jacob seeing that their enemies were more numerous than they**, he being the king of the band, therefore he **commanded his people that they should take their flight** [*move*] **into the northernmost part of the land**, and **there build up unto themselves a kingdom, until they were joined by dissenters** [*people leaving other tribes to join them*], (for he flattered them that there would be many dissenters) and they become sufficiently strong to contend with the tribes of the people; and they did so.

13 And **so speedy was their march that it could not be impeded** [*stopped*] until they had gone forth out of the reach of the people. And thus ended **the thirtieth year**; and thus were the affairs of the people of Nephi.

14 And it came to pass in **the thirty and first year** that they were **divided into tribes**, every man according to his family, kindred and friends; **nevertheless they had come to an agreement that they would not go to war one with another**; but they were not united as to their laws, and their manner of government, for they were established according to the minds of those who were their chiefs

and their leaders. But **they did establish very strict laws that one tribe should not trespass against another**, insomuch that **in some degree they had peace in the land; nevertheless, their hearts were turned from the Lord their God, and they did stone the prophets and did cast them out from among them**.

Next, Mormon turns our attention to Nephi, who over thirty years earlier had been told by the voice of the Savior that He would be born the next day. (See 3 Nephi 1:12–13.)

As is the case with our modern prophets and Apostles, Nephi spoke plainly and boldly and provided strong leadership upon which the faithful Saints could rely in a world which had largely departed from the standards of the gospel.

Mormon points out many of Nephi's qualifications to be a mighty prophet at this point, which is shortly before the Savior's coming to them. They are similar qualifications to those of our general authorities today.

15 And it came to pass that **Nephi—having been visited by angels** and **also the voice of the Lord**, therefore having seen angels, and **being eye-witness**, and **having had power given unto him that he might know concerning the ministry of Christ**, and also **being eye-witness to their quick return from righteousness unto their wickedness and abominations**;

16 Therefore, being grieved for the hardness of their hearts and the blindness of their minds—**went forth among them** in that same year, and **began to testify, boldly, repentance and remission** [*forgiveness*] **of sins through faith on the Lord Jesus Christ**.

17 And he did minister many things unto them; and all of them cannot be written, and a part of them would not suffice, therefore they are not written in this book [*Mormon's abridgement*]. And **Nephi did minister with power and with great authority**.

18 And it came to pass that **they were angry with him**, even **because he had greater power than they, for it were not possible that they could disbelieve his words**, for so great was his faith on the Lord Jesus Christ that **angels did minister unto him daily**.

19 And **in the name of Jesus did he cast out devils and unclean spirits**; and even **his brother** [*Timothy; see 3 Nephi 19:4*] **did he raise from the dead, after he had been stoned** [*had rocks thrown at him*] and suffered death by the people.

20 And **the** people saw it, and did witness of it, **and were angry with him because of his power**; and he did also do many more miracles, in the sight of the people [*in other words, there was much obvious evidence of God and the truthfulness of the gospel*], in the name of Jesus.

Next, the number of converts to the Church drops off as the Savior's coming to the Nephites gets very close.

21 And it came to pass that **the thirty and first year** did pass away, and there were but **few** who were **converted** unto the Lord; but as many as were converted did truly signify unto the people that they had been visited by the power and Spirit of God, which was in Jesus Christ, in whom they believed.

Just a thought about having "devils cast out from them," in verses 19, above, and 22, next, as well as elsewhere in scripture. Obviously, it is literal; but in a symbolic sense, "devils" can refer to false beliefs, false philosophies, inappropriate behaviors and fears, etc., that can be "cast out" through understanding and living the gospel of Christ.

22 And as **many** as **had devils cast out from them, and were healed of their sicknesses and their infirmities** [*other problems and troubles*], did truly manifest unto the people that they had been wrought upon [*worked upon*] by the Spirit of God, and had been healed; and they did show forth signs also and did do some miracles among the people.

23 Thus passed away **the thirty and second year** also. And **Nephi** did cry unto the people in the commencement [*beginning*] of **the thirty and third year**; and he **did preach unto them repentance and remission of sins**.

In other words, forgiveness is still available to these people in spite of their wickedness.

Next, Mormon reminds us that baptism is necessary in order for a person to be forgiven of sins. This might sound somewhat harsh as far as doctrine is concerned. Some would insist that anyone, regardless of religious belief or lack thereof, can be forgiven of sins simply by expressing sorrow for them and stopping the particular behaviors considered to be sin. That would seem to some to be logical. However, if we truly understand the laws of justice and mercy, such would be neither logical nor true.

In the "big picture" of things as they really are, in the universe, two laws cover all behaviors; namely, the law of justice and the law of mercy. The law of justice simply requires that all sins be paid for. This keeps things in proper balance in the universe. The law of mercy allows Christ's Atonement to pay for all sins and for Him to require any who desire to take advantage of His payment to repent, be baptized, and receive the Holy Ghost. Thus, baptism is a completely necessary part of the requirement for being forgiven of sins.

If, after a person has had a complete opportunity to understand and accept or reject the gospel of Christ, he or she ultimately refuses the "payment" required by the Savior (of repenting, being baptized, receiving the gift of the Holy Ghost, and living true to gospel covenants) in order to access His Atonement, that person must be subject to the law of justice rather than the law of mercy. In such cases, those people must suffer for their own sins (D&C 19:15–19).

Now, on to Mormon's teaching that baptism is required for forgiveness of sins.

24 **Now I** [*Mormon*] **would have you to remember also, that there were none who were brought unto repentance who were not baptized with water.**

Next, Mormon explains that, among other reasons for being baptized (such as those given in Mosiah 18:8–13), a major purpose is to show others that you have repented and have been forgiven of sins.

25 Therefore, there were ordained of Nephi, men unto this ministry, that **all such as should come unto them should be baptized** with water, and this **as a witness and a testimony** before God, and **unto the people, that they had repented and received a remission of their sins.**

After having had a time when there was a drop in the number of convert baptisms (verse 21, above), baptisms increased significantly immediately before Christ's coming.

26 And **there were many in the commencement of this year that were baptized unto repentance**; and thus the more part of the year did pass away.

THIRD NEPHI 8

In this chapter you will see the terrible destruction that took place in America at the time of the Savior's Crucifixion. Samuel the Lamanite told the wicked Nephites that this would happen, and it did. Not only were the wicked people destroyed, but the land was changed dramatically by earthquakes and fire and great storms, etc. The people who survived were the ones who were more righteous. You will also see the three days of absolute darkness prophesied by Samuel.

This chapter is one where the Holy Ghost can bear strong testimony to you that the prophecies given by prophets of the Lord are indeed fulfilled, including the many prophecies now, in our day, in which many prophecies leading up to the Second Coming of Christ are being fulfilled right before our eyes.

1 AND now it came to pass that **according to our record**, and we know our record to be true, for behold, it was a just [*righteous*] man [*Nephi; see 3 Nephi 23:7*] who did keep the record—for he truly did many miracles in the name of Jesus; and **there was not any man who could do a miracle in the name of Jesus save** [*unless*] **he were cleansed every whit** [*every bit*] **from his iniquity** [*sins*]—

2 And now it came to pass, if there was no mistake made by this man [*Nephi*] in the reckoning [*calculating*] of our time, **the thirty and third year had passed away** [*since the birth of Christ*];

3 And **the people began to look with great earnestness** [*seriousness*] **for the sign which had been given by the prophet Samuel, the Lamanite**, yea, for the time that there should be **darkness for the space of three days** over the face of the land.

4 And **there began to be great doubtings and disputations** among the people, notwithstanding [*in spite of the fact that*] so many signs had been given.

5 And it came to pass **in the thirty and fourth year, in the first month, on the fourth day of the month, there arose a great storm**, such an one as never had been known in all the land.

As far as the Nephite calendar was concerned, remember that they changed their calendar system after the sign of Christ's birth was given (3 Nephi 2:7–8). They began to calculate time from the day, night, and day without darkness. Thus, the "first month" in their new calendar system would be the month when Christ was born.

President Spencer W. Kimball said that Christ was born on April 6. (See Conference Report, April 1975, 3–4.)

With this as a background, one possibility for the "first month," in verse 5, above, would be the month of April in our modern-day calendar system.

6 And there was also **a great and terrible tempest**; and there was terrible **thunder**, insomuch that it **did shake the whole earth** as if it was about to divide asunder [*as if it were going to break apart*].

7 And there were **exceedingly sharp lightnings**, such as never had been known in all the land.

8 And **the city of Zarahemla did take fire**.

9 And **the city of Moroni did sink into the depths of the sea**, and the inhabitants thereof were drowned.

10 And the **earth was carried up upon the city of Moronihah, that in the place of the city there became a great mountain**.

11 And there was a great and terrible **destruction in the land southward**.

12 But behold, there was **a more great and terrible destruction in the land northward**; for behold, **the whole face of the land was changed**, because of the **tempest** [*high winds*] and the **whirlwinds**, and the **thunderings** and the **lightnings**, and the exceedingly **great quaking of the whole earth**;

13 And the **highways were broken up**, and the level **roads were spoiled**, and many **smooth places became rough**.

14 And many great and notable **cities were sunk**, and many were **burned**, and many were **shaken** till the buildings thereof had fallen to the earth, and the **inhabitants** thereof were **slain**, and the places were left desolate.

15 And there were **some cities** which **remained**; but the **damage thereof was exceedingly great**, and there were many in them who were slain.

16 And there were **some** who **were carried away in the whirlwind**; and whither [*where*] they went no man knoweth, save they know that they were carried away.

17 And thus **the face of the whole earth became deformed**, because of the tempests, and the thunderings, and the lightnings, and the quaking of the earth.

18 And behold, **the rocks were rent in twain** [*torn apart*]; they were broken up upon the face of the whole earth, insomuch that they were found in **broken fragments, and in seams and in cracks, upon all the face of the land**.

Next, Mormon tells us how long this terrible destruction lasted.

19 And it came to pass that **when the thunderings**, and the **lightnings**, and the **storm**, and the **tempest**, and the **quakings of the earth did cease**—for behold, **they did last for about the space of three hours**; and it was said by some that the time was greater; nevertheless, **all these great and terrible things were done in about the space of three hours—and then behold, there was darkness** upon the face of the land.

As described by Mormon, next, the darkness which followed the destruction was "thick" and those who were still alive could "feel the vapor of darkness." You may remember that one of the ten plagues caused by the Lord through Moses in Egypt was "thick darkness" for three days (Exodus 10:22).

As mentioned previously, this is symbolic. When Christ was born, there was light. When He was taken from the world by wicked and cruel men, there was darkness. Likewise, when we invite the Savior into our lives, there is "light" in our souls. When we cast Him out of our lives, there is "darkness."

20 And it came to pass that there was **thick darkness** upon all the face of the land, insomuch that **the inhabitants** thereof who had not fallen [*who had not been killed*] **could feel the vapor of darkness**;

The darkness that came, signifying that the Savior had been crucified, was absolute. The surviving Nephites were unable to create any light at all (see verses 21–22, next). This could be symbolic of the fact that no other light can be made that can take the place of Christ. In other words, "there is no other way or means whereby man can be saved, only in and through Christ" (see Alma 38:9).

Such darkness is an important and clear reminder of how dependent we are on Christ and the light of His gospel.

21 And **there could be no light, because of the darkness, neither candles**, neither **torches; neither could there be fire kindled** with their fine and exceedingly dry wood, so that **there could not be any light at all**;

22 And **there was not any light seen**, neither **fire**, nor **glimmer** [*the slightest light*], neither the **sun**, nor the **moon**, nor the **stars**, for so great were the mists of darkness which were upon the face of the land.

23 And it came to pass that **it did last for the space of three days** [*basically, the time that Christ's body was in the tomb*] that **there was no light seen**;

and **there was great mourning** and **howling** and **weeping** among all the people **continually**; yea, great were the **groanings** of the people, **because of the darkness and the great destruction which had come upon them**.

24 And in one place they were heard to cry, saying: **O that we had repented before this great and terrible day**, and then would our brethren have been spared, and they would not have been burned in that great city Zarahemla.

25 And in another place they were heard to cry and mourn, saying: **O that we had repented before this great and terrible day**, and had not killed and stoned the prophets, and cast them out; then would our mothers and our fair daughters, and our children have been spared, and not have been buried up in that great city Moronihah. And **thus were the howlings of the people great and terrible**.

THIRD NEPHI 9

Remember that it is still completely dark at this point, as described in 3 Nephi 8:20–21. The absolute darkness will continue for three days until it is lifted, as told in 3 Nephi 10:9.

It is in this darkness that the people who were not destroyed hear a voice. It is the voice of the Savior (verse 15) telling them what has happened to those who were so wicked that they were destroyed, and inviting these people who survived the destruction to repent and come unto Him and be healed (verse 13).

You will notice some important symbolism here, namely, that the voice of the Lord penetrated through spiritual darkness, calling to the survivors to repent and come to Him and enjoy the light of the gospel.

1 AND it came to pass that **there was a voice heard among all the inhabitants** of the earth, **upon all the face of this land**, [*meaning the Book of Mormon lands; see next, in this verse*], crying:

Next, Jesus tells us how the devil and his evil spirits react to destruction of so many wicked people.

2 **Wo** [*deep trouble is coming*], **wo, wo unto this people**; wo unto the inhabitants of the whole earth except [*unless*] they shall repent; **for the devil laugheth, and his angels rejoice, because of the slain of the fair sons and daughters of my people**; and it is because of their iniquity [*wickedness*] and abominations [*extreme wickedness*] that they are fallen [*have been killed by the destructions*]!

The next verses provide an important clarification. Occasionally you may hear someone claim that God himself does not punish His wayward children here on earth. Rather, He withdraws from them and lets Satan punish and destroy them.

While this is certainly the case in many instances, it is definitely not always the case, as shown in the next several verses. As you will clearly see, the Lord Himself caused the destruction of many cities. Perhaps one lesson to be learned here is that disciplining and punishing, when the occasion demands, is an integral part of "parenting."

Bold italics **and underlining** will be used to point out this principle.

3 Behold, that great city Zarahemla have ***I*** burned with fire, and the inhabitants thereof.

4 And behold, that great city Moroni have ***I*** caused to be sunk in the depths of the sea, and the inhabitants thereof to be drowned.

5 And behold, that great city Moronihah have ***I*** covered with earth, and the inhabitants thereof, to hide their iniquities and their abominations [*extreme wickedness*] from before my face, that the blood of the prophets and the saints shall not come any more unto me against them.

The phrase "the blood of the prophets and the Saints," in verse 5, above, means "the responsibility for killing the prophets and Saints." "Come any more unto me against them" means, in effect, that until people either repent or are punished for sins, the law of justice keeps reminding God that they must be punished.

6 And behold, the city of Gilgal have ***I*** caused to be sunk, and the inhabitants thereof to be buried up in the depths of the earth;

7 Yea, and the city of Onihah and the inhabitants thereof, and the city of Mocum and the inhabitants thereof, and the city of Jerusalem and the inhabitants thereof; and waters have ***I*** caused to come up in the stead thereof, to hide their wickedness and abominations from before my face, that the blood of the prophets and the saints shall not come up any more unto me against them.

8 And behold, the city of Gadiandi, and the city of Gadiomnah, and the city of Jacob, and the city of Gimgimno, all these have ***I*** caused to be sunk, and made hills and valleys in the places thereof; and the inhabitants thereof have ***I*** buried up in the depths of the earth, to hide their wickedness and abominations from before my face, that the blood of the prophets and the saints should not come up any more unto me against them.

9 And behold, that great city Jacobugath, which was inhabited by the people of king Jacob [*who was the leader of the secret combination; see 3 Nephi 7:9–10*], have ***I*** caused to be burned with fire because of their sins and their wickedness, which was above all the wickedness of the whole earth, **because of their secret murders and combinations; for it was they that did destroy the peace of my people and the government of the land**; therefore ***I*** did cause them to be burned, to destroy them from before my face, that the blood of the prophets and the saints should not come up unto me any more against them.

10 And behold, the city of Laman,

and the city of Josh, and the city of Gad, and the city of Kishkumen [*perhaps named after the Kishkumen who founded the secret combination which later became the Gadianton robbers; see Helaman 1:9, 2:3–4*], have ***I*** caused to be burned with fire, and the inhabitants thereof, because of their wickedness in casting out the prophets, and stoning those whom I did send to declare unto them concerning their wickedness and their abominations.

In verse 11, next, we once again are told, in effect, that when a society gets to the point that there are no righteous among them, usually because they have killed them or driven them out, that society will be destroyed by God.

11 And **because they did cast them all out, that there were none righteous among** them, ***I*** did send down fire and destroy them, that their wickedness and abominations might be hid from before my face, that the blood of the prophets and the saints whom I sent among them might not cry unto me from the ground against them.

12 And many great destructions have ***I*** caused to come upon this land, and upon this people, because of their wickedness and their abominations.

Next, the Savior tells those who were not destroyed that the reason they are still alive is that they were not as wicked as those who were destroyed. He then invites them to repent and allow Him to heal them from the effects of their sins. He teaches them about the law of mercy. A major message to all of us in these verses is that the Savior loves to forgive us!

13 O all **ye that are spared because ye were more righteous than they, will ye not now return unto me, and repent of your sins, and be converted, that I may heal you**?

14 Yea, verily I say unto you, **if ye will come unto me ye shall have eternal life** [*exaltation*] Behold, mine arm of **mercy is extended towards you** [*you can still repent and be completely cleansed and healed*] and **whosoever will** [*wants to*] **come, him will I receive**; and blessed are those who come unto me.

Next, the Savior introduces Himself as the one who is speaking through the darkness to them.

15 Behold, **I am Jesus Christ** the Son of God. I created the heavens and the earth, and all things that in them are. I was with the Father from the beginning [*in other words, I have been working for your salvation for a long time*]. I am in the Father, and the Father in me [*the Father and Son work in perfect unity and harmony, to help us be saved*]; and in me hath the Father glorified his name [*through My work and Atonement, many souls have been and will be brought to the Father; compare with Moses 1:39*].

16 **I came unto my own** [*to Israel, particularly the Jews*], and **my own received me not** [*rejected Me*]. And the scriptures concerning my coming are fulfilled.

The phrase "sons of God" (compare with "begotten sons and daughters unto God" in D&C 76:24), as used in verse 17, next, is another term for eternal life, which always means exaltation in the highest degree of glory in the celestial kingdom (see D&C 14:7).

17 And **as many as have received me, to them have I given to become the sons of God**; and even so will I to as many as shall [*now and in the future*] believe on my name, for behold, **by me redemption cometh**, and in me is the law of Moses fulfilled.

By way of review, the "law of Moses" was a "schoolmaster" law (Galatians 3:24) given to prepare the Old Testament Israelites for the gospel of Christ. It consisted of laws, rituals, performances and ordinances required by the Lord, as given through Moses in the books of Exodus, Leviticus, Numbers, and Deuteronomy in the Bible. The various requirements of the Law of Moses were designed by the Lord to raise the standards of the children of Israel and to point their minds toward the Savior.

As stated by the Savior, in verse 17, above, His coming to earth fulfilled the purposes of the Law of Moses.

18 **I am the light and the life of the world**. I am Alpha and Omega [*the first and last letters of the Greek alphabet*], the beginning and the end.

In other words, among other things, the Savior worked for our welfare in the beginning, which includes the premortal spirit world and the creation of our earth, and He will be involved with us in the end, which includes the final judgment.

Next, Jesus commands the Nephites to no longer offer blood sacrifices, such as sacrificing lambs, as they have done up to now, in keeping with the Law of Moses.

19 And **ye shall offer up unto me no more the shedding of blood**; yea, your sacrifices and your burnt offerings shall be done away, for I will accept none of your sacrifices and your burnt offerings.

Next, the Master explains the type of sacrifice He wants in place of animal sacrifices. The phrase "broken heart and contrite spirit," used in verse 20, next, can be explained in many ways. One way is that "broken heart" implies not only humble but also obedient, as in a well-trained or well-broken horse. The word "contrite," in addition to meaning humble, also is defined as "desiring correction as needed."

20 And **ye shall offer for a sacrifice unto me a broken heart and a contrite spirit**. And whoso cometh unto me with a broken heart and a contrite spirit, **him will I baptize with fire and with the Holy Ghost** [*they will receive the Gift of the Holy Ghost*], even as the Lamanites, because of their faith in me at the time of their conversion, were baptized with fire and with the Holy Ghost, and **they knew it not**.

Sometimes we do not realize how much the Holy Ghost affects our lives.

21 Behold, **I have come unto the world to bring redemption unto the world, to save the world from sin**.

Next, in verse 22, the Savior summarizes what He has taught these people so far.

22 Therefore, **whoso repenteth and cometh unto me as a little child** [*in simple, obedient, trusting faith*], **him will I receive**, for of such is the kingdom of God. [*These are the types of people who obtain celestial glory.*] **Behold, for such I have laid down my life, and have taken it up again; therefore repent, and come unto me ye ends of the earth** [*all people everywhere*] **and be saved.**

The phrase "for such I have laid down my life," in verse 22, above, is an important doctrinal statement. It must be kept in the context of verse 22, as well as the larger context of all of the scriptures. It is saying, in effect, that those who obtain celestial glory are the ones whose sins will be forgiven because of the Atonement.

We know from 1 Corinthians 15:22 and 2 Nephi 9:22 and other such scriptures that all mortals will be resurrected because of Christ's resurrection, regardless of whether or not they repent of their sins.

Therefore, Christ paid for resurrection for all who ever have been born or who ever will be born. He also paid for all of the sins of these people (see 2 Nephi 9:21). However, once they are properly taught and thus become fully accountable (whether in this life or in the missionary work that goes on beyond the grave), if they choose not to repent of their sins, the law of justice (see Alma 42) requires that the Savior's payment for their sins be taken back and that they suffer for their own sins (see D&C 19:15–17).

THIRD NEPHI 10

Silence is an effective way to get people's attention and to promote deep thinking and serious analyzing. Perhaps you've been in attendance at a general conference of the Church when the Prophet entered the Conference Center and you have "heard" the silence as it spread throughout the building by way of respect and honor for him. There will be "silence in heaven for the space of half an hour" just before the Savior's Second Coming, which is sometime in the future for our generation (D&C 88:95).

As we begin chapter 10, there are several hours of silence following the words of Christ recorded in chapter 9. It is still completely dark. We sense that the people are in a state of deep readiness to receive the next message of the Savior.

1 AND now behold, it came to pass that **all the people of the land did hear these sayings** [*chapter 9*], and did witness of it. And **after these sayings there was silence in the land for the space of many hours**;

2 For so great was the astonishment of the people that they did cease lamenting [*mourning and weeping*] and howling for the loss of their kindred [*relatives*] which had been slain; **therefore, there was silence in all the land for the space of many hours.**

The Savior's voice comes again to these people, reminding them of how often He has gathered His people and blessed them in times past. He also invites them to repent and return to Him and enjoy the warmth and comfort He has for them. He compares this warmth and security to chicks gathered under the soft, warm, secure wing of a mother hen.

3 And it came to pass that **there came a voice** [*the Savior's voice*] **again unto the people**, and all the people did hear, and did witness of it, **saying**:

4 O ye people of these great cities which have fallen, who are descendants of Jacob [*Israel; Jacob's name was changed to "Israel" as recorded in Genesis 32:28*], yea, who are of the house of Israel, **how oft have I gathered you as a hen gathereth her chickens under her wings, and have nourished you**.

5 And again, **how oft would I have gathered you** [*how often have I tried to gather you*] as a hen gathereth her chickens under her wings, yea, O ye people of the house of Israel, who have fallen [*who have fallen away from God*]; yea, O ye people of the house of Israel, ye that dwell at Jerusalem, as ye that have fallen; yea, **how oft would I have gathered you as a hen gathereth her chickens, and ye would not** [*you refused to be gathered*].

Next, the Savior reminds all people that He will keep trying to gather them and bring them safely back to the Father. He also warns them of the consequences if they refuse.

6 O ye house of Israel whom I have spared [*who are still alive*], **how oft will I gather you** as a hen gathereth her chickens under her wings, **if ye will repent and return unto me with full purpose of heart**.

7 **But if not**, O house of Israel [*descendants of Abraham, Isaac, and Jacob; in other words, the "covenant people;" see Abraham 2:9–11 for the Lord's promises to His covenant people*], **the places of your dwellings shall become desolate** [*you will be scattered and driven throughout the world*] until the time of the fulfilling of the covenant to your fathers [*ancestors; in other words, until I gather you again, which I promised your ancestors I would do*].

8 And now it came to pass that **after the people had heard these words**, behold, **they began to weep and howl again** because of the loss of their kindred and friends.

Next, Mormon tell us that the darkness left. He also gives us a very brief summary of conditions in nature during the past three days.

9 And it came to pass that **thus did the three days pass away**. And it was **in the morning**, and **the darkness dispersed** [*left*] from off the face of the land, and **the earth did cease to tremble**, and **the rocks did cease to rend** [*tear and break up*], and **the dreadful groanings did cease**, and **all the tumultuous** [*terrible, rumbling, frightening*] **noises did pass away** [*stopped*].

There is symbolism in the tremblings, tearings, groanings, and noises in verse 9, above. It can be symbolic of what happens deep within a person as he or she goes through deep godly sorrow for sin during the process of repenting. Such deep concern for sin causes cleansing and permanent change for the better. Paul described these aspects of godly sorrow to the Corinthians (2 Corinthians 7:10–11):

10 For **godly sorrow worketh repentance** [*causes us to repent*] to salvation [*and thus obtain exaltation*] *not to be repented of* [*and leaves us with no regrets*]: but **the sorrow of the world** [*being sorry you got caught, or sorry because you are embarrassed, or sorry that your opportunity to continue committing that sin has been taken away, etc.*] **worketh death** [*leads to spiritual death*].

Now, Paul describes some components of "godly sorrow" that make it so effective in cleansing us from sin and leading to our truly changing and becoming more righteous. The disturbances among the elements of the earth during the three days of darkness can symbolize these.

11 For behold this selfsame thing [*this godly sorrow, the very thing I'm teaching you about*], that ye sorrowed [*were sorry for sins*] after a godly sort [*in the way God wants you to be*], what carefulness [*sincerity, anxiety*] it wrought [*caused*] in you, yea, what clearing of yourselves [*eagerness to become clear of the sin*], yea, what indignation [*irritation, anger at yourself for committing the sin*], yea, what fear [*alarm*], yea, what vehement desire [*strong desire to change*], yea, what zeal [*enthusiasm to change*], yea, what revenge [*punishment; suffering whatever is necessary to make permanent change*]! In all things ye have approved yourselves to be clear in this matter [*in everything you have done, you have demonstrated that you understand godly sorrow*].

After having gone through godly sorrow for sin, as described by Paul, above, it is absolutely necessary to allow one's self to advance to the joy and thanksgiving described in verse 10, next. This is one of the clearest verses in all of scripture in teaching the next step of repentance after godly sorrow.

10 And the earth did cleave together again [*the ground came together again*], that it stood [*stopped shaking*]; and **the mourning, and the weeping, and the wailing of the people who were spared alive did cease** [*stop*]; and **their mourning was turned into joy**, and their lamentations [*sorrow for past behaviors, etc.*] **into the praise and thanksgiving unto the Lord Jesus Christ, their Redeemer**.

Next, in verse 11, Mormon bears his testimony to us of the fulfillment of prophecy. He will continue this testimony in verses 14–17.

11 And **thus far were the scriptures fulfilled which had been spoken by the prophets**.

As we approach the Second Coming of Christ in the future, many wonder where the line will be drawn between who will be burned and who will be spared. Verse 12, next, has the basic answer. We understand the "more righteous" to be those who are at least living a terrestrial lifestyle. You can read Doctrine and Covenants 76:71–80 for a description of this lifestyle. Celestial people are described in Doctrine and Covenants 76:51–53.

It was the wicked who were destroyed, those who were living either a telestial or sons of perdition type of life. You can read about telestial lifestyle in Doctrine and Covenants 76:81–85, 98–106, and about sons of perdition lifestyle in Doctrine and Covenants 76:31–49.

12 And **it was the more righteous part of the people who were saved**, and it was they who received the prophets and stoned them not; and it was they who had not shed the blood of the saints, who were spared—

In verse 13, next, Mormon mentions two additional ways in which the wicked were destroyed in the Americas at the time of Christ's Crucifixion and death.

13 And they were spared and were not sunk and buried up in the earth; and they were not drowned in the depths of the sea; and they were not burned by fire, neither were they fallen upon and crushed to death; and they were not **carried away in the whirlwind**; neither were they **overpowered by the vapor of smoke and of darkness**.

14 And now, **whoso readeth, let him understand; he that hath the scriptures, let him search** [*study*] **them, and see and behold if all these deaths and destructions by fire, and by smoke, and by tempests, and by whirlwinds, and by the opening of the earth to receive them, and all these things are not unto the fulfilling of the prophecies of many of the holy prophets**.

15 Behold, I [*Mormon*] say unto you, **Yea, many have testified of these things** at the coming of Christ, and **were slain because they testified of these things**.

Next, Mormon tells us that both Zenos (whom Jacob quoted as he gave us the allegory of the tame and wild olive trees; see Jacob 5) and Zenock were killed (verse 15, above) because they prophesied of Christ's coming to the Nephites and the destruction of the wicked that would accompany it.

16 Yea, the prophet **Zenos did testify of these things**, and also **Zenock spake concerning these things**, because they testified particularly concerning us, who are the remnant [*a remaining part*] of their seed [*posterity, descendants*].

Next, Mormon refers to the prophecies about Joseph's descendants who came to America in Lehi's group.

17 Behold, **our father** [*ancestor*] **Jacob** [*the son of Isaac, grandson of Abraham*] **also testified concerning a remnant of the seed of Joseph** [*who was sold into Egypt; Jacob's prophecy about Joseph's descendants is found in Genesis 49:22–26*]. And behold, **are not we a remnant of the seed of Joseph**? And **these things which testify of us, are they not written upon the plates of brass** which our father Lehi brought out of Jerusalem?

18 And it came to pass that **in the ending of the thirty and fourth year**, behold, I will show unto you that the people of Nephi who were spared, and also those who had been

called Lamanites, who had been spared, did have great favors shown unto them, and great blessings poured out upon their heads, insomuch that **soon after the ascension of Christ into heaven he did truly manifest himself unto them**—

19 Showing his body unto them, and ministering unto them; and an account of his ministry shall be given hereafter. **Therefore for this time I make an end of my sayings**.

THIRD NEPHI 11

In chapters 11 through 26, you will read about the appearance of Jesus to the people in America who survived the terrible destruction. You will read His teachings to them and how He tenderly ministered to them.

First, in chapter 11, we will be given a description of Heavenly Father's voice as He bears witness of His Son to those who have gathered around the temple in the land of Bountiful. Then, through the words recorded here by Mormon, we will have the privilege, along with those who were there, of seeing the Savior come down out of heaven.

Jesus will then invite each of the 2,500 people assembled there to come forth individually and feel the wound in His side and the prints of the nails in His hands and feet. He will then teach them to avoid contention (arguing and quarreling with each other) and will bear witness of the Father to them. Finally, He will teach them the first principles of the gospel.

1 AND now it came to pass that there were **a great multitude** [*about 2,500, according to 3 Nephi 17:25*] **gathered together**, of the people of Nephi, **round about the temple** which was in the land Bountiful; and they were **marveling and wondering** one with another, and were **showing one to another the great and marvelous change which had taken place**.

2 And they were also **conversing** [*talking*] **about this Jesus Christ, of whom the sign had been given concerning his death**.

Next, these people are privileged to hear the Father's voice, bearing witness of the Son. They thus join the select few, including Peter, James, and John (Mount of Transfiguration, Matthew 17:5), and Joseph Smith (First Vision, Joseph Smith—History 1:17), who have been privileged to hear His voice during their mortal lives.

Mormon describes His voice and its effect on the people who heard it, in some detail. This is a most precious description which is available nowhere else in scripture. Note that they will not understand the voice until the third time they hear it.

3 And it came to pass that while they were thus conversing one with another, **they heard a voice** as if it came out of heaven; **and they cast their eyes round about** [*they looked around*], for **they understood not the voice** which they heard; and **it was not** a **harsh voice**, **neither was it** a **loud** voice; nevertheless, and notwithstanding [*even though*] it being a

small voice **it did pierce them that did hear to the center** [*it went clear to the center of their bodies*], **insomuch that** [*so that*] **there was no part of their frame** [*body*] **that it did not cause to quake** [*shake*]; **yea, it did pierce them to the very soul, and did cause their hearts to burn** [*to have a very warm feeling*].

4 And it came to pass that **again** [*the second time*] **they heard the voice, and they understood it not.**

> As you read verse 5, next, note what they did differently this time, which enabled them to understand the voice the third time they heard it.

5 And again **the third time they did hear the voice, and did open their ears** to hear it; and **their eyes were towards the sound** thereof; and **they did look steadfastly** [*very focused*] **towards heaven**, from whence [*where*] the sound came.

6 And behold, **the third time they did understand the voice** which they heard; **and it said unto them**:

> There are many lessons that could be taught from what the people did in verse 5, which led to their understanding the voice. One lesson might be that they opened their spiritual ears and focused completely toward heaven, tuning out all distractions. This would certainly be an example of how we may receive revelation and inspiration from above.
>
> We will now listen to the message from Heavnly Father regarding His Beloved Son and then watch the Savior come.

7 **Behold my Beloved Son, in whom I am well pleased, in whom I have glorified my name—hear ye him.**

8 And it came to pass, **as they understood they cast their eyes** [*looked*] **up again towards heaven**; and behold, **they saw a Man descending out of heaven**; and he was **clothed in a white robe** [*symbolic of purity and celestial glory; see Revelation 3:4–5, 7:9*]; and **he came down and stood in the midst of** [*among*] **them**; and **the eyes of the whole multitude were turned upon him**, and they durst not open their mouths, even one to another, and wist [*knew*] not what it meant, for **they thought it was an angel** that had appeared unto them.

9 And it came to pass that **he stretched forth his hand and spake** [*spoke*] unto the people, saying:

10 Behold, **I am Jesus Christ, whom the prophets testified shall come into the world.**

11 And behold, **I am the light and the life of the world**; and **I have drunk out of that bitter cup which the Father hath given me** [*I have fulfilled the extremely difficult assignment (see D&C 19:15–19) given me by the Father*], and **have glorified the Father** [*have brought glory and honor to the Father*] **in taking upon me the sins of the world**, in the which **I have suffered** [*accepted and fulfilled*] **the will of the Father in all things from the beginning** [*from premortality*].

12 And it came to pass that **when Jesus had spoken these words the**

whole multitude fell to the earth; for they remembered that it had been prophesied among them that Christ should show himself unto them after his ascension [*going up*] **into heaven**.

In other words, it finally occurred to them what was happening—that the prophecies about Jesus appearing were actually being fulfilled in front of their very eyes!

For those of us who have been taught of these events many times, it may seem a bit strange in verse 12, above, that it took a while before it finally occurred to these people what was actually happening. It is not strange. Remember that even with the Savior's Apostles and disciples, it took a while for them to realize that the prophecies regarding his death and resurrection had been fulfilled. They apparently didn't fully realize that this was what was happening, even though Jesus had told them several times, especially during the last week of His life. In fact, even when the resurrected Jesus appeared to His disciples in the room, "They were terrified and affrighted, and supposed that they had seen a spirit" (Luke 24:37).

Next, the Savior invites each individual to come forth and feel the wound in His side and the prints of the nails in His hands and feet. There is beautiful symbolism here, including that each of us is an individual to the Lord. He knows each of us personally. Each of us is invited to let His Atonement be applied very personally in our lives.

It is interesting to try to get a perspective as to how much time this individual attention to each person might take. While we obviously don't know how much time the Savior took with each individual, if we were to suppose for a moment that each person took an average of just ten seconds, it would take about seven hours for each of the 2,500 (3 Nephi 17:25) people to have their precious, individual witness of the resurrected Christ.

13 And it came to pass that **the Lord spake unto them saying**:

14 **Arise and come forth unto me, that ye may thrust** [*put*] **your hands into my side, and also that ye may feel the prints of the nails in my hands and in my feet, that ye may know** that I am the God of Israel, and the God of the whole earth, and have been slain for the sins of the world.

15 And it came to pass that **the multitude went forth, and thrust their hands into his side, and did feel the prints of the nails in his hands and in his feet**; and this they did do, going forth **one by one** until they had all gone forth, **and did see with their eyes and did feel with their hands, and did know of a surety** [*for sure*] and did bear record [*bear testimony*], that it was he, of whom it was written by the prophets, that should come.

As mentioned above, there is much symbolism in these scenes. One of the most important symbolic messages is the worth of each individual in the sight of God. Perhaps you've noticed that one of Satan's most devastating goals is to do away with the worth of the individual. Throughout history, political philosophies have been adopted that make the masses more important than the individual. Governments based upon this false philosophy devastate individuals and eventually destroy the masses. On the other hand, when the rights of individuals are respected and carefully protected, and individuals rise to the challenge of fulfilling their moral obligations to such governments, peace and prosperity rule. So it is in the kingdom of God. The worth of the individual soul is all-important. (See D&C 18:10.)

16 And when they had all gone forth and had witnessed for themselves, **they did cry out with one accord** [*in unity*], **saying**:

17 **Hosanna! Blessed be the name of the Most High God!** And **they did fall down at the feet of Jesus, and did worship him.**

The word "hosanna," as used in verse 17, above, has much significance in our day to those of us who have had the privilege of attending temple dedications. The "Hosanna Shout" is used during these sacred dedicatory services. Each participant is invited to bring a clean, white handkerchief for use during the "Hosanna Shout." We will take a moment here to define "hosanna" and explain its background. First, we will quote Bruce R. McConkie (bold added for emphasis):

"Included in the Feast of Tabernacles was a holy convocation, which in this instance was called also a solemn assembly. **In our modern solemn assemblies** [*including temple dedications*] **we give the Hosanna Shout**, which also was associated with the Feast of Tabernacles anciently, except that ancient **Israel waved palm branches instead of white handkerchiefs** as they exulted in such declarations as **'Hosanna, Hosanna, Hosanna, to God and the Lamb'"** (McConkie, *The Mortal Messiah*, 1:179–80).

Our Bible Dictionary, under "Hosanna," defines "Hosanna" as meaning "save now." Another definition of "Hosanna" is found in Psalm 118:25, where it is rendered, "Save now, I beseech thee, O Lord." Other wordings used in the defining of "Hosanna" include:

- "O, please, Jehovah, save (us) now, please!"
- "O save, help (us), O Son of David (Christ), please!"
- "O save, help (us), O (thou) Highest, please!"

The waving of palm branches in ancient Biblical times, in addition to use in greeting a king, symbolized victory and triumph over the powers of the enemy. Thus, the waving of white handkerchiefs (in place of palm fronds) in our temple dedications today is symbolic of our deep gratitude to God because of our gaining victory over sin and being brought into the presence of the Lord through the Atonement of Christ.

We will now continue with Mormon's account of the visit of the resurrected Christ to the people of Nephi. Next, the Savior will talk directly to Nephi. Imagine the feelings of this humble prophet as the Lord Himself invited him to come forth to Him.

18 And it came to pass that **he spake unto Nephi** (for Nephi was among the multitude) **and he commanded him that he should come forth**.

19 And **Nephi arose and went forth, and bowed himself before the Lord and did kiss his feet**.

20 And **the Lord commanded him that he should arise**. And he arose and stood before him.

21 And **the Lord said unto him: I give unto you power that ye shall baptize this people when I am again ascended into** [*when I have gone back to*] **heaven**.

22 And again the **Lord called others**, and said unto them **likewise**; and **he gave unto them power to baptize**. And he said unto them: **On this wise shall ye baptize** [*this is how you should perform baptisms*]; **and there shall be no disputations among** you [*there must be no disagreements among you as to how to do this*].

Some are caught off guard at this point and wonder why these men are being given power to baptize when they have already been baptizing people all along in the Book of Mormon. See Mosiah 18:16 and Helaman 16:4, for example.

The answer is simple. These men are being given authorization to baptize people now for entrance into the Church of Jesus Christ, which is new for them and which the Savior will now establish among them. Up to this point, the people were living the Law of Moses and were being baptized in connection with it. The Law of Moses has now been fulfilled by the Savior.

A similar thing happened in the early days of the Church after Joseph Smith was called to restore the gospel. Many were baptized before the Church was officially organized on April 6, 1830. They were rebaptized for admission into The Church of Jesus Christ of Latter-day Saints after its organization. In fact, in Doctrine and Covenants section 20 (in which the Savior told them to organize the Church on April 6, 1830; see section 20, verse 1), the Lord gave exact instructions as to how to baptize and as to the prayer that was to be used for baptism into the restored Church (D&C 20:72–74).

Next, Jesus will give specific instructions to these Nephites about baptizing.

23 Verily I say unto you, that **whoso repenteth of his sins** through your words, and **desireth** [*wants*] **to be baptized** in my name, **on this wise shall ye baptize them**—Behold, ye shall **go down and stand in the water, and in my name** [*in the name of Jesus Christ*] **shall ye baptize them**.

24 And now behold, **these are the words which ye shall say, calling them by name, saying**:

25 **Having authority given me of Jesus Christ, I baptize you in the name of the Father, and of the Son, and of the Holy Ghost. Amen**.

Occasionally someone will ask why we don't use this form of the baptismal prayer when we baptize today. Again, the answer is simple. The Lord instructed us in Doctrine and

Covenants 20:73 to use that form of the baptismal prayer in our day.

26 And **then shall ye immerse them in the water, and come forth again out of the water.**

27 And **after this manner shall ye** [*this is how you should*] **baptize in my name**; for behold, verily [*"verily" means "listen carefully"*] I say unto you, that **the Father, and the Son, and the Holy Ghost are one** [*united*]; **and I am in the Father, and the Father in me, and the Father and I are one.**

Jesus is making a very strong point here about unity among His people. In verse 27, above, He pointed out that the members of the Godhead work in unity and harmony. In other words, there are no "disputations" or contentions among them. The instructions about baptism, just given, should be the final word. Jesus will say this again at the beginning of verse 28, next. Apparently, there had been some contention up to now regarding some aspects of baptizing as well as upon some points of doctrine.

28 **And according as I have commanded you thus shall ye baptize. And there shall be no disputations** [*arguing*] **among you, as there have hitherto been; neither shall there be disputations among you concerning the points** [*exact explanations and meanings*] **of my doctrine, as there have hitherto been.**

One of the first major messages to the people of Nephi here is that of avoiding contention. He will emphasize it in several ways in the next verses, warning that Satan uses contention as one of his very successful tools against us. This is a major message to all of us.

29 For verily, verily I say unto you, **he that hath the spirit of contention is not of me, but is of the devil, who is the father** [*the originator*] **of contention**, and he stirreth up the hearts of men to contend with anger, one with another.

30 Behold, **this is not my doctrine, to stir up the hearts of men with anger, one against another**; but this is my doctrine, that such things should be done away.

No doubt you have had experience that verifies that contention drives the Holy Ghost away. When a spirit of contention enters, one can immediately feel the withdrawal of the Spirit.

You will see why the Savior emphasized this principle so strongly before He went on to the next part of His message to these people. He will now teach us His "doctrine." "Doctrine" means specific teachings and facts taught by the gospel.

31 Behold, verily, verily [*listen very carefully*], I say unto you, **I will declare unto you my doctrine.**

32 And **this is my doctrine**, and it is the doctrine which the Father hath given unto me; and I bear record of the Father, and the Father beareth record of me, and the Holy Ghost beareth record of the Father and me; and I bear record that the Father commandeth all men, everywhere, to **repent and believe in me.**

33 And **whoso believeth in me, and is baptized, the same shall be saved**; and they are they who **shall inherit the kingdom of God** [*celestial glory*].

34 And **whoso believeth not in me, and is not baptized, shall be damned** [*stopped in their eternal progression*].

We used the term "eternal progression" in the note in verse 34, above. Many members of the Church misunderstand the meaning of this expression. They think that everyone, regardless of status at the Final Judgment, will continue to have eternal progression. That is not true. "Eternal progression" applies only to those who gain exaltation in the highest degree of the celestial kingdom. All others will have limits placed on them. Even those who attain either of the lower two categories in the celestial kingdom will not have eternal progression. See Doctrine and Covenants 131:1–4 where it says "that is the end of his kingdom; he cannot have an increase."

35 Verily, verily, I say unto you, that **this is my doctrine**, and I bear record of it from the Father [*it is My Father's doctrine also*]; and **whoso** [*whoever*] **believeth in me believeth in the Father also**; and unto him **will the Father bear record of me, for he will visit him with fire and with the Holy Ghost** [*the Father will testify of this to them through the Holy Ghost*].

At this point, it becomes clear why the Savior prefaced His "doctrine" of repentance and baptism by warning against contention. Once a person is baptized, the gift of the Holy Ghost is given as a guide and teacher in all things leading to exaltation. Contentious members drive the Holy Ghost away and thus do not have the testimony, help, and guidance essential to obtain exaltation.

36 And **thus will the Father bear record of me, and the Holy Ghost will bear record unto him of the Father and me**; for the Father, and I, and the Holy Ghost are one [*We are united and you must be too*].

Next, the Savior repeats His "doctrine" (verses 31–35) again.

37 And again I say unto you, **ye must repent**, and **become as a little child** [*which includes pure faith*], and **be baptized** in my name, **or ye can in nowise receive these things** [*including what the Holy Ghost will teach you about gaining exaltation*].

38 And again I say unto you, **ye must repent, and be baptized in my name, and become as a little child**, or ye can in nowise [*otherwise, it will be impossible for you to*] inherit the kingdom of God.

39 Verily, verily, I say unto you, that **this is my doctrine**, and **whoso buildeth upon this buildeth upon my rock, and the gates of hell shall not prevail** [*win*] **against them**.

Understanding the word "prevail" in verse 39, above, is very important doctrinally. It does not mean that Satan and his evil hosts cannot try to "prevail" against the Saints and cause trouble and trials for them. But it does guarantee to the faithful that Satan will not win. And that is what counts eternally.

Next, the Savior warns us not to twist, change, or water down "His doctrine."

40 And **whoso shall declare more or less than this, and establish it for my doctrine** [*say this is what the Lord really means*], **the same cometh of evil, and is not built upon my rock**; but **he buildeth upon a sandy foundation** [*an unstable foundation*], **and the gates of hell stand open to receive such when the floods come and the winds beat upon them** [*compare with Matthew 7:26–27*].

41 Therefore, **go forth unto this people, and declare** [*teach and explain*] **the words which I have spoken**, unto the ends of the earth [*everywhere*].

Chapters 12–14 (next), sometimes referred to as the "Sermon at the Temple," are similar to the Sermon on the Mount that was given by the Savior in the Bible in Matthew, chapters 5–7. However, there are several very significant differences and clarifications in Third Nephi.

Many Book of Mormon critics claim that Joseph Smith simply copied the Sermon on the Mount from the Bible and put it in his "Gold Bible." They need to read 3 Nephi 15:1, where Jesus tells the Book of Mormon people that He had just taught them the things He taught His people in the Holy Land before He returned to heaven. The Sermon on the Mount was among these teachings. He was, in effect, quoting what He taught His disciples on the mount in Galilee (Matthew 4:23–25).

However, as stated above, there are significant differences between the Sermon on the Mount and the Sermon at the Temple in the Book of Mormon. Before continuing, let's look at these differences; words and phrases in the Sermon at the Temple are **bolded** where they differ from those of the Sermon on the Mount.

Not all differences between the two texts have been noted, but I'm hoping that enough of them are so that you can appreciate that Joseph Smith did not simply copy the Sermon on the Mount and put it in the Book of Mormon.

When we are done doing this, we will return to Third Nephi, chapter 12, and continue like we have been doing.

See the Sermon at the Temple compared to the Sermon on the Mount on the following pages.

3 Nephi 12

Compared to Matthew 5

1 **AND it came to pass that when Jesus had spoken these words unto Nephi, and to those who had been called, (now the number of them who had been called, and received power and authority to baptize, was twelve) and behold, he stretched forth his hand unto the multitude, and cried unto them, saying: Blessed are ye if ye shall give heed unto the words of these twelve whom I have chosen from among you to minister unto you, and to be your servants; and unto them I have given power that they may baptize you with water; and after that ye are baptized with water, behold, I will baptize you with fire and with the Holy Ghost; therefore blessed are ye if ye shall believe in me and be baptized, after that ye have seen me and know that I am.**

2 **And again, more blessed are they who shall believe in your words because that ye shall testify that ye have seen me, and that ye know that I am. Yea, blessed are they who shall believe in your words, and come down into the depths of humility and be baptized, for they shall be visited with fire and with the Holy Ghost, and shall receive a remission of their sins.**

3 Yea, blessed are the poor in spirit **who come unto me**, for theirs is the kingdom of heaven.

4 And again, blessed are **all** they that mourn, for they shall be comforted.

5 And blessed are the meek, for they shall inherit the earth.

6 And blessed are **all** they **who** do hunger and thirst after righteousness, for they shall be **filled with the Holy Ghost**.

7 And blessed are the merciful, for they shall obtain mercy.

8 And blessed are **all** the pure in heart, for they shall see God.

9 And blessed are **all** the peacemakers, for they shall be called the children of God.

10 And blessed are **all** they **who** are persecuted for **my name's** sake, for theirs is the kingdom of heaven.

11 And blessed are ye when men shall revile you and persecute, and shall say all manner of evil against you falsely, for my sake;

12 **For ye shall have great joy** and be exceedingly glad, for great **shall be** your reward in heaven; for so persecuted they the prophets **who** were before you.

13 **Verily, verily, I say unto you, I give unto you to be** the salt of the earth; but if the salt **shall lose** its savor wherewith shall **the earth** be salted? **The salt shall be** thenceforth good for nothing, but to be cast out and to be trodden under foot of men.

14 **Verily, verily, I say unto you, I give unto you to be** the light of **this**

people. A city that is set on a hill cannot be hid.

15 **Behold, do men** light a candle and put it under a bushel? **Nay**, but on a candlestick, and it giveth light **to** all that are in the house;

16 **Therefore** let your light so shine before **this people**, that they may see your good works and glorify your Father **who** is in heaven.

17 Think not that I am come to destroy the law or the prophets. I am not come to destroy but to fulfil;

18 For verily I say unto you [*"Till heaven and earth pass" is omitted*], one jot **nor** one tittle **hath not passed away** from the law, **but in me it hath all been** fulfilled.

19 **And behold, I have given you the law and the commandments of my Father, that ye shall believe in me, and that ye shall repent of your sins, and come unto me with a broken heart and a contrite spirit. Behold, ye have the commandments before you, and the law is fulfilled.**

20 **Therefore come unto me and be ye saved; for verily I say unto you, that except ye shall keep my commandments, which I have commanded you at this time**, ye shall in no case enter into the kingdom of heaven.

21 Ye have heard that it **hath been** said by them of old time, **and it is also written before you, that** thou shalt not kill, and whosoever shall kill shall be in danger of the judgment **of God**;

22 But I say unto you, that whosoever is angry with his brother [*"without a cause" is omitted*] shall be in danger of his judgment. And whosoever shall say to his brother, Raca, shall be in danger of the council; and whosoever shall say, Thou fool, shall be in danger of hell fire.

23 Therefore, **if ye shall come unto me, or shall desire to come unto me**, and rememberest that thy brother hath aught against thee—

24 [*"Leave there thy gift before the altar, and" is omitted*] Go thy way **unto thy brother**, and first be reconciled to thy brother, **and then come unto me with full purpose of heart, and I will receive you**.

25 Agree with thine adversary quickly while thou art in the way with him, lest at any time **he shall get thee**, and thou **shalt** be cast into prison.

26 Verily, **verily**, I say unto thee, thou shalt by no means come out thence **until** thou hast paid the uttermost **senine. And while ye are in prison can ye pay even one senine? Verily, verily, I say unto you, Nay.**

27 **Behold, it is written** by them of old time, **that** thou shalt not commit adultery;

28 But I say unto you, that whosoever looketh on a woman, to lust after her, hath committed adultery [*"with her" is omitted*] already in his heart.

29 **Behold, I give unto you a commandment, that ye suffer none of these things to enter into your heart**;

30 **For it is better that ye should deny yourselves of these things, wherein ye will take up your cross, than that ye** should be cast into hell.

31 It hath been **written, that** whosoever shall put away his wife, let him give her a writing of divorcement.

32 **Verily, verily**, I say unto you, that whosoever shall put away his wife, saving for the cause of fornication, causeth her to commit adultery; and **whoso** shall marry her **who** is divorced committeth adultery.

33 **And** again **it is written**, thou shalt not forswear thyself, but shalt perform unto the Lord thine oaths;

34 But **verily, verily**, I say unto you, swear not at all; neither by heaven, for it is God's throne;

35 Nor by the earth, for it is his footstool [*"neither by Jerusalem; for it is the city of the great King" is omitted*];

36 Neither shalt thou swear by thy head, because thou canst not make one hair **black or white** [*reversed order*];

37 But let your communication be Yea, yea; Nay, nay; for whatsoever **cometh of more than these** [*reversed order*] is evil.

38 **And behold, it is written**, an eye for an eye, and a tooth for a tooth;

39 But I say unto you, that ye **shall not resist evil**, but whosoever shall smite thee on thy right cheek, turn to him the other also;

40 And if any man will sue thee at the law and take away thy coat, let him have thy cloak also;

41 And whosoever shall compel thee to go a mile, go with him twain.

42 Give to him that asketh thee, and from him that would borrow of thee turn thou not away.

43 **And behold it is written also, that** thou shalt love thy neighbor and hate thine enemy;

44 But **behold** I say unto you, love your enemies, bless them that curse you, do good to them that hate you, and pray for them **who** despitefully use you and persecute you;

45 That ye may be the children of your Father **who** is in heaven; for he maketh his sun to rise on the evil and on the good [*"and sendeth rain on the just and on the unjust" is omitted*].

46 **Therefore those things which were of old time, which were under the law, in me are all fulfilled.**

47 **Old things are done away, and all things have become new.**

48 **Therefore I would that ye should** be perfect even as **I, or** your Father who is in heaven is perfect.

3 Nephi 13
Compared to Matthew 6

1 **VERILY, verily, I say that I would that ye should do alms unto the poor; but** take heed that ye do not your alms before men to be seen of them; otherwise ye have no reward of your Father **who** is in heaven.

2 Therefore, when **ye shall do your** alms do not sound a trumpet before **you**, as **will** hypocrites do in the synagogues and in the streets, that they may have glory of men. Verily I say unto you, they have their reward.

3 But when thou doest alms let not thy left hand know what thy right hand doeth;

4 That thine alms may be in secret; and thy Father **who** seeth in secret, himself shall reward thee openly.

5 And when thou prayest thou shalt not **do** as the hypocrites, for they love to pray, standing in the synagogues and in the corners of the streets, that they may be seen of men. Verily I say unto you, they have their reward.

6 But thou, when thou prayest, enter into thy closet, and when thou hast shut thy door, pray to thy Father **who** is in secret; and thy Father, **who** seeth in secret, shall reward thee openly.

7 But when ye pray, use not vain repetitions, as the heathen, for they think that they shall be heard for their much speaking.

8 Be not ye therefore like unto them, for your Father knoweth what things ye have need of before ye ask him.

9 After this manner therefore pray ye: Our Father **who** art in heaven, hallowed be thy name.

10 [*"Thy kingdom come" omitted*] Thy will be done **on** earth as it is in heaven.

[*Matt. 6:11, "Give us this day our daily bread," is omitted.*]

11 And forgive us our debts, as we forgive our debtors.

12 And lead us not into temptation, but deliver us from evil.

13 For thine is the kingdom, and the power, and the glory, forever. Amen.

14 For, if ye forgive men their trespasses your heavenly Father will also forgive you;

15 But if ye forgive not men their trespasses neither will your Father forgive your trespasses.

16 Moreover, when ye fast be not as the hypocrites, of a sad countenance, for they disfigure their faces that they may appear unto men to fast. Verily I say unto you, they have their reward.

17 But thou, when thou fastest, anoint thy head, and wash thy face;

18 That thou appear not unto men to fast, but unto thy Father, **who** is in secret; and thy Father, **who** seeth in secret, shall reward thee openly.

19 Lay not up for yourselves treasures upon earth, where moth and rust doth corrupt, and thieves break through and steal;

20 But lay up for yourselves treasures in heaven, where neither moth nor rust doth corrupt, and where thieves do not break through nor steal.

21 For where your treasure is, there will your heart be also.

22 The light of the body is the eye; if, therefore, thine eye be single, thy whole body shall be full of light.

23 But if thine eye be evil, thy whole body shall be full of darkness. If, therefore, the light that is in thee be darkness, how great is that darkness!

24 No man can serve two masters; for either he will hate the one and love the other, or else he will hold to the one and despise the other. Ye cannot serve God and Mammon.

25 **And now it came to pass that when Jesus had spoken these words he looked upon the twelve whom he had chosen, and said unto them: Remember the words which I have spoken. For behold, ye are they whom I have chosen to minister unto this people.** Therefore I say unto you, take no thought for your life, what ye shall eat, or what ye shall drink; nor yet for your body, what ye shall put on. Is not the life more than meat, and the body than raiment?

26 Behold the fowls of the air, for they sow not, neither do they reap nor gather into barns; yet your heavenly Father feedeth them. Are ye not much better than they?

27 Which of you by taking thought can add one cubit unto his stature?

28 And why take ye thought for raiment? Consider the lilies of the field how they grow; they toil not, neither do they spin;

29 And yet I say unto you, that even Solomon, in all his glory, was not arrayed like one of these.

30 Wherefore, if God so clothe the grass of the field, which today is, and tomorrow is cast into the oven, **even so will he** clothe you, **if ye are not** of little faith.

31 Therefore take no thought, saying, What shall we eat? or, What shall we drink? or, Wherewithal shall we be clothed?

32 [*"For after these things do the Gentiles seek:" is omitted.*] For your heavenly Father knoweth that ye have need of all these things.

33 But seek ye first the kingdom of God and his righteousness, and all these things shall be added unto you.

34 Take therefore no thought for the morrow, for the morrow shall take thought for the things of itself. Sufficient **is** the day **unto** the evil thereof.

3 Nephi 14
Compared to Matthew 7

1 **AND now it came to pass that when Jesus had spoken these words he turned again to the multitude, and did open his mouth unto them again, saying: Verily, verily, I say unto you,** Judge not, that ye be not judged.

2 For with what judgment ye judge, ye shall be judged; and with what measure ye mete, it shall be measured to you again.

3 And why beholdest thou the mote that is in thy brother's eye, but considerest not the beam that is in thine own eye?

4 Or how wilt thou say to thy brother: Let me pull the mote out of thine eye—and behold, a beam is in thine own eye?

5 Thou hypocrite, first cast the beam out of thine own eye; and then shalt thou see clearly to cast the mote out of thy brother's eye.

6 Give not that which is holy unto the dogs, neither cast ye your pearls before swine, lest they trample them under their feet, and turn again and rend you.

7 Ask, and it shall be given **unto** you; seek, and ye shall find; knock, and it shall be opened unto you.

8 For every one that asketh, receiveth; and he that seeketh, findeth; and to him that knocketh, it shall be opened.

9 Or what man is there of you, **who,** if his son ask bread, will give him a stone?

10 Or if he ask a fish, will he give him a serpent?

11 If ye then, being evil, know how to give good gifts unto your children, how much more shall your Father **who** is in heaven give good things to them that ask him?

12 Therefore, all things whatsoever ye would that men should do to you, do ye even so to them, for this is the law and the prophets.

13 Enter ye in at the strait gate; for wide is the gate, and broad is the way, **which** leadeth to destruction, and many there be **who** go in thereat;

14 Because strait is the gate, and narrow is the way, which leadeth unto life, and few there be that find it.

15 Beware of false prophets, **who** come to you in sheep's clothing, but inwardly they are ravening wolves.

16 Ye shall know them by their fruits. Do men gather grapes of thorns, or figs of thistles?

17 Even so every good tree bringeth forth good fruit; but a corrupt tree bringeth forth evil fruit.

18 A good tree cannot bring forth evil fruit, neither a corrupt tree bring forth good fruit.

19 Every tree that bringeth not forth good fruit is hewn down, and cast into the fire.

20 Wherefore, by their fruits ye shall know them.

21 Not every one that saith unto me, Lord, Lord, shall enter into the kingdom of heaven; but he that doeth the will of my Father **who** is in heaven.

22 Many will say to me in that day: Lord, Lord, have we not prophesied in thy name, and in thy name have cast out devils, and in thy name done many wonderful works?

23 And then will I profess unto them: I never knew you; depart from me, ye that work iniquity.

24 Therefore, **whoso** heareth these sayings of mine and doeth them, I will liken him unto a wise man, **who** built his house upon a rock—

25 And the rain descended, and the floods came, and the winds blew, and beat upon that house; and it fell not, for it was founded upon a rock.

26 And every one that heareth these sayings of mine and doeth them not shall be likened unto a foolish man, **who** built his house upon the sand—

27 And the rain descended, and the floods came, and the winds blew, and beat upon that house; and it fell, and great was the fall of it.

28 And it came to pass, when Jesus had ended these sayings, the people were astonished at his doctrine:

29 For he taught them as one having authority, and not as the scribes [***italic text omitted in Third Nephi***].

Now let's go through 3 Nephi 12–14, with notes and commentary added, like we have been doing. By the way, since this is the version of the "Sermon on the Mount" that the Savior gave to the Book of Mormon people, it will be interesting when we get the records of the lost ten tribes (2 Nephi 29:13 says we will) and others to see if they, too, have scriptures with the Sermon on the Mount in them.

One other quick comment regarding those who criticize the Book of Mormon for having parts of other scriptures in it. If they are going to criticize Joseph Smith, they should also criticize the New Testament and Angel Gabriel for using language similar to Old Testament, Isaiah 9:7, when he was telling Mary about the Child she was going to bear (Luke 1:33).

THIRD NEPHI 12

Remember, as we said previously, that chapter 12 here is comparable to Matthew 5. However, 3 Nephi 12:1–2 are not in Matthew 5, and they contain very important background for the Sermon on the Mount. From these two verses, we find that this sermon is directed to baptized members of the Church, and that it is a "formula" outlining the process we must follow in attaining exaltation and perfection after baptism. In other words, this sermon is much more than a system of ethics for all people. Rather, it is the "lesson manual" for members to follow after they have been baptized and have received the gift of the Holy Ghost, as they strive to learn how to continue toward exaltation.

1 AND it came to pass that when Jesus had spoken these words unto Nephi, and to those who had been called, (now **the number of them who had been called, and received power and authority to baptize, was twelve**) and behold, **he stretched forth his hand unto the multitude**, and cried unto them, **saying: Blessed are ye if ye shall give heed unto** [*follow and obey*] **the words of these twelve** whom I have chosen from among you to minister unto you, and to be your servants; and **unto them I have given power that they may baptize you** [*into the Church of Jesus Christ, which will now replace the Law of Moses*] **with water**; and after that ye are baptized with water, behold, **I will baptize you with fire and with the Holy Ghost** [*the gift of the Holy Ghost*]; therefore blessed are ye if ye shall believe in me and be baptized, after that ye have seen me and know that I am.

In verse 1, we are told by Mormon that Jesus had called twelve, including Nephi, to serve as the equivalent of the Twelve Apostles in Jerusalem for the people of Nephi. It is appropriate to call the Nephite Twelve "Apostles," because Joseph Smith did in the Wentworth Letter (**bold** added for emphasis): "This book also tells us that our Savior made His appearance upon this continent after His Resurrection; that He planted the Gospel here in all its fulness, and richness, and power, and blessing; that they had **Apostles**, Prophets, Pastors, Teachers, and Evangelists; the same order, the same priesthood, the same ordinances, gifts, powers, and blessings, that were enjoyed on the eastern continent" (Joseph Smith, *History of The Church of Jesus Christ of Latter-day Saints*, 4:537–38).

The word "fire," in verse 1, is often used in conjunction with the Holy Ghost. The imagery is that a refiner of gold uses fire to melt the gold ore and thus separate the pure gold from the rock and other unwanted elements. The pure gold symbolizes the faithful Saints, and the rock represents sins and imperfections, immaturity, etc., that must be "burned" out of our souls by the Holy Ghost as He guides us and testifies to us.

Next, in verse 2, we are reminded that this "Sermon at the Temple" is given to baptized and confirmed members of the Church, or to those who soon will be.

2 And again, more blessed are they who shall believe in your words because that ye shall testify that ye have seen me, and that ye know that I am. Yea, blessed are they who shall believe in your words, and come down into the depths of humility and be **baptized**, for they shall be visited with fire and with the **Holy Ghost**, and shall **receive a remission of their sins**.

Verses 3–12 are commonly known as the "Beatitudes." There are many ways to study them. We will go through them four times. First, we will go through them pointing out with bold the changes in the Beatitudes here in Third Nephi as compared to the Beatitudes in Matthew 5:1–12. This is a repetition of part of what we did at the beginning of this chapter, but is worth doing again here. By the way, the word "blessed," among other things, means "to be happy" (see Matthew 5:3, footnote a, in our Bible). Therefore, each time we read "blessed are" in the Beatitudes, we can think "happy are."

3 Yea, blessed are the poor in spirit **who come unto me**, for theirs is the kingdom of heaven.

4 And again, blessed are **all** they that mourn, for they shall be comforted.

5 And blessed are the meek, for they shall inherit the earth.

6 And blessed are **all** they **who** do hunger and thirst after righteousness, for they shall be filled **with the Holy Ghost**.

7 And blessed are the merciful, for they shall obtain mercy.

8 And blessed are **all** the pure in heart, for they shall see God.

9 And blessed are **all** the peacemakers, for they shall be called the children of God.

10 And blessed are **all** they who are persecuted for **my name's** sake, for theirs is the kingdom of heaven.

11 And blessed are ye when men shall revile you and persecute [*the "you" in Matthew 5:11 is left out here in Third Nephi*], and shall say all manner of evil against you falsely, for my sake;

12 **For ye shall have great joy** and be exceedingly glad, for great **shall be** your reward in heaven; for so

persecuted they the prophets **who** were before you.

Next, we will go through the Beatitudes in Third Nephi again, this time pointing out that they contain instructions for obtaining the celestial kingdom once you are baptized (verses 1 and 2). We will **bold** words and phrases that mean celestial glory.

3 Yea, blessed are the poor in spirit who come unto me, for theirs is **the kingdom of heaven**.

4 And again, blessed are all they that mourn, for they shall be comforted.

5 And blessed are the meek, for **they shall inherit the earth** [*which will become the celestial kingdom; see D&C 131:9–11*].

6 And blessed are all they who do hunger and thirst after righteousness, for they shall be filled with the Holy Ghost.

7 And blessed are the merciful, for they shall obtain mercy.

8 And blessed are all the pure in heart, for **they shall see God** [*including when they associate with Him in celestial glory*].

9 And blessed are all the peacemakers, for they shall be called **the children of God** [*meaning those who attain exaltation in celestial glory; see D&C 76:24, Mosiah 5:7, 15:10–11*].

10 And blessed are all they who are persecuted for my name's sake, for theirs is **the kingdom of heaven**.

11 And blessed are ye when men shall revile you and persecute, and shall say all manner of evil against you falsely, for my sake;

12 For ye shall have great joy and be exceedingly glad, for great shall be **your reward in heaven**; for so persecuted they the prophets who were before you.

Now, we will go through these Beatitudes yet again, this time watching for additional teachings and lessons.

3 Yea, blessed are the **poor in spirit who come unto me**, for theirs is the kingdom of heaven.

Among many possible meanings of "poor in spirit," we can include the following:

a. Those who lack spirituality and thus need to repent in order to "come unto me."

b. Those who lack confidence in their own abilities, who come unto Christ, can obtain celestial glory with his help.

c. Those who avoid pride (as mentioned in Matthew 5:3, footnote b) and thus come unto Christ.

4 And again, **blessed are all they that mourn, for they shall be comforted**.

Here are two of many possible lessons from this verse:

a. Those who mourn the loss of a loved one will be comforted by the Spirit.

b. Those who mourn for their sins, and thus repent, are comforted by the forgiveness they obtain.

5 And **blessed are the meek, for they shall inherit the earth.**

The word "meek" can be defined as "being patient and mild, not inclined to anger or resentment." See *Webster's Collegiate Dictionary*, 1980 edition. It is also often defined as being teachable and voluntarily humble. Thus, being meek implies being kind, pleasant, and humble as a result of having deep inner strength.

6 And **blessed are all they who do hunger and thirst after righteousness, for they shall be filled with the Holy Ghost.**

Among the several things we could teach from this verse are:

a. "Happy are" the people who don't level out and quit progressing in their striving for personal righteousness.

b. "Happy are" the people who truly want to be good.

c. "Happy are" those who continually strive to serve others righteously.

d. "Righteousness," in scripture, is sometimes a synonym for God (2 Nephi 26:9). Therefore, to "hunger and thirst after righteousness" can mean to seek Christ, the result of which is being filled with the Holy Ghost who bears witness of Him.

7 And **blessed are the merciful, for they shall obtain mercy** [*from the Savior now and during Final Judgment; Matthew 6:14*].

Merciful behavior toward others is a sign of true personal righteousness. Sincere mercy offered to others is a very strong purifier of the soul.

8 And **blessed are all the pure in heart, for they shall see God.**

"Heart" is often used in scriptures to represent the true inner person. Thus, true personal purity, in thought and action, is required to see God and to ultimately be in His presence.

9 And **blessed are all the peacemakers, for they shall be called the children of God.**

Whether or not you are a "peacemaker" is a significant measure of personal spirituality. Also, the more pure you become, the more offensive contention becomes to you.

Verses 10 and 11, next, go together. It would seem that being persecuted is sometimes a significant indicator that the members of the Church are doing well at living the gospel. We must, of course, be careful that we do not intentionally heap persecution upon our heads by being obnoxious in living our religion.

10 And **blessed are all they who are persecuted for my name's sake, for theirs is the kingdom of heaven.**

11 And blessed are ye when men shall revile [*mock, ridicule, make fun of*] you and persecute, and shall say all manner of evil against you **falsely** [*we must live such that their accusations are false*], for my sake;

12 For ye shall have great joy and be exceedingly glad, for **great shall be**

your reward in heaven; for so persecuted they the prophets who were before you.

The future is always ultimately bright for those who live the gospel.

We will go through the Beatitudes one last time now and point out that another way to study them is to view them as a "progression" that leads ultimately to salvation in celestial glory. We will present this "progression" as a series of steps.

Step 1. (Verse 3) When you recognize that you are truly lacking in spirituality, and blame no one but yourself for it, personal progress begins.

3 Yea, **blessed are the poor in spirit who come unto me**, for theirs is the kingdom of heaven.

Step 2. (Verse 4) When you begin to mourn for your sins, true repentance begins, and the Holy Ghost comforts you and assures you that you are on the right path.

4 And again, **blessed are all they that mourn** [*for their sins*], for they shall be comforted.

Step 3. (Verse 5) This mourning for your sins makes you meek and humble as you recognize your dependence on Christ. Pride and arrogance melt away.

5 And **blessed are the meek**, for they shall inherit the earth.

Step 4. (Verse 6) With newly found light and spirituality in your life, your thirst and hunger for this gospel lifestyle continues to grow. The gospel is exciting to a degree you never thought possible for you. Activity and service in the Church become your constant goal. The Holy Ghost keeps giving you new knowledge and insights into the gospel.

6 And **blessed are all they who do hunger and thirst after righteousness**, for they shall be filled with the Holy Ghost.

Step 5. (Verse 7) As you are filled with gospel light and truth, and as you find yourself much closer to the Spirit, you become much more merciful toward others. You are truly becoming more Christlike.

7 And **blessed are the merciful**, for they shall obtain mercy.

Step 6. (Verse 8) Things that were not particularly offensive to you are now very objectionable and disturbing to you. You want nothing to do with filth, vulgarity, mean-spirited behaviors, etc. You want nothing entering your life that will prevent you from feeling the Spirit and from "seeing" the Savior in His teachings and counsels. You have come a long way from when you first realized that you were "poor in spirit," and chose to begin doing something about it.

8 And **blessed are all the pure in heart**, for they shall see God.

Step 7. (Verse 9) Contention is extremely offensive to you now. You have progressed to the point that you desire peace and to be at peace with others. Whereas, you formerly sometimes enjoyed contention, you now seek to promote peace.

9 And **blessed are all the peacemakers**, for they shall be called the children of God.

Step 8. (Verses 10 and 11) Former friends and associates who have not changed are now wondering what happened to you. They are no longer comfortable around you and sometimes mock your standards and values. You have found that as you gently and humbly live the gospel, some delight in making fun of you for it. You are glad for the company of those who respect you and for those of like standards and find yourself bracing for persecution as it comes.

10 And **blessed are all they who are persecuted for my name's sake**, for theirs is the kingdom of heaven.

11 And **blessed are ye when men shall revile you and persecute, and shall say all manner of evil against you falsely, for my sake**;

12 For **ye shall have great joy and be exceedingly glad, for great shall be your reward in heaven**; for so persecuted they the prophets who were before you.

As we move to verse 13, next, it is helpful to know that salt, in Old Testament culture, among other things, represented covenants. The following quote from the *Book of Mormon Student Manual*, used by the institutes of religion in the Church, is helpful:

"In the Mosaic sacrificial ritual, **salt was a token of covenants with God** (see Numbers 18:19 and 2 Chronicles 13:5). In a similar sense, Saints should be tokens or symbols of the Christlike life. Doctrine and Covenants 101:39–40 indicates what one must do to be accounted as the 'salt of the earth'" (*Book of Mormon Student Manual*, 1996 edition, 118).

Also, you no doubt know from personal experience that a little salt is a powerful influence in making an entire meal taste better. Therefore, one aspect of symbolism here is that salt makes the environment better. So also, true Saints make their environment better and more pleasant for those around them.

13 Verily, verily, I say unto you, **I give unto you to be the salt of the earth**; but **if the salt shall lose its savor** [*flavor, ability to season food*] **wherewith shall the earth be salted** [*one way to look at this is, if the Saints don't keep their covenants, how are they going to improve things for those around them*]**? The salt shall be thenceforth good for nothing, but to be cast out and to be trodden under foot of men**.

This is a rather stern warning to members of the Church who don't keep their covenants, because those members who "lose their saltiness or savor" will ultimately be "walked on" and scattered and smitten by others, by Satan, or by both.

Next, in verses 14–16, the Savior teaches the people of Nephi the importance of living the gospel in order to help others see its value. It has been said that what people see in the lives of members is far more important than what they hear when it comes to influencing them to want to know more about the Church.

14 Verily, verily, I say unto you, **I give unto you to be the light of this people. A city that is set on a hill cannot be hid**.

15 Behold, **do men light a candle and put it under a bushel? Nay, but on a candlestick, and it giveth light to all that are in the house;**

16 Therefore **let your light so shine before this people, that they may see your good works and glorify your Father who is in heaven.**

Verses 17–18, next, require some background to understand. The "law" generally means the first five books in the Old Testament, namely, Genesis, Exodus, Leviticus, Numbers, and Deuteronomy. Specifically, in this context, the "law" means the Law of Moses (see 3 Nephi 12:18, footnote b). The "prophets" means the prophets in the Old Testament, such as Isaiah, Jeremiah, Ezekiel, Daniel, etc. Thus, "the law or the prophets" refers especially to the Law of Moses, which was designed to point the people's minds toward Christ, and to the words of the prophets, such as Isaiah, who had prophesied of Christ.

17 **Think not that I am come to destroy the law or the prophets** [*don't think I have come to render the Law of Moses and the words of the prophets to be of no value*]. **I am not come to destroy but to fulfil** [*on the contrary; I have come to prove their value by fulfilling everything they said about Me*];

18 For verily I say unto you, **one jot nor one tittle** [*one tiny bit*] **hath not passed away** [*gone unfulfilled by Me*] **from the law, but in me it hath all been fulfilled.**

Verses 17 and 18, above, are a strong validation by the Savior Himself of the worth of the teachings of Moses and other Old Testament prophets. If you keep in mind that Christ is taught very strongly in the "law and the prophets" of the Old Testament, it will help you greatly as you study it.

Next, Jesus explains to these people that He has given them what the Old Testament pointed toward; namely, the higher law, which His Father had instructed that He now give them. These are the higher laws of the Church of Jesus Christ, including faith, repentance, baptism, the gift of the Holy Ghost (chapter 11), and the Beatitudes, which were given at the first of this chapter. He will continue to give these people more instruction on these higher laws as Third Nephi continues.

19 And behold, **I have given you the law and the commandments of my Father**, that ye shall **believe in me** [*have faith in Christ*], and that ye shall **repent of your sins**, and come unto me **with a broken heart and a contrite spirit** [*in humility, with sorrow for your sins, desiring correction as needed*]. Behold, **ye have the commandments before you** [*the higher laws of the restored gospel; see verse 20, next*], **and the law** [*of Moses; see 3 Nephi 9:17*] **is fulfilled.**

20 Therefore **come unto me and be ye saved**; for verily I say unto you, that **except ye shall keep my commandments, which I have commanded you at this time** [*rather than the Law of Moses*], **ye shall in no case enter into the kingdom of heaven.**

In other words, the Law of Moses cannot save you.

Jesus will now compare and contrast the higher laws that accompany the Church of Jesus Christ, which He is now restoring to the people of Nephi, and which include the laws that were part of the Law of Moses.

Just a note regarding the Law of Moses, so that we do not mistakenly think it was a low law. The children of Israel were slaves in Egypt for hundreds of years. During that time, they adopted many of the false beliefs and philosophies of their Egyptian slave drivers. Thus, the Law of Moses was a high law for them. For example, an "eye for an eye, a tooth for a tooth, a hand for a hand, and a foot for a foot" (Exodus 21:24) is part of the Law of Moses and commands, in effect, that punishment be limited to the exact value of what was taken by an enemy. It eliminates revenge, wherein, for example, the person wronged by a thief who stole two of his sheep might burn the thief's house and sell his wife and children into slavery.

Indeed, the Law of Moses would be a high law for most of the world even today. Read, for example, Exodus 22:1–5, 23:1–8.

Thus, the Law of Moses was actually a rather high standard, with a great number of behaviors in a large number of situations spelled out in much detail. The higher law, brought now to the people of Nephi by the Savior, is principle-based and requires deep inner conviction rather than mostly outward pressure to live it.

In the next verses you can recognize the "old law" by the phrase "Ye have heard" or "It is written by them of old," etc., referring to the Law of Moses. You will recognize the "new law," given by Christ, by the phrase "But I say," "I give unto you," etc.

21 **Ye have heard that it hath been said by them of old time** [*the Law of Moses, etc.*], and it is also written before you [*you have it in your records, including the Brass Plates*], that **thou shalt not kill** [*first degree murder*], and whosoever shall kill shall be in danger of the judgment of God;

22 **But I say unto you, that whosoever is angry with his brother shall be in danger of his judgment** [*"the judgment"; Matthew 5:22*]. And **whosoever shall say to his brother, Raca** [*derision, ridicule, contempt; see Matthew 5:22, footnote d*], **shall be in danger of the council** [*will be in danger of being brought before the highest religious disciplinary council; see Matthew 5:22, footnote e*]; **and whosoever shall say, Thou fool, shall be in danger of hell fire** [*the punishment of God*].

Near the beginning of verse 22, above, there is a seldom-noticed but significant difference between the Book of Mormon and Matthew 5:22. The Book of Mormon reads, "shall be in danger of his judgment," implying "the judgment of the person," whereas, Matthew reads, "the judgment," implying "the judgment of God."

Using the Book of Mormon version, we have a "progression" or logical sequence of more serious "dangers" as follows:

1. Danger from the person.
2. Danger from disciplinary council.
3. Danger from God's displeasure.

This is another one of those places where we see that the Prophet Joseph Smith did not simply copy the Sermon on the Mount from the Bible. Rather, we see a significant difference in clarity and meaning, even if it comes from just one small word that differs between the two texts.

The phrase "Thou fool," at the end of verse 22, above, must be kept in the context of mocking, ridiculing, or belittling someone for something he or she did, as if you had never made any mistakes yourself. Otherwise, we would have conflicting scriptures in cases such as Romans 1:22, Ephesians 5:15, and many other places in scripture (see Topical Guide under "Fool") where the word "fool" or "fools" is used to mean unwise, short-sighted, etc.

23 Therefore, **if ye shall come unto me** [*if you are coming to worship Me*], or shall desire to come unto me, **and rememberest that thy brother hath aught against thee** [*if you remember that there is contention between you and someone else*]—

24 **Go** thy way **unto thy brother**, and first **be reconciled** to [*make peace with*] thy brother, and **then come unto me** with full purpose of heart, and I will receive [*accept*] you.

Next, we are taught a vital lesson about the value of being a peacemaker and of the terrible prison we put ourselves in if we refuse this counsel. You will see several differences between the next two verses and the corresponding verses in Matthew 5:25–26.

25 **Agree with thine adversary quickly while thou art in the way with him, lest** [*for fear that*] at any time he shall get thee, and **thou shalt be cast into prison** [*including the "prison" of bitterness, hatred, grudges, etc., that surround those who refuse to forgive*].

26 Verily, verily, I say unto thee, **thou shalt by no means come out thence** [*get out of that prison*] **until thou hast paid the uttermost senine** [*the highest price*]. And while ye are in prison can ye pay even one senine? Verily, verily, I say unto you, Nay.

In other words, such self-built "prisons" often make it nearly impossible for you to think rationally and clearly. Thus, you are emotionally paralyzed and find it very difficult to work your way out.

Next, the topic switches to sexual immorality.

27 Behold, **it is written by them of old time** [*under the law of Moses*], **that thou shalt not commit adultery**;

28 **But I say unto you**, that **whosoever looketh on a woman, to lust after her** [*to entertain sexual desires for her*], **hath committed adultery already in his heart**.

29 Behold, **I give unto you a commandment, that ye suffer** [*allow*] **none of these things to enter into your heart**;

It would seem significant that the Savior used the word "heart" rather than "mind" in verse 29, above. Merely by being alive and being normal, such thoughts can enter or be put into our minds. But, if we keep them and "entertain" them, they will soon work their way into our hearts, or center of feelings and emotions. Thus, we will become lustful individuals.

In *True to the Faith*, published by the First Presidency in 2004, page 32, our prophets said (**bold** added for emphasis), "If you allow your thoughts to linger on obscene or immoral things you have already taken the first step toward immorality. Flee immediately from situations that may lead to sin. Pray for constant strength to resist temptation and **control your thoughts**. Make this a part of your daily prayers."

30 For **it is better that ye should deny yourselves of these things** [*"lingering" lustful thoughts*], wherein ye will take up your cross [*which can be difficult to overcome*], than that ye should be cast into hell [*being turned over to Satan to be punished for your sins, and eventually put in telestial glory; see D&C 76:103*].

Next, Jesus gives instructions regarding divorce. These next two verses, if taken out of the context of the scriptures and the teachings of our Church leaders, can cause much heartache and discouragement if misunderstood. We will first read verses 31–32, giving some explanation within the verses. Then, we will give additional commentary.

31 **It hath been written**, that **whosoever shall put away** [*divorce*] **his wife**, let him give her a writing of divorcement [*a document in writing legalizing the divorce*].

32 Verily, verily, **I say unto you**, that whosoever shall put away his wife, saving for the cause of fornication [*except in the case of fornication*], **causeth her to commit adultery**; and **whoso shall marry her who is divorced committeth adultery**.

First of all, marriage is serious and sacred. In an ideal society, there would be no divorce. Marriage vows would be held sacred by both husband and wife. The love and respect that led to marriage in the first place would continue to grow in the marriage. But we do not live in a perfect society. In fact, divorce is everywhere in today's society and has plagued many other societies throughout history.

Divorce is not desirable. Yet, to interpret verse 32 as an absolute law not to marry a divorced person would be to deny divorcees the opportunity for repentance, if needed, and to deny innocent victims of divorce the option of marrying again.

Also, when the interpretation of a passage of scripture, such as verse 32, is unclear, there is wisdom in turning to the Brethren (the Apostles and prophets of the Church) to see what they do with respect to it. The leaders of the Church clearly permit divorced individuals to remarry and be sealed in the temple. It is thus clear that marrying someone who has been divorced does not, in and of itself, make one an "adulterer." Otherwise, no one who marries a divorced person could get a temple recommend and be sealed in the temple. No doubt you know faithful Saints who have been sealed in the temple, even though one or both of them were previously divorced.

If we had no other answer to verses 31 and 32, other than observing that the Brethren (the prophets and Apostles of our day) permit temple sealings between divorced persons, then we would have all we need to know as far as proper procedure and God's laws are concerned.

This being the case, we will now take one more look at verses 31 and 32, in the big context of the scriptures and the words of the Brethren, to see what may be missing in our understanding of them.

By way of background, divorce had become extremely easy in New Testament times. In fact, about all a man had to do in order to divorce his wife was to say to her, in the presence of a witness, "I divorce you" three times. She would then be put out of his house and out of his life.

Verse 31 reminds the people of Nephi that Old Testament law required more than just a verbal divorce. It implies that similar attitudes and behaviors concerning divorce had come to exist among the Book of Mormon peoples before the coming of Christ to them.

Verse 32 requires that we take a closer look at vocabulary, especially the word "fornication." It is interesting that, in the usual definition, "fornication" means sexual relations between unmarried persons. The context of verse 32 is marriage. "Adultery" would seem to be the more appropriate word.

However, the word "fornication" is often used in the scriptures to mean total disloyalty and breaking of covenants. See Isaiah 23:17 and Revelation 14:8. In fact, both "fornication" and "adultery" are commonly used in scripture to mean extreme disloyalty and breaking of commitments and covenants. In our Bible Dictionary under "Adultery," we read the following: "Adultery . . . is sometimes used to illustrate the apostasy of a nation or a whole people from the ways of the Lord, such as Israel forsaking her God and going after strange gods and strange practices (Exodus 20:14; Jeremiah 3:7–10; Matthew 5:27–32; Luke 18:11; D&C 43:24–25)."

With this in mind, we conclude that one possible explanation of verses 31 and 32 is as follows: Marriage is sacred and serious. If marriage is treated lightly and basically as a license to have sexual relations, with no thought as to the seriousness of vows and commitments, and is followed by divorce and remarriage on the basis of lust, people are basically committing "legalized" adultery, which doesn't work in the eyes of God.

One possible meaning of the phrase "saving for the cause of fornication" (verse 32) is "except in the case of very serious breaking of trust, loyalty, vows, commitments, covenants, etc., including abuse."

Finally, according to the policies of the Church established by our Apostles and prophets, a person whose life is in order, who marries a divorced person whose life is also in order, is not committing adultery by getting married. The blessings of the temple are available to them, just as with other worthy individuals.

Verses 33–37, next, deal with keeping your word, that is, keeping your promises.

33 And again **it is written** [*in the old law that you have been living*], **thou shalt not forswear thyself** [*perjure yourself; break your word*], **but shalt perform unto the Lord thine oaths** [*keep your covenants to the Lord*];

To understand the next verses, it is helpful to know that in Biblical society, people had come to the point where they would put all kinds of conditions in contracts, which allowed them to easily go back on their word if they felt it was to their advantage. A simple example might be, "I swear by the full moon that this chariot is in top condition as I sell it to you." Actually, the moon was not quite full, rather, just one day short of being full. But on that technicality, you could get a lawyer to defend you and tell the disappointed client that it is his problem that the chariot is defective, because he should have noticed that the moon was not quite full.

The above example is the background for the Savior's teachings in verses 34–37.

34 But verily, verily, **I say unto you, swear** [*promise*] **not at all; neither by heaven, for it is God's throne** [*don't add all kinds of conditions to your promises, contracts, etc.*];

35 **Nor by the earth**, for it is his footstool;

36 **Neither shalt thou swear by thy head**, because thou canst not make one hair black or white;

37 **But let your communication be Yea, yea; Nay, nay** [*just say "Yes" if you mean "Yes" and "No" if you mean "No;" don't complicate it; let your word be good*]; for whatsoever cometh of more than these is evil.

If you keep adding complicating details, you are paving the way for you and others to be dishonest and break your word.

In verses 38–45, next, Jesus teaches the importance of gaining self-control over our own emotions if we want to enter celestial exaltation and become gods. Remember, this Sermon at the Temple, or Sermon on the Mount, is a "blueprint" for becoming gods, who must have self-control, or they would not be reliable for their children on their earths. Again, the issue in these next verses is control over your own emotions and behaviors rather than control over other people.

38 And behold, **it is written** [*in the old law, which you have been living*], **an eye for an eye, and a tooth for a tooth**;

39 **But I say unto you**, that **ye shall not resist evil, but whosoever shall smite thee on thy right cheek, turn to him the other also**;

40 And **if any man will sue thee at the law** [*take you to court*] **and take away thy coat, let him have thy cloak also**;

41 And **whosoever** [*whoever*] **shall compel** [*force*] **thee to go a mile, go with him twain** [*two*].

42 **Give to him that asketh thee, and from him that would borrow of thee turn thou not away** [*don't tell him to go away and not bother you*].

43 And behold **it is written also**, that thou shalt **love thy neighbor and hate thine enemy**;

44 **But behold I say unto you, love your enemies, bless them that curse you, do good to them that hate you, and pray for them who**

despitefully use you [*are mean to you*] **and persecute you;**

45 **That ye may be the children of your Father who is in heaven** [*so you can become exalted beings; see D&C 76:24*]; **for he maketh his sun to rise on the evil and on the good.**

If you are going to become gods, you must be willing to do nice things for the wicked as well as the righteous on your worlds.

46 Therefore **those things which were of old time** [*times past in the Old Testament*], **which were under the law** [*of Moses*], **in me are all fulfilled.**

47 **Old things are done away**, and **all things have become new.**

The last phrase in verse 47, above, reminds us that the Savior is setting up a new, or restored, church among these people. This is one of the reasons they need to be rebaptized (3 Nephi 11:21), that is, for membership in this "new" church.

There is a significant difference between verse 48, next, and Matthew 5:48 in the Bible. We will quote Matthew 5:48 right after 3 Nephi 12:48. See if you can pick out the main difference between the two.

48 **Therefore, I would that ye should be perfect even as I, or your Father who is in heaven is perfect.**

Matthew 5:48: Be ye therefore perfect, even as your Father which is in heaven is perfect.

The main difference is that in 3 Nephi 12:48 Jesus includes Himself along with the Father as a perfect being. He is now resurrected and has a glorified, resurrected body like the Father. In this sense He was not yet completely perfected when He gave the Sermon on the Mount to the people in the Holy Land.

Another important message from 3 Nephi 12:48 is that we are commanded to become perfect like the Savior and our Father in Heaven. This means that it is possible, even though it will be well into the next life before we attain it. Footnote 48a, which accompanies 3 Nephi 12:48, instructs us that this verse is teaching us that we have the "potential to become like Heavenly Father."

THIRD NEPHI 13

This chapter is a lot like Matthew, chapter 6 in the Bible. As mentioned in the notes at the beginning of Third Nephi, chapter 12, in this study guide, Jesus told the Book of Mormon people that He was going to teach them what He had taught the people in the Holy Land before He went up into heaven. (See 3 Nephi 15:1.)

In chapter 13, here, the Savior continues teaching and explaining personal attributes needed for entrance into celestial glory. Remember that the people "did cry out with one accord, saying Hosanna!" (See 3 Nephi 11:16–17.) "Hosanna" means, in effect, "save us now" (see Bible Dictionary under "Hosanna") or "teach us how to be saved in celestial glory." In this chapter, the Savior continues to grant their request to be taught personal attributes needed in order to return to live in the presence of God forever.

As we continue studying, we will suggest some possible interpretations and applications of the Master's teachings here. Obviously, you will be able to come up with many more yourself.

In verse one, we are reminded that our motives in providing help for the poor should be pure rather than to make ourselves look good in the eyes of other people.

1 VERILY, verily [*listen very carefully*], I say that **I would** [*I desire*] **that ye should do alms** [*give donations*] **unto the poor; but take heed that ye do not your alms before men to be seen of them**; otherwise ye have no reward of your Father who is in heaven.

> One lesson we learn from the end of verse 1, above, is that heaven rewards us for what we really are rather than what we outwardly appear to be.

2 **Therefore** [*for this reason*], **when ye shall do your alms do not sound a trumpet before you** [*to signal to others that you are now going to do your "righteous" acts*], **as will hypocrites** [*those who want to appear to be righteous but don't really want to be righteous*] **do** in the synagogues and in the streets, **that they may have glory of men** [*so they can be praised by others*]. Verily I say unto you, they have their reward [*perhaps meaning that they have the praise of men, which is what they wanted*].

3 **But when thou doest alms let not thy left hand know what thy right hand doeth** [*keep it as quiet and low-key as possible*];

4 **That thine alms may be in secret**; and **thy Father who seeth in secret, himself shall reward thee openly.**

> The blessings you receive for genuine service will be obvious to you.

5 **And when thou prayest thou shalt not do as the hypocrites**, for they love to pray, standing in the synagogues and in the corners of the streets, that they may be seen of men [*their true motive*]. Verily I say unto you, they have their reward [*which is to have others think they are righteous*].

6 **But thou, when thou prayest, enter into thy closet** [*do it in private*], and when thou hast shut thy door, pray to thy Father who is in secret; and thy Father, who seeth in secret, shall reward thee openly.

> Some people interpret verse 6, above, as well as Matthew 6:6 in the Bible, to mean that all prayers should be said in private and that public prayers should not be said. To teach that from this verse would be twisting the scriptures. Jesus prayed in public many times; for example, when He blessed the "five loaves and the two fishes" before feeding the 5,000 (Matthew 14:19). In Doctrine and Covenants 19:28, the Lord commanded Martin Harris to "pray vocally as well as in thy heart; yea, before the world as well as in secret, in public as well as in private."
>
> The context (background and setting) of verse 6 is referring to personal motives or reasons for praying. If your purpose in praying is to communicate with your Heavenly Father, He will hear and respond to

your prayer according to His wisdom.

Next, in verse 7, we are given counsel regarding the content of our prayers. We will quote commentary from the 1996 edition of the *Book of Mormon Student Manual* for help with the term "vain repetitions."

"The word *vain* means empty, hollow, deceiving, lacking genuineness. Vain repetitions in prayer can refer to words or phrases that are used without real thought, feeling, or meaning. It can also refer to set prayers that are repeated over and over. An example is the Zoramites' rote prayer from the Rameumptom, which was thoughtlessly repeated each week (see Alma 31:14–22). For additional insight into what constitutes vain prayers, see Alma 34:28."

7 But **when ye pray, use not vain repetitions** [*useless repeating of many words*], as the heathen [*non-Christians*], for they think that they shall be heard for their much speaking.

We need to be careful not to include "sincere repetitions" in the category of "vain repetitions." There may be many parts of our daily prayers that are basically the same each time we pray but are not "empty" or "vain." Examples might include our prayers for the Prophet and our loved ones, or for the strength to avoid temptation, and expressions of gratitude.

8 **Be not ye therefore like unto them**, for your Father knoweth what things ye have need of before ye ask him [*you don't have to use lots of words because Heavenly Father already knows what you need*].

Next, the Lord gives an example of prayer. It is similar to the "Lord's Prayer" in Matthew 6:9–13. It obviously suggests a pattern and isn't the only way to pray since Jesus said many different prayers Himself in the course of His mortal mission.

9 After this manner therefore pray ye: **Our Father who art in heaven, hallowed** [*holy, sanctified*] **be thy name.**

10 **Thy will be done on earth as it is in heaven.**

11 **And forgive us our debts, as we forgive our debtors** [*forgive us as we forgive others*].

12 **And lead us not into temptation, but deliver us from evil.**

13 **For thine is the kingdom, and the power, and the glory, forever. Amen.**

Jesus now gives additional emphasis to verse 11, above. In effect, we are writing part of the script for our own Judgment Day when we do not forgive others.

14 For, **if ye forgive men their trespasses** [*things they do that bother you*] **your heavenly Father will also forgive you;**

15 **But if ye forgive not men their trespasses neither will your Father forgive your trespasses.**

The theme of developing pure, righteous motives in our personal worship is continued in verses 16–18, next.

16 Moreover, **when ye fast be not as the hypocrites, of a sad**

countenance [*doing their best to look hungry and sad because they are going without food*], for **they disfigure their faces that they may appear unto men to fast**. Verily I say unto you, they have their reward.

Others can easily notice that they are fasting, which is what they want.

17 But thou, when thou fastest, **anoint thy head, and wash thy face** [*do your best to look normal*];

In other words, groom yourself neatly as usual.

18 **That thou appear not unto men to fast**, but unto thy Father, who is in secret; and thy Father, who seeth in secret [*who is all knowing; see 3 Nephi 13:6, footnote b*], shall reward thee openly.

Verses 19–21 continue the theme of pure motives and priorities that will lead to exaltation.

19 **Lay not up for yourselves treasures upon earth** [*don't make worldly things your top priorities*], **where moth and rust doth corrupt** [*where they won't last long*], and thieves break through and steal [*because they can easily be lost and are temporary*];

20 **But lay up for yourselves treasures in heaven** [*rather, make things of lasting and eternal value your top priorities*], where neither moth nor rust doth corrupt, and where thieves do not break through nor steal [*because they can't be taken away from you*].

21 For **where your treasure is, there will your heart be also**.

One interpretation of "eye," in verse 22, next, is your focus or priorities in life. We will add notes in harmony with this approach.

22 **The light of the body is the eye** [*what you focus on affects your whole life*]; **if, therefore, thine eye be single** [*Joseph Smith Translation of the Bible for Matthew 6:22 says, "single to the glory of God"; or, in other words, focused on the things that bring glory to God*], **thy whole body shall be full of light** [*your whole life will be filled with the light of the gospel*].

Remember that the suggested lessons and interpretations given here are only a few of several possibilities. With the inspiration and help of the Spirit, you can come up with many other important meanings and messages for your life.

23 **But if thine eye be evil, thy whole body** [*your whole life*] **shall be full of darkness**. If, therefore, the light that is in thee be darkness, how great is that darkness [*spiritual darkness*]!

Next, we are reminded that it is impossible to be loyal to God while being loyal to sin and worldliness. Some people seem to spend their entire lives trying to find a balance between being religious and enjoying unrighteous things of the world; or, in other words, serving "Mammon." As verse 24 clearly states, it is impossible.

24 **No man can serve two masters**; for either he will hate the one and love the other, or else he will hold to the one and despise the other. **Ye cannot serve God and Mammon** [*worldliness*].

Matthew 6:25–34, next, were addressed specifically to the Twelve Apostles. Unfortunately, many groups and individuals throughout history have tried to adopt these verses as guidelines for their own lives. It doesn't work, because they don't work for a living like normal people have to.

As you will see, verse 25, next, clearly indicates that these verses were given to the Nephite Twelve, who had been called to full-time service in the Church that Jesus established among the people of Nephi. Similarly, Matthew 6:25–27, in the JST (Joseph Smith Translation of the Bible), indicates that these verses in the Sermon on the Mount were addressed to the Twelve Apostles, who were to go to all the world teaching and baptizing (Matthew 28:19–20). These same instructions also basically apply to full-time missionaries today.

25 And now it came to pass that **when Jesus had spoken these words** [*to the multitude; 3 Nephi 12:1*] **he looked upon the twelve** whom he had chosen [*3 Nephi 12:1*], **and said unto them**: Remember the words which I have spoken. For behold, **ye are they whom I have chosen to minister unto this people. Therefore** I say unto you, **take no thought for your life, what ye shall eat, or what ye shall drink; nor yet for your body, what ye shall put on.** Is not the life more than meat [*food*], and the body than raiment [*clothing*]?

The word, "meat," as used in verse 25, above, and elsewhere in the Bible and Book of Mormon, means "food." The word "flesh" is used to mean the meat of animals, birds, and fish.

26 **Behold** [*look at*] **the fowls** [*birds*] **of the air**, for they sow not [*do not plant crops*], neither do they reap [*harvest*] nor gather into barns; yet your heavenly Father feedeth them. **Are ye not much better than they** [*aren't you more important than they are*]?

In our day, we are faced with many philosophies, some true and some false. The scriptures are given to us to serve as the "standard works," meaning the standard by which all things are to be measured.

There are "rights" groups today, whose philosophy is that people are merely higher-functioning animals. Thus, they claim that animals, birds, fish, bugs, etc., are just as important as mankind. Often, such groups and individuals become radical in their views and advocate policies and laws that actually make people less important than the animal kingdom.

The last phrase of verse 26, above, is the standard set by God, against which such ideologies should be measured.

27 **Which of you by taking thought can add one cubit** [*about 18 inches*] **unto his stature** [*height*]?

Remember, the Savior is telling these newly-called Apostles that He will take care of their physical needs as they go around doing His work full-time.

28 And **why take ye thought for raiment** [*clothing*]? Consider the lilies of the field how they grow; they toil

not, neither do they spin [*spin thread with which to make fabric for clothes*];

29 And yet I say unto you, that **even Solomon** [*King Solomon, a very wealthy Old Testament king*], **in all his glory, was not arrayed** [*dressed*] **like one of these.**

30 Wherefore [*and so*], **if God so clothe the grass of the field**, which today is, and tomorrow is cast into the oven, **even so will he clothe you**, if ye are not of little faith [*if you have sufficient faith*].

31 Therefore **take no thought** [*don't worry*], **saying, What shall we eat? or, What shall we drink? or, Wherewithal shall we be clothed** [*what shall we do for clothing*]?

32 For **your heavenly Father knoweth that ye have need of all these things.**

33 But **seek ye first the kingdom of God and his righteousness, and all these things shall be added unto you.**

34 **Take therefore no thought for the morrow** [*tomorrow*], for the morrow shall take thought for the things of itself. **Sufficient is the day unto the evil thereof.**

The above verse (Matthew 6:34) was translated in the NIV Bible as "each day has enough trouble of its own," perhaps meaning, "You will face plenty of trouble and evil in fulfilling your Church callings—teaching, baptizing, and spreading the gospel—without adding more worries to your lives by being concerned about food, clothing, and housing, which God will provide for you if you have faith."

THIRD NEPHI 14

This is the concluding chapter of what is commonly referred to as the "Sermon on the Mount" or the "Sermon at the Temple" since it was given to the people of Nephi as they gathered "round about the temple which was in the land Bountiful" (3 Nephi 11:1).

The next thing (verses 1–5) Jesus will teach these people as He continues to instruct them on how they can qualify to be exalted in celestial glory and become gods is that they must learn to avoid unrighteously judging others. We use the phrase "unrighteously judging," because Joseph Smith does so in JST Matthew 7:1–2. He said, "Judge not unrighteously, that ye be not judged: but judge righteous judgment."

We know that we have to judge righteously and wisely in all kinds of situations in our lives. We would be foolish not to. The message here is not to unrighteously or unfairly judge people and thus, damage their reputations unfairly.

Alma 41:14 also uses this terminology as follows: "Therefore, my son, see that you are merciful unto your brethren; deal justly, judge righteously, and do good continually."

1 AND now it came to pass that **when Jesus had spoken these words** [*to the Nephite twelve disciples*] **he turned again to the multitude**

[*crowd*], and did open his mouth unto them again, **saying**: Verily, verily [*listen very carefully*], I say unto you, **Judge not, that ye be not judged**.

2 For **with what judgment ye judge, ye shall be judged** [*God will judge you according to how you judge others*]; and **with what measure ye mete** [*what you do to others*], **it shall be measured to you again** [*will be done to you*].

Next, Jesus will explain what He means by not judging others. He will give a simple example.

3 And **why beholdest thou** [*call attention to, point out*] **the mote** [*tiny speck; symbolic of small imperfections in others*] **that is in thy brother's eye, but considerest not** [*don't even worry about*] **the beam** [*large piece of timber*] **that is in thine own eye?**

In other words, why do you concern yourself with small imperfections in others when you, yourself, have such large imperfections?

4 **Or how** [*why*] **wilt thou say to thy brother: Let me pull the mote out of thine eye** [*let me work on your faults and imperfections*]**—and behold, a beam is in thine own eye** [*and you are the one who needs to be worked on*]?

5 **Thou hypocrite** [*a person who acts like he or she is perfect*], **first cast the beam out of thine own eye** [*first, take care of your own imperfections*]; and then shalt thou see clearly to cast the mote out of thy brother's eye [*to help others improve and progress*].

Next, the Savior teaches that some things are especially sacred and should not be shared with people who will not respect them.

6 **Give not that which is holy unto the dogs, neither cast ye your pearls before swine**, lest they trample them under their feet [*treat them with terrible disrespect*], and turn again and rend you [*tear up your emotions and feelings for what is sacred*].

Next, in verses 7–11, Jesus reminds us that Heavenly Father loves to have us ask Him for help and blessings. This is a pleasant reminder that our Father has tender feelings toward us and loves to bless us.

7 **Ask**, and it shall be given unto you; **seek**, and ye shall find; **knock**, and it shall be opened unto you.

8 **For every one that asketh, receiveth; and he that seeketh, findeth; and to him that knocketh, it shall be opened**.

Remember that the above teachings are in the context of the Father's knowledge of what is best for us. Therefore, the things we request, if in harmony with His knowledge of our needs, will be given according to His timetable, not ours.

As you reflect back on some of the foolish or unwise things you have asked God for in times past, you will no doubt be greatly relieved that He either did not grant it or that He waited until the timing was right.

We continue now with the Savior's tender teachings that the Father loves to help us, His children.

9 Or **what man is there of you, who, if his son ask bread, will give him a stone?**

10 **Or if he ask a fish, will he give him a serpent** [*a snake*]**?**

11 **If ye then, being evil** [*mortal; imperfect; subject to the evils of the "natural man"—Mosiah 3:19*], **know how to give good gifts unto your children, how much more shall your Father who is in heaven give good things to them that ask him?**

Verse 12, next, is often referred to as "the Golden Rule."

12 Therefore, **all things whatsoever ye would that men should do to you, do ye even so to them**, for this is the law and the prophets.

This is what the Law of Moses (Genesis, Exodus, Leviticus, Numbers, Deuteronomy) and the Old Testament prophets taught. See Leviticus 19:18.

It seems that the teaching of the majority of religions, as well as the thinking of many individuals, is that "all roads lead to Rome." In other words, "There are many ways to get to heaven."

Verses 13–14, next, as well as Matthew 7:13–14, teach otherwise.

13 **Enter ye in at the strait** [*narrow*] **gate** [*baptism; see 2 Nephi 31:7–8, 17–18; D&C 22:2–4*]; for **wide is the gate, and broad is the way, which leadeth to destruction, and many there be who go in thereat**;

14 Because **strait is the gate, and narrow is the way** [*the path you must stay on, after you are baptized*], **which leadeth unto life** [*heaven, eternal life; exaltation*], and **few there be that find it**.

Next, Jesus teaches us to be very careful as to whom we choose to follow. "False prophets" don't necessarily have to be religious leaders. They can be anyone we follow, including media celebrities and friends. In fact, beware of anyone whose teachings depart from those that lead us along the covenant path.

15 **Beware of false prophets, who come to you in sheep's clothing** [*who look harmless*], but inwardly they are ravening [*vicious*] wolves.

16 **Ye shall know them by their fruits** [*by the results of their lives and teachings*]. **Do men gather grapes of thorns** [*from thorn bushes*], **or figs of** [*from*] **thistles** [*a type of weed*]?

17 Even so **every good tree bringeth forth good fruit; but a corrupt** [*no good*] **tree bringeth forth evil fruit**.

18 **A good tree cannot bring forth evil fruit, neither a corrupt tree bring forth good fruit**.

Next, we are taught that all philosophies, teachings, examples, etc. that do not agree with God's teachings will lead to failure to enter the celestial kingdom.

19 **Every tree that bringeth not forth good fruit is hewn** [*cut*] **down, and cast into the fire**.

20 **Wherefore** [*therefore*], **by their fruits ye shall know them**.

Verses 21–23, next, are still in the context of verses 15–19, above, which warn us to beware of false prophets "in sheep's clothing." In other words, we must constantly be on guard against false teachers and philosophers whose teachings may appear good but which water down and dilute the pure teachings of Christ or totally disagree with them. Such teachers and leaders themselves cannot enter celestial glory except based upon the laws, ordinances, and commandments of God. Again, "all roads do not lead to Rome." There is but one "gate" (authorized baptism) and one "path" (the doctrines and ordinances of the plan of salvation).

21 **Not every one that saith unto me, Lord, Lord** [*not everybody who asks to enter heaven*], **shall enter into the kingdom of heaven; but he that doeth the will of my Father who is in heaven**.

22 **Many will say to me in that day** [*on Judgment Day*]: **Lord, Lord, have we not prophesied in thy name**, and in thy name have **cast out devils**, and in thy name **done many wonderful works**?

23 And **then will I profess unto them** [*formally declare to them on Judgment Day*]: **I never knew you** [*JST, "ye never knew me"*]; **depart from me** [*go away, you cannot enter celestial glory*], **ye that work iniquity** [*you who have done evil*].

While the final phrase ("ye that work iniquity"), in verse 23, above, may sound harsh, it is a strong reminder that anything that gets in the way of our staying firmly on the covenant path and returning home to live with our Father forever is extremely serious. Therefore, even if it is something like going to a concert on Sunday rather than going to church, it is appropriately referred to as iniquity or wickedness.

The Savior closes the Sermon on the Mount or the Sermon at the Temple by giving a short parable in which we are counseled to be wise and build upon a "rock." You have probably noticed that "rock," as used in the scriptures, usually refers to the "Rock," namely, Christ. "House" is often used to mean "lives" (as in "put your house in order") and also can mean "family unit." For instance, the "house of Israel" is the family of Jacob.

Thus, a "house" built upon a "rock" can be symbolic of a life built upon the teachings of Christ, or of a family who will be together forever, because they are built upon the gospel of Christ.

24 Therefore, **whoso heareth these sayings of mine and doeth them**, I will liken him unto a **wise man, who built his house upon a rock**—

Verse 25, next, represents troubles, hardships, trials, tribulations, and temptations that are a part of our mortal journey.

25 And **the rain descended**, and the **floods came**, and the **winds blew**, and **beat upon that house; and it fell not, for it was founded** [*built*] **upon a rock**.

26 And **every one that heareth these sayings of mine** [*who has a fair*

opportunity to hear and understand the gospel of Christ] **and doeth them not shall be likened unto** [*compared to*] **a foolish man, who built his house upon the sand**—

27 And the rain descended, and the **floods came**, and the **winds blew, and beat upon that house; and it fell**, and great was the fall of it.

It is interesting to observe that in JST (the Joseph Smith Translation of the Bible) Revelation 13:1 the "beast," which represents Satan's kingdom, is standing upon sand (see Revelation 13:1, footnote a, in our LDS Bible). Thus, the "foolish man who built his house upon the sand," in verse 26, above, was, in effect, building his life upon Satan's values.

THIRD NEPHI 15

As we begin this chapter, Jesus tells these people of Nephi that He has just taught them the things He taught His followers in the Holy Land before He went back up into heaven after His Crucifixion and Resurrection. Like we have already said, this helps us understand why the "Sermon at the Temple" (Third Nephi, chapters 12–14) is so similar to the "Sermon on the Mount" (Matthew, chapters 5–7).

He then answers questions in the people's minds concerning what they should do about the Law of Moses, which they have been living up to now.

We will also learn about the Savior's relationship with the Father as He addresses the Twelve, and we will learn about the "other sheep" referred to in John 10:16.

1 AND now it came to pass that **when Jesus had ended these sayings he cast his eyes round about** [*He looked around*] on the multitude [*crowd of people*], **and said** unto them: Behold, **ye have heard the things which I taught** [*in Jerusalem*] **before I ascended** [*returned up*] **to my Father**; therefore, **whoso remembereth these sayings of mine and doeth them, him will I raise up** [*give exaltation*] **at the last day** [*at the Final Judgment*].

Next, Jesus explains what these people should do regarding the Law of Moses, which they have been living up to now.

2 And it came to pass that **when Jesus had said these words he perceived that there were some among them who** marveled, and **wondered what he would** [*wondered what He wanted them to do*] **concerning the law of Moses**; for **they understood not the saying that old things had passed away, and that all things had become new** [*which He had explained and told them in 3 Nephi 12:46–47*].

3 And **he said** unto them: **Marvel not** [*don't keep being surprised*] **that I said unto you that old things had passed away, and that all things had become new.**

4 Behold, I say unto you that **the law** [*the law of Moses*] **is fulfilled that was given unto Moses**.

5 Behold, **I am he that gave the law** [*I am the God of the Old Testament*], and **I am he who covenanted with my people Israel**; therefore, **the law in**

me is fulfilled [*the purpose of the law of Moses is fulfilled by My coming to earth and fulfilling My mission*], **for I have come to fulfil the law; therefore it hath an end** [*it has fulfilled its purpose*].

6 Behold, **I do not destroy the prophets** [*I am not here to do away with what the Old Testament prophets prophesied and instructed*], **for as many as have not been fulfilled in me** [*whatever they said that has not yet been fulfilled*], verily I say unto you, **shall all be fulfilled**.

Next, in verse 7, Jesus repeats what He said in verse 6.

7 And because I said unto you that old things have passed away, **I do not destroy** [*set aside*] **that which hath been spoken concerning things which are to come** [*things that will yet be fulfilled in the future*].

8 For behold, **the covenant which I have made with my people is not all fulfilled** [*including the covenant made with Abraham through which exaltation can be attained; see Abraham 2:9–11*]; **but the law which was given unto Moses** [*the "schoolmaster law"; see Galatians 3:24*] **hath an end in me** [*has been fulfilled by Me*].

9 Behold, **I am the law, and the light. Look unto me, and endure to the end, and ye shall live** [*gain eternal life*]; for **unto him that endureth to the end will I give eternal life** [*exaltation in celestial glory*].

Notice that Jesus is, in effect, creating a distance between the laws and commandments He is giving now and the Law of Moses. He is emphasizing that He is the God who gave the Law of Moses.

You may recall that the Jews failed to see that the Law of Moses, which they were living, was designed to prepare them to receive Christ. Instead, they claimed that Jesus was working against what Moses taught and crucified Him.

Jesus is thus instructing the people of Nephi to distance themselves from the rituals and "schoolmaster" requirements of the Law of Moses and to move ahead to the higher laws He gave them in the Sermon on the Mount. Most people in the Holy Land failed to do this. These people will succeed.

10 Behold, **I have given unto you the commandments**; therefore **keep my commandments**. And **this is the law and the prophets** [*this is the whole purpose of the Law of Moses and the Old Testament prophets*], for **they truly testified of me**.

Next, Jesus specifically teaches the new Twelve disciples or Apostles among the Nephites in America. His instructions and teachings to them will continue through chapter 16.

11 And now it came to pass that when Jesus had spoken these words [*to the multitude*], **he said unto those twelve** whom he had chosen [*as mentioned in 3 Nephi 12:1*]:

12 **Ye are my disciples**; and **ye are a light unto this people**, who are a remnant of the house of Joseph [*who are descendants of Joseph who was sold into Egypt*].

As the Savior continues His instructions to the Nephite Twelve Apostles (Joseph Smith called them Apostles. See *History of the Church*, volume 4, page 538.), He emphasizes that He works under the direction of the Father. Among other things, this reminds us that the Father and the Son are two separate beings. It also teaches the unity and harmony that exist between them. A third thing, and we will emphasize it here, is that Jesus always gives credit to His Father. In other words, He gives glory and honor to the Father rather than seeking it for Himself. The word "Father" is in ***bold italics and underlined*** each time it occurs in this context in verses 13–24.

13 And behold, this is the land of your inheritance; and **the *<u>Father</u>* hath given it unto you**.

In the next verses, Jesus tells the people of Nephi that knowledge about them has largely been kept from the people at Jerusalem.

14 And **not at any time hath the *<u>Father</u>* given me commandment that I should tell it** unto your brethren at Jerusalem.

15 **Neither at any time hath the *<u>Father</u>* given me commandment that I should tell unto them concerning the other tribes of the house of Israel** [*including the Ten Lost Tribes; see footnote 15a, given for this verse in your Book of Mormon*], **whom the *<u>Father</u>* hath led away out of the land**.

16 **This much did the *<u>Father</u>* command** me, that I should tell unto them:

17 That **other sheep I have which are not of this fold; them also I must bring, and they shall hear my voice; and there shall be one fold** [*one true church*], **and one shepherd** [*see John 10:16*].

18 And now, **because of stiffneckedness** [*pride; stubbornness*] **and unbelief they understood not** my word; therefore **I was commanded to say no more of** [*by*] **the *<u>Father</u>*** concerning this thing unto them.

19 But, verily, I say unto you that **the *<u>Father</u>* hath commanded me, and I tell it unto you**, that **ye were separated from among them because of their iniquity** [*Lehi left Jerusalem because of the wickedness of the people there*]; therefore **it is because of their iniquity that they know not of you**.

20 And verily, I say unto you again that **the other tribes hath the *<u>Father</u>* separated from them**; and it is **because of their iniquity** [*wickedness and sin*] **that they know not of them**.

Next, Jesus tells these people that they are the ones He referred to in the Bible in John 10:16.

21 And verily I say unto you, that **ye are they of whom I said: Other sheep I have which are not of this fold; them also I must bring, and they shall hear my voice; and there shall be one fold, and one shepherd**.

22 And **they** [*the people in Jerusalem*] **understood me not**, for they supposed it had been the Gentiles [*they thought I

was referring to the Gentiles; in other words, non-Jews or non-Israelites]; for they understood not that the Gentiles should be converted through their preaching.

23 And **they** [*the people in Jerusalem*] **understood me not that I said they** [*the people of Nephi in America*] **shall hear my voice; and they understood me not that the Gentiles should not at any time hear my voice**—that I should not manifest myself unto them save it were [*except*] by the Holy Ghost.

24 But behold, **ye have both heard my voice, and seen me; and ye are my sheep**, and ye are numbered among those whom **the *Father* hath given me**.

> In other words, you are among those who will gain salvation in celestial glory; see John 6:37.

THIRD NEPHI 16

In this chapter Jesus continues teaching and instructing the newly-called Twelve Apostles here among the surviving Nephites in America. In fact, He has been doing so since 3 Nephi 15:11. He has been instructing them on their new responsibilities as the leaders of His Church in the Americas.

In verses 1–3, the Savior speaks of "other sheep" He will also visit. We understand that He is referring to the lost ten tribes because of 3 Nephi 17:4, wherein He said, "Now I go unto the Father, and also to show myself unto the lost tribes of Israel."

You may recall that, in the Old Testament, Moses led the children of Israel out of Egyptian slavery and captivity. The children of Israel were the twelve tribes of Israel, or the descendants of the twelve sons of Jacob, whose name was changed to Israel. These twelve sons and their families came to Egypt to survive a terrible famine and ended up staying in Egypt for hundreds of years. They were eventually put into slavery by the Egyptians.

When these twelve tribes of Israel finally escaped from Egypt, under the leadership of Moses, they entered the Holy Land (basically where the nation of Israel is today) and each tribe was given a specific territory to settle in that country. Over many years, ten of those twelve tribes united together as a nation and became known as the ten tribes of Israel.

About 722 years before Christ was born in Bethlehem, the ten tribes were captured and taken away somewhere far to the north by an enemy nation called Assyria. They became known as the "Lost Ten Tribes." Nobody knows for sure where they ended up, but someday they will return (see D&C 133:26–35.)

Now, Jesus tells the Nephite Twelve Apostles that He still has to visit these lost ten tribes. No doubt, someday we will be told more about His visit to them.

1 AND **verily, verily** [*listen carefully, this is important*], I say unto you that **I have other sheep**, which are not of this land [*America*], neither of the land of Jerusalem [*the Holy Land*], neither in any parts of that land round about whither [*where*] I have been to minister.

2 For they of whom I speak are they **who have not as yet heard my voice**; neither have I at any time manifested [*shown*] myself unto them.

3 But **I have received a commandment of the Father** [*Heavenly Father*] **that I shall go unto them**, and that they shall hear my voice, and shall be numbered [*counted*] among my sheep [*they will be part of My people, My Church*], that there may be one fold [*one big group to which all of them will belong*] and one shepherd [*Christ*]; **therefore I go to show myself unto them**.

Regarding the lost ten tribes, it is interesting that in 1831, the Prophet Joseph Smith said that the Apostle John was at that time working with the lost ten tribes, preparing them for their return. See *History of the Church*, volume 1, page 176.

We read more about the return of these tribes in Doctrine and Covenants 133:26–33. And in 2 Nephi 29:13, we are told that we will someday be privileged to read the records of the lost ten tribes. We anticipate that when that day comes, we will read about the Savior's visit to them, as indicated in verses 1–3, above.

The next four paragraphs are a bit complicated. You may want to skip them. However, if you take the time and put forth the effort to understand what they teach about the word "Gentile," it will be very helpful to you as you study the rest of this chapter. In fact, it will help you a lot throughout your life in your gospel study because you will have a good basic understanding of what the word "Gentiles" means in the scriptures and in other gospel conversations.

In order to understand verses 4–15, we will need to define the word "Gentiles." The term "Gentiles" is context-sensitive. That is, its meaning depends on the words around it, the background and setting in which you are reading it. In its simplest modern-day generic sense, it basically means anyone who is not part of the group to which you belong.

In the scriptures, Gentiles often means non-Israelites, in other words, people who are not members of the twelve tribes of Israel. Your patriarchal blessing tells you which tribe you belong to. The word "Gentile" can also refer to Israelites who are not members of the true Church of God. When the Jews are speaking, "Gentile" often means anyone who is not a Jew. When members of the Church are speaking, it can be used to refer to nonmembers. You may wish to review the definitions of "Gentile" in our Bible Dictionary at the back of our Bible.

The most common usage of the word "Gentile" in the Book of Mormon is "non-Jews." Thus, Joseph Smith and most members of the Church today are referred to as "Gentiles" in Book of Mormon prophecies.

We will go through verses 4–15 now, giving one possible interpretation based on the Book of Mormon use of "Gentile." Remember, this is just one possible explanation of these verses. You could probably go several directions, depending on which definition of "Gentiles" and which definition of "my people" you use.

Next, Jesus tells these men to write down what He is saying to them, after He is gone.

4 And **I command you that ye shall write these sayings after I am gone**, that if it so be that my people [*the Jews*] at Jerusalem, they who have seen me and been with me in my ministry [*Christ's mortal ministry in the Holy Land*], do not ask the Father in my name, **that they** [*the Jews*] **may receive a knowledge of you** by the Holy Ghost, **and also of the other tribes** [*the lost ten tribes and perhaps others*] whom they know not of, that **these sayings** [*this part of the Book of Mormon that records Christ's visit*] **which ye shall write shall be kept and shall be manifested** [*shown*] **unto the Gentiles** [*the members of the Church in the last days, through the Book of Mormon*], **that through the fulness of the Gentiles** [*the fulness of the gospel, restored through Joseph Smith*], **the remnant** [*what's left*] **of their seed** [*the posterity of the Jews*], who shall be scattered forth upon the face of the earth because of their unbelief, **may be brought in** [*gathered*], **or may be brought to a knowledge of me, their Redeemer**.

Based on the last phrase of verse 4, above, we see that the "gathering of the Jews" is more than a physical gathering. It is also a spiritual gathering. Indeed, the more important part of any gathering of people, including individuals, is that of being "gathered" to Christ. See 3 Nephi 5:25–26.

5 And **then will I gather them** [*the last days' gathering of the Jews, as well as all Israel; see Isaiah 5:26*] in from the four quarters of the earth [*from all over the earth*]; and then will I fulfil the covenant which the Father hath made unto all the people of the house of Israel [*Isaiah 54:7*].

6 And **blessed are the Gentiles** [*the faithful members of the Church, Israelites who are non-Jews, in the last days, before the Jews are converted in large numbers*], **because of their belief in me, in and of the Holy Ghost, which witnesses unto them of me and of the Father**.

7 Behold, **because of their belief in me**, saith the Father, **and because of the unbelief of you, O house of Israel** [*people who have Israelite blood but turn to gross wickedness*], **in the latter day shall the truth come unto the Gentiles** [*non-Jews; people who have Israelite blood, including Ephraim and Manasseh, who accept the gospel and live it*], **that the fulness of these things shall be made known unto them** [*the Jews and wicked Israelites*].

Next, Christ prophesies about the Gentiles who come to the Americas and scatter the Lamanites.

8 But **wo** [*big trouble*], saith the Father, **unto the unbelieving of the Gentiles** [*those who came to America, after Columbus discovered it, most of whom are of Israelite blood*]—for notwithstanding [*even though*] they have come forth upon the face of this land [*America*], and have scattered my people [*the Lamanites; see footnote 8b in your Book of Mormon, which refers you to 1 Nephi 13:14*] who are of the house of Israel; and my people who

are of the house of Israel have been cast out from among them, and have been trodden under feet by them;

9 And **because of the mercies of the Father unto the Gentiles** [*who discovered and settled America*], **and also the judgments** [*punishments*] **of the Father upon my people** [*the Jews*] who are of the house of Israel [*who are descendants of Abraham, Isaac, and Jacob*], verily, verily, I say unto you, that after all this, and **I have caused my people** [*the Jews, and also the Lamanites, in the context of these verses*] who are of the house of Israel **to be smitten**, and to be **afflicted**, and to be **slain**, and to be **cast out** from among them, and to become **hated** by them, and to **become a hiss and a byword** [*a term of disrespect; in a way, a cuss word*] among them—

10 And thus commandeth the Father that I should say unto you [*Jesus is again reminding the Twelve that He works under the direction of the Father*]: **At that day** [*probably referring to the last days, when wickedness sweeps the earth*] **when the Gentiles** [*in this context, this could especially refer to the United States; see verse 8, above*] **shall sin against my gospel**, and shall **reject the fulness of my gospel**, and **shall be lifted up in the pride** of their hearts **above all nations** [*the most powerful nation on earth leads all other nations in wide open wickedness*], and **above all the people of the whole earth**, and **shall be filled with** all manner of **lyings**, and of **deceits** [*dishonesty*], and of **mischiefs**, and all manner of **hypocrisy** [*wanting to look good while secretely being bad*], and **murders**, and **priestcrafts** [*preaching what people want to hear in return for wealth and power; see Alma 1:16*], and **whoredoms** [*sexual immorality*], and of **secret abominations**; and **if they shall do all those things, and shall reject the fulness of my gospel, behold, saith the Father, I will bring the fulness of my gospel from among them**.

11 And **then will I remember** [*keep*] **my covenant which I have made unto my people, O house of Israel, and I will bring my gospel unto them**.

Verse 11, above, could well refer to the Millennium.

12 And I will show unto thee, O house of Israel, that the Gentiles shall not have power over you; but **I will remember** [*keep*] **my covenant unto you, O house of Israel, and ye shall come unto the knowledge of the fulness of my gospel**.

Verse 13, next, is a reminder that all people, no matter who they are, can be "gathered" and remain with the Lord's people forever.

13 But **if the Gentiles will repent and return unto me, saith the Father, behold they shall be numbered among** [*will become part of*] **my people, O house of Israel**.

Verses 14–15, next, basically say that the day will come when those who follow Christ faithfully will gain triumph and victory over all people who have stood in the way of living their religion, throughout history. Indeed, those who gain exaltation and become gods will ultimately triumph over all their enemies.

14 And **I will not suffer** [*permit; instruct*] **my people, who are of the house of Israel, to go through among them** [*the Gentiles mentioned in verse 13*]**, and tread them down** [*gain victory over them*], **saith the Father**.

15 But **if they will not turn unto me**, and hearken unto my voice [*if the wicked will not repent*], I will suffer them, yea, **I will suffer** [*allow, instruct*] **my people, O house of Israel, that they shall go through among them, and shall tread them down**, and they shall be as salt that hath lost its savor [*symbolic of people who are no longer doing good and helping the gospel spread; compare with 3 Nephi 12:13*], which is thenceforth good for nothing but to be cast out, and to be trodden under foot of my people, O house of Israel.

16 Verily, verily, I say unto you, **thus hath the Father commanded me—that I should give unto this people** [*the Nephites and Lamanites; the descendants of Joseph who was sold into Egypt*] **this land** [*America*] **for their inheritance**.

17 And **then the words of the prophet Isaiah shall be fulfilled, which say**:

18 **Thy watchmen** [*prophets, leaders*] **shall lift up the voice; with the voice together** [*in unity and harmony*] **shall they** [*faithful Israel*] **sing, for they shall see eye to eye** [*live in peace and harmony with each other and the gospel*] **when the Lord shall bring again Zion.**

19 **Break forth into joy**, sing together, ye waste places of Jerusalem; for the Lord hath comforted his people [*the Jews*], he hath redeemed Jerusalem.

Jerusalem will be restored and will become a headquarters for the Savior during the Millennium.

Verse 20, next, is speaking of the future as though it has already taken place.

20 **The Lord hath made bare his holy arm** [*has shown His power in keeping His covenants with Israel*] in the eyes of all the nations; and **all the ends of the earth** [*everybody in the whole world*] **shall see the salvation of God** [*will see the promises and work of God fulfilled*].

THIRD NEPHI 17

The Resurrected Savior is now finished specifically teaching the newly-called twelve disciples, who will lead the Church in America, and will turn around to face the large group of people who are gathered at the temple in the land Bountiful (3 Nephi 11:1). You can see from verse 25 of this chapter that there were about 2,500 people. He will tell them that He must leave now to visit His Father as well as the lost ten tribes. However, He can see that they really don't want Him to leave yet, so He will stay with them and continue to teach and minister to them until the end of chapter 18.

As we study this chapter, you will once again see how kind and gentle the Savior is.

1 BEHOLD, now it came to pass that **when Jesus had spoken these words** [*to the Nephite twelve disciples*] **he looked round about again on the multitude**, and he said unto them: Behold, my time is at hand [*I must leave now*].

In verses 2–3, next, we are taught that some things take time to settle in our minds and hearts. Pondering, in other words, thinking more about it and prayer is necessary for gaining deeper understanding of the gospel and its teachings. Such behavior prepares our minds for additional gospel understanding.

President Marion G. Romney of the First Presidency expressed his feelings about pondering as follows: "Pondering is, in my feeling, a form of prayer" ("Magnifying One's Calling in the Priesthood," general conference, Apr. 1973).

2 I perceive that ye are weak, that **ye cannot understand all my words** which I am commanded of the Father to speak unto you at this time.

3 **Therefore, go ye unto your homes**, and **ponder** [*think more about it*] upon the things which I have said, **and ask of the Father, in my name** [*pray in the name of Jesus Christ*], **that ye may understand**, and **prepare your minds for the morrow** [*tomorrow*], and I come unto you again.

Next, Jesus tells these people why He must leave now.

4 But now **I go unto the Father**, and **also to show myself unto the lost tribes of Israel**, for they are not lost unto the Father, for he knoweth whither he hath taken them.

As you will see next, Jesus did not leave as scheduled. The tender desires of these humble people touched His heart deeply, and He stayed and healed their sick, had them bring their children to Him, spent time praying to the Father while the people in the multitude listened, blessed their children one at a time, called angels down from heaven to minister to the children, conducted a sacrament service and taught the multitude about the sacrament, taught them about prayer and the importance of holding up the Savior's light to the world, instructed them as to what to do with unworthy people as far as church attendance is concerned, and finally, He touched each one of the twelve disciples, giving them power to give the gift of the Holy Ghost.

All of this would have taken considerable time. As an interesting side issue, we wonder what the lost ten tribes did while waiting for Him to come. Of course, we don't know, but it will be interesting at a future time to hear a report on this.

5 And it came to pass that **when Jesus had thus spoken** [*had told them He must leave and would be back tomorrow*], he cast his eyes round about [*He looked around*] again on the multitude, and beheld [*saw that*] **they were in tears**, and did look steadfastly [*gazed steadily*] upon him as if they would ask him to tarry [*stay*] a little longer with them.

6 And **he said unto them: Behold, my bowels are** [*My whole being is*] **filled with compassion** [*deep love and feeling*] **towards you**.

As you can sense, this is a very tender and rewarding time for the Savior Himself. Remember, He has recently left an environment of hatred against Him—mocking, scourging, and crucifixion—and is now among people who want Him to stay and teach and heal them physically and spiritually.

Perhaps this is one fulfillment of Isaiah 53:11 in which we read, "He [*Jesus*] shall see of the travail of his soul [*the results of His suffering and Atonement*], and shall be satisfied." See also the last sentence of verse 20, below.

While we understand the healings, which Jesus performs next, to be literal, in other words, really happened, there is also beautiful symbolism. Physical healing can symbolize spiritual healing, emotional healing, the healing of lack of confidence, and so on. When verse 7 says that the Savior healed those who were "afflicted in any manner," it is a reminder that the Atonement has the power to heal any kind of spiritual needs.

7 **Have ye any that are sick among you**? Bring them hither [*to Me*]. Have ye any that are **lame**, or **blind**, or **halt** [*who walk with a limp*], or **maimed** [*crippled, deformed*], or **leprous** [*who have a terrible disease called leprosy*], or that are **withered** [*shrunk*], or that are **deaf**, or that are **afflicted in any manner** [*sick in any way*]? Bring them hither [*here to Me*] and **I will heal them**, for **I have compassion upon you; my bowels are filled with mercy**.

8 For **I perceive** [*I can tell*] **that ye desire that I should show unto you what I have done unto your brethren** [*relatives*] **at Jerusalem**, for **I see that your faith is sufficient that I should heal you**.

9 And it came to pass that **when he had thus spoken, all the multitude**, with one accord [*in unity*], **did go forth with their sick and their afflicted, and their lame, and with their blind, and with their dumb** [*not able to talk*], **and with all them that were afflicted in any manner; and he did heal them every one as they were brought forth unto him**.

Did you notice the symbolism at the end of verse 9, above? It is that when they came "unto Him" they were healed.

10 And **they did all**, both they who had been healed and they who were whole [*were healthy and did not need physical healing*], **bow down at his feet, and did worship him**; and as many as could come for the multitude [*because of the size of the group*] **did kiss his feet**, insomuch that they **did bathe his feet with their tears**.

Next, the little children, who often symbolize innocence and purity in the scriptures, are brought to the Savior.

11 And it came to pass that **he commanded that their little children should be brought**.

12 So **they brought their little children** and set them down upon the ground round about him, and Jesus stood in the midst; and the multitude gave way [*moved out of the way*] till they had all been brought unto him.

13 And it came to pass that when they had all been brought, and Jesus stood in the midst, **he commanded the multitude that they should kneel down upon the ground**.

> Again, in verse 14, we see that Jesus is filled with deep emotions. No doubt the contrast between these humble people and their children and the wickedness of the people He had just left in the Holy Land caused the deepest of feelings in the Savior's heart and soul.
>
> As He prays, we are reminded that there are some spiritual experiences for which words are totally inadequate.

14 And it came to pass that **when they had knelt upon the ground, Jesus groaned within himself, and said: Father, I am troubled because of the wickedness of the people of the house of Israel**.

15 And when he had said these words, he himself also knelt upon the earth; and behold **he prayed unto the Father, and the things which he prayed cannot be written, and the multitude did bear record** [*were witnesses and bore testimony*] who heard him.

16 And **after this manner do they bear record** [*this is what these people had to say about what they experienced when the Savior prayed*]: **The eye hath never seen, neither hath the ear heard, before, so great and marvelous things as we saw and heard Jesus speak unto the Father**;

17 And **no tongue can speak, neither can there be written by any man, neither can the hearts of men** [*people who have not experienced what we did*] **conceive** [*imagine*] **so great and marvelous things as we both saw and heard Jesus speak; and no one can conceive of the joy which filled our souls at the time we heard him pray for us unto the Father**.

18 And it came to pass that **when Jesus had made an end of praying unto the Father, he arose**; but so great was the joy of **the multitude** that they **were overcome**.

19 And it came to pass that **Jesus spake unto them, and bade them** [*asked them to*] **arise.**

20 And they arose from the earth, and **he said unto them: Blessed** [*happy*] **are ye because of your faith. And now behold, my joy is full** [*this brought Jesus, Himself, much joy*].

> Next, Jesus will take the time to bless each of the little children individually and to offer a prayer to the Father for them. We understand that this was also a tender time for Heavenly Father.

21 **And when he had said these words, he wept, and the multitude bare record of it, and he took their little children, one by one, and blessed them, and prayed unto the Father for them**.

22 And when he had done this **he wept again** [*His emotions are brimming with joy; see verse 20, above*];

23 And **he spake unto the multitude, and said unto them: Behold your little ones** [*look closely at your little children*].

24 And **as they looked** to behold they cast their eyes towards heaven, and **they saw the heavens open**, and **they saw angels descending** [*coming down*] **out of heaven** as it were in the midst of fire [*perhaps meaning clothed with glory*]; and **they came down and encircled those little ones about, and they were encircled about with fire; and the angels did minister unto them**.

25 And **the multitude** did see and hear and bear record; and they know that their record is true for they all of them **did see and hear, every man for himself**; and **they were in number about two thousand and five hundred souls**; and they did consist of men, women, and children.

> You may wish to add yourself to the 2,500 who witnessed these marvelous things, thus making 2,501 who have felt and witnessed the truth of these things by the power of the Holy Ghost.

THIRD NEPHI 18

As the Savior continues to stay (3 Nephi 17:5–6) with these people in the land Bountiful, He will give the sacrament to them and teach them about it. We can learn much about this sacred ordinance from what they are taught.

Jesus had already told these people that the Law of Moses (the rules and laws that people in the Old Testament lived by), which they had been living, was no longer in force (3 Nephi 15:2–5). The flesh and blood sacrifices of animals, which up to now had pointed toward the coming sacrifice of the Son of God (Moses 5:4–8) and which had been a constant part of the Law of Moses, were now to be replaced with the sacrament, which was designed to point the minds of worthy members back to the Savior and His Atoning sacrifice for our sins.

In this chapter, Jesus also teaches more about prayer and about worthiness to partake of the sacrament. He then gives the Nephite twelve disciples instructions about their role in preserving the sacred character of the sacrament, their responsibility to excommunicate members of the Church who won't repent of very serious sins, if needed, and the importance of welcoming all people to their public worship services.

1 AND it came to pass that **Jesus commanded his Disciples that they should bring forth some bread and wine unto him**.

2 And while they were gone for bread and wine, **he commanded the multitude that they should sit themselves down** upon the earth.

3 And when the Disciples had come with bread and wine, **he took of the bread and brake** [*broke*] **and blessed it**; and **he gave unto the Disciples and commanded that they should eat**.

4 And **when they had eaten and were filled, he commanded that they should give unto the multitude**.

The Lord's true Church is a kingdom of order. All ordinances must be done by proper priesthood authority and in proper order. Next, in verse 5, Jesus emphasizes this principle to the disciples, who will be the leaders of the Church among the people of Nephi when He leaves.

5 And when the multitude had eaten and were filled, **he said unto the Disciples**: Behold **there shall one be ordained among you**, and **to him will I give power that he shall break bread and bless it and give it unto the people of my church, unto all those who shall believe and be baptized in my name**.

Next, Christ teaches the symbolism and promise that accompanies partaking of the sacrament bread. Pay close attention to what He says.

6 And **this shall ye always observe to do**, even as I have done, even as I have broken bread and blessed it and given it unto you.

7 And **this shall ye do in remembrance of my body**, which I have shown unto you. And **it shall be a testimony unto the Father that ye do always remember me**. And **if ye do always remember me ye shall have my Spirit to be with you**.

8 And it came to pass that **when he said these words, he commanded his Disciples that they should take of the wine of the cup and drink of it, and that they should also give unto the multitude that they might drink of it**.

9 And it came to pass that **they did so**, and did drink of it and were filled; **and they gave unto the multitude, and they did drink**, and they were filled.

One principle attending the proper administering and partaking of the sacrament is the principle of obedience, as taught in verse 10, next.

10 And when the Disciples had done this, Jesus said unto them: Blessed are ye for this thing which ye have done, for this is fulfilling my commandments, and **this doth** [*does*] **witness unto the Father that ye are willing to do that which I have commanded you**.

Next, we are taught the symbolism and promise attending the partaking of the wine (water in our day; see D&C 27, heading and verse 2).

11 And this shall ye [*speaking still to His twelve disciples; see verse 10*] always do to those who repent and are baptized in my name; and **ye shall do it in remembrance of my blood, which I have shed for you, that ye may witness unto the Father that ye do always remember me**. And **if ye do always remember me ye shall have my Spirit to be with you**.

12 And I give unto you a commandment that ye shall do these things. And **if ye shall always do these things blessed are ye, for ye are built upon my rock** [*symbolic of*

building our lives upon the Savior as the foundation for all we do].

One great challenge throughout the ages has been that of keeping the Church doctrinally pure, in other words, keeping the teachings in the gospel from being changed. That is one of the great blessings of having Apostles and prophets to lead the Church.

One of the ways people go into apostasy (fall away from the Church) is by adding to, or taking away from the simple ordinances and teachings which Jesus has given us. In verse 13, next, He warns the Twelve against doing this. This warning applies to all of us.

13 But **whoso among you shall do more or less than these are not built upon my rock** [*My firm, solid foundation*], but are built upon a sandy foundation; and when the rain descends, and the floods come, and the winds blow, and beat upon them, they shall fall, and the gates of hell are ready open to receive them.

14 Therefore **blessed are ye if ye shall keep my commandments**, which the Father hath commanded me that I should give unto you.

Next, Jesus gives instruction regarding prayer, using Himself as the example. He is still speaking directly to His twelve disciples.

15 Verily, verily, I say unto you, **ye must watch and pray always, lest ye be** [*so that you are not*] **tempted by the devil, and** ye be **led away captive by him**.

16 And **as I have prayed among you even so shall ye pray in my church**, among my people who do repent and are baptized in my name. Behold I am the light; **I have set an example for you**.

Next, Jesus turns His attention once more to the multitude, instructing them in the matter of prayer.

17 And it came to pass that **when Jesus had spoken these words unto his Disciples, he turned again unto the multitude** and said unto them:

18 Behold, verily, verily [*now listen carefully*], I say unto you, **ye must watch and pray always lest ye enter into temptation**; for Satan desireth to have you, that he may sift you as wheat.

19 Therefore **ye must always pray unto the Father in my name**;

In verse 20, next, there is important instruction regarding getting answers to prayer in addition to having faith; namely, that we must ask for that "which is right." In other words, what we ask for must be in harmony with the will of the Lord so that it is for our best good.

You may wish to read more on this subject in Doctrine and Covenants 46:30 and 50:30 wherein we are told that if we are in tune, the Holy Ghost will tell us what we may properly ask for.

20 And **whatsoever** [*whatever*] **ye shall ask the Father in my name, which is right, believing that ye shall receive, behold it shall be given unto you.**

21 **Pray in your families** unto the Father, always in my name [*always in the name of Jesus Christ*], that your wives and your children may be blessed.

Sometimes people ask why we can't pray to the Father without using the name of Christ, or why we can't pray to Jesus. The answer is simple. Jesus told us to pray to the Father in His name. He never did authorize praying to Him or to the Father without using His name. Anyone who does so or teaches to do so is violating the principle given in verse 13, above, where it tells us not to change the teachings of the gospel.

Next, the Savior teaches the importance of meeting together often in our church meetings and of allowing anyone who desires the privilege of attending to do so.

22 And behold, **ye shall meet together oft** [*often*]; and **ye shall not forbid any man from coming unto you when ye shall meet together**, but suffer [*permit*] them that they may come unto you and forbid them not;

23 But ye shall **pray for them**, and shall **not cast them out**; and if it so be that they come unto you oft ye shall pray for them unto the Father, in my name.

24 Therefore, **hold up your light that it may shine unto the world** [*be good examples*]. Behold **I am the light which ye shall hold up—that which ye have seen me do** [*in other words, use the example I have set for you in how you treat nonmembers*]. Behold ye see that **I have prayed unto the Father**, and ye all have witnessed.

25 And ye see that **I have commanded that none of you should go away**, but **rather have commanded that ye should come unto me, that ye might feel and see** [*the purpose of attending our church meetings*]; **even so shall ye do unto the world** [*people who are not members of the Church*]; and whosoever breaketh this commandment suffereth [*allows*] himself to be led into temptation.

Next, Jesus focuses His attention once again on the Apostles He called. (Remember that Joseph Smith called them Apostles in *History of the Church*, volume 4, page 538.) As the leaders of the Church who hold the keys of the priesthood, the Apostles received instruction from Jesus concerning those who might take the sacrament unworthily.

These instructions are the same today. A bishop or a stake president may request that a member not take the sacrament until a worthiness concern is appropriately taken care of. We often refer to these priesthood leaders with keys as "judges in Israel."

26 And now it came to pass that when Jesus had spoken these words, **he turned his eyes again upon the Disciples** whom he had chosen, and said unto them:

27 Behold verily, verily, I say unto you, **I give unto you another commandment**, and then I must go unto my Father [*remember that at the beginning of chapter 17, he told the people that He had to go to the Father and to the Lost Ten Tribes*] that I may fulfil other commandments which he hath given me.

28 And now behold, **this is the commandment which I give unto you**, that **ye shall not suffer** [*allow*] **any one knowingly** [*this is a key word*] **to partake of my flesh and blood** [*the sacrament*] **unworthily, when ye shall minister it**;

Next, we see how important it is to take the sacrament worthily.

29 For **whoso eateth and drinketh my flesh and blood** [*the sacrament*] **unworthily eateth and drinketh damnation to his soul**; therefore **if ye know that a man is unworthy to eat and drink of my flesh and blood ye shall forbid him**.

If you have a question as to whether or not you are worthy to take the sacrament, you should ask your "judge in Israel," or, in other words, your bishop or branch president. Some people are too hard on themselves and think they should be nearly perfect in order to partake of the sacrament.

In general, people who are sincerely striving to live the gospel are worthy to take the sacrament. If they are in violation of worthiness standards for temple recommends, they should ask their bishop about it.

Next, Jesus continues by giving more instructions concerning those who are not worthy to take the sacrament.

30 Nevertheless, **ye shall not cast him out from among you** [*you should let the person attend your sacrament meetings*], but ye shall **minister unto him** and shall **pray for him** unto the Father, in my name; and **if it so be that he repenteth and is baptized in my name, then shall ye receive him, and shall minister unto him of my flesh and blood** [*give him the sacrament*].

31 But **if he repent not he shall not be numbered among my people** [*if he is a nonmember, don't baptize him; if he is a member, he will have to be excommunicated*], **that he may not destroy my people** [*cause damage to the Church*], for behold I know my sheep, and they are numbered.

32 **Nevertheless, ye shall not cast him out of your synagogues** [*church buildings*], **or your places of worship**, for **unto such shall ye continue to minister**; for **ye know not but what they will return and repent**, and **come unto me with full purpose of heart, and I shall heal them**; and ye shall be the means of bringing salvation unto them.

It is important to pay attention to what would happen if Church leaders failed to refuse baptism to seriously unworthy individuals or to administer appropriate Church discipline to members who are grossly unworthy. In verse 31, above, the Savior taught the Nephite Twelve that if not properly dealt with, such people would destroy the Church.

Church leaders have serious responsibilities to look after the Church in these matters, as stated by Christ in verse 33, next.

33 Therefore, **keep these sayings** which I have commanded you **that ye come not under condemnation**

[*so that you don't get in trouble yourselves*]; **for wo unto him whom the Father condemneth**.

Based on verse 34, next, it appears that before the Savior's appearance to the people of Nephi, they had serious contention among them as to whether they should allow non-members or seriously unworthy members to attend church meetings.

34 And **I give you these commandments because of the disputations which have been among you**. And blessed are ye if ye have no disputations among you.

35 And **now I go unto the Father** [*as He said He must, in 3 Nephi 17:4 and 18:27*], because it is expedient [*necessary*] that I should go unto the Father for your sakes.

It appears in verses 36 and 37, next, that Jesus gave more authority to the Twelve. We look forward to getting more information on this in the future.

36 And it came to pass that **when Jesus had made an end of these sayings, he touched with his hand the disciples whom he had chosen, one by one**, even until he had touched them all, **and spake unto them as he touched them**.

37 And the multitude heard not the words which he spake, therefore they did not bear record [*couldn't tell us what was said*]; but **the disciples bare record that he gave them power to give the Holy Ghost**. And I [*Mormon*] will show unto you hereafter that this record is true.

38 And it came to pass that when Jesus had touched them all, **there came a cloud and overshadowed the multitude that they could not see Jesus**.

39 And **while they were overshadowed he departed from them, and ascended into heaven**. And the disciples saw and did bear record that he ascended again into heaven.

THIRD NEPHI 19

The people will now wait for Jesus to come to them again the next day. They will all go home and look forward to His return the next morning. In the meantime, they will spread the news to everybody they can to be there when He returns. They will spend most of the night doing this. Imagine the surprise and joy of these other people when they are invited to come see the Savior the next morning!

In verse 4, we will be given the names of the Nephite twelve disciples, three of whom will become the Three Nephites later on. We will read about the Three Nephites in Third Nephi, chapter 28.

We will see the Twelve already fulfilling the instructions of the Savior as they teach the multitude that is waiting for Him to appear that morning as promised in 3 Nephi 17:3.

We will watch as these disciples are baptized, receive the gift of the Holy Ghost, and are ministered to by angels.

Jesus will come as promised and minister to the Twelve. We will learn more concerning prayer and unity and will be taught that the heart is capable of feeling far more than intellect and vocabulary can describe.

1 AND now it came to pass that when Jesus had ascended [*gone up*] into heaven, **the multitude did disperse** [*everybody left*], and every man did take his wife and his children and did return to his own home.

2 And **it was noised abroad** [*the news spread*] among the people immediately, before it was yet dark, **that the multitude had seen Jesus**, and that **he had ministered unto them, and that he would also show himself on the morrow** [*tomorrow*] **unto the multitude**.

3 Yea, and even **all the night it was noised abroad** [*the news was spread*] concerning Jesus; and insomuch did they send forth unto the people that there were **many**, yea, an exceedingly great number, **did labor exceedingly all that night, that they might be on the morrow in the place where Jesus should show himself unto the multitude**.

Next, we are given the names of the Nephite twelve disciples.

4 And it came to pass that on the morrow [*the next day*], when the multitude was gathered together, behold, **Nephi** and his brother whom he had raised from the dead, whose name was **Timothy**, and also his son, whose name was **Jonas**, and also **Mathoni**, and **Mathonihah**, his brother, and **Kumen**, and **Kumenonhi**, and **Jeremiah**, and **Shemnon**, and **Jonas**, and **Zedekiah**, and **Isaiah**—now these were the names of the disciples whom Jesus had chosen—and it came to pass that **they went forth and stood in the midst of the multitude**.

Jesus hasn't arrived yet, so these righteous men, who have been given the keys and responsibility to lead these people in the Restored Church that the resurrected Christ is establishing among them, are running things.

5 And behold, **the multitude was so great** [*large*] that they did cause that they should be **separated into twelve bodies** [*groups*].

There are twelve groups so that one of the Twelve can instruct each group.

6 And **the twelve did teach the multitude**; and behold, **they did cause that the multitude should kneel down upon the face of the earth, and should pray** unto the Father in the name of Jesus.

7 And **the disciples did pray unto the Father also** in the name of Jesus. And it came to pass that **they arose and ministered unto the people**.

Next, the Twelve teach the people, many of whom were not in attendance the day before. They teach exactly what Jesus taught yesterday.

We see the same pattern established among the people of Nephi that we have today. The Savior is in charge of the Church under the

Father's direction. The First Presidency and the Twelve teach us His will.

8 And **when they had ministered those same words which Jesus had spoken**—nothing varying [*exactly the same things*] from the words which Jesus had spoken—behold, **they knelt again and prayed to the Father in the name of Jesus**.

Next, we are taught the value of the gift of the Holy Ghost. Of all the things these disciples could pray for, they prayed for the Holy Ghost. When we have this marvelous gift and heed it, all other things fall into proper place in our lives, including being given strength to pass tests and trials and troubles, which are part of the lessons we need to learn during this life.

9 And **they did pray for that which they most desired**; and they desired **that the Holy Ghost should be given unto them**.

Next, we see Nephi get baptized first, and then he baptizes the rest of the Twelve.

Later (4 Nephi 1:1, etc.), virtually all of these people, many of whom had been baptized previously (Helaman 16:3–4), will likewise be baptized into the Church of Jesus Christ (of "former-day Saints") for membership into the Church, which was being restored among them by the Savior Himself. Up to now, they had been baptized in compliance with the Law of Moses (1 Nephi 20:1).

10 And **when they had thus prayed they** [*the Twelve*] **went down unto the water's edge**, and the multitude followed them.

11 And it came to pass that **Nephi** went down into the water and **was baptized**.

12 And **he came up out of the water and began to baptize**. And **he baptized all those whom Jesus had chosen** [*the rest of the Twelve*].

Next, the prayer of the disciples is granted (verse 9), namely, they receive the Holy Ghost.

13 And it came to pass when they [*the Twelve*] were all baptized and had come up out of the water, **the Holy Ghost did fall upon them, and they were filled with the Holy Ghost and with fire**.

Next, the twelve disciples receive the ministering of angels. The people in the multitude are privileged to see this.

14 And behold, **they were encircled about as if it were by fire; and it came down from heaven, and the multitude did witness it**, and did bear record; and **angels did come down out of heaven and did minister unto them**.

Next, as promised, the Savior appears.

15 And it came to pass that **while the angels were ministering unto the disciples**, behold, **Jesus came** and stood in the midst and ministered unto them.

16 And it came to pass that **he spake unto the multitude, and commanded them that they should kneel down again upon the earth, and also that his disciples should kneel down** upon the earth.

17 And it came to pass that **when they had all knelt down upon the earth, he commanded his disciples that they should pray.**

18 And behold, they began to **pray**; and **they did pray unto Jesus, calling him their Lord and their God.**

Some people are concerned that the disciples are praying to Jesus, as indicated in verse 18, above. We know from the scriptures that we are to pray to the Father and no one else. Jesus commands us to pray to the Father in His name in numerous passages of scripture (see verse 6, above).

We will need to wait for a final clarification on this matter (of their praying to Christ) from someone who knows for sure. In the meantime, we note that at the end of verse 22, it seems that Jesus is explaining why they are praying to Him. Also, we see that they were being inspired by the Holy Ghost as to what to say (verse 24), and the Savior's "countenance did smile upon them" (verse 25) as they prayed to Him. It may even be that the word "pray" in this limited context could mean that they were praising and expressing appreciation and adoration to Him directly since He was with them. This is a special and unique situation, and the fact that Jesus did not stop them should be sufficient for now.

Whatever the case, it will be interesting to someday get the final, correct explanation from the proper authority on this. In the meantime, we ought to feel the sweetness of this marvelous blessing to these Twelve who have the privilege of seeing the Savior and Him ministering to them.

As we continue, Mormon will point out to us the things he is inspired to include about the Savior's ministry to these people.

19 And it came to pass that **Jesus departed out of the midst of them** [*the Twelve*], **and went a little way off from them and bowed himself** to the earth, and **he said:**

20 **Father, I thank thee that thou hast given the Holy Ghost unto these whom I have chosen**; and it is because of their belief in me that I have chosen them out of the world.

21 **Father, I pray thee that thou wilt give the Holy Ghost unto all them that shall believe in their words.**

22 Father, thou hast given them the Holy Ghost because they believe in me; and thou seest that they believe in me because thou hearest them, and **they pray unto me**; and **they pray unto me because I am with them.**

23 And now Father, **I pray unto thee for them, and also for all those who shall believe on their words,** that they may believe in me, that I may be in them as thou, Father, art in me, **that we may be one** [*that they, too, may have unity and harmony*].

You may have noticed that when the Holy Ghost is upon you, you have a feeling of peace, and you love and respect everyone. This is one of the "fruits of the Spirit."

Next, we are taught that when we pray and the Holy Ghost is upon us, we say the things that He inspires us to say. Thus, there are no "vain repetitions," in other words, unnecessary repetitions, and our expressions of gratitude and our requests are guided by inspiration. You may wish to read Doctrine and Covenants 46:30 and 50:30 on this subject.

24 And it came to pass that **when Jesus had thus prayed unto the Father, he came unto his disciples**, and behold, they did still continue, without ceasing [*stopping*], to **pray** unto him; and **they did not multiply many words, for it was given unto them what they should pray**, and they were filled with desire.

In verse 25, next, we see the glory of God upon these humble disciples, and we and are taught that nothing on earth can compare with the purity and glory of celestial realms.

25 And it came to pass that **Jesus blessed them as they did pray unto him**; and **his countenance** [*face*] **did smile upon them, and the light of his countenance did shine upon them**, and behold **they were as white as the countenance and also the garments** [*clothing*] **of Jesus**; and behold the whiteness thereof did exceed all the whiteness, yea, even **there could be nothing upon earth so white as the whiteness thereof**.

26 And **Jesus said unto them: Pray on**; nevertheless they did not cease to **pray**.

Perhaps the word "nevertheless" refers back to verse 25 and the "transfiguration" that they themselves were experiencing. Thus, "nevertheless, in spite of what they themselves were experiencing, they did not cease to pray."

27 And **he turned from them** [*the Twelve*] again, **and went a little way off and bowed himself to the earth**; and **he prayed again unto the Father, saying:**

In verses 28–29, next, we are given a brief course in the end result of the Atonement as far as our sins and imperfections are concerned. In other words, we are shown that, through the Atonement of Christ, we can become completely clean and pure.

28 Father, I thank thee that **thou hast purified those whom I have chosen** [*the twelve disciples*], because of their faith, and **I pray for them, and also for them who shall believe on their words, that they may be purified in me** [*through the Atonement*], through faith on their words [*through faith in the teaching of Church leaders*], even as **they** [*Church leaders*] **are purified in me**.

29 Father, **I pray not for the world** [*not all will be saved, because of their agency choices*], **but for those whom thou hast given me out of the world, because of their faith**, that **they may be purified in me**, that I may be in them [*united with them*] as thou, Father,

art in me, that we may be one, that I may be glorified in them.

Perhaps inferring "as Thou art glorified in Me," meaning that when we do what is right, we bring glory to God.

30 And **when Jesus had spoken these words he came again unto his disciples**; and behold **they did pray steadfastly**, without ceasing, unto him; and he did smile upon them again; and behold they were white [*clothed with glory; radiated, glowed; were transfigured*], even as Jesus.

31 And it came to pass that **he went again a little way off and prayed unto the Father**;

In verses 32–34, next, we are taught that when the Holy Ghost is upon us, our heart and spirit can understand and feel far more than words can express.

32 And **tongue cannot speak** the words which he **prayed, neither can be written** by man **the words which he prayed**.

33 And **the multitude did hear and do bear record**; and **their hearts were open** and **they did understand in their hearts the words which he prayed**.

34 Nevertheless, **so great and marvelous were the words which he prayed that they cannot be written neither can they be uttered** [*spoken or expressed*] **by man**.

Next, we learn that our faith or lack of faith plays a significant role in determining what God can show and teach us.

35 And it came to pass that when Jesus had made an end of praying he came again to the disciples, and said unto them: So great faith have I never seen among all the Jews; **wherefore** [*for this reason*] **I could not show unto them so great miracles, because of their unbelief**.

36 Verily I say unto you, **there are none of them that have seen so great things as ye have seen; neither have they heard so great things as ye have heard**.

THIRD NEPHI 20

You have no doubt heard our prophets today say much about the gathering of Israel. "Israel" is the name for the covenant people of the Lord, in other words His chosen people. Ever since the beginning, God has promised Israel that He would gather them back onto the covenant path and into the Church in large numbers before the Second Coming of the Savior. We hear much about this from our prophets and leaders today. It is happening right before our eyes and we have a lot to do with it!

The central theme of chapters 20–23 is the gathering of Israel in the last days before the Second Coming of Christ. Some of the verses in these chapters can be somewhat difficult to understand. If you find them difficult, go ahead and read them, of course, but just remember that the gathering of Israel is a big thing that has to be done as we prepare the world for the

Savior's Second Coming. If you at least remember this as you read, you will get the main idea of what you are reading.

By the way, the coming forth of the Book of Mormon is a key event signaling that the last days' gathering of Israel has begun and that we are in the final days of the world before the Savior comes and the Millennium begins.

The second day of Christ's appearance to the people in America began with chapter 19, and this chapter, chapter 20, is a continuation of His second day of ministering to them.

In chapter 20, the Savior miraculously provides bread and wine and administers the sacrament to the multitudes who had gathered to meet Him when He returned to them that morning. Remember that He administered the sacrament to a multitude of about 2,500 the previous day (see chapter 18).

After providing and administering the sacrament, Jesus prophesies a number of specific aspects of the latter-day gathering of Israel. We are watching much of this now as it takes place in our day.

First, remember that there was much praying in chapter 19. Now the Savior will command these people to stop praying but not to stop praying "in their hearts" (verse 1). There are many lessons we can learn from this. One is that we should have a prayer in our hearts at all times. One way we can do this is to constantly be aware of who we are as a child of God and that Heavenly Father is always aware of us. Another way is to say a lot of little prayers of gratitude throughout the day. This is a good way to keep a prayer in our heart all the time. Yet another thing this can mean is that we should be constantly aware of who we are and of our covenants and commitments to God.

Yet another lesson for us from what happened to the people here might be that we can't just pray all the time as has been taught by some people and groups. Rather, we must be up and doing and getting on with other matters of importance in our lives.

1 AND it came to pass that **he commanded the multitude that they should cease to pray**, and **also his disciples**. And **he commanded them that they should not cease to pray in their hearts**.

2 And **he commanded them that they should arise and stand up upon their feet**. And they arose up and stood upon their feet.

> Next, Jesus miraculously provides bread and wine and gives instructions regarding the sacrament to this much larger group than the previous day's multitude. Many of these people have spent all night gathering (3 Nephi 19:2–3). As was the case the previous day (3 Nephi 18:3–4), He gives the sacrament first to His disciples and then has them administer it to the multitude. This is no doubt part of the disciples' schooling to prepare them to lead the Church when Jesus departs, just as it was part of the schooling of Joseph Smith and Oliver Cowdery to learn the proper procedure for baptizing for the remission of sins, as well as ordaining men to the Aaronic Priesthood with John the Baptist as their instructor (see Joseph Smith—History 1:68–72).

Thus, we see that these Twelve Disciples are being given practical experience in leading and governing the Church that the resurrected Lord is establishing among them.

3 And it came to pass that **he brake bread** [*broke the sacrament bread*] **again and blessed it**, and **gave to the disciples to eat.**

4 And **when they had eaten he commanded them that they** [*the disciples*] **should break bread, and give unto the multitude.**

5 And when they had given unto the multitude **he also gave them wine to drink, and commanded them that they should give unto the multitude.**

Next, Mormon reminds us that the Savior's providing the bread and wine was indeed a miracle. This might be compared to him feeding 5,000 men plus women and children (Matthew 14:17–21), and feeding 4,000 men plus women and children (Matthew 15:32–38) during His ministry in the Holy Land. These miracles are symbolic of the fact that the Savior can provide things for us that cannot come from our own resources.

6 Now, **there had been no bread, neither wine, brought by the disciples, neither by the multitude;**

7 **But he truly gave unto them bread to eat, and also wine to drink.**

Next, the Savior instructs them again as to the symbolism of the bread and wine. Remember that according to the instructions given by the Lord in Doctrine and Covenants 27:1–4, water is used today in place of wine. (See also the heading to D&C 7.) We are taught in these verses the precious benefits of partaking of the sacrament righteously.

8 And he said unto them: **He that eateth this bread eateth of my body** [*partakes of My Atonement*] **to his soul** [*to the benefit and nourishing of his soul*]; and **he that drinketh of this wine drinketh of my blood** [*partakes of My atoning blood*] **to his soul** [*to the benefit of his spirituality*]; and **his soul shall never hunger nor thirst, but shall be filled** [*with the Holy Ghost; see 3 Nephi 12:6 and verse 9, next*].

It may be that verse 8, above, among other things, refers back to the Savior's instructions in the Sermon at the Temple (3 Nephi 12–14). Thus, "never hunger nor thirst," in verse 8, above, can be a reference to those who "hunger and thirst after righteousness," and who "shall be filled with the Holy Ghost" (see 3 Nephi 12:6) as they partake worthily of the sacrament emblems and keep covenants in their daily lives. (See also verse 9, below.)

Being "filled" (end of verse 8, above) could also include being filled with the peace that attends faithful members of the Church because they know they have found and are striving to faithfully live the true gospel of Christ.

9 Now, **when the multitude had all eaten and drunk**, behold, **they were filled with the Spirit**; and they did cry out with one voice, and gave glory to Jesus, whom they both saw and heard.

Next, the Savior will teach the people of Nephi about the scattering and gathering of Israel. This is both literal and symbolic. Israel (the children of Israel, the twelve tribes of Israel; Abraham's descendants) has literally been scattered throughout the world. It is literally being gathered in the last days before the second coming.

Symbolically, Satan and his evil followers attempt to "scatter" us away from the gospel of Christ and away from the possibility of being "gathered" back home to our Father to live with Him in celestial glory. The gospel of Jesus Christ is the means of "gathering" us back into the fold. As we follow the Good Shepherd and make covenants in His name, we intentionally take the covenant path home.

Jesus will now begin the final instruction that His Father had commanded Him to give this people. In so doing, He will remind them of some prophecies of Isaiah and will instruct them to study the words of this great prophet.

10 And it came to pass that when they had all given glory unto Jesus, he said unto them: **Behold now I finish the commandment which the Father hath commanded me concerning this people**, who are a remnant [*part*] of the house of Israel.

11 **Ye remember that I spake unto you** [*about the gathering of Israel; see 3 Nephi 16:5, 11–12, and so on*], **and said that when the words of Isaiah should be fulfilled** [*3 Nephi 16:17*]—behold they are written, **ye have them before you** [*in 2 Nephi 6:4–18, 2 Nephi 7–8, 12–24, and so on*], **therefore search them**—

As you can see in the references given in the notes in verse 11, above, Isaiah speaks much concerning the scattering and gathering of Israel. This is evident in what Jesus teaches next.

12 And verily, verily, I say unto you, **that when they** [*Isaiah's prophecies*] **shall be fulfilled then is the fulfilling of the covenant** [*then will the covenant be fulfilled that Israel will be gathered*] **which the Father hath made unto his people, O house of Israel**.

13 And **then shall the remnants** [*of Israel*], **which shall be scattered** abroad upon the face of the earth, **be gathered in from the east and from the west, and from the south and from the north**; and **they shall be brought to the knowledge of the Lord their God** [*learning of Christ and accepting His gospel is the "spiritual" gathering that motivates the children of Israel to physically gather to various lands to the stakes of Zion throughout the world*], **who hath redeemed them**.

14 And **the Father hath commanded me** [*3 Nephi 15:13, 16:16*] **that I should give unto you this land** [*America*] **for your inheritance**.

"Gentiles" is used in verse 15, next, as well as elsewhere in this chapter. Remember that this word is context sensitive; in other words, what it means depends on the setting and background in which it is used.

As explained in our Bible Dictionary, under "Gentiles," it can mean non-Israelites, but often, especially in the Book of Mormon, it is used to mean those who do not have the gospel, even though they may have Israelite lineage. Sometimes it is used to mean non-Jews. Sometimes it means non-Lamanites. There are several possible meanings. Each time it is used, we will need to look at the specific context.

As we continue, we will give one of several possible interpretations of verses 15–18.

15 And I say unto you, that **if the Gentiles** [*people throughout the world who do not have the gospel and the wicked who reject the gospel*] **do not repent after the blessing which they shall receive** [*after the restored gospel is made available to them*], after they have scattered my people [*including the Lamanites and the Jews*]—

16 **Then shall ye, who are a remnant of the house of Jacob** [*the righteous throughout the world, who have been gathered to the gospel of Christ*], **go forth among them** [*the wicked*]; and ye shall be in the midst of them [*the wicked*] who shall be many [*there will be multitudes of wicked people in the last days*]; and **ye shall be among them as a lion among the beasts of the forest** [*none will stop you; see 1 Nephi 14:13–15*], **and as a young lion among the flocks of sheep** [*none will stop the spread of the gospel in the last days*], who, if he goeth through both treadeth down and teareth in pieces, and **none can deliver** [*no one can prevent this from happening*].

17 **Thy** [*righteous Israel in the last days*] **hand shall be lifted up upon thine adversaries** [*your enemies; in other words, you will have power to proceed against all odds*], and all thine enemies shall be cut off [*by the Lord so that the righteous will ultimately triumph*].

18 And **I will gather my people together** as a man gathereth his sheaves [*bundles of grain*] into the floor [*threshing floor*].

In other words, the "grain" is gathered; the "wheat" is separated from the "tares;" the Lord will gather the righteous in the last days, and none will stop Him. He will send righteous members of the Church to do this.

Next, we see Bible symbolism in use. The word "horn" is symbolic of power and protection. For instance, in ancient Israel, the altar had four horns on it, and anyone who was in danger from another could grab hold of the horns of the altar and be safe and protected. (See 1 Kings 1:50.)

Also, "horses" symbolized military might, triumph, and victory in Biblical culture. See Jeremiah 8:16 and Revelation 19:11. Therefore, "hoofs [*of*] brass," in verse 19, next, could symbolize horses, in other words, victory over those who try to prevent Israel from being gathered in the last days. In addition, "brass" is sometimes associated with Christ, as in Revelation 1:15, wherein the Savior's feet are described as being "like unto fine brass, as if they burned in a furnace." Thus, "I will make thy hoofs brass," in verse 19, could symbolize that righteous Israel will have the help and power of the Lord in ultimately triumphing over all their enemies.

Pay special attention to the word "I" as the Savior tells these Book of Mormon people that the reason

Israel will be gathered in the last days is that He, the Lord, will be involved, and will use His power to fulfill the prophecies of the gathering.

19 For **I will make my people** [*I will strengthen Israel*] **with whom the Father hath covenanted** [*through Abraham; see Abraham 2:9–11*], yea, **I will make thy horn** [*symbolic of power in Bible culture*] **iron** [*strong*], **and I will make thy hoofs brass** [*hoofs can be symbolic of horses, which symbolize military might and power, in Biblical culture*]. **And thou** [*Israel*] **shalt beat in pieces many people** [*triumph over all enemies; perhaps referring to the Millennium*]; and **I will consecrate their gain unto the Lord, and their substance unto the Lord of the whole earth**. And behold, **I** [*Christ*] **am he who doeth it**.

In other words, the reason that this prophecy will be fulfilled is that Christ will do it.

20 And it shall come to pass, saith the Father, that **the sword of my justice shall hang over them** at that day [*the law of justice will take over because they refuse to take advantage of the law of mercy by repenting*]; and **except** [*unless*] **they repent it shall fall upon them**, saith the Father, yea, **even upon all the nations of the Gentiles**.

In context, "Gentiles," at the end of verse 20, above, can mean all the wicked, regardless of whether or not they belong to the house of Israel. Note also that this prophecy applies to "all the nations of the Gentiles," not just the Gentiles in America. This is important, because some people tend to apply verses 16–19 only to the Lamanites and the Gentiles in America.

21 And it shall come to pass that **I will establish my people, O house of Israel**.

Next, the Savior teaches Nephi's people about New Jerusalem. We learn that a city called New Jerusalem will be established in America, as specified in the tenth Article of Faith, and that the Savior Himself will visit the inhabitants of New Jerusalem. This city will be built in Independence, Missouri. (See D&C 57:2–3, 84:3–4.)

22 And behold, **this people** [*the people of Joseph—see 3 Nephi 20, footnote 22a—which includes people of Manasseh and Ephraim*] **will I establish in this land** [*America*], unto the fulfilling of the covenant which I made with your father Jacob; and **it shall be a New Jerusalem**. And **the powers of heaven shall be in the midst of this people**; yea, even **I will be in the midst of you**.

Elder Bruce R. McConkie explains more about New Jerusalem as follows: "'We believe . . . that Zion (the New Jerusalem) will be built upon the American continent." So specified the seer of latter days in our Tenth Article of Faith. Zion, the New Jerusalem, on American soil! And we hasten to add, so also shall there be Zions in all lands and New Jerusalems in the mountains of the Lord in all the earth. But the American Zion shall be the capital city, the source whence the law shall go forth to govern all the earth [*during the Millennium*]. It shall be the city of the Great King. His throne shall be there, and from there he shall reign gloriously over all the earth" (Bruce R. McConkie, *The Millennial Messiah: The Second Coming of the Son of Man* [Salt Lake City: Deseret Book, 1982], 301).

Next, Christ explains that He is the one prophesied of by Moses in Deuteronomy 18:15 and 18. The Savior is bearing witness to us that He is the Christ, the Messiah, prophesied about by Old Testament prophets.

23 Behold, **I am he of whom Moses spake**, saying: A prophet shall the Lord your God raise up unto you of your brethren, like unto me; him shall ye hear in all things whatsoever he shall say unto you. And **it shall come to pass that every soul who will not hear that prophet** [*Christ*] **shall be cut off from among the people** [*will be cut off from the people of the Lord*].

24 Verily I say unto you, yea, and **all the prophets from Samuel and those that follow after, as many as have spoken, have testified of me.**

What the Savior tells these people who have gathered at the temple in the land Bountiful also applies to us as modern-day Israelites. His teachings help us understand the significance of our being part of Israel and of having our lineage designated as we receive our patriarchal blessings.

25 And behold, **ye are the children** [*descendants*] **of the prophets** [*Abraham, Isaac, and Jacob*]; and **ye are of the house of Israel**; and **ye are of the covenant** [*the covenant applies to you*] which the Father made with your fathers [*ancestors*], **saying unto Abraham**: And **in thy seed shall all the kindreds of the earth be blessed** [*see Abraham 2:9–11*].

26 **The Father having raised me** [*Christ*] **up unto you** [*Israel, including the people of Nephi to whom the Savior is speaking*] **first, and sent me to bless you in turning away every one of you from his iniquities** [*these Book of Mormon people will have about two hundred years of peace and righteousness after the Savior departs; they are the ones who survived the destruction of the wicked on the American continent at the time of Christ's Crucifixion*]; and this because ye are the children of the covenant—

Next, the Savior teaches more about the scattering of Israel and explains that through the descendants of Abraham, all people of the world will be blessed. He tells them that the Holy Ghost will ultimately give all people the opportunity to understand and accept or reject the gospel.

27 And after that ye were blessed **then fulfilleth the Father the covenant which he made with Abraham, saying: In thy seed shall all the kindreds of the earth be blessed** [*Abraham 2:11*]—unto the pouring out of the Holy Ghost through me [*in conjunction with the gospel of Jesus Christ*] upon the Gentiles, which blessing upon the Gentiles shall make them mighty above all, unto **the scattering of my people, O house of Israel.**

Verse 28 focuses on America and the scattering of the Lamanites in

America by the Gentiles who settled America. You may wish to review 1 Nephi 22:7–9, in which Nephi prophesies of this scattering.

28 And **they** [*the settlers of America*] **shall be a scourge** [*big trouble*] **unto the people of this land** [*the Lamanites*]. Nevertheless, **when they shall have received the fulness of my gospel** [*restored through the Prophet Joseph Smith*], then **if they** [*the non-Lamanites in America*] shall **harden their hearts against me I will return their iniquities upon their own heads** [*they will be punished for and by their wickedness*], saith the Father.

Next, in verses 29–31, Jesus speaks of the gathering of the Jews and their future conversion to Him.

29 And **I will remember** [*fulfill*] **the covenant which I have made with my people** [*the Jews; see last half of this verse*]; and **I have covenanted with them that I would gather them together in mine own due time** [*when I consider the timing to be right*], **that I would give unto them again the land of their fathers** [*ancestors*] **for their inheritance, which is the land of Jerusalem, which is the promised land unto them forever**, saith the Father.

The "land of Jerusalem," in verse 29, above, is obviously more than the city of Jerusalem.

Next, Jesus teaches that the time will come when the gospel will be preached on a large scale to the Jews. This time has not yet come. The most common thinking on this is that it will begin when the Savior appears to the Jews as He stands on the Mount of Olives, and that this conversion of the Jews will extend into the Millennium (see Zechariah 14:1–9).

Whatever the case, when this time does come, there will be a large-scale conversion of the Jews. This is a wonderful time to anticipate.

30 And it shall come to pass that **the time cometh, when the fulness of my gospel shall be preached unto them** [*the Jews*];

31 And **they shall believe in me, that I am Jesus Christ, the Son of God**, and shall pray unto the Father in my name [*an acceptance of the fact that Jesus is the promised Messiah, for whom the Jews have been waiting over the centuries*].

32 **Then shall their watchmen** [*"watchmen" usually means "prophets;" perhaps meaning that the day will come when the Jews will listen to the prophets of God*] **lift up their voice, and with the voice together** [*in harmony and unity*] **shall they sing** [*sing praises to Christ*]; for **they shall see eye to eye** [*one possible meaning of this is that they will be united in their belief in Christ*].

As we read verse 33 in context, next, it becomes clear that this gathering of the Jews includes a spiritual gathering. In other words, they will be converted and gathered to Christ. This is the most important gathering eternally for any of us. Their physical gathering back to Jerusalem is also important and significant.

33 **Then will the Father gather them together again, and give unto**

them Jerusalem for the land of their inheritance.

As we continue, starting with verse 34, next, it primarily sounds like a description of conditions during the Millennium when the spiritual gathering of Israel will happen in very large numbers. Much of what we read in the next verses is seen in Isaiah, chapter 52.

The word "sing," as used in verse 34, next, as well as other verses, is often used in scripture to mean rejoicing and joy at the fulfillment of a prophesied event. For example, in Doctrine and Covenants 84:98, speaking of the beginning of the Millennium, the inhabitants of the earth sing a "new song" (D&C 84:99–102), which is a "song" of rejoicing in millennial conditions that have come with the arrival of Christ to reign on earth for a thousand years.

34 **Then shall they break forth into joy—Sing** together, ye waste places of Jerusalem [*Jerusalem has been devastated by apostasy, as well as wars and other things*]; **for the Father hath comforted his people, he hath redeemed Jerusalem.**

35 The **Father hath made bare his holy arm** [*has shown His power*] **in the eyes of all the nations** [*by sending the Savior back to earth for the Second Coming*]; and **all the ends of the earth shall see the salvation of the Father** [*all people will know of God at the Second Coming of Christ*]; and the Father and I are one [*work in complete unity and harmony*].

36 And **then** [*at the beginning of the Millennium*] **shall be brought to pass that which is written** [*in Isaiah 52:1*]: **Awake, awake** [*wake up spiritually*] again, and **put on thy strength** [*put on the true gospel of Christ with its priesthood authority; see D&C 113:7–8*], **O Zion** [*people of the Lord*]**; put on thy beautiful garments** [*make priesthood covenants with God; see D&C 82:14–15*], O Jerusalem, the holy city, for henceforth [*from the beginning of the Millennium on*] **there shall no more come into thee the uncircumcised** [*the wicked; those who refuse to make sacred priesthood covenants with God*] **and the unclean** [*wicked*].

37 **Shake thyself from the dust** [*remove yourself from your past, which has reduced you to "dust"*]; **arise** [*elevate yourself through the Atonement of Christ*], **sit down** [*in honor and dignity*], O Jerusalem; **loose thyself** [*"return to the Lord"; D&C 113:10*] **from the bands of thy neck** [*"the curses of God upon her, or the remnants of Israel in their scattered condition among the Gentiles"; see D&C 113:9–10*], O captive daughter of Zion.

Remember that the Savior has been quoting Isaiah and explaining his prophecies about the gathering of various groups of Israel in the last days. (See 3 Nephi 20:10–13.)

He now explains to these people, who have gathered near the temple in the land Bountiful to hear Him (3 Nephi 11:1), how Israel got themselves into such wickedness, and how they can get away from it and return to Him and the Father.

38 For thus saith the Lord: **Ye have sold yourselves for naught** [*for absolutely nothing of value, or, in other words, for*

wickedness], **and ye shall be redeemed without money** [*through the Atonement of Christ, something money cannot buy*].

39 Verily, verily, I say unto you, that **my people** [*Israel; see Isaiah 52:4*] **shall know my name** [*Jesus Christ*]; yea, in that day they shall know that I am he that doth speak.

40 And then shall they say: **How beautiful upon the mountains are the feet of him that bringeth good tidings** [*good news; the gospel*] **unto them** [*perhaps meaning that the day will come when Israel will once again rejoice at having true prophets who teach them about Christ*], that publisheth peace; that bringeth good tidings [*the gospel of Christ*] unto them of good, that publisheth salvation; that saith unto Zion: Thy God reigneth!

41 And then shall a cry go forth: **Depart ye, depart ye, go ye out from thence** [*flee from wickedness and evil*], **touch not that which is unclean** [*don't even get close to being wicked*]; go ye out of the midst of her [*possibly a reference to Babylon (1 Nephi 20:20), to Satan's kingdom, the "whore of all the earth" (1 Nephi 14:11)*]; **be ye clean that bear the vessels** [*administer priesthood ordinances*] **of the Lord** [*see Isaiah 52:11*].

Next, the Lord teaches them that the gathering of Israel is to be done in an orderly fashion, not in panic or disorder. Perhaps you've noticed that the Church moves forward with great carefulness and in peaceful order under the direction of the First Presidency and the Quorum of the Twelve.

42 For **ye shall not go out with haste nor go by flight**; for the Lord will go before you [*will prepare the way*], and the God of Israel shall be your rearward [*your protection*].

The servant spoken of in verse 43, next, could be Joseph Smith Jr., as mentioned on page 428 of the 1986 *Book of Mormon Student Manual*'s discussion of 3 Nephi 21:10–11. Or it could be Christ, modern servants, prophets of God, or all of the above working together to fulfill 3 Nephi 20:46.

43 Behold, **my servant shall deal prudently** [*wisely*]**; he shall be exalted and extolled** [*praised*] **and be very high**.

Verses 44 and 45 seem to refer to the Savior.

44 As many were astonished at thee—**his visage** [*appearance, face*] **was so marred, more than any man** [*Christ went through more than any mortal could in carrying out the Atonement for us*] and his form more than the sons of men—

45 **So shall he** [*the Lord*] **sprinkle** [*Joseph Smith Translation of the Bible, Isaiah 52:15, uses the word, "gather"*] **many nations**; the kings shall shut their mouths at him [*will be speechless in His presence*], for that which had not been told them shall they see; and that which they had not heard shall they consider.

Kings and rulers of nations will not be able to stop the work of the Lord from progressing in the last days. (See 3 Nephi 21:8 in context.)

Next, Jesus bears testimony that the gathering of Israel will take place just as prophesied.

46 **Verily, verily** [*listen very carefully*], **I say unto you, all these things shall surely come, even as the Father hath commanded me**. Then shall this covenant [*to gather Israel again in the last days*] which the Father hath covenanted [*promised*] with his people be fulfilled; and **then shall Jerusalem be inhabited again with my people** [*the Jews*], **and it shall be the land of their inheritance**.

THIRD NEPHI 21

This chapter is a continuation of prophecies about the last days' gathering of Israel, which you have no doubt noticed is a major emphasis in the Church today. In this chapter, you will see considerable repetition of 3 Nephi 20, no doubt for emphasis about the gathering.

Remember, "Israel" is another name for the descendants of Abraham, Isaac, and Jacob, through whom the Lord said that He would take the gospel and the blessings of the priesthood to all the world (see Abraham 2:9-11, in the Pearl of Great Price). Their descendants are the Lord's covenant people.

The 12 tribes of Israel were scattered throughout the world in Old Testament times and are to be gathered back to the gospel and Christ in our day. It is one of the most important things members of the Church are doing today. It includes missionary work and temple work, where we are gathering Israel in the postmortal spirit world.

In verses 1 and 2, next, the Savior will tell these people that the coming forth of the Book of Mormon will be a major sign that the much-prophesied gathering of Israel in the last days is about to begin. The gathering of Israel is a major sign of the times, telling us that the Second Coming of the Savior is getting close.

1 AND verily I say unto you, **I give unto you a sign**, that ye may know the time when these things [*the gathering of Israel*] shall be about to take place—**that I shall gather in, from their long dispersion** [*scattering*], **my people, O house of Israel, and shall establish again among them my Zion**;

2 And behold, **this is the thing which I will give unto you for a sign**—for verily I say unto you that **when these things** [*what the Savior has taught these Book of Mormon people*] **which I declare unto you, and which I shall declare unto you hereafter** of myself, **and by the power of the Holy Ghost** which shall be given unto you of the Father, **shall be made known unto the Gentiles that they may know concerning this people** [*the Book of Mormon people*] **who are a remnant of the house of Jacob** [*who are a part of covenant Israel*], and concerning this my people who shall be scattered by them;

In other words, the sign is the coming forth of the Book of Mormon so all the world can know about the dealings of the Lord with the people of the Western Hemisphere. Compare with 1 Nephi 13:35.

3 Verily, verily, I say unto you, **when these things shall be made known unto them** of the Father, **and shall come forth** of the Father, **from them** [*the Gentiles; the restored Church, established through the Prophet Joseph Smith*] **unto you** [*the descendants of the Book of Mormon people; the Lamanites*];

Next, we are shown that the United States of America was to be established by the power of God in the last days. This was necessary in order for the Church to be established and for the Book of Mormon to be brought forth and taken to the Lamanites as part of the fulfillment of the covenant leading to the gathering of Israel.

4 For **it is wisdom in the Father that they** [*the Gentiles; the Pilgrims and settlers of America; see 1 Nephi 13:12–19*] **should be established in this land** [*America*], **and be set up as a free people** by the power of the Father, **that these things** [*the Book of Mormon*] **might come forth from them unto a remnant of your seed** [*the Lamanites*], **that the covenant of the Father may be fulfilled which he hath covenanted** [*promised*] **with his people, O house of Israel**;

5 Therefore, **when these works and the works** [*things*] **which shall be wrought** [*done*] **among you hereafter** [*in other words, the Book of Mormon*] **shall come forth from the Gentiles** [*members of the Church, restored by Joseph Smith*], **unto your seed** [*descendants, in other words, the Lamanites*] **which shall dwindle** [*gradually leave the gospel*] **in unbelief because of iniquity** [*wickedness*];

Next, Jesus explains why the Book of Mormon will come forth from the Gentiles. Remember that in this context, "Gentiles" are Joseph Smith and the early members of the Restored Church, as well as nonmembers in the United States. (See Bible Dictionary, under "Gentiles," for help in understanding various uses of the word "Gentiles.")

6 For thus **it behooveth the Father** [*it is the will of the Father*] that it [*the Book of Mormon*] should come forth from the Gentiles, **that he may show forth his power unto the Gentiles**, for this cause [*for this purpose*] **that the Gentiles**, if they will not harden their hearts, that they **may repent and come unto me and be baptized** in my name and **know of the true points of my doctrine, that they may be numbered among my people, O house of Israel**;

Next, Jesus repeats the fact that the coming forth of the Book of Mormon is a sign that the gathering of Israel is beginning to take place.

7 And **when** these things come to pass that **thy seed** [*the Lamanites*] **shall begin to know these things** [*start to learn about the Book of Mormon*]—**it shall be a sign** unto them, that they may know **that the work of the Father hath already commenced** [*begun*] unto the fulfilling of the covenant [*to gather Israel*] which he hath made unto the people who are of the house of Israel.

8 And **when that day shall come** [*when the gathering of Israel begins*], it shall come to pass that **kings shall shut their mouths** [*leaders of nations will not

stop the gathering of Israel]; for that which had not been told them shall they see [*perhaps meaning that great leaders and influential people will express amazement at the "unexpected" progress of the Church*]; and that which they had not heard shall they consider [*perhaps meaning that influential people in the last days will reconsider their opinions of the Church as they witness its progress*].

9 **For in that day** [*when the Church is restored, when the Book of Mormon comes forth, and when the gathering of Israel begins*], for my sake **shall the Father work a work, which shall be a great and a marvelous work among them**; and there shall be among them those who will not believe it, although a man shall declare [*explain*] it unto them.

Next, the Savior speaks of Joseph Smith (see 3 Nephi 21:10, footnote a, which takes you to D&C 135:1–3 and the martyrdom of the Prophet Joseph Smith). This ties in with verses 1–6, above, because Joseph Smith was the one through whom the Lord restored the true Church among the Gentiles, who, consequently, are the ones who bring the Book of Mormon and the Church to the Lamanites and to all of Israel.

10 But behold, **the life of my servant** [*Joseph Smith*] **shall be in my hand**; therefore they shall not hurt him [*as far as eternity is concerned*], although he shall be marred [*killed, martyred*] because of them. Yet I will heal him, for I will show unto them that my wisdom is greater than the cunning of the devil.

11 Therefore it shall come to pass that **whosoever will not believe in my words**, who am Jesus Christ, **which the Father shall cause him** [*Joseph Smith*] **to bring forth unto the Gentiles**, and shall give unto him [*Joseph Smith*] power that he shall bring them forth unto the Gentiles, (it shall be done even as Moses said [*as quoted by Christ in 3 Nephi 20:23]*) **they shall be cut off from among my people** [*Israel*] who are of the covenant.

In other words, they will ultimately lose the opportunity for celestial exaltation, which is the end result of making and keeping covenants.

12 And **my people** [*Israel*] **who are a remnant** [*a remaining part*] **of Jacob** [*of Jacob's posterity; the father of the Twelve Tribes of Israel*] **shall be among the Gentiles**, yea, in the midst of them **as a lion among the beasts of the forest** [*unstoppable*], **as a young lion among the flocks of sheep**, who, if he go through both treadeth down and teareth in pieces, and none can deliver [*nobody can save them*].

Nothing can stop the gospel from spreading and the resulting gathering of Israel in the last days prior to the Second Coming of Christ.

13 **Their** [*the people of the Lord; "my people" in verse 12, above*] **hand shall be lifted up upon their adversaries** [*enemies*], and all their enemies shall be cut off [*no one will stop them*].

Next, Christ prophesies the ultimate destruction of all wickedness. We understand that the final destruction of these things will take place when the Savior returns and the Millennium begins.

14 Yea, **wo be unto the Gentiles** [*all the wicked who reject the gospel*] **except** [*unless*] **they repent**; for it shall come to pass in that day, saith the Father, that **I will cut off thy horses** [*symbolic of power, military might, in Biblical culture*] out of the midst of thee, and **I will destroy thy chariots** [*likewise symbolic of power and military might*];

15 And **I will cut off the cities** of thy land, and **throw down all thy strongholds**;

16 And **I will cut off witchcrafts** out of thy land, and thou shalt have no more **soothsayers**;

17 Thy **graven images** [*idols*] I will also cut off, and thy **standing images** [*idols*] out of the midst of thee, and **thou shalt no more worship the works of thy hands** [*idols*]**;**

18 And I will pluck up thy **groves** [*centers of sexual immorality*] out of the midst of thee; **so will I destroy thy cities**.

19 And it shall come to pass that all **lyings**, and **deceivings**, and **envyings**, and **strifes**, and **priestcrafts** [*preaching for the sake of wealth and honor of men; see Alma 1:16*], and **whoredoms** [*sexual immorality*], **shall be done away**.

Next, the Savior repeats the basic message of the above verses.

20 For it shall come to pass, **saith the Father**, that at that day **whosoever will not repent and come unto my Beloved Son, them will I cut off from among my people, O house of Israel.**

In other words, they will be cut off from the privilege of returning to live with God in celestial exaltation—the highest degree in the celestial kingdom—and becoming gods themselves and living in the family unit forever;

21 And **I will execute vengeance and fury upon them**, even as upon the heathen [*people who don't worship the true God*], such as they have not heard [*conditions among the wicked will be very bad in the last days*].

Perhaps you've noticed that the Savior constantly interjects an invitation and reminder for the wicked to repent. He does it again in verse 22, next.

22 But **if they** [*the gentiles mentioned in verse 14, above*] **will repent** and hearken unto my words, and harden not their hearts, I will establish my church among them, and **they shall come in unto the covenant** and be numbered among this the remnant of Jacob, unto whom I have given this land for their inheritance;

Next, Jesus speaks again of the city of New Jerusalem. He spoke of it in 3 Nephi 20:22.

23 And they [*converts from all over the world; see bold later in this verse*] shall assist my people, the remnant of Jacob [*especially Ephraim and Manasseh, who are prominent in the Church*], and **also as many of the house of Israel as shall come, that they may build a city, which**

shall be called the New Jerusalem.

24 And **then shall they** [*converts from among the Gentiles; see 3 Nephi 21:6 as referred to in 3 Nephi 21:24, footnote a*] **assist my** people that they may be gathered in, who are scattered upon all the face of the land, in **unto the New Jerusalem.**

Next, the Savior explains that He will visit those in New Jerusalem. Remember that the city of New Jerusalem will become one of two headquarters of the Savior during the Millennium. The other city will be old Jerusalem. You can read more about these two cities in Ether 13:1–12.

25 And **then shall the power of heaven come down among them; and I also will be in the midst.**

Next, the Savior once again repeats that the pivotal sign for the Restoration of the gospel and the gathering of Israel in the last days is the coming forth of the Book of Mormon.

26 And **then shall the work of the Father commence** at that day, even **when this gospel shall be preached among the remnant of this people** [*when the Lamanites hear about the Book of Mormon*]. Verily I say unto you, at that day shall the work of the Father commence **among all the dispersed** [*scattered*] **of my people**, yea, **even the tribes which have been lost**, which the Father hath led away out of Jerusalem.

In other words, when the Book of Mormon comes forth, the work of gathering will begin among all of Israel, including the lost ten tribes.

In conjunction with the end of verse 26, above, it is interesting to note that in 1831, the Prophet Joseph Smith said that John the Beloved Apostle, who was translated (has not died yet), was now working with the lost ten tribes, preparing them for their return. (See *History of the Church* 1:176.)

27 Yea, **the work shall commence among all the dispersed of my people** [*among all of scattered Israel*], with the Father to prepare the way **whereby they may come unto me**, that they may call on the Father in my name.

You have no doubt noticed that throughout all these verses, Jesus humbly gives credit and honor to the Father for what will take place rather than taking any honor or credit to Himself.

28 Yea, and then shall the work commence, **with the Father** among all nations in preparing the way whereby his people may be gathered home to the land of their inheritance.

29 And they shall go out [*be gathered*] from all nations; and they shall not go out in haste, nor go by flight [*the gathering will be a gradual, orderly process*], for I will go before them [*I will prepare the way*], **saith the Father**, and I will be their rearward [*their protection*].

THIRD NEPHI 22

As you have probably already noticed, in Third Nephi, chapters 20–21, the

Savior quoted much from Old Testament prophets, especially Isaiah, concerning the promised gathering of Israel in the last days. That is the day we are living in right now. He will now quote what is known in the Bible as Isaiah, chapter 54. After doing so, He will command the people of Nephi to study Isaiah (3 Nephi 23:1–2).

The imagery that Isaiah uses in verse 1, next, in order to show us what he wants us to know, is that of a woman (Israel) who has not been able to have children (righteous children). The message is that Israel, in Old Testament times, did not bear children who remained righteous, but in the last days, she will have righteous, faithful Saints, who will make and keep covenants with the Lord. You are part of the fulfillment of this prophecy of Isaiah.

1 And **then** [*in the last days*] **shall that which is written** [*the prophecies concerning the gathering of Israel*] **come to pass**: Sing, O barren [*Israel, who has not produced*], thou that didst not bear [*righteous children*]; break forth into singing [*rejoice*], and cry aloud, thou that didst not travail [*go into labor*] with child [*in former days, you did not succeed in bringing forth that which you were supposed to, namely righteous people loyal to Christ*]; for more are the children of the desolate [*converts from scattered Israel*] than the children of the married wife [*perhaps meaning converts from Israelites who remained in the Holy Land*], saith the Lord [*now, in the last days, you've got more righteous Israelites than you ever thought possible*].

One of the characteristics of Isaiah's prophesying is that he repeats the main point of the prophecy and then repeats it again and again. Some people get confused by this when they read and study Isaiah's writings. They don't realize that he is simply and skillfully repeating to emphasize the point he is making.

2 **Enlarge the place of thy tent** [*make the tent bigger in the last days; make more room for righteous Israel in the last days!*], and let them **stretch forth the curtains of thy habitations** [*make more room*]; spare not [*spare no effort in making more room*], **lengthen thy cords and strengthen thy stakes** [*make more room; the Church will greatly expand in the last days as righteous Israel is gathered*];

3 For thou [*righteous Israel*] shalt **break forth on the right hand and on the left** [*righteous Israel will be popping up everywhere!*], and **thy seed** [*the descendants of Israel*] **shall inherit the Gentiles** [*will spread throughout the world in the last days*] and **make the desolate cities** [*cities without the gospel*] **to be inhabited** [*with righteous members of the Church*].

4 Fear not, for **thou shalt not be ashamed** [*you won't fail*]; **neither be thou confounded** [*stopped; confused*], for **thou shalt not be put to shame** [*you won't fail again*]; for **thou shalt forget the shame of thy youth** [*forget past failures—a major message of the Atonement*], and **shalt not remember the reproach** [*embarrassing times*] **of thy youth, and shalt not remember the reproach of thy widowhood** [*when you broke your covenants with the Lord and were thus left alone*] any more [*you can forget the failures of the past when Israel was*

apostate; the once "barren" Church is going to bear much fruit in the last days].

5 For **thy maker, thy husband, the Lord of Hosts** [*the true God*] **is his name** [*you will return to your Creator, the Lord, in the last days*]; and **thy Redeemer, the Holy One of Israel** [*Christ*]—the God of the whole earth shall he be called [*reference to the Millennium*].

6 For **the Lord hath called thee as a woman forsaken and grieved in spirit** [*Israel has been through some rough, discouraging times*], **and a wife of youth, when thou wast refused** [*you didn't bear righteous children when you were young*], saith thy God.

7 **For a small moment** [*for a short while in the Lord's time*] **have I forsaken thee** [*I had to leave you, because you apostatized*], **but with great mercies will I gather thee** [*the Atonement in action as Israel is gathered in the last days*].

8 **In a little wrath** [*anger*] **I hid my face from thee for a moment** [*I had to quit blessing you when you rejected Me*], **but with everlasting kindness will I have mercy on thee** [*when you return to Me*], saith the Lord thy Redeemer [*Christ*].

9 **For this, the waters of Noah unto me** [*your situation is similar to the days of Noah and the Flood*], for **as I have sworn** [*promised, covenanted*] that **the waters of Noah should no more go over the earth, so have I sworn that I would not be wroth** [*angry*] **with thee** [*just as I (the Lord) promised not to flood the earth again, so have I promised to accept you back as you return to Me in the last days*].

10 For **the mountains shall depart and the hills be removed** [*other things may change over time*], **but my kindness shall not depart from thee, neither shall the covenant of my peace** [*which brings lasting peace*] **be removed,** saith the Lord that hath mercy on thee.

God keeps His promises; Isaiah is reminding us of the true nature of God—a kind and merciful God indeed!

Isaiah continues to repeat the main message, which the Savior has emphasized in the past two chapters, to the survivors of the destruction in America; namely, that God is merciful and that Israel can indeed be gathered because of the Atonement of Christ. This applies to us all.

11 **O thou** [*Israel*] **afflicted, tossed with tempest, and not comforted** [*you've had a rough past with lots of troubles*]! **Behold, I will lay thy stones with fair colors, and lay thy foundations with sapphires** [*I will make your eternal homes with Me in heaven very beautiful; compare with the description of the celestial kingdom in Revelation 21:18–21*].

12 And **I will make thy windows of agates** [*beautiful jewel stones*], **and thy gates of carbuncles** [*a bright red precious stone in Isaiah's day*], **and all thy borders of pleasant stones** [*the righteous will have it really good*].

13 And **all thy children** [*Israel*] **shall be taught of the Lord**; and **great shall be the peace of thy children** [*likely referring mainly to the Millennium*].

14 **In righteousness** [*through Christ*] **shalt thou** [*Israel*] **be established** [*gathered into the fold in the last days*]; **thou shalt be far from oppression for thou shalt not fear, and from terror for it shall not come near thee** [*Millennial conditions*].

15 Behold, **they** [*enemies of righteousness*] **shall surely gather together against thee, not by me** [*not brought by the Lord as in times past when Israel was wicked; example: 2 Nephi 20:5–6*]; **whosoever shall gather together against thee shall fall for thy sake** [*I will protect you; you will finally have peace*].

Next, the Lord, through Isaiah, explains why He has power to bless and protect Israel if they repent and return to Him. The explanation is simple. He is the Creator!

16 Behold, **I have created the smith** [*the blacksmith*] that bloweth the coals in the fire, and that bringeth forth an instrument [*who creates tools, weapons, etc.*] for his work; and I have created the waster to destroy [*I have power over those who choose to destroy, including Satan; in other words, over the wicked; you will be safe with Me*].

In verse 17, next, Isaiah repeats and summarizes the main message in the previous verses.

17 **No weapon that is formed against thee** [*righteous Israel*] **shall prosper** [*succeed*]; and every tongue that shall revile [*speak evil things*] against thee in judgment thou shalt condemn [*your righteous actions will bear witness against*]. **This is the heritage** [*inheritance; blessing*] **of the servants of the Lord**, and their righteousness is of me [*comes because of My Atonement and gospel and power to save*], saith the Lord [*in other words, there is safety for the righteous with Me*].

THIRD NEPHI 23

Next, Jesus commands the people to study the prophecies of Isaiah concerning the gathering of Israel. Isaiah's words are important for all of us, especially because they teach the power of the Atonement of Jesus Christ to cleanse us and heal us from our sins completely. For example, see Isaiah 1:18 in the Bible.

1 AND now, behold, I say unto you, that **ye ought to search these things** [*the words of Isaiah*]. Yea, **a commandment I give unto you that ye search these things diligently**; for **great are the words of Isaiah**.

Imagine how humble Isaiah feels knowing that the Savior Himself said "great are the words of Isaiah."

2 For surely **he** [*Isaiah*] **spake** [*spoke*] **as touching all things concerning my people which are of the house of Israel**; therefore it must needs be [*it is necessary*] that he must speak also to the Gentiles [*everyone must ultimately have a chance to understand the gospel*].

Next, Jesus explains that everything Isaiah said either has been fulfilled or will be fulfilled.

3 And **all things that he spake have been and shall be**, even according to the words which he spake.

Next, Jesus instructs that His words which He is teaching the people in America now are to be written down so that in due time they can go forth to all the world. We are witnessing the fulfillment of this as the Book of Mormon goes forth to more and more nations and peoples.

4 Therefore give heed to [*pay close attention to and obey*] my words; **write the things which I have told you**; and **according to the time and the will of the Father they shall go forth unto the Gentiles**.

Next, we are reminded that the gospel is for everyone. This is another way of saying that all people everywhere are invited to come unto Christ, make covenants with Him, and join with Israel, which, in the overall sense, means those who make and keep covenants with God the Father through the gospel of Christ.

5 And **whosoever will hearken unto** [*listen and obey*] **my words and repenteth and is baptized, the same shall be saved**. Search the prophets [*search the scriptures; study the words of the prophets*], for many there be that testify of these things.

Next, Christ explains that there are yet other scriptures that He wants them to write down. It appears that He is now addressing the twelve Nephite disciples. He will remind them that they have failed to write down the words of Samuel the Lamanite. Among other things, this can be a reminder to us of the importance of recording significant events in our own lives.

6 And now it came to pass that **when Jesus had said these words** he said unto them again, after he had expounded [*explained*] all the scriptures unto them which they had received, **he said unto them: Behold, other scriptures I would that ye should write, that ye have not**.

7 And it came to pass that **he said unto Nephi: Bring forth the record which ye have kept**.

8 And, **when Nephi had brought forth the records, and laid them before him he** [*Christ*] **cast his eyes upon** [*looked at*] **them and said**:

9 Verily I say unto you, **I commanded my servant Samuel, the Lamanite, that he should testify unto this people**, that at the day that the Father should glorify his name in me that there were many saints who should arise from the dead, and should appear unto many, and should minister unto them. And he said unto them: **Was it not so?**

10 And **his disciples answered him and said: Yea, Lord**, Samuel did prophesy according to thy words, and they were all fulfilled.

11 And Jesus said unto them: **How be it** [*why is it*] **that ye have not written this thing**, that many saints did arise and appear unto many and did minister unto them?

Next, we will see some swift repenting, which is certainly a good example for us.

12 And it came to pass that **Nephi remembered that this thing had not been written**.

13 And it came to pass that Jesus commanded that it should be written; **therefore it was written** according as he commanded.

14 And now it came to pass that **when Jesus had expounded** [*explained and taught*] **all the scriptures** in one, which they had written, **he commanded them** [*the disciples*] **that they should teach the things which he had expounded unto them**.

> Once again, in verse 14, above, we see the pattern in which Jesus teaches and instructs the Apostles and prophets. And they, in turn, instruct us. This is why it is safe to "follow the Brethren."

THIRD NEPHI 24

In 3 Nephi 23:6, Jesus told the twelve disciples that He had other scriptures for them to write down. He then had them write the words of Samuel the Lamanite (3 Nephi 23:9–13), and here, in chapter 24, Christ will command them to write what we know as Malachi, chapter 3, in the Old Testament.

Malachi is the last recorded prophet in the Old Testament, and his prophecies were given about 430 BC. (430 years before the birth of Christ—see Bible Dictionary, under "Malachi.") Since he lived almost two hundred years after Lehi left Jerusalem (600 BC), the Book of Mormon people could not know of Malachi's prophecies. Thus, the Savior tells them what Malachi wrote.

In this chapter, the Savior quotes Malachi, especially with respect to the Second Coming and the payment of tithing. Note how Jesus continues to give His Father credit in all things, thus reminding us that Christ works under the direction of our Heavenly Father.

1 AND it came to pass that he commanded them [*the disciples*] that they should **write the words which the Father had given unto Malachi**, which he [*Jesus*] should [*would*] tell unto them. And it came to pass that after they were written he expounded [*explained*] them. And these are the words which he did tell unto them, saying: **Thus said the Father unto Malachi**—Behold, **I will send my messenger** [*we don't know who this "messenger" is; it could be several different messengers, including angels of the Restoration, the Prophet Joseph Smith, and others; it could include the restored gospel—see D&C 45:9*], **and he shall prepare the way before me**, and the Lord whom ye seek shall suddenly come to his temple, even the messenger of the covenant, whom ye delight in; behold, he shall come, saith the Lord of Hosts.

> The phrase "suddenly come to his temple," as used in verse 1, above, could refer to appearances of the Savior in the last days, including His appearance in the Kirtland Temple (D&C 110:2). It could also refer directly to His Second Coming and the Millennium, during which time temples will be all over the earth. Perhaps you've noticed that many passages of scripture lend themselves to many different interpretations and fulfillments. Thus, it is often wise not to restrict such verses to just one meaning.

Whatever the case, we understand from the heading of this chapter in our Book of Mormon that this chapter deals with the Second Coming, and that verse 2, next, basically asks who will survive the Coming of the Lord.

2 But **who may abide the day of his coming, and who shall stand** [*remain standing*] **when he** [*Christ*] **appeareth?** For he is like a refiner's fire [*the Savior is a "purifier"*], and like fuller's soap [*a strong cleansing soap, used in Biblical times to remove stains and clean laundry*].

3 And **he** [*Christ*] **shall sit as a refiner and purifier of silver** [*symbolic of bringing out the best that is in us*]; and **he shall purify the sons of Levi** [*the holders of the priesthood in the last days; see D&C 84:31–32, 128:24*], **and purge** [*cleanse*] **them** as gold and silver, **that they may offer unto the Lord an offering in righteousness** [*that they may be worthy to officiate in priesthood ordinances, etc.*].

It may be that verse 4, next, has reference mainly to the large-scale conversion of the Jews to Christ and His gospel, which leads up to and into the Millennium.

4 **Then shall the offering of Judah** [*the Jews*] and Jerusalem [*the Jews*] **be pleasant** [*acceptable*] **unto the Lord,** as in the days of old, and as in former years.

Next, Malachi speaks of the judgment of God that will fall upon the wicked at the time of the Second Coming.

5 And **I will come near to you to judgment**; and I will be a swift witness a**gainst the sorcerers** [*the occult, devil worshipers, and so forth*], and against the **adulterers** [*those involved in sexual immorality*], and against **false swearers** [*including those who make but don't keep covenants*], and against **those that oppress the hireling in his wages** [*those who cheat their employees out of due wages*], **the widow and the fatherless** [*against those who oppress widows and orphans*], and **that turn aside the stranger** [*who reject foreigners; in other words, against those who are prejudiced against others because of race or ethnic origins*], and **fear not me**, saith the Lord of Hosts.

6 For **I am the Lord, I change not** [*I keep My word, My covenants*]; therefore [*this is the reason that*] ye sons of Jacob [*descendants of Abraham, Isaac, and Jacob*] are not consumed [*destroyed*].

Next, the Lord says that Israel has been a difficult people to work with over the centuries. Still, He invites them to repent and join with Him in salvation.

7 **Even from the days of your fathers** [*ancestors*] **ye are gone away from mine ordinances** [*you have rebelled and rejected My gospel*], and have not kept them. **Return unto me and I will return unto you**, saith the Lord of Hosts. But ye say: Wherein shall we return [*how can we return when we have never left You*]?

Next, we are given a powerful sermon on the importance of paying our tithes and offerings. It is interesting that this lesson applied directly to these Book of Mormon people. Perhaps many of them had not been paying their tithes and offerings.

8 **Will a man rob God? Yet ye have robbed me. But ye say: Wherein** [*how*] **have we robbed thee?** [*Answer*] **In tithes and offerings.**

9 **Ye are cursed with a curse** [*your progress is stopped*], **for** [*because*] **ye have robbed me**, even this whole nation.

Next, the Savior extends an invitation to repent. We often read and hear verse 10, but we need to continue on through verse 12 in order to catch the full beauty of the blessings promised to faithful Saints who are full tithe payers.

10 **Bring ye all the tithes into the storehouse** [*pay your tithing*], **that there may be meat in my house** [*so that the Church has the means to take care of its members*]; **and prove me now herewith** [*test Me*], saith the Lord of Hosts, **if I will not open you the windows of heaven** [*including revelation and spiritual guidance*], **and pour you out a blessing that there shall not be room enough to receive it.**

11 And **I will rebuke the devourer for your sakes**, and **he shall not destroy the fruits of your ground** [*your crops*]; **neither shall your vine cast her fruit before the time in the fields** [*your crops will grow and ripen as they are supposed to*], saith the Lord of Hosts.

12 And **all nations shall call you blessed**, for **ye shall be a delightsome land**, saith the Lord of Hosts.

Next, the Lord returns to scolding Israel for their rebellious attitude.

13 **Your words have been stout** [*strong*] **against me**, saith the Lord. **Yet ye say** [*you pretend innocence by saying*]: **What have we spoken against thee?**

14 **Ye have said: It is vain** [*useless*] **to serve God**, and **what doth it profit** [*what good has it done us*] **that we have kept his ordinances** [*laws and commandments*] **and that we have walked mournfully before the Lord of Hosts?**

Perhaps you've noticed that these verses sound a bit like a drama or stage production in which the Lord's covenant people are complaining that it doesn't do any good to live the gospel. No doubt this is exactly what Malachi intended as he delivered the message from God to his people.

Next, the people complain that the wicked prosper and that there are no real consequences for being wicked.

15 And now **we call the proud happy** [*the proud seem to be happy*]; yea, **they that work wickedness are set up** [*the wicked are prospering*]; yea, **they that tempt God are even delivered** [*those who openly defy God don't get smitten or punished*].

Perhaps these people, to whom Malachi is speaking, do not realize that the Lord is patient and doesn't immediately punish the wicked. If He did, there would be, in effect, no real agency, nor would this earth life be a valid test.

Next, the Lord tells the people that He understands their concerns and that He is keeping track of the righteous, and that their righteousness is being recorded in heaven.

16 **Then they that feared the Lord** [*the truly righteous people*] **spake** [*spoke*] **often one to another** [*supported and sustained one another*], **and the Lord hearkened and heard**; and **a book of remembrance was written before him** [*was recorded in heaven*] for them that feared [*respected and honored*] the Lord, and that thought upon his name [*who remembered and kept their covenants with the Lord*].

17 And **they shall be mine** [*they will enter celestial glory*], saith the Lord of Hosts, **in that day when I make up my jewels** [*on Final Judgment Day*]; and **I will spare them** as a man spareth his own son that serveth him.

18 **Then shall ye return** [*in the last days Israel will be gathered literally and spiritually*] **and discern between the righteous and the wicked** [*and will have the gift of the Holy Ghost to help them discern between good and evil, the ways of the righteous and the ways of the wicked*], **between him that serveth God and him that serveth him not**.

THIRD NEPHI 25

This chapter is one of the places where we are told that wicked people will be burned at the time of the Savior's Second Coming. You will see this in verse 1. Verse 2 is good news for the righteous people. They will not be burned but will continue to live as the Millennium starts, now that Jesus is here on earth. These people will live without disease or illness until they are 100 years old. Then they will die and be resurrected in the "twinkling of an eye" as mentioned in Doctrine and Covenants 101:31. The Millennium is the 1,000 years of peace on earth when Satan can't even tempt people.

This chapter can be compared with Malachi, chapter 4, the last chapter in the Old Testament. As was the case with Third Nephi, chapter 24, the Savior quotes Malachi so these Book of Mormon people can have his prophecy about things relating to the Second Coming. In this case, it is the prophecy of the destruction of the wicked, and also, that before the burning of the wicked, the Prophet Elijah will bring the priesthood keys of temple work which includes sealing families for eternity.

We often speak of the "Spirit of Elijah," which is a reference to the inspiration that comes upon people to seek out their genealogy and do the work for them in the temple.

1 FOR behold, **the day cometh that shall burn as an oven** [*the destruction of the wicked at the time of the Second Coming of Christ*]; and **all the proud, yea, and all that do wickedly** [*pride is the root cause of wickedness*], **shall be stubble** [*will be like dry straw ready to be burned*]; and the day that cometh [*the Second Coming*] shall burn them up [*they will be burned by the glory of the Lord; see D&C 5:19; 2 Nephi 12:10, 19, and 21*], saith the Lord of Hosts [*Christ*], that it shall leave them neither root nor branch.

In verse 2, next, the contrast between the righteous and the wicked when the Savior comes is given. For the righteous, the Second Coming will be a day of rejoicing and healing from the cares and worries of living in a wicked world.

2 **But unto you that fear my name** [*the righteous who respect God and strive to live the gospel*], **shall the Son of Righteousness arise** [*shall Christ come*] **with healing in his wings** [*with His healing power*]; and ye shall go forth and grow up as calves in the stall [*you will have peace and protection in the Millennium that follows*].

The imagery of growing up "as calves in the stall," in verse 2, above, has reference to calves that are kept safe and protected from animals that would kill them.

Next, the tables are turned. Whereas, until the Second Coming, the righteous were often trampled upon by the wicked, the wicked who were destroyed at the Second Coming will, in effect, be "ashes" under the feet of the righteous.

3 And ye shall tread down **the wicked**; for they **shall be ashes under the soles of your feet** in the day that I shall do this [*when I destroy the wicked*], saith the Lord of Hosts.

4 **Remember ye the law of Moses**, my servant, which I commanded unto him in Horeb [*another name for Sinai; see Bible Dictionary under "Horeb"*] **for all Israel, with the statutes and judgments** [*with the laws and commandments, as well as the punishments that go along with violating them*].

Verses 5–6, next, are some of the most famous and oft-quoted of all scripture. These people of Nephi are told that Elijah, the prophet who lived at the end of the Old Testament, will come before the Second Coming of the Lord, and that his coming will pave the way for family history and temple work. This, of course, will lead them to the opportunity to be sealed together as families for time and eternity. In other words, the doors will be opened for the crowning ordinances that lead to exaltation and becoming gods.

5 Behold, **I will send you Elijah the prophet before the coming of the great and dreadful day of the Lord** [*the Second Coming, a terrible and fearful day for the wicked*];

6 And **he shall turn the heart of the fathers to the children, and the heart of the children to their fathers** [*he will get family history and temple work going*], lest I come and smite the earth with a curse [*the "curse" of not being sealed together as families*].

Elijah has already come. He came to the Kirtland, Ohio, Temple, seven days after it was dedicated. His coming is recorded in Doctrine and Covenants 110. It took place on Sunday, April 3, 1836 (see heading of D&C 110).

THIRD NEPHI 26

In this chapter, the Nephites hear Jesus teach and explain all things from the beginning to the time of His future Second Coming and on to the Final Judgment Day. He will teach them about the laws of justice and mercy and the fact that He was chosen to be the Redeemer in premortality.

Mormon will then explain that Jesus taught far more to these people than is recorded in his abridgment or summary of the Nephite records. He will then summarize the Savior's ministry to these people in America.

1 AND now it came to pass that **when Jesus had told these things** [*including Isaiah's prophecies about the gathering of Israel in the last days and the prophecies of Malachi*] he expounded [*explained*] them unto the multitude; and **he did expound** [*teach and explain*] **all things unto them, both great and small** [*a reminder that details of the gospel are important too*].

2 And **he saith: These scriptures, which ye had not with you** [*Malachi chapters 3 and 4*], **the Father commanded that I should give unto you**; for it was wisdom in him that they should be given unto future generations.

3 And **he did expound all things, even from the beginning until the time that he should come in his glory** [*the Second Coming*]—yea, even **all things which should come upon the face of the earth**, even until **the elements should** [*will*] **melt with fervent heat** [*something that will happen at the time of the Second Coming, see 2 Peter 3:10 and 12; Mormon 9:2*], and **the earth should be wrapt together as a scroll** [*possibly a reference to the continents coming together to form one land (see D&C 133:23–24) in conjunction with the Second Coming*], and the heavens and the earth should pass away;

Perhaps referring to the fact that the earth as we know it will undergo a great change and become a "paradisiacal glory" for the Millennium. (See tenth article of faith.)

4 And **even unto the great and last day** [*Final Judgment Day*], **when all people**, and all kindreds [*extended families*], and all nations and tongues **shall stand before God, to be judged of their works**, whether they be good or whether they be evil—

5 **If they be good**, to the resurrection of everlasting life [*they will gain exaltation in celestial glory and get celestial bodies (see D&C 88:28) in the resurrection*]; and **if they be evil**, to the resurrection of damnation [*they will also be resurrected, but their progression will be stopped as far as the privilege of living with God is concerned*]; being on a parallel [*there is symmetry in this*], the one on the one hand and the other on the other hand, **according to** the **mercy**, and the **justice**, **and the holiness which is in Christ**, who was before the world began [*who became the Redeemer in premortality*].

The reference to the laws of justice and mercy, in verse 5, above, is significant. Ultimately, because of agency choices, each of us will come under the power of either the law of justice or the law of mercy.

If we have chosen "good," the law of mercy allows us to be forgiven of sin and made pure and clean, fit to comfortably live in the presence of God forever because of the Atonement of Christ.

If we have chosen "evil," we have placed ourselves under the law of justice, which requires that we suffer for our own sins (see D&C 19:15–17) and places us outside of celestial glory (see D&C 76:112).

Next, Mormon talks to us about what he has written in his abridgment, which includes the Savior's visit and teachings to the people of Nephi.

6 And now **there cannot be written in this book** [*Mormon's abridgment, which became the gold plates, delivered to Joseph Smith by Moroni*] **even a hundredth** part of the things which Jesus did truly teach unto the people;

7 But behold **the plates of Nephi** [*the Large Plates of Nephi; see "A Brief Explanation about the Book of Mormon" at the front of your Book of Mormon; also see 4 Nephi 1:19*] **do contain the more part of the things which he taught the people**.

Next, Mormon tells us what he intends to have happen with the account of Christ's ministry to the Nephites in America, which he included in what was to become the Book of Mormon.

8 And **these things** [*which include what we have in the Book of Mormon*] **have I written, which are a lesser part of the things which he taught the people**; and **I have written them to the intent that they may be brought again unto this people** [*the Lamanites*], **from the Gentiles** [*Joseph Smith and the members of the Restored Church*], according to the words which Jesus hath spoken.

Next, Mormon explains to us that if we are faithful to the knowledge and testimony brought to us by his writings in the Book of Mormon, then the "greater" things taught by Christ to these people will be given to us.

9 And **when they** [*referring to us, in our day*] **shall have received this** [*the "lesser part of the things which he taught the people," verse 8, above*], **which is expedient** [*necessary*] that they should have first, **to try** [*test*] **their faith**, and **if** it shall so be that **they shall believe these things then shall the greater things be made manifest unto them**.

10 And **if** it so be that **they will not believe these things, then shall the greater things be withheld** [*kept*] **from them**, unto their condemnation [*which will stop their eternal progression*].

Next, Mormon tells us that he was going to tell us more of what Jesus taught these people but was forbidden to do so by the Lord. As a result, he limits what he writes on these plates to what the Lord authorizes us to know at this point.

11 Behold, **I was about to write them**, all which were engraven upon the plates of Nephi, **but the Lord forbade it**, saying: I will try [*test*] the faith of my people.

12 **Therefore I, Mormon, do write the things which have been commanded me of the Lord**. And now I, Mormon, make an end of my sayings [*my own comments about what I have written*], and proceed to write the things which have been commanded me.

Next, Mormon tells us that the Savior taught the Nephites for three days, and then came often to them to teach them more and to have the sacrament with them.

13 Therefore, I would that ye should behold [*I desire that you should see*] that **the Lord truly did teach the people, for the space of three days; and after that he did show himself unto them oft, and did break bread oft, and bless it** [*the sacrament*], **and give it unto them**.

14 And it came to pass that **he did teach and minister unto the children of the multitude** of whom hath been spoken, and **he did loose their tongues** [*make it so they could talk and teach marvelous things*], **and they did speak unto their fathers great and marvelous things**, even greater than he had revealed unto the people; and he loosed their tongues that they could utter.

15 And it came to pass that **after he had ascended into** [*gone back up to*] **heaven—the second time that he showed himself unto them**, and had gone unto the Father, **after having healed all their sick**, and their **lame**, and opened the eyes of their **blind** and unstopped the ears of the **deaf**, and even had done **all manner of cures** among them, and **raised a man from the dead**, and had shown forth his power unto them, and had ascended unto the Father—

16 Behold, it came to pass **on the morrow** [*the next day*] that the multitude gathered themselves together, and **they both saw and heard these children**; yea, **even babes did open their mouths and utter** [*say, speak*] **marvelous things**; and the things which they did utter were forbidden that there should not any man write them.

The above reminds us that some things are so sacred that they cannot be or should not even be written; see verse 18, below.

Next, the Nephite twelve disciples go about their responsibilities as the leaders of the church that Jesus established among them.

17 And it came to pass that **the disciples whom Jesus had chosen began from that time forth to baptize and to teach as many as did come unto them**; and **as many as were baptized in the name of Jesus were filled with the Holy Ghost**.

18 And **many of them saw and heard unspeakable things, which are not lawful to be written**.

Next, we are told that these people lived what is called the "Law of Consecration," or the "United Order," as it is often called. In other words, they shared everything with each other.

19 And **they taught, and did minister one to another**; and **they had all things common among them** [*shared their possessions with each other*], **every man dealing justly** [*fairly and righteously*], **one with another**.

20 And it came to pass that **they did do all things even as Jesus had commanded them** [*which will lead to*

about two hundred years of wonderful peace and prosperity].

21 And **they who were baptized in the name of Jesus were called the church of Christ**.

THIRD NEPHI 27

We know exactly what the full name of the Church is, namely, "The Church of Jesus Christ of Latter-day Saints." But, as we begin this chapter, we see that there had been some confusion among the people as to exactly what the name of the Church should be that Jesus established during His visit to the Nephites.

It is interesting to watch the Savior as He patiently teaches these humble leaders of the Church. Obviously, He could have told them, along with other things He taught during the three days (3 Nephi 26:13), exactly what the name of the Church should be. But, He waits until they want to know.

As you have probably noticed, there are many things we are taught only after we have wondered about them. In fact, Doctrine and Covenants 76:15–18 teaches us that the Spirit can inspire us to wonder about some things as a way of preparing us to be taught.

Thus, the Nephite Twelve are prepared to be taught as we will see in the next verses.

1 AND it came to pass that as the disciples of Jesus were journeying and were preaching the things which they had both heard and seen, and were baptizing in the name of Jesus, it came to pass that **the disciples were gathered together and were united in mighty prayer and fasting**.

2 **And Jesus again showed himself unto them**, for they were praying unto the Father in his name; and Jesus came and stood in the midst of them, **and said unto them: What will ye that I shall give unto you?**

3 And **they said** unto him: **Lord, we will that thou wouldst** [*we would like You to*] **tell us the name whereby we shall call this church**; for there are disputations [*there have been arguments*] among the people concerning this matter.

As we continue, we see Jesus, who is the Master Teacher demonstrate the use of questions in effective teaching.

4 And the Lord said unto them: Verily, verily, I say unto you, **why is it that the people should murmur** [*grumble and complain*] **and dispute** [*argue*] **because of this thing** [*what the name of the Church should be*]?

5 **Have they not read the scriptures, which say ye must take upon you the name of Christ, which is my name?** For by this name shall ye be called at the last day;

6 And **whoso** [*whoever*] **taketh upon him my name, and endureth** [*stays faithful*] **to the end**, the same **shall be saved at the last day** [*on Judgment Day*].

Next, the Savior answers their question and then asks another question to point out how important it is that the Church be named after Him.

7 Therefore, **whatsoever ye shall do, ye shall do it in my name; therefore ye shall call the church in my name**; and ye shall call upon the Father in my name that he will bless the church for my sake.

8 And **how be it my church save** [*how can it be My church unless*] **it be called in my name?** For if a church be called in Moses' name then it be Moses' church; or if it be called in the name of a man then it be the church of a man; but if it be called in my name then it is my church, **if** it so be that **they are built upon my gospel**.

In other words, merely naming a church after Christ does not make it the true Church.

The early members of the Church in our dispensation also struggled with what to call the Church. When the Lord was ready, He gave them the answer. ("The Church of Jesus Christ of Latter-day Saints." See D&C 115:4.)

Jesus summarizes the above discussion in verses 9–11, next. He also points out in verse 9 that Heavenly Father hears our prayers, which is an important truth, because some people believe that other heavenly beings hear our prayers and then, if the prayers are good enough, they send them on to the Father. That is false doctrine!

9 Verily I say unto you, that **ye are built upon my gospel; therefore ye shall call whatsoever** [*whatever*] **things ye do call, in my name**; therefore, **if ye call upon the Father, for the church, if it be in my name the Father will hear you;**

10 And **if** it so be that **the church is built upon my gospel** then will the Father show forth his own works in it.

11 But **if it be not built upon my gospel**, and is built upon the works of men, or upon the works of the devil, verily I say unto you **they have joy in their works for a season**, and by and by the end cometh, and they are hewn [*cut*] down and cast into the fire, from whence [*where*] there is no return [*the Final Judgment is indeed final*].

12 For **their works do follow them, for it is because of their works** [*it is because they are false churches*] **that they are hewn down** [*destroyed*]; therefore remember the things that I have told you.

Next, in verses 13–21, Jesus gives a brief but beautiful summary of His gospel, which He has just taught these people.

13 Behold **I have given unto you my gospel**, and **this is the gospel** which I have given unto you—**that I came into the world to do the will of my Father, because my Father sent me.**

14 And **my Father sent me that I might be lifted up upon the cross** [*be crucified; in other words, perform the Atonement*]; and after that I had been lifted up upon the cross, **that I might draw all men unto me, that as I have been lifted up by men** [*crucified*]

even so should men be lifted up [*resurrected*] **by the Father, to stand before me** [*Christ is the final judge; see John 5:22*], **to be judged of their works**, whether they be **good or** whether they be **evil**—

15 And **for this cause have I been lifted up** [*this is why I carried out the Atonement; this is why I was lifted up upon the cross; this is why I was lifted up as a light to all the world*]; **therefore**, according to the power of the Father **I will draw all men unto me, that they may be judged according to their works**.

In other words, because of Christ's Atonement, all people are placed under His power and authority; He has power to save them; He has power to judge them; He has power to condemn them.

Next, Jesus emphasizes His power to save those who will come to the Father through Him. He speaks of the blessings of membership in His Church, of the importance of remaining faithful to the end, and of His role as our final judge.

When you have finished studying this summary, you will be more familiar with many words and phrases that are commonly used in the scriptures and in the teaching of our church leaders today. Once you are familiar with such gospel terms, you can be given an entire sermon in just a phrase or two.

16 And it shall come to pass, that **whoso repenteth and is baptized in my name shall be filled** [*with the Holy Ghost, with gospel light, with joy and happiness, with security and peace, etc.*]; and **if he endureth** [*remains faithful*] **to the end**, behold, **him will I hold guiltless** [*he will be pure and clean*] **before my Father** [*Christ has the power to make us completely pure and clean on Judgment Day*] at that day when **I shall** stand to **judge the world**.

A necessary part of the gospel of Christ is the warning of those who choose not to remain faithful to the covenants they have made with God. Thus, all will have ownership of their final status on Judgment Day.

17 And **he that endureth not unto the end**, the same is he that **is also hewn down and cast into the fire** [*they must suffer for their own sins*], **from whence they can no more return** [*their final placement on Judgment Day is a permanent, eternal placement*], **because of the justice of the Fathe**r [*because of the requirements of the law of justice*].

18 And **this is the word** [*the gospel*] **which he** [*the Father*] **hath given unto the children of men** [*to all people*]. And for this cause [*to make "immortality and eternal life"—Moses 1:39—available to all people*] he fulfilleth the words which he hath given, and he lieth not, but fulfilleth all his words.

19 And **no unclean thing can enter into his kingdom** [*celestial glory*]; therefore **nothing entereth into his rest** [*exaltation; see D&C 84:24*] **save it be** [*except*] **those who have washed** [*cleansed*] **their garments** [*their lives*] **in my blood** [*through My Atonement*], **because of their faith, and the repentance of all their sins, and their faithfulness unto the end**.

In effect, next, Jesus summarizes His "summary" above of what the gospel is.

20 Now **this is the commandment: Repent**, all ye ends of the earth [*everyone, everywhere*], and **come unto me** and **be baptized** in my name, **that ye may be sanctified** [*be made clean and pure, fit to be in the presence of God forever*] **by the reception of the Holy Ghost** [*by receiving and using the gift of the Holy Ghost*], **that ye may stand spotless** [*perfectly clean*] **before me** [*your final judge*] **at the last day** [*on Final Judgment Day*].

21 **Verily, verily** [*this is the whole point to what I have been saying*], I say unto you, **this is my gospel**; and **ye know the things that ye must do** in my church [*you are accountable*]; for **the works which ye have seen me do that shall ye also do** [*in other words, follow My example*]; for **that which ye have seen me do even that shall ye do**;

22 Therefore, **if ye do these things** blessed are ye, for **ye shall be lifted up at the last day** [*you will receive exaltation*].

Apparently, Jesus now addresses the Nephite twelve disciples and gives them instructions.

23 **Write the things which ye have seen and heard**, save [*except*] it be those which are forbidden.

24 **Write the works of this people**, which shall be [*continue to keep records of this people, including future events and doings*], even as hath been written [*the same as has been done in the past on the large plates of Nephi, etc.*], of that which hath been [*of things that have happened in the past*].

Next, the Savior explains that records kept by the Church on earth will be used in the process of the Final Judgment.

25 For behold, **out of the books which have been written, and which shall be written, shall this people be judged**, for by them shall their works be known unto men.

Jesus also explains that there are records kept in heaven that will likewise be used in the judgment.

26 And behold, **all things are written by the Father**; therefore **out of the books which shall be written shall the world be judged**.

Next, the Savior explains that there is an order of things on Judgment Day and that our leaders who hold priesthood keys will assist in judging.

27 And know ye that **ye shall be judges of this people, according to the judgment which I shall give unto you, which shall be just** [*no mistakes will be made in the Final Judgment, because Christ is ultimately the last word*]. Therefore, **what manner of men ought ye to be? Verily I say unto you, even as I am** [*a much-quoted and beautiful instruction from our Savior*].

The Savior now explains that He must leave and go to His Father. He gives final counsel about how to continue receiving guidance and revelation from God.

28 And **now I go unto the Father**.
And verily I say unto you, **whatsoev-
er things ye shall ask the Father in
my name shall be given unto you**.

29 Therefore, **ask, and ye shall re-
ceive; knock, and it shall be opened
unto you**; for **he that asketh, re-
ceiveth; and unto him that knock-
eth, it shall be opened**.

As you know from this and preceding chapters detailing the ministry of Christ to these Book of Mormon people, the Savior's heart has been full of sweet emotion as He met with and taught these humble people. Imagine the contrast between His reception among these Saints, who in their hearts begged Him to stay and teach them more (3 Nephi 17:5), compared to those who had recently mocked and jeered as they crucified Him. No wonder His joy is complete, as stated in verse 30, next.

Not only that, but He informs them of the joy in Heavenly Father's heart and in the hearts of the angels in heaven.

30 And now, behold, **my joy is great,
even unto fulness** [*complete*], **because
of you**, and also this generation; yea,
and even **the Father rejoiceth**, and
also all the holy angels, because of
you and this generation; for none of
them are lost [*every one of these people will
be saved in celestial glory*].

Next, Jesus makes sure that they have understood what he has just told them.

31 Behold, **I would that ye should
understand** [*I want to be sure you under-
stand*]; for **I mean them who are now
alive of this generation**; and **none
of them are lost**; and **in them I have
fulness of joy**.

"In them I have fulness of joy" can remind us of Isaiah's words, quoted by Abinadi in King Noah's court, when he explains that the Savior will have great joy and satisfaction through His saving of souls. Isaiah said, referring to Christ, "He shall see the travail of his soul [*the results of His Atonement*], and shall be satisfied [*will have much satisfaction and joy*]." See Mosiah 14:11 and Isaiah 53:11.

Next, Jesus expresses His sadness because of the souls who will be lost in future generations of these people because they will reject Him. He explains why they will go astray and fall away.

32 **But behold, it sorroweth me
because of the fourth generation
from this generation**, for they are
led away captive by him [*Satan*] even
as was the son of perdition [*this ap-
pears to be a reference to Judas Iscariot; see
John 17:12*]; for **they will sell me for
silver and for gold** [*materialism*], **and
for that which moth doth corrupt**
[*destroy*] [*worldliness, temporary pleasures,
earthly priorities*] and which thieves can
break through and steal [*which can be
taken away*]. And in that day will I visit
them [*the people in the last days of the Book of
Mormon*], even in turning their works
upon their own heads [*they will be de-
stroyed by the results of their own choices*].

Before leaving, the Savior summarizes the narrow path, in other words, the covenant path, that will lead to salvation and warns against the many ways that lead us away from God. Notice how "strait" is spelled. It is not "straight." "Strait" means "narrow."

33 And it came to pass that when Jesus had ended these sayings he said unto his disciples: **Enter ye in at the strait** [*narrow, restricted, only*] **gate**; for **strait is the gate, and narrow is the way that leads to life** [*eternal life, exaltation*], and few there be that find it; but **wide is the gate, and broad the way which leads to death** [*spiritual death; being cut off from living in God's presence forever*], and many there be that travel therein, until the night cometh [*final Judgment Day*], wherein no man can work [*when it is everlastingly too late*].

THIRD NEPHI 28

Perhaps you have heard of the Three Nephites. They are three of the Nephite Twelve Disciples who have not died yet. They go around doing good wherever they are needed. They will stay alive until the Second Coming of Christ and then they will die and be resurrected in an instant and join Him as He comes to earth to minister for a thousand years during the Millennium.

This chapter is perhaps best known for its information about these three Nephite Apostles. They were "translated," which means that their mortal bodies were changed. They are no longer subject to pain and death and can be wherever they want to be by praying to be there.

As we begin this chapter, the Savior asks the twelve Nephite disciples individually if they have any special requests of Him. We see His tenderness as He responds to their requests.

1 AND it came to pass when Jesus had said these words [*as recorded in chapter 27*], **he spake** [*spoke*] **unto his disciples, one by one**, saying unto them: **What is it that ye desire of me, after that I am gone to the Father?**

Next, nine of the twelve request the privilege of returning speedily to the Savior when they die. Their desires are granted.

2 And **they all spake, save it were three** [*except for three of them*], saying: **We desire that after we have lived unto the age of man** [*seventy-two years of age according to verse 3, below*], that our ministry, wherein thou hast called us, may have an end, **that we may speedily come unto thee in thy kingdom**.

Notice how Jesus quickly puts them at ease regarding their request.

3 And he said unto them: **Blessed are ye because ye desired this thing of me**; therefore, **after that ye are seventy and two years old ye shall come unto me in my kingdom**; and with me ye shall find rest.

Next, He turns His attention to the three who had not dared say what they wanted.

4 And when he had spoken unto them [*the nine*], **he turned himself unto the three**, and said unto them: **What will ye** [*what do you want*] **that I should do unto you, when I am gone unto the Father**?

5 And **they sorrowed in their hearts** [*probably meaning that they were worried about what they wanted to ask*], **for they durst not speak unto** [*didn't dare tell*] **him the thing which they desired.**

Notice again how kind and tender the Savior is. He immediately tells them that John the Beloved Apostle (one of the Twelve Apostles), in the Holy Land, had requested the same thing. Imagine how this would put these disciples' minds at ease!

6 And **he said** unto them: Behold, **I know your thoughts**, and **ye have desired the thing which John, my beloved**, who was with me in my ministry, before that I was lifted up [*crucified*] by the Jews, **desired of me.**

7 **Therefore, more blessed are ye** [*you will yet have many more blessings in mortality*], **for ye shall never taste of death** [*This does not mean that they will not die; rather that they will die and be resurrected immediately at the time of the Second Coming (see verse 40). Thus, they won't "taste" death, which often includes the aches and pains leading up to death. (See verse 8, below.)*]; **but ye shall live to behold** [*see*] **all the doings of the Father unto the children of men** [*on earth*], even **until** all things shall be fulfilled according to the will of the Father, when **I shall come in my glory** with the powers of heaven [*the Second Coming*].

Next, Mormon tells us some of the changes that were made in their mortal bodies. In effect, this is a description of a "translated" being.

Before we continue, let's talk about the difference between the words "translated" and "transfigured." "Translated" means being changed so they can continue living as mortals over a much-extended period of time. Moses and Elijah were both "translated," which allowed them to remain alive until they were resurrected at the time of Christ's Resurrection. As translated beings, they were privileged to minister to the Savior on the Mount of Transfiguration several months before His Crucifixion. (See Matthew 17:3.)

"Transfigured" means a temporary change that allows someone to be in the presence of the Lord without being destroyed by His glory. An example of this was Moses when he saw the Lord. (See Moses 1:11.) It can also mean the radiance that comes upon an individual on sacred occasions when the Spirit of the Lord is upon him or her in extra measure.

8 And **ye shall never endure the pains of death**; but **when I shall come in my glory** [*the Second Coming*] **ye shall be changed** [*resurrected*] **in the twinkling of an eye from mortality to immortality**; and **then shall ye be blessed in the kingdom of my Father** [*you will be blessed with exaltation in celestial glory; see verse 10, below*].

9 And again, **ye shall not have pain** while ye shall dwell in the flesh [*during mortality*], **neither sorrow save** [*except*] **it be for the sins of the world**; and all this will I do because of the thing which ye have desired of me, for **ye have desired that ye might bring the souls of men unto me**, while the world shall stand [*while the world exists, up to the Second Coming*].

10 And for this cause **ye shall have fulness of joy** [*exaltation*]; and **ye shall sit down in the kingdom of my Father**; yea, **your joy shall be full**, even as the Father hath given me fulness of joy [*you will be like I am; joint heirs with Christ*]; and **ye shall be even as I am**, and **I am even as the Father** [*in other words, you will become gods*]; and the Father and I are one;

11 And **the Holy Ghost beareth record** [*bears witness, bears testimony*] **of the Father and me**; and the Father giveth the Holy Ghost unto the children of men [*people*], because of me [*because of My gospel, which includes baptism and confirmation*].

Next, Jesus finalizes the blessings granted to each of the Twelve.

12 And it came to pass that when Jesus had spoken these words, **he touched every one of them with his finger save** [*except*] it were **the three who were to tarry** [*remain on earth until the Second Coming*], **and then he departed**.

13 And behold, **the heavens were opened, and they** [*the three; see verse 36*] **were caught up into heaven**, and **saw and heard unspeakable things** [*things too sacred to be talked about or that cannot be described with words; see verse 14, next*].

14 And it **was forbidden them that they should utter** [*talk about it*]**; neither was it given unto them power that they could utter the things which they saw and heard**;

15 And **whether they were in the body or out of the body, they could not tell**; for **it did seem unto them like a transfiguration of them, that they were changed from this body of flesh into an immortal state**, that they could behold the things of God.

16 But it came to pass that **they did again minister upon the face of the earth** [*they returned to earth after they had temporarily been taken up*]; nevertheless they did not minister of the things which they had heard and seen, because of the commandment which was given them in heaven.

17 And now, **whether they were mortal or immortal, from the day of their transfiguration, I know not**;

As indicated in verse 17, above, at this point in his engraving of the plates, Mormon does not know if the Three Nephites' bodies were changed to immortal bodies or not. In verses 36–39, he will explain that by the time he wrote those verses, he was told by the Lord that these men were still mortal and had what we call "translated" bodies.

18 But **this much I know**, according to the record which hath been given—**they did go forth upon the face of the land, and did minister unto all the people**, uniting as many to the church as would believe in their preaching; baptizing them, and as many as were baptized did receive the Holy Ghost.

One would think that enemies of the Three Nephites would catch on to the fact that they could not be stopped. Obviously, as indicated in the next verses, wickedness does not promote clear thinking or smart behavior.

19 And **they were cast into prison** by them who did not belong to the church. **And the prisons could not hold them**, for they were rent in twain [*were torn apart, a bit expensive for the local tax payers*].

20 And **they were cast down into the earth** [*into holes the wicked people dug to throw them into*]; but they did smite the earth with the word of God, insomuch that **by his power they were delivered out of the depths of the earth**; and **therefore they could not dig pits sufficient** [*deep enough*] **to hold them**.

21 And **thrice** [*three times*] **they were cast into a furnace and received no harm**.

22 And **twice were they cast into a den of wild beasts**; and behold **they did play with the beasts** as a child with a suckling lamb [*a baby, nursing, lamb*], and **received no harm**.

23 And it came to pass that **thus they did go forth among all the people of Nephi, and did preach the gospel of Christ unto all people upon the face of the land**; and they were converted unto the Lord, and were united unto the church of Christ [*joined the Church*], and thus the people of that generation were blessed, according to the word of Jesus.

The Three Nephites continued to serve and teach among the Nephites for about three hundred years before the Lord took them away to serve elsewhere on earth. (See Mormon 1:13, combined with the chronology note given in Mormon, chapter 1 in the Book of Mormon.) As Mormon finishes telling us about the Three Nephites, he gives a few more fascinating details about them. He has seen them, and they have been a blessing to him.

24 And now **I, Mormon, make an end of speaking concerning these things for a time**.

25 Behold, **I was about to write the names of those who were never to taste of death** [*the Three Nephites*], **but the Lord forbade**; therefore I write them not, for they are hid from the world.

26 But behold, **I have seen them, and they have ministered unto me.**

27 And behold **they will be among the Gentiles** [*all people who are not Jews*], **and the Gentiles shall know them not** [*won't recognize them*].

28 **They will also be among the Jews, and the Jews shall know them not**.

29 And it shall come to pass, when the Lord seeth fit in his wisdom that **they shall minister unto all the scattered tribes of Israel, and unto all nations, kindreds, tongues and people, and shall bring out of them unto Jesus many souls, that their desire may be fulfilled** [*their desire to remain on earth and bring souls unto Christ;*

see verse 9, above], and also because of the convincing power of God which is in them.

Next, Mormon tells us how the Three Nephites travel from place to place.

30 And they are as the angels of God, **and if they shall pray unto the Father in the name of Jesus they can show themselves unto whatsoever man it seemeth them good** [*whoever they want to*].

31 Therefore, **great and marvelous works shall be wrought** [*accomplished*] **by them**, before the great and coming day when all people must surely stand before the judgment-seat of Christ;

32 Yea even **among the Gentiles shall there be a great and marvelous work wrought by them**, before that judgment day.

Next, Mormon teaches the importance of studying and following the words of the scriptures.

33 And **if ye had all the scriptures which give an account of all the marvelous works of Christ, ye would**, according to the words of Christ, **know that these things must surely come.**

34 And **wo be unto him that will not hearken unto** [*listen and obey*] **the words of Jesus, and also to them** [*including our general authorities and missionaries today*] **whom he hath chosen and sent among them; for whoso receiveth not** [*rejects*] **the words of Jesus and the words of those whom he hath sent receiveth not him**; and **therefore he will not receive them** [*into celestial glory*] at the last day [*on the Final Judgment Day*];

35 And **it would be better for them if they had not been born**. For **do ye suppose that ye can get rid of the justice of an offended God, who hath been trampled under feet of men** [*rejected, mocked, and crucified*]**, that thereby salvation might come** [*to make salvation available to all people*]?

The context "And it would be better for them if they had not been born," in verse 35, above, seems to be saying, in effect, do you think that you can be wicked, reject Christ and His gospel, and get away with it? When the wicked realize what they have done, they will wish they had not been born.

We know from Doctrine and Covenants 76:89 that even the telestial kingdom is far better than we can imagine.

Next, Mormon gives a few more details about the Three Nephites, which he has learned since his previous engravings about them. This is a reminder to us that engraving is a painstaking endeavor, and that it is apparently an ongoing project for Mormon.

36 And now behold, **as I spake concerning** those [*the Three Nephites*] whom the Lord hath chosen, yea, even **three** who were caught up into the heavens, **that I knew not whether they were cleansed from mortality to immortality**—

37 But behold, **since I wrote, I have inquired** [*asked*] **of the Lord**, and **he hath made it manifest unto me that there must needs be** [*had to be*] **a change wrought** [*take place*] **upon their bodies**, or else it needs be that they must taste of death [*otherwise, they would die when they get old*];

38 **Therefore**, that they might not taste of death **there was a change wrought** [*made*] **upon their bodies**, that they might not suffer pain nor sorrow save it were for the sins of the world.

39 Now **this change was not equal to that which shall take place at the last day** [*it was not equal to resurrection into an immortal body*]; **but there was a change wrought upon them, insomuch that** [*such that*] **Satan could have no power over them**, that **he could not tempt them**; and **they were sanctified** [*made pure and holy; calling and election made sure*] **in the flesh** [*here in mortality*], that they were holy, and that **the powers of the earth could not hold them**.

In other words, they can move about as they wish, perhaps even between heaven and earth. Also, it will not be "dangerous" to their salvation for them to remain on earth for such a long time.

40 And **in this state** [*translated condition*] **they were to remain until the judgment day of Christ** [*apparently meaning the judgments and destructions upon the wicked at the second coming; see verses 7–8*]; and **at that day they were to receive a greater change** [*resurrection*], **and to be received into the kingdom of the Father** to go no more out [*forever*], but **to dwell with God eternally in the heavens**.

THIRD NEPHI 29

As Mormon finishes the Book of Third Nephi, he now gives his own brief summary and adds his own testimony to that of the Savior. He is a great prophet and you can feel his goodness as he carefully warns all of us who have the gospel not to ignore its teachings.

In 3 Nephi 21:1, and elsewhere, Jesus told the people of Nephi that the coming forth of the Book of Mormon would be a sign that the last days' gathering of Israel had begun. The Book of Mormon has now come forth, through the Prophet Joseph Smith, and the last days are here. This dispensation is the one in which the Second Coming will take place.

1 AND **now behold, I** [*Mormon*] **say unto you that when the Lord shall see fit, in his wisdom, that these sayings** [*the Book of Mormon*] **shall come unto the Gentiles** [*everyone but the Jews, in this context*] according to his word, **then ye may know that the covenant which the Father hath made with the children of Israel** [*covenant Israel; we are part of them*], **concerning their restoration to the lands of their inheritance, is already beginning to be fulfilled**.

2 **And ye may know that the words of the Lord, which have been spoken by the holy prophets, shall all**

be fulfilled; and ye need not say that the Lord delays his coming unto the children of Israel.

3 **And ye need not imagine in your hearts that the words which have been spoken are vain** [*won't be fulfilled*], for behold, **the Lord will remember** [*keep*] **his covenant** which he hath made unto his people of the house of Israel [*to gather them in the last days*].

4 **And when ye shall see these sayings** [*the Book of Mormon*] **coming forth among you**, then **ye need not any longer spurn** [*scoff*] **at the doings of the Lord**, for **the sword of his justice is in his right hand** [*covenant hand; in other words, the promised destructions of the wicked will also take place; therefore, sinners beware*]; and behold, at that day, **if ye shall spurn at his doings he will cause that it** [*the sword of justice; the destruction of the wicked*] **shall soon overtake you**.

5 Wo [*trouble*] unto him that spurneth at the doings of the Lord; yea, **wo unto him that shall deny the Christ and his works**!

Verses 6–7, next, deal directly with the false philosophies and teachings of many in our day, because they deny the gifts of the Spirit. (See D&C 46:13–25, 1 Corinthians 12:3–11, and Moroni 10:9–18 for lists of the gifts of the Spirit.)

6 Yea, **wo unto him that shall deny the revelations of the Lord, and that shall say the Lord no longer worketh by revelation**, or by **prophecy**, or by **gifts**, or by **tongues**, or by **healings**, or by the power of the **Holy Ghost!**

7 Yea, and **wo unto him that shall say at that day, to get gain** [*to be popular and to earn money preaching what people want to hear in place of the gospel of Christ; priestcraft; see Alma 1:16*], **that there can be no miracle wrought by Jesus Christ; for he that doeth this shall become like unto the son of perdition, for whom there was no mercy**, according to the word of Christ!

Next, Mormon warns those who fight against and mock the Jews, or any Israelites.

8 Yea, and **ye need not any longer hiss** [*as prophesied in 1 Nephi 19:14*], **nor spurn** [*avoid, shun*], **nor make game of the Jews, nor any of the remnant of the house of Israel**; for behold, **the Lord remembereth** [*will keep*] **his covenant** [*promise*] **unto them**, and he will do unto them according to that which he hath sworn [*promised*].

In other words, He will gather them back into the Church, as well as gather them back to the lands of their inheritance.

Next, Mormon finally warns that no one can stop the Lord in carrying out His plans and promises.

9 **Therefore ye need not suppose that ye can turn the right hand of the Lord unto the left** [*make the Lord change His plans*], **that he may not execute** [*carry out*] **judgment unto the**

fulfilling of the covenant which he hath made unto the house of Israel [*including that He will gather them back unto Himself in the last days*].

THIRD NEPHI 30

In this final chapter of Third Nephi, the Savior, through Mormon, issues a gentle but firm invitation to the Gentiles to come unto Him.

1 **HEARKEN, O ye Gentiles, and hear the words of Jesus Christ, the Son of the living God**, which he hath commanded me [*Mormon*] that I should speak concerning you, for, behold he commandeth me that I should write, saying:

2 **Turn, all ye Gentiles, from your wicked ways**; and **repent of your evil doings**, of your **lyings** and **deceivings** [*fraud, dishonesty*], and of your **whoredoms** [*sexual immorality*], and of your **secret abominations**, and your **idolatries** [*worshipping things other than God*], and of your **murders**, and your **priestcrafts** [*twisting and changing the true gospel so that people like what you preach and give you money*], and your **envyings**, and your **strifes**, and **from all your wickedness and abominations** [*extra-bad wickedness*], and **come unto me**, and **be baptized** in my name, that ye may **receive a remission** [*be forgiven*] **of your sins**, and **be filled with the Holy Ghost**, that ye may **be numbered** [*joined*] **with my people who are of the house of Israel** [*covenant Israel*].

FOURTH NEPHI

THE BOOK OF NEPHI

Fourth Nephi is a very short book in the Book of Mormon. It has just forty-nine verses and covers about 285 years. It lets you see the huge difference between the results of personal righteousness upon an entire society (verses 1–23) and the devastating results of personal wickedness upon a nation (verses 24–47).

Mormon took his material for this book from the writings of four record keepers: Nephi, the son of Nephi, the disciple of Christ; Amos, the son of Nephi; and Amos and Ammaron, the sons of the first Amos. (See 4 Nephi 1:19–21, 47–48.)

FOURTH NEPHI 1

There are many possible lessons you could learn from this chapter. For our purposes, we will list things that help a nation remain righteous and make it so that the citizens can lead pleasant and prosperous lives. Then we will list some steps, summarized by Mormon, beginning with verse 24, that show how Satan goes about destroying and taking apart a righteous society. These steps become a pattern for how the devil fools people into following him and serve as a warning for us to avoid falling into his traps.

Perhaps you have wondered what would happen if everyone in our current world were truly converted to the gospel of Jesus Christ and started living the gospel faithfully every day. The answer comes in verses 1–23, next, as we see that within about two years after the Savior's departure, everyone in the Book of Mormon lands was converted.

As we go along, notice the things that righteous people do to make sure they stay strong in the gospel. We will point these things out by using ***bold italics***.

1 AND it came to pass that **the thirty and fourth year passed away, and also the thirty and fifth**, and behold the disciples of Jesus had formed a church of Christ in all the lands round about. And as many as did come unto them, and ***did truly repent of their sins, were baptized in the name of Jesus; and they did also receive the Holy Ghost.***

2 And it came to pass **in the thirty and sixth year, the people were all converted unto the Lord**, upon all the face of the land, **both Nephites and Lamanites**, and there were ***no contentions and disputations*** [*no arguing and fighting and quarreling*] ***among them***, and ***every man did deal justly*** [*fairly*] ***one with another***.

3 And ***they had all things common*** [*they shared everything*] ***among them*** [*they were unselfish*]; therefore ***there were not rich and poor, bond*** [*servants, slaves*]

and free, but they were all made free, and partakers of the heavenly gift [*the special blessings and gifts of the Spirit that accompany the gift of the Holy Ghost among faithful Saints*].

4 And it came to pass that **the thirty and seventh year** passed away also, and there still continued to be peace in the land.

5 And there were ***great and marvelous works wrought*** [*performed*] by the disciples of Jesus, insomuch that ***they did heal the sick, and raise the dead, and cause the lame*** [*crippled*] ***to walk, and the blind to receive their sight, and the deaf to hear; and all manner of*** [*all kinds of*] ***miracles did they work among the children of men*** [*the people*]; and in nothing did they work miracles save it were in the name of Jesus. [*No false prophets and false miracles were among them.*]

In verse 6, next, you can almost see Mormon thumbing through the records as he engraved his gold plates, to see what he should record next. We get the sense that, because of the righteousness of these people, it was basically the same wonderful story throughout many years.

6 And thus did the **thirty and eighth year** pass away, and also the **thirty and ninth**, and **forty and first**, and the **forty and second**, yea, even until **forty and nine years had passed away**, and also the **fifty and first**, and the **fifty and second**; yea, and even **until fifty and nine years had passed away**.

7 And ***the Lord did prosper them exceedingly in the land***; yea, insomuch that they did build cities again where there had been cities burned [*during the destruction of the wicked at the time of the Crucifixion of the Savior; see 3 Nephi 8–9*].

8 Yea, even **that great city Zarahemla did they cause to be built again**.

9 But there were **many cities which had been sunk**, and waters came up in the stead thereof; therefore **these cities could not be renewed**.

10 And now, behold, it came to pass that ***the people of Nephi did wax*** [*grow*] ***strong***, and ***did multiply exceedingly fast*** [*had large families*], and ***became an exceedingly fair and delightsome people***.

11 And ***they were married, and given in marriage*** [*the institution of marriage and family was held to be sacred and vital to society*], and were ***blessed according to the multitude of the promises which the Lord had made unto them***.

12 And **they did not walk any more after the performances and ordinances of the law of Moses** [*their religion was not superficial, as was the case with many who lived the law of Moses*]; but ***they did walk after*** [*keep*] ***the commandments which they had received from their Lord and their God*** [*including those given in the Sermon on the Mount; see 3 Nephi 12–14*], ***continuing in fasting***

and prayer, and in ***meeting together oft both to pray and to hear the word of the Lord*** [*they attended their meetings regularly*].

13 And it came to pass that there was ***no contention among all the people***, in all the land; but there were ***mighty miracles wrought among the disciples of Jesus.***

In verse 14, next, Mormon tells us that nine of the Nephite Twelve Disciples finally passed away. You may recall that nine were given the privilege of living until they reached seventy-two years of age, and then dying and joining the Savior in His kingdom in heaven (3 Nephi 28:3). He also informs us that the Three Nephites continued to minister and live among the people, and that other disciples were called to replace the others as they passed away, as is done with the Apostles in the Church today.

14 And it came to pass that **the seventy and first year** passed away, and also **the seventy and second year**, yea, and in fine [*in summary*], till the **seventy and ninth year had passed away**; yea, even **an hundred years had passed away, and the disciples of Jesus, whom he had chosen, had all gone to the paradise of God, save** [*except*] **it were the three who should tarry** [*stay alive on earth*]**; and there were other disciples ordained in their stead**; and also many of that generation had passed away.

15 And it came to pass that ***there was no contention in the land, because of the love of God which did dwell in the hearts of the people.***

16 And there were ***no envyings, nor strifes, nor tumults*** [*big disturbances*], ***nor whoredoms*** [*sexual immorality*], ***nor lyings, nor murders, nor any manner of lasciviousness*** [*sexual immorality*]; and ***surely there could not be a happier people among all the people who had been created by the hand of God.***

Among the things in a Zion society (one in which all the people live the gospel faithfully), which Mormon points out, next, in verse 17, is that among truly righteous people there are no class distinctions, no "manner of "-ites," as he puts it. This is one of the most difficult Christlike qualities for people to achieve.

17 There were ***no robbers, nor murderers, neither were there Lamanites, nor any manner of -ites***; but ***they were in one*** [*united*], ***the children of Christ*** [*true followers of Christ*], and ***heirs to the kingdom of God*** [*they earned celestial glory*].

18 And how blessed were they! For ***the Lord did bless them in all their doings***; yea, even they were ***blessed and prospered*** until an **hundred and ten years had passed away**; and the first generation from Christ had passed away, and there was ***no contention in all the land.***

Remember, the word "contention" in the last line of verse 18, above, means arguing, quarreling, fighting, being mean to one another, and so forth. Contention not only makes life miserable, but it also drives the Holy Ghost away and makes it so that He can't help, inspire, teach, warn, and comfort people. Have you noticed how many times "no contention" has been mentioned in relation to becoming a true follower of Christ, here in the Book of Mormon? This is one of the highest manifestations of self-control and Christlike living. Satan is a master at stirring up contention among well-meaning Saints, as well as among the deeply wicked.

Next, in verses 19–23, Mormon explains who the record keepers were during these years of peace and provides a brief transition between the years of righteousness and prosperity and the beginning of the downfall of these people.

19 And it came to pass that **Nephi** [*who had prayed the day before Christ was born (3 Nephi 1:11–13), who was chosen as one of the twelve Nephite disciples (3 Nephi 11:18–22), and who kept the Nephite records (3 Nephi 23:7–8)*], **he that kept this last record**, (and he kept it upon the plates of Nephi [*the Large Plates of Nephi*]) **died**, and **his son Amos kept it in his stead** [*in his place*]; and he kept it upon the plates of Nephi [*the Large Plates of Nephi*] also.

20 And **he kept it eighty and four years**, and **there was still peace in the land, save** [*except*] **it were a small part of the people who had revolted from the church and taken upon them the name of Lamanites**; therefore there began to be Lamanites again in the land.

It is important to be aware that one of the ways the devil entices some members to distance themselves from the leaders of the Church and from the faithful members is to get them to pattern their lives after other cultures who have rejected God. We see this happening among the Nephites in verse 20, above, and we see it among some members of the Church in our day. Their subculture becomes a substitute for the Church in their lives.

21 And it came to pass that **Amos died also**, (and it was **an hundred and ninety and four years from the coming of Christ**) and **his son Amos** [*Nephi's grandson*] **kept the record in his stead** [*in his place*]; and he also kept it upon the plates of Nephi; and it was also written in the book of Nephi [*Fourth Nephi*], which is this book.

A quote from the *Book of Mormon Student Manual*, used in the institutes of religion of the Church, gives helpful commentary regarding the "book of Nephi" mentioned in verse 21, above.

"When the Book of Mormon was first printed, 3 and 4 Nephi were each called Book of Nephi. In 1879 Elder Orson Pratt, authorized to prepare a new edition of the Book of Mormon for the Church, added Third and Fourth to the two books in order to help distinguish one from the other" (*Book of Mormon Student Manual* [1996], 128).

At this point in the Book of Mormon, we are at about AD 201, as Mormon explains in verse 22, next.

22 And it came to pass that **two hundred years had passed away**; and the second generation had all passed away save it were a few.

23 And now I, Mormon, would that ye should know that ***the people had***

multiplied, insomuch that they were spread upon all the face of the land, and that ***they had become exceedingly rich, because of their prosperity in Christ*** [*because of the blessings of the Lord, which came as a result of the righteousness of their society*].

In studying the last half of Fourth Nephi, we will follow Mormon's description of the downfall of this righteous nation, using a different format than we did to highlight the elements of a Zion society in verses 1–23.

We will list the steps that Mormon points out and will bold the actual text of the Book of Mormon that describes these tools of the devil, which he uses to destroy nations and individuals. You will no doubt see additional steps to the ones we list.

Step 1. Pride and Materialism.

24 And now, in this **two hundred and first year** there began to be among them those who were **lifted up in pride**, such as the **wearing of costly apparel** [*clothing*], and all manner of **fine pearls**, and of the **fine things of the world**.

Step 2. Selfishness.

25 And from that time forth **they did have their goods and their substance no more common among them** [*they didn't share their possessions equally with each other*].

Step 3. Divide into classes; look down on others; priestcraft; apostasy.

26 **And they began to be divided into classes** [*different social groups*]; and they began to **build up churches unto themselves to get gain**, and began to **deny the true church of Christ**.

Step 4. Pick and choose which parts of the gospel to live.

Step 5. Allow, but not necessarily participate in, wickedness in society.

Step 6. Lower the standards of the Church as far as the sacrament and worthiness is concerned.

27 And it came to pass that when **two hundred and ten years had passed away** there were many churches in the land; yea, there were many churches which professed to know the Christ, and yet **they did deny the more parts of his gospel**, insomuch that **they did receive** [*accept*] **all manner of wickedness**, and **did administer that which was sacred** [*the sacrament*] **unto him to whom it had been forbidden because of unworthiness**.

Step 7. Start desiring to be wicked.

28 And **this church did multiply exceedingly** [*grow fast*] **because of iniquity** [*wickedness and sin*], and because of the power of **Satan** who **did get hold upon their hearts** [*symbolic of feelings and desires; in other words, they wanted to be wicked*].

Step 8. Put pressure on members of the Church who still want to live the gospel with exactness. Many in society begin trying to impose their "beliefs" upon faithful Saints.

29 And again, there was another church which denied the Christ; and **they did persecute the true church**

of Christ, because of their humility and their belief in Christ; and they did despise [*look down on*] them because of the many miracles which were wrought among them.

30 Therefore **they did exercise power and authority over the disciples of Jesus** [*the Three Nephites*] who did tarry with them, and they did **cast them into prison**; but by the power of the word of God, which was in them, **the prisons were rent in twain** [*torn apart*], **and they went forth doing mighty miracles among them**.

Step 9. Become angry at the Lord's anointed, the leaders of the Church.

31 Nevertheless, and notwithstanding [*in spite of*] all these miracles, **the people did harden their hearts, and did seek to kill them** [*the Three Nephites*], even as the Jews at Jerusalem sought to kill Jesus, according to his word.

Next, Mormon tells us of several attempts of the wicked to destroy the Three Nephites. It is a reminder that the wicked lose their ability to think reasonably as they surrender their agency to Satan.

32 And **they did cast them into furnaces of fire**, and they came forth receiving no harm.

33 And **they also cast them into dens of wild beasts**, and they did play with the wild beasts even as a child with a lamb; and they did come forth from among them, receiving no harm.

Step 10. Select leaders whose values reflect their own desires for personal wickedness, support them, and follow them in persecuting the righteous.

34 Nevertheless, **the people did harden their hearts**, for they were **led by many priests and false prophets** to build up many churches, and **to do all manner of iniquity** [*they first accepted evil into their culture (verse 27), and now they are participating in it themselves*]. And **they did smite upon** [*persecute, physically harm*] **the people of Jesus**; but the people of Jesus did not smite again. And **thus they did dwindle in unbelief and wickedness**, from year to year, even until **two hundred and thirty years** had passed away.

35 And now it came to pass in this year, yea, in the **two hundred and thirty and first year**, there was **a great division** [*separation*] **among the people**.

36 And it came to pass that in this year there arose a people who were called **the Nephites**, and they **were true believers in Christ**; and among them there were those who were called by the Lamanites—Jacobites, and Josephites, and Zoramites;

37 Therefore **the true believers in Christ, and the true worshipers of Christ**, (among whom were the three disciples of Jesus [*the Three Nephites*] who should tarry) **were called Nephites, and Jacobites, and Josephites, and Zoramites**.

Step 11. Openly and blatantly rebel against standards set by the scriptures, and intentionally teach their children to do the same.

38 And it came to pass that **they who rejected the gospel were called Lamanites, and Lemuelites, and Ishmaelites**; and they did not dwindle in unbelief, but **they did wilfully rebel against the gospel of Christ**; and **they did teach their children that they should not believe**, even as their fathers, from the beginning, did dwindle.

Step 12. Teach ethnic hatred to their children, in other words, teach them to hate people of other races and cultures.

39 And it was because of the wickedness and abomination of their fathers, even as it was in the beginning. And **they were taught to hate the children of God, even as the Lamanites were taught to hate the children of Nephi from the beginning**.

Step 13. The majority of the people desire wickedness and evil.

40 And it came to pass that **two hundred and forty and four years** had passed away, and thus were the affairs of the people. And **the more wicked part of the people did wax** [*grow*] **strong, and became exceedingly more numerous than were the people of God**.

Step 14. Continue to make own rules.

41 And they did still continue to **build up churches unto themselves** [*making up their own teachings rather than holding firmly to the gospel of Jesus Christ*], and adorn them with all manner of precious things. And thus did **two hundred and fifty years** pass away, and also **two hundred and sixty years**.

Step 15. Build up secret combinations and support murder and terrorism to gain desired goals.

42 And it came to pass that **the wicked part of the people began again to build up the secret oaths and combinations of Gadianton**.

Step 16. The few remaining righteous begin to follow the same pattern the wicked are following, thinking that because they are not as wicked, they are somehow righteous.

43 And also the people who were called **the people of Nephi began to be proud** in their hearts, because of their exceeding riches [*great wealth*], a**nd become vain like unto their brethren** [*relatives*], the Lamanites.

44 And from this time **the disciples** [*the Three Nephites*] **began to sorrow for the sins of the world** [*as they were told would be the case; see 3 Nephi 28:9*].

Step 17. Almost everyone becomes extremely wicked. You can't tell the difference between many who are members of the Church and the wicked.

45 And it came to pass that when **three hundred years** had passed away, **both the people of Nephi and**

the Lamanites had become exceedingly wicked one like unto another.

> **Step 18.** Society is riddled with dishonesty, murder, robbing, and plundering, and materialism is everywhere.

46 And it came to pass that **the robbers of Gadianton did spread over all the face of the land**; and there were none that were righteous save [*except*] it were the disciples of Jesus. And **gold and silver did they lay up in store in abundance, and did traffic in all manner of traffic** [*gaining wealth has become top priority*].

> In the next verses, Mormon sets the stage to tell us more about himself and his youth, in Mormon, chapter 1. Ammaron, the record keeper (verse 47, next), will meet with Mormon when Mormon is ten years old (see Mormon 1:1).

47 And it came to pass that a**fter three hundred and five years** had passed away, (and the people did still remain in wickedness) **Amos died**; and his brother, **Ammaron, did keep the record in his stead** [*in his place*].

48 And it came to pass that when **three hundred and twenty years** had passed away, **Ammaron**, being constrained [*inspired*] by the Holy Ghost, **did hide up the records** which were sacred—yea, even **all the sacred records which had been handed down from generation to generation**, which were sacred—even until the **three hundred and twentieth year** from the coming of Christ.

49 And **he did hide them up unto the Lord, that they might come again unto the remnant of the house of Jacob** [*as the Book of Mormon, which signals the beginning of the gathering of Israel–the "house of Jacob"—in the last days*], according to the prophecies and the promises of the Lord. And thus is the end of the record of Ammaron.

THE BOOK OF MORMON

You will find much in this book, the Book of Mormon within the Book of Mormon, that will help you remain strong and faithful in the Church and the gospel, no matter what difficulties you run into in your own life.

In this book, Mormon records his own life and history. It consists of nine chapters and contains much sorrow, bloodshed, wars, and wickedness. In fact, Mormon was asked at age fifteen to serve as the commander-in-chief of all the Nephite armies. This is indeed a compliment to him, but it could also be a sad commentary on what wickedness had done to the men in his nation.

We are told that the word "Mormon" means "more good." See *History of the Church*, volume 5, pages 399–400. Mormon certainly exemplified his noble name.

Before we study the nine chapters in this book, we will take time to consider how this humble prophet survived spiritually in such a wicked world around him. There are many lessons for us in the principles taught by Mormon's life.

We will list six steps out of many that we find in this book and will narrow our approach down to "How to Survive When Your World Is Falling Apart around You," using Mormon as our example. We will quote from his writings to support each step.

How to Survive When Your World Is Falling Apart around You

STEP 1 Gain your own strong testimony of the gospel.

> "I was visited of the Lord, and tasted and knew of the goodness of Jesus" (Mormon 1:15).

STEP 2 Personal, strict obedience to righteous commitments and covenants.

> "I remembered the things which Ammaron had commanded me [*in Mormon 1:3–4*]. I had gone according to the word of Ammaron, and taken the plates of Nephi, and did make a record according to the words of Ammaron" (Mormon 1:5, 2:17).

STEP 3 Confidence in your personal standing with God.

> "I know that I shall be lifted up [*gain exaltation in the celestial kingdom*] at the last day [*on Judgment Day*]" (Mormon 2:19).

STEP 4 Allow for "time out" when things become overwhelming, and try again later, after you've regained your strength.

> "I, Mormon, did utterly refuse from this time forth to be a commander and a leader of this people, because

of their wickedness and abomination" (Mormon 3:11).

STEP 5 Try again, and keep trying, even though there may seem to be little or no hope of success because of seemingly "impossible" people. It is Christlike to keep trying with people.

> "I did go forth among the Nephites, and did repent of the oath which I had made [*changed my mind*] that I would no more assist them; . . . But behold, I was without hope" (Mormon 5:1–2).

STEP 6 Love your enemies. Desire good for them. Do good for them. Such feelings and actions provide stability and are a means to spiritual survival for your self-confidence in your personal standing with God.

> "And now, behold, I would speak somewhat unto the remnant of this people who are spared [*the Lamanites, the bitter enemies of Mormon who have virtually destroyed his people*] if it so be that God may give unto them my words, that they may know of the things of their fathers [*the gospel of Christ, which their ancestors had*]; yea, I speak unto you" (Mormon 7:1).

As stated above, Mormon is a wonderful example of someone who maintained his spirituality and Christlike attributes while surrounded by terrible wickedness and insensitivity to spiritual things.

We will follow his life from age ten (Mormon 1:2) through about age seventy-four (Mormon 6:5).

MORMON 1

This chapter covers about 5 years, from about AD 321 to about AD 326. A little over 285 years have passed since the Savior appeared to the people of Nephi after His Crucifixion and Resurrection and established His church among them. The Three Nephites are still among these people, but they will soon be taken away because of their terrible wickedness (verse 13).

As you will see, Mormon is sensitive to spiritual things at a very young age, and is given a heavy responsibility by Ammoron, the keeper of the records, including the large plates of Nephi.

First, Mormon tells us that he is going to call his book here "the Book of Mormon."

1 AND **now I, Mormon, make a record of the things which I have both seen and heard, and call it the Book of Mormon**.

2 And **about the time that Ammaron** [*the grandson of Nephi, the Disciple of Christ; 3 Nephi 12:1*] **hid up the records** unto the Lord [*4 Nephi 1:48–49*], **he came unto me, (I being about ten years of age**, and I began to be learned somewhat after the manner of the learning of my people) **and Ammaron said unto me: I perceive** [*see*] **that thou art a sober** [*serious-minded*] **child, and art quick to observe** [*probably meaning "very observant" (see verse 3); also used as "obedient" in many scriptures*];

3 **Therefore, when ye are about twenty and four years old I would that ye should** [*I want you to*] **remember the things that ye have observed concerning this people**; and when ye are of that age **go to the land Antum, unto a hill which shall be called Shim**; and **there have I deposited unto the Lord all the sacred engravings concerning this people**.

4 And behold, ye shall **take the plates of Nephi unto yourself, and the remainder shall ye leave in the place where they are; and ye shall engrave on the plates of Nephi all the things that ye have observed concerning this people**.

Next, Mormon informs us that his father's name was also Mormon. As he continues, we see that the wickedness and wars that would surround him throughout his life are already underway.

5 And I, Mormon, being a descendant of Nephi, (and **my father's name was Mormon**) **I remembered** [*part of keeping commitments is remembering them*] **the things which Ammaron commanded me**.

6 And it came to pass that **I, being eleven years old, was carried by my father** into the land southward, even **to the land of Zarahemla**.

7 **The whole face of the land had become covered with buildings**, and the people were as numerous almost, as it were the sand of the sea [*there were huge numbers of people living there*].

8 And it came to pass **in this year there began to be a war between the Nephites**, who consisted of the Nephites and the Jacobites and the Josephites and the Zoramites; and this war was between the Nephites, **and the Lamanites** and the Lemuelites and the Ishmaelites.

Next, Mormon explains that he will refer simply to Nephites and Lamanites hereafter in his record, rather than listing the various tribes and ethnic groups in each category.

9 Now the Lamanites and the Lemuelites and the Ishmaelites were called Lamanites, and **the two parties were Nephites and Lamanites**.

10 And it came to pass that **the war began to be among them in the borders of Zarahemla**, by the waters of Sidon.

Some readers of the Book of Mormon tend to think we are dealing with relatively small groups of people in the Americas. As you will see throughout the next several chapters, especially chapter 6 where 230,000 Nephite men plus women and children are killed, this is not the case.

11 And it came to pass that **the Nephites had gathered together a great number of men**, even to **exceed the number of thirty thousand**. And it came to pass that **they did have in this same year a number of battles**, in which the Nephites did beat the Lamanites and did slay many of them.

12 And it came to pass that **the Lamanites withdrew their design** [*backed off*], and there was peace settled in the land; and **peace did remain for the space of about four years**, that there was no bloodshed [*killing*].

Next, we see that the Three Nephites finally leave these people because of their terrible wickedness. The Three Nephites are still upon the earth today, and many have been ministered to by them.

Mormon also teaches us that the loss of miracles and the gifts of the Spirit accompany wickedness. It is a tragic loss.

13 But wickedness did prevail upon the face of the whole land, insomuch that **the Lord did take away his beloved disciples** [*the Three Nephites*], and **the work of miracles and of healing did cease because of the iniquity** [*wickedness*] **of the people**.

14 And there were **no gifts from the Lord, and the Holy Ghost did not come upon any**, because of their wickedness and unbelief.

Next, Mormon tells us that by age fifteen he already had a strong testimony of Christ because of his many spiritual blessings.

15 And **I, being fifteen years of age and being somewhat of a sober mind** [*serious-minded, mature for his age*], **therefore I was visited of the Lord, and tasted and knew of the goodness of Jesus.**

You have probably been taught that in some situations, you should not even attempt to teach or preach the gospel because of the spiritual insensitivity of the person or people involved. Next, we see this with Mormon.

16 And **I did endeavor** [*attempt*] **to preach unto this people, but my mouth was shut, and I was forbidden that I should preach unto them**; for behold they had wilfully rebelled against their God; and the beloved disciples were taken away out of the land, because of their iniquity [*extreme wickedness*].

17 **But I did remain among them**, but **I was forbidden to preach unto them, because of the hardness of their hearts**; and because of the hardness of their hearts the land was cursed for their sake.

Next, we see that this society has deteriorated to the point that "anything goes," in other words, the people don't think there is such thing as sin or good and evil, with the result that people can't even hold on to their material possessions. They keep getting robbed. Nobody is honest anymore. Also, we see that the Gadianton robbers have spread throughout the land.

18 And **these Gadianton robbers**, who were among the Lamanites, **did infest the land**, insomuch [*so*] that the inhabitants thereof **began to hide up their treasures** in the earth; and they **became slippery**, because the Lord had cursed the land, that **they could not hold them, nor retain them again**.

As you read verse 19, next, you can see that Satan uses the same things today, as in times past, to lead people away from God.

19 And it came to pass that there were **sorceries**, and **witchcrafts**, and **magics** [*the occult, like black magic, seances, etc.*]; and **the power of the evil one** [*the devil*] **was wrought upon all the face of the land**, even unto the fulfilling of all the words of Abinadi [*perhaps referring to Abinadi's warning that extreme wickedness would lead to their utter destruction—Mosiah 12:8—which is coming to Mormon's people*], and also Samuel the Lamanite [*see Helaman 13:31*].

MORMON 2

This chapter covers about 23 years, from about AD 327 to AD 350. At the young age of fifteen, Mormon will be appointed as the commander-in-chief of all the Nephite armies. In other words, he will be the leader of all of the soldiers of his people. As you will see, he keeps getting his hopes up that his soldiers and people will repent and turn to God for help, but time and time again he is disappointed. Just think how difficult it would be to lead an army of wicked, unrepentant people who "curse God and wish to die" (verse 14), when you know God and know He has the power to rescue and save from physical enemies as well as spiritual foes.

Perhaps one of the comforting lessons we can gain from this chapter, as well as the rest of Mormon, is that the Lord keeps working with wicked people, sometimes against all odds, in order to have His Atonement and healing power immediately available to begin rescuing them if and when they exercise their agency to start repenting and turning toward Him.

1 AND it came to pass in that same year **there began to be a war again between the Nephites and the Lamanites.** And **notwithstanding** [*even though*] **I being young, was large in stature** [*was big for my age*]; therefore **the people of Nephi appointed me that I should be their leader, or the leader of their armies.**

2 Therefore it came to pass that **in my sixteenth year** [*fifteen years old; on his next birthday he would be sixteen*] **I did go forth at the head of an army of the Nephites**, against the Lamanites; therefore **three hundred and twenty and six years** had passed away [*about AD 327*].

Next, Mormon tells us how his soldiers refused to fight. Compare these men with the righteous Nephite armies, including the two thousand stripling warriors under Helaman and Captain Moroni.

3 And it came to pass that in the three hundred and twenty and seventh year **the Lamanites did come upon us** with exceedingly great power, insomuch that **they did frighten my armies; therefore they would not fight, and they began to retreat** towards the north countries.

4 And it came to pass that **we did come to the city of Angola**, and we did take possession of the city, a**nd**

make preparations to defend ourselves against the Lamanites. And it came to pass that we did fortify the city with our might; but notwithstanding [*in spite of*] all our fortifications **the Lamanites did come upon us and did drive us out of the city.**

5 And **they did also drive us forth out of the land of David.**

Remember that one of the lessons we are being taught here is that without God's help, we will be driven back rather consistently, not only by others, but also by Satan and the forces of evil. You have often heard that there is no rest for the wicked. It is true.

6 And **we marched forth and came to the land of Joshua**, which was in the borders west by the seashore.

7 And it came to pass that **we did gather in our people as fast as it were possible, that we might get them together in one body** [*group*].

8 **But behold, the land was filled with robbers and with Lamanites; and notwithstanding** [*in spite of*] **the great destruction which hung over my people, they did not repent of their evil doings** [*these people seem to have gotten to the point that they are "past feeling" (1 Nephi 17:45), and the idea of repenting and turning to God for protection no longer even enters their minds; when people get to this point, they seem incapable of even thinking like faithful Saints*]; **therefore there was blood and carnage** [*gore, bloody wounds and dead bodies*] **spread throughout all the face of the land**, both on the part of the Nephites and also on the part of the Lamanites; and it was one complete revolution throughout all the face of the land.

Once again, in verse 9, we see that these are rather large numbers of people. Keep in mind that there are women and children above and beyond the numbers of men listed in the armies.

9 And now, **the Lamanites** had a king, and his name was Aaron; and he came against us **with an army of forty and four thousand**. And behold, **I** [*Mormon*] **withstood him with forty and two thousand**. And it came to pass that **I beat him with my army** that he fled before me. And behold, all this was done, and three hundred and thirty years had passed away.

Mormon is about nineteen years old at this point.

Next, in verses 10–15, we see Mormon get his hopes up that his people are actually beginning to sincerely repent, but such was not the case.

10 And it came to pass that **the Nephites began to repent of their iniquity, and began to cry even as had been prophesied by Samuel the prophet** [*Helaman 13:31–32*]; for behold **no man could keep that which was his own**, for [*because of*] the thieves, and the robbers, and the murderers, and the magic art, and the witchcraft which was in the land.

11 Thus **there began to be a mourning and a lamentation** [*crying and moaning and sadness*] **in all the land**

because of these things, and **more especially among the people of Nephi**.

12 And it came to pass that **when I, Mormon, saw their lamentation and their mourning and their sorrow before the Lord, my heart did begin to rejoice within me**, knowing the mercies and the long-suffering [*patience*] of the Lord [*knowing that it was still possible for them to repent*], therefore **supposing that he would be merciful unto them that they would again become a righteous people**.

13 **But behold this my joy was vain** [*turned out to not be what I thought it was*], for **their sorrowing was not unto repentance** [*it turned out that they did not want to repent*], because of the goodness of God; but **it was rather the sorrowing of the damned** [*they were not sorry for their wickedness, rather, they were sorry that their wickedness wasn't paying off anymore*], because the Lord would not always suffer them [*permit them to continue*] to take happiness in sin.

14 And **they did not come unto Jesus** with broken hearts [*humble, submissive*] and contrite [*desiring correction from God as needed*] spirits, but **they did curse God, and wish to die**. Nevertheless they would struggle with the sword for their lives.

Verse 15, next, is a straightforward warning to all of us that it is possible for us to get so far away from God that all desire to return to Him is gone. At this point, it can become "everlastingly too late" (Helaman 13:38), simply because the desire to repent is completely gone. The invitation to repent is still in place (Helaman 13:39), but people who are this far gone don't want it.

15 And it came to pass that **my sorrow did return unto me again**, and I saw that **the day of grace** [*help from God*] **was passed with them** [*they were past that point in their hearts*], both **temporally and spiritually**; for I saw thousands of them hewn [*cut*] down in **open rebellion against their God**, and heaped up as dung upon the face of the land. And thus **three hundred and forty and four years** had passed away.

Mormon is now about thirty-two to thirty-three years old.

16 And it came to pass that in the **three hundred and forty and fifth year the Nephites did begin to flee before the Lamanites**; and they were pursued [*chased*] until they came even to the land of Jashon, before it was possible to stop them in their retreat.

Next, in verses 17–18, Mormon tells us that he had kept his word to Ammaron, who had turned the responsibility of keeping the records of the Nephites over to him (Mormon 1:1–4). He was instructed by Ammoron that when he was twenty-four years old, he was to go to where the plates were hidden, take the large plates of Nephi, leave the other plates behind, and keep an ongoing record of the Nephites.

17 And now, **the city of Jashon was near the land where Ammaron**

had deposited the records unto the Lord, that they might not be destroyed. And behold **I had gone according to the word of Ammaron, and taken the plates of Nephi, and did make a record according to the words of Ammaron**.

18 And **upon the plates of Nephi** [*the large plates of Nephi*] **I did make a full account** of all the wickedness and abominations [*extra-evil sins*]; **but upon these plates** [*Mormon's abridgment; in other words, the gold plates that were given to Joseph Smith*] **I did forbear to make** [*hold back from making*] **a full account** of their wickedness and abominations, for behold, **a continual scene of wickedness and abominations has been before mine eyes ever since I have been sufficient to behold the ways of man** [*ever since I was old enough to understand what was going on*].

19 And wo is me because of their wickedness; for **my heart has been filled with sorrow because of their wickedness, all my days; nevertheless, I know that I shall be lifted up at the last day** [*Mormon knows he will be saved in heaven because of his personal righteousness, no matter what his people do; a powerful key to surviving sorrow and discouragement in our lives, brought on by the behaviors of others*].

20 And it came to pass that in this year **the people of Nephi again were hunted and driven**. And it came to pass that we were driven forth until we had come northward to the land which was called Shem.

21 And it came to pass that **we did fortify the city of Shem, and we did gather in our people as much as it were possible, that perhaps we might save them from destruction**.

22 And it came to pass in the **three hundred and forty and sixth year** they began to come upon us again.

Mormon is about thirty-five years old now. His loyalty to his people is Christlike, even though they reject his values and standards. Perhaps you have noticed that the Lord does not often destroy people. Rather, he makes the gospel available to them time and time again throughout their lives. No doubt Mormon is continuing to work with his people, hoping that someday they will rethink their position on the gospel he loves.

Next, Mormon rallies his people to stand up and fight for their preservation against the Lamanites. Though badly outnumbered, the Nephites will win this one.

23 And it came to pass that **I did speak unto my people, and did urge them with great energy, that they would stand boldly before the Lamanites and fight for their wives, and their children, and their houses, and their homes** [*contains some but not all of the elements of Captain Moroni's title of liberty; see Alma 46:12*].

24 And **my words did arouse them somewhat to vigor** [*energy and action*], insomuch that **they did not flee from before the Lamanites, but did stand with boldness against them**.

25 And it came to pass that we did contend **with an army of thirty**

thousand against an army of fifty thousand. And it came to pass that we did stand before them with such firmness that **they did flee from before us**.

26 And it came to pass that when they had fled **we did pursue them** with our armies, and did meet them again, and **did beat them**; nevertheless [*however*] the strength of **the Lord was not with us**; yea, **we were left to ourselves**, that **the Spirit of the Lord did not abide** [*stay*] **in us**; therefore **we had become weak like unto our brethren** [*the Lamanites; compare with Helaman 4:24*].

It is difficult in a significant way to be a loyal follower of Christ with the understanding and perspectives it brings, and to have to stand by and watch other people make agency choices that you know will bring them nothing but heartache. There is great happiness and joy in living the gospel, yet we must allow for the sorrow that occasionally comes upon us and wish that loved ones could or would allow themselves to see things as God sees them.

We see this, next, in Mormon's heart.

27 And **my heart did sorrow because of this the great calamity** [*disaster*] **of my people, because of their wickedness and their abominations**. But behold, we did go forth against the Lamanites and the robbers of Gadianton, until **we had again taken possession of the lands of our inheritance**.

Next, the Nephites and Lamanites will sign a peace treaty, which will provide ten years of peace (see Mormon 3:1).

28 And the three hundred and forty and ninth year had passed away. And in the three hundred and fiftieth year **we made a treaty with the Lamanites and the robbers of Gadianton**, in which we did get the lands of our inheritance divided.

29 And **the Lamanites did give unto us the land northward**, yea, even to the narrow passage which led into the land southward. And **we did give unto the Lamanites all the land southward**.

MORMON 3

This chapter covers two to three years, from about AD 360–362. Mormon is now about forty-nine years old.

In Mormon 1:16–17, Mormon was forbidden by the Lord to preach to his people because of their terrible, gross wickedness. But in chapter 3, verse 2, the Lord gives the people yet another chance to repent by instructing Mormon to preach the gospel to them. He even promises them that they will be saved from physical destruction by the Lamanites if they will repent. We will see how they respond.

1 AND it came to pass that **the Lamanites did not come to battle again until ten years more** had passed away [*AD 360*]. And behold, I had employed my people [*kept them busy*], the Nephites, in preparing their lands and their arms against the time of battle.

2 And it came to pass that **the Lord did say unto me: Cry unto this people—Repent ye, and come unto me, and be ye baptized, and build up again my church, and ye shall be spared**.

In verse 3, next, we are taught that the Lord often spares the wicked from destruction and gives them additional opportunities to repent. This applies to individuals as well as nations. They usually do not even realize that God is involved in keeping them from being destroyed.

3 And **I did cry unto this people, but it was in vain** [*didn't do any good*]; and **they did not realize that it was the Lord that had spared them, and granted unto them a chance for repentance**. And behold they did harden their hearts [*became insensitive to the Spirit and proud and mean*] against the Lord their God.

Next, in verses 4–16, the Nephites, who have continued to refuse to repent, will be successful in some battles, which will increase their pride, arrogance, and disrespect for God even more. Mormon will refuse to be their leader (verses 11 and 16; see also chapter 5, verse 1).

This is a reminder that the Lord withdraws His Spirit from wicked people and leaves them on their own. Sometimes they wake up. Sometimes they don't. It is still an agency choice at this point.

4 And it came to pass that after this tenth year had passed away, making, in the whole, **three hundred and sixty years** from the coming of Christ, the king of **the Lamanites sent an epistle** [*letter, communication*] **unto me**, which gave unto me to know **that they were preparing to come again to battle against us**.

5 And it came to pass that **I did cause my people that they should gather themselves together at the land Desolation**, to a city which was in the borders, by the narrow pass which led into the land southward.

6 And **there we did place our armies, that we might stop the armies of the Lamanites**, that they might not get possession of any of our lands; therefore **we did fortify against them with all our force**.

7 And it came to pass that in the **three hundred and sixty and first year the Lamanites did come down to the city of Desolation to battle against us**; and it came to pass that in that year **we did beat them**, insomuch that they did return to their own lands again.

Mormon is now about fifty-one years old.

8 And in the **three hundred and sixty and second year** they did come down again to battle. And **we did beat them again**, and did slay [*kill*] a great number of them, and their dead were cast [*thrown*] into the sea.

9 And now, because of this great thing which my people, **the Nephites**, had done, they **began to boast in their own strength**, and began **to swear before the heavens that they would avenge themselves of** [*get

revenge for] **the blood of their brethren** who had been slain by their enemies.

10 And **they did swear by the heavens, and also by the throne of God** [*such talk is often called "blasphemy;" it is against God's commandments to talk like this (see verse 14)*], that they would go up to battle against their enemies, and would cut them off from the face of the land.

11 And it came to pass that **I, Mormon, did utterly refuse from this time forth to be a commander and a leader of this people**, because of their wickedness and abomination.

Next, we see that Mormon's heart is broken because of the wickedness of his people. He tells us that the reason he had continued leading them was because he loved them. Again, we are seeing the love of God for His wayward children reflected in the love of Mormon for his rebellious people.

12 Behold, **I had led them, notwithstanding** [*in spite of*] **their wickedness** I had led them many times to battle, and **had loved them, according to the love of God which was in me, with all my heart**; and my soul had been poured out in prayer unto my God all the day long for them; **nevertheless, it was without faith, because of the hardness of their hearts.**

13 And **thrice** [*three times*] **have I delivered them out of the hands of their enemies, and they have repented not of their sins**.

14 And **when they had sworn by all that had been forbidden them by our Lord and Savior Jesus Christ** [*see verse 10, above*], that they would go up unto their enemies to battle, and avenge themselves of the blood of their brethren, behold **the voice of the Lord came unto me, saying:**

15 **Vengeance** [*revenge*] **is mine, and I will repay; and because this people repented not after I had delivered them, behold, they shall be cut off from the face of the earth**.

16 And it came to pass that **I utterly refused to go up against mine enemies; and I did even as the Lord had commanded me**; and **I did stand as an idle witness to manifest unto the world the things which I saw and heard**, according to the manifestations of the Spirit which had testified of things to come [*including the restoration of the gospel in the last days, which Mormon will speak of in verses 17–22, next*].

Imagine how difficult it must have been for Mormon to stand by as an idle witness (verse 16, above)! He was obedient and continued to record what was happening to his people.

Next, Mormon writes to all those, including you and me, who will eventually read the Book of Mormon. He warns them that all people will be held accountable for their actions and will someday stand before Christ to be judged. He invites everyone to believe in Christ and accept the gospel when it is made available to them.

17 Therefore **I write unto you, Gentiles, and also unto you, house of Israel**, when the work shall commence [*when the Book of Mormon comes forth and the last days' gathering begins*], that ye shall be about to prepare to return to the land of your inheritance;

18 Yea, behold, **I write unto all the ends of the earth**; yea, **unto you, twelve tribes of Israel** [*you will know from your patriarchal blessing that you are part of Israel*], who shall be judged according to your works by the twelve [*the Twelve Apostles*] whom Jesus chose to be his disciples in the land of Jerusalem.

19 And I write **also unto the remnant of this people** [*the Lamanites*], **who shall also be judged by the twelve** [*the twelve disciples*] **whom Jesus chose in this land**; and they shall be judged by the other twelve whom Jesus chose in the land of Jerusalem.

Next, in verses 20–22, Mormon summarizes the purpose for his writing to all people.

20 And these things doth the Spirit manifest unto me; therefore **I write unto you all**. And **for this cause** [*for this purpose*] I write unto you, **that ye may know that ye must all stand before the judgment-seat of Christ**, yea, every soul who belongs to the whole human family of Adam; and ye must stand **to be judged of your works**, whether they be **good or evil**;

21 And **also that ye may believe the gospel of Jesus Christ**, which ye shall have among you [*which you will have the opportunity to accept or reject*]; and **also that the Jews**, the covenant people of the Lord, **shall have other witness** besides him whom they saw and heard, **that Jesus**, whom they slew, **was the very Christ and the very God** [*the God of this earth, the Creator, under the direction of the Father; see Mosiah 15:1–3*].

22 And **I would** [*wish*] **that I could persuade** [*convince*] **all ye ends of the earth** [*everybody, everywhere*] **to repent and prepare to stand before the judgment-seat of Christ.**

MORMON 4

This chapter covers about 12 years, from about AD 363 to AD 375. The wickedness and wars between the Nephites and the Lamanites continue. Remember that Mormon has quit leading the Nephite armies because they have become so wicked (see Mormon 3:11 and 16).

This chapter will remind us of how low people can get when they completely let go of the gospel and God's standards.

1 AND now it came to pass that in **the three hundred and sixty and third year** the Nephites did go up with their armies to battle against the Lamanites, out of the land Desolation.

2 And it came to pass that the armies of **the Nephites were driven back again** to the land of Desolation. And while they were yet weary, a fresh

army of the Lamanites did come upon them; and they had a sore battle, insomuch that **the Lamanites did take possession of the city Desolation, and did slay** [*kill*] **many of the Nephites, and did take many prisoners**.

3 And **the remainder did flee** [*run*] **and join the inhabitants of the city Teancum**. Now the city Teancum lay in the borders by the seashore; and it was also near the city Desolation.

Next, Mormon tells us that because the Nephites were the aggressors, meaning they were the ones who were attacking, they were defeated at this point.

4 And **it was because the armies of the Nephites went up unto the Lamanites that they began to be smitten** [*beaten and killed*]; **for were it not for that** [*if they hadn't been the agressors*], **the Lamanites could have had no power over them**.

Next, Mormon teaches us one significant way through which the wicked are punished.

5 But, behold, the judgments [*punishments*] of God will overtake the wicked; and **it is by the wicked that the wicked are punished**; for it is the wicked that stir up the hearts of the children of men unto bloodshed.

6 And it came to pass that **the Lamanites did make preparations to come against the city Teancum**.

7 And it came to pass in the **three hundred and sixty and fourth year the Lamanites did come against the city Teancum**, that they might take possession of the city Teancum also.

8 And it came to pass that **they were repulsed** [*stopped*] **and driven back by the Nephites**. And when **the Nephites** saw that they had driven the Lamanites they **did again boast** [*brag*] **of their own strength**; and they went forth in their own might, and took possession again of the city Desolation.

9 And now all these things had been done, and **there had been thousands slain** [*killed*] **on both sides**, both the Nephites and the Lamanites.

10 And it came to pass that the **three hundred and sixty and sixth year** had passed away, and the Lamanites came again upon the Nephites to battle; and **yet the Nephites repented not of the evil they had done, but persisted in their wickedness** [*kept being wicked*] **continually**.

We see much of this in the world today; many seem to be beyond the point where they see any connection between personal wickedness and destruction.

11 And **it is impossible for the tongue to describe, or for man to write a perfect description of the horrible scene of the blood and carnage** [*gore, mangled and dead bodies*] **which was among the people, both of the Nephites and of the Lamanites**; and **every heart was hardened**, so that **they delighted**

in the shedding of blood [*killing*] continually.

12 And **there never had been so great wickedness among all the children of Lehi, nor even among all the house of Israel**, according to the words of the Lord, **as was among this people**.

13 And it came to pass that **the Lamanites did take possession of the city Desolation**, and this because their number did exceed the number of the Nephites [*they had more soldiers than the Nephites*].

14 And **they did also march forward against the city Teancum**, and did drive the inhabitants forth out of her, **and did take many prisoners both women and children, and did offer them up as sacrifices unto their idol gods**.

15 And it came to pass that in the three hundred and sixty and seventh year, **the Nephites being angry because the Lamanites had sacrificed their women and their children**, that they did go against the Lamanites with exceedingly great anger, insomuch that **they did beat again the Lamanites, and drive them out of their lands**.

16 And the Lamanites did not come again against the Nephites until the **three hundred and seventy and fifth year**.

Once again, in verse 17, next, we are reminded by Mormon that we are dealing with very large populations of people. We also see the change in which the Nephites no longer hold their own, and the prophesied destruction begins to speed up.

17 And in **this year they did come down against the Nephites** with all their powers; and **they were not numbered** [*couldn't be counted*] **because of the greatness of their number** [*because there were so many of them*].

18 And **from this time forth did the Nephites gain no power over the Lamanites, but began to be swept off** [*destroyed*] **by them even as a dew before the sun**.

19 And it came to pass that **the Lamanites did come down against the city Desolation**; and there was an exceedingly sore [*bad*] battle fought in the land Desolation, in the which **they did beat the Nephites**.

20 And **they** [*the Nephites*] **fled again from before them**, and they came to the city Boaz; and there they did stand against the Lamanites with exceeding boldness, insomuch that the Lamanites did not beat them until they had come again the second time.

21 And when they had come the second time, **the Nephites were driven and slaughtered** with an exceedingly great slaughter [*big amount of killing*]; **their women and their children were again sacrificed unto idols** [*killed by being offered to the Lamanite's idols*].

22 And it came to pass that **the Nephites did again flee from before**

them, taking all the inhabitants with them, both in towns and villages.

Next, Mormon transports all the Nephite plates and records elsewhere. It is our understanding from what Ammoron told Mormon in Mormon 1:3 that there were many other records besides the large plates of Nephi that Mormon was using for his abridgment or summary of all the records to create what we have now as the Book of Mormon. Thus, we imagine that it would be a large task to transport all these precious records to another location where they would be safe from the invading Lamanite armies.

23 And now **I, Mormon, seeing that the Lamanites were about to overthrow the land**, therefore I did go to the hill Shim, and **did take up all the records which Ammaron had hid up unto the Lord**.

MORMON 5

This chapter covers about nine years, from about AD 375–384. Mormon is about sixty-four years old as we begin this chapter.

First, Mormon decides to once again serve his people by leading their armies, even though he considers it hopeless that they will repent. He is an example of someone who continues working with "impossible" people because of the Christlike love he has in his heart for them.

1 AND it came to pass that **I did go forth among the Nephites, and did repent of the oath which I had made** [*I changed my mind*] **that I would no more assist them; and they gave me command again of their armies**, for they looked upon me as though I could deliver them from their afflictions.

Remember when you see "I was without hope" in verse 2, next, that Mormon is not without hope for his own soul. As mentioned previously in Mormon 2:19, confidence in your standing with God and knowing that your life is acceptable unto Him can be a great source of strength for you as you work with those who do not share your values.

2 But behold, **I was without hope** [*for these people, not the case for his own soul*], **for I knew the judgments** [*punishments*] **of the Lord which should** [*would*] **come upon them**; for **they repented not of their iniquities** [*sin and wickedness*], but **did struggle for their lives without calling upon that Being** [*God*] **who created them**.

3 And it came to pass that **the Lamanites did come against us as we had fled to the city of Jordan**; but behold, **they were driven back** that they did not take the city at that time.

4 And it came to pass that **they came against us again, and we did maintain** [*kept*] **the city**. And there were **also other cities** which were maintained by the Nephites, which strongholds did cut them off that they could not get into the country which lay before us, to destroy the inhabitants of our land.

5 And it came to pass that **whatsoever** [*whatever*] **lands we had passed by,**

and the inhabitants thereof were not gathered in, were destroyed by the Lamanites, and their towns, and villages, and cities were burned with fire; and thus **three hundred and seventy and nine years** passed away.

6 And it came to pass that in the **three hundred and eightieth year the Lamanites did come again** against us to battle, and we did stand against them boldly; but it was all in vain [*useless*], for so great were their numbers [*they had so many soldiers*] that **they did tread the people of the Nephites under their feet.**

Mormon is about sixty-nine years old now.

7 And it came to pass that **we did again take to flight** [*we ran again*], and those whose flight was swifter than the Lamanites' did escape, and those whose flight did not exceed [*those who could not stay ahead of*] the Lamanites' were swept down and destroyed.

Next, Mormon tells us that he is sensitive about showing us such a horrible picture of what is happening to these people, but he knows that he needs to at least give us some idea of how bad it gets among the wicked. We see much of this type of blood and carnage on the daily news now.

8 And now behold, **I, Mormon, do not desire to harrow up** [*torment—to break up or tear, as a harrow does behind a tractor as it breaks up the dirt in a field*] **the souls of men in casting before them such an awful scene of blood and carnage** as was laid before mine eyes; **but I, knowing that these things must surely be made known**, and that all things which are hid must be revealed upon the housetops—

9 And **also that a knowledge of these things** [*the Book of Mormon*] **must come unto the remnant** [*the descendants of the people who survive*] **of these people, and also unto the Gentiles**, who the Lord hath said should scatter this people [*the descendants of the Lamanites*], and this people should be counted as naught [*nothing*] among them—**therefore I write a small abridgment** [*summary; a condensation*], daring not to give a full account of the things which I have seen, because of the commandment which I have received, and **also that ye might not have too great sorrow because of the wickedness of this people** [*he doesn't want to be too graphic or describe it too much in detail for fear of causing us too much pain*].

Next, Mormon refers to the righteous, who accept the gospel with all their hearts and thus are sensitive to the pain and suffering of others.

10 And now behold, **this I speak unto their seed** [*descendants*]**, and also to the Gentiles who have care for the house of Israel**, that realize and know from whence [*where*] their blessings come [*who believe in God and know where their blessings come from*].

11 For I know that **such will sorrow for the calamity** [*disaster*] **of the house of Israel**; yea, **they will**

sorrow for the destruction of this people; they will **sorrow that this people had not repented** that they **might have been clasped in the arms of Jesus** [*protected physically and could have felt the love of the Savior in their daily lives*].

12 Now **these things** [*the Book of Mormon*] **are written unto the remnant of the house of Jacob** [*to all of scattered Israel*]; and they are written **after this manner** [*written upon gold plates*], because it is known of God that **wickedness will not bring them forth** unto them [*the wicked would not preserve and pass on these teachings and truths*]; and **they are to be hid up unto the Lord** [*buried by Moroni in the Hill Cumorah*] **that they may come forth in his own due time** [*through Joseph Smith*].

13 And **this is the commandment which I have received**; and behold, **they shall come forth according to the commandment of the Lord, when he shall see fit, in his wisdom** [*when He decides it is time for them to be published*].

Mormon has been telling us how widespread the Book of Mormon will eventually be. Next, he informs us that the day will come when the Jews will also have and believe the Book of Mormon. Then he repeats that the Book of Mormon will go to all the world, including the Lamanites.

14 And behold, **they** [*the teachings of the Book of Mormon*] **shall go unto the unbelieving of the Jews**; and for this intent shall they go—**that they may be persuaded that Jesus is the Christ, the Son of the living God**; that the Father may bring about, through his most Beloved [*Christ*], his great and eternal purpose, in **restoring the Jews**, or **all the house of Israel**, to the land of their inheritance, which the Lord their God hath given them, unto the fulfilling of his covenant;

15 And **also that the seed** [*descendants*] **of this people** [*the Lamanites*] **may more fully believe his gospel, which shall go forth unto them from the Gentiles** [*Joseph Smith and the members of the Church, which got its start in the United States of America*]; for **this people** [*the Book of Mormon people who have become so extremely wicked in Mormon's day*] **shall be scattered**, and **shall become a dark, a filthy, and a loathsome people, beyond the description of that which ever hath been amongst us**, yea, even that which hath been among the Lamanites, and this **because of their unbelief and idolatry** [*worshiping things other than God*].

16 For behold, **the Spirit of the Lord hath already ceased to strive** [*stopped working*] **with their fathers** [*ancestors*]**; and they are without Christ and God in the world**; and they are driven about as chaff [*scattered all over, like the lightweight fragments of husks of grain, after the heads of grain are separated from them*] before the wind.

In other words, they are not anchored to truth and righteousness; therefore, they are blown around by Satan however he chooses.

17 **They were once a delightsome people**, and **they had Christ for their shepherd**; yea, **they were led even by God the Father.**

18 **But now**, behold, **they are led about by Satan, even as chaff is driven before the wind**, or **as a vessel** [*ship*] **is tossed about upon the waves, without sail or anchor, or without anything wherewith to steer her** [*without a rudder*]; and **even as she is, so are they**.

19 And behold, **the Lord hath reserved their** [*the people in Mormon's day, in America*] **blessings**, which they might have received in the land [*America*], **for the Gentiles** [*the immigrants who settle America*] who shall possess the land.

20 But behold, it shall come to pass that **they** [*the Lamanites*] **shall be driven and scattered by the Gentiles** [*early settlers of America; see 1 Nephi 13:14*]; and **after they have been driven and scattered by the Gentiles, behold, then will the Lord remember** [*fulfill*] **the covenant which he made unto Abraham and unto all the house of Israel** [*that Abraham's descendants will take the gospel to all the world; see Abraham 2:9–11*].

21 And **also the Lord will remember the prayers of the righteous** [*such as Mormon*], which have been put up unto him **for them.**

Next, Mormon reminds all people everywhere that they must repent and come unto Christ, or they will stand in misery before Him on Judgment Day.

22 And **then, O ye Gentiles** [*people everywhere who do not have the gospel; see Bible Dictionary, under "Gentile"*], **how can ye stand before the power of God, except ye shall repent and turn from your evil ways?**

23 **Know ye not that ye are in the hands of God? Know ye not that he hath all power**, and at his great command the earth shall be rolled together as a scroll [*when the continents come back together at the Second Coming of Christ; see D&C 133:23–24*]?

24 Therefore, **repent ye, and humble yourselves before him**, lest he shall come out in justice [*according to the law of justice*] against you—lest a remnant of the seed of Jacob [*the righteous who are gathered to the Church in the last days*] shall go forth among you as a lion [*unstoppable*], and tear you in pieces, and there is none to deliver [*no one to save you*].

None can stop the spread of the gospel in the last days, which will bring accountability to the wicked, and their wicked lifestyles will be "torn to pieces" or destroyed by the power of God when the time is right.

MORMON 6

This chapter takes place about AD 385. In it, we see the final destruction of the Nephites. It is a very sad chapter. Mormon will tell of the deaths of two hundred and thirty thousand of his men, plus women and children. Mormon was about seventy-four years old at the time he wrote this.

It is a sad warning about what happens to a nation and a people who are given repeated opportunities to understand the gospel and repent but then openly refuse to do so.

Mormon will hide all the Nephite records in the Hill Cumorah, except for the plates that contain his abridgment, which he will give to his son, Moroni.

1 AND **now I finish my record concerning the destruction of my people, the Nephites**. And it came to pass that **we did march forth before the Lamanites**.

2 And **I, Mormon, wrote an epistle** [*a letter*] **unto the king of the Lamanites**, and desired of him that he would **grant unto us that we might gather together our people unto the land of Cumorah**, by a **hill** which was called **Cumorah**, and there we could give them battle.

3 And it came to pass that **the king of the Lamanites did grant unto me the thing which I desired**.

4 And it came to pass that **we did march forth to the land of Cumorah**, and we did **pitch our tents around about the hill Cumorah**; and it was in a land of many waters, rivers, and fountains [*springs*]; and here we had hope to gain advantage over the Lamanites.

5 And when **three hundred and eighty and four years** had passed away, we had gathered in all the remainder of our people unto the land of Cumorah.

6 And it came to pass that when we had gathered in all our people in one to the land of Cumorah, behold **I, Mormon, began to be old** [*apparently meaning that he was starting to feel his age, which was seventy-four years old*]; and knowing it to be the last struggle of my people, and **having been commanded of the Lord that I should not suffer** [*allow*] **the records which had been handed down by our fathers** [*ancestors*], **which were sacred, to fall into the hands of the Lamanites**, (for the Lamanites would destroy them) therefore I made this record [*the gold plates, which would be given to Joseph Smith by Moroni*] out of the plates of Nephi [*the large plates of Nephi*], **and hid up in the hill Cumorah all the records** which had been entrusted to me by the hand of the Lord, **save it were** [*except*] **these few plates which I gave unto my son Moroni**.

Next, Mormon speaks of the fear that fills the souls of the intentionally wicked when they know that destruction is finally coming upon them. The Lamanites will kill all but twenty-four of his people, other than a few who escaped or deserted, by the time this battle is over. Mormon was wounded but not killed in the battle.

He tells the numbers of the men of his armies who were killed in this final battle, which totaled up to two hundred and thirty thousand men.

7 And it came to pass that my people, with their wives and their children, did now behold [*could see*] the armies of the Lamanites marching towards them; and **with that awful fear of**

death which fills the breasts of all the wicked, did they await to receive them.

8 And it came to pass that they came to battle against us, and **every soul was filled with terror** because of the greatness of their numbers.

9 And it came to pass that **they did fall upon my people** with the sword, and with the bow, and with the arrow, and with the ax, and with all manner of weapons of war.

10 And it came to pass that my men were hewn [*cut*] down, yea, even **my ten thousand** who were with me, and **I fell wounded** in the midst; and they passed by me that they did not put an end to my life.

11 And **when they had gone through and hewn down all my people save it were twenty and four of us**, (among whom was my son Moroni) and **we** having survived the dead of our people, **did behold** [*we saw*] **on the morrow** [*the next day*], when the Lamanites had returned unto their camps, **from the top of the hill Cumorah**, the ten thousand of my people who were hewn down, being led in the front by me [*Mormon, going at the front, led his men into battle*].

12 And we also beheld the **ten thousand** of my people who were **led by my son Moroni**.

13 And behold, the **ten thousand** of Gidgiddonah had fallen, and he also in the midst.

14 And Lamah had fallen with his **ten thousand**; and Gilgal had fallen with his **ten thousand**; and Limhah had fallen with his **ten thousand**; and Jeneum had fallen with his **ten thousand**; and Cumenihah, and Moronihah, and Antionum, and Shiblom, and Shem, and Josh, had fallen with their **ten thousand each**.

15 And it came to pass that there were **ten more** who did fall by the sword, **with their ten thousand each**; yea, even all my people, save it were those twenty and four who were with me, and **also a few who had escaped** into the south countries, and **a few who had deserted over unto the Lamanites, had fallen**; and their flesh, and bones, and blood lay upon the face of the earth, being left by the hands of those who slew them to molder [*rot*] upon the land, and to crumble and to return to their mother earth.

Next, we have one of the most heart-wrenching lamentations in all of scripture as this gentle, Christlike man of God, Mormon, mourns the loss of his people.

16 And **my soul was rent** [*torn*] **with anguish** [*grief*], because of the slain of my people, and I cried:

17 **O ye fair ones, how could ye have departed from the ways of the Lord! O ye fair ones, how could ye have rejected that Jesus, who stood with open arms to receive you!**

18 Behold, **if ye had not done this, ye would not have fallen. But behold, ye are fallen, and I mourn your loss.**

19 **O ye fair sons and daughters, ye fathers and mothers, ye husbands and wives, ye fair ones, how is it that ye could have fallen!**

20 But behold, **ye are gone, and my sorrows cannot bring your return**.

21 And **the day soon cometh that your mortal must** [*will*] **put on immortality** [*you will be resurrected*], and these bodies which are now moldering in corruption [*rotting*] must soon become incorruptible [*resurrected*] bodies; and **then ye must stand before the judgment-seat of Christ, to be judged according to your works**; and if it so be that ye are righteous, then are ye blessed with your fathers who have gone before you.

22 **O that ye had repented before this great destruction had come upon you.** But behold, ye are gone, and the Father, yea, the Eternal Father of heaven, knoweth your state [*condition*]; and he doeth with you according to his justice and mercy.

MORMON 7

Mormon loves his enemies. This is a beautiful chapter in which this man of God expresses his hope and the desire of his heart that his bitter enemies might someday be brought to Christ. He wants the best for them!

No example, other than that of the Savior Himself, could be greater than that of Mormon. This chapter is written about AD 385.

1 **AND now, behold, I would speak somewhat unto the remnant of this people** [*the Lamanites in the latter days; see heading to this chapter in your Book of Mormon*] who are spared, **if it so be that God may give unto them my words, that they may know of the things of their fathers** [*ancestors*]; yea, **I speak unto you, ye remnant** [*remaining part*] **of the house of Israel** [*the covenant people of the Lord*]; and **these are the words which I speak**:

2 Know ye that **ye are of the house of Israel**.

3 Know ye that **ye must come unto repentance, or ye cannot be saved**.

4 Know ye that **ye must lay down your weapons of war, and delight no more in the shedding of blood** [*killing people*], **and take them not again, save it be that God shall command you**.

The last phrase in verse 4, above, is important, because it teaches us that sometimes war is necessary. The key to if and when is whether God has approved it. We look to the First Presidency and the Twelve in our day for counsel on this subject as it applies to our day.

5 Know ye that **ye must come to the knowledge of your fathers** [*to the knowledge of God that your righteous ancestors had*], **and repent of all your sins and iniquities** [*wickedness*], **and believe in Jesus Christ, that he is the Son of God, and that he was slain** [*killed*] **by the Jews, and by the power of the Father he hath risen**

again [*has been resurrected*], **whereby he hath gained the victory over the grave; and also in him is the sting of death swallowed up.**

6 **And he bringeth to pass the resurrection of the dead, whereby man must** [*will*] **be raised to stand before his judgment-seat.**

Next, Mormon assures us that the Atonement of Christ has the power to cleanse and heal from sin, and that all who are willing can have a pleasant Judgment Day.

7 And **he hath brought to pass the redemption of the world**, whereby [*the forgiveness of sins through the Atonement of Christ*] **he that is found guiltless before him at the judgment day hath it given unto him to dwell in the presence of God** in his kingdom, **to sing ceaseless praises** [*to have gratitude and rejoicing*] with the choirs above [*with the angels in heaven*], **unto the Father, and unto the Son, and unto the Holy Ghost**, which are one God [*who work in complete harmony with each other*], **in a state of happiness which hath no end.**

8 Therefore [*because this forgiveness is available to you*] **repent, and be baptized in the name of Jesus, and lay hold** [*take hold*] **upon the gospel of Christ**, which shall be set before you [*the Lamanites in the latter days*], **not only in this record** [*the Book of Mormon*] **but also in the record** [*the Bible*] **which shall come unto the Gentiles from the Jews**, which record shall come from the Gentiles unto you.

9 For behold, **this** [*the Book of Mormon*] **is written for the intent** [*for the purpose*] **that ye may believe that** [*the Bible*]; and if ye believe that [*the Bible*] **ye will believe this** [*the Book of Mormon*] also; **and if ye believe this** [*the Book of Mormon*] **ye will know concerning your fathers** [*ancestors, in the Book of Mormon*], and **also the marvelous works which were wrought** [*accomplished*] **by the power of God among them.**

As you are aware, many in our day, who come from a family heritage of believing in the Bible, no longer believe in it, or, at least, do not take its teachings seriously. Perhaps you remember also that some years ago, the First Presidency and the Quorum of the Twelve Apostles added the phrase "Another Testament of Jesus Christ" to the name of the Book of Mormon in our scriptures.

With this in mind, we see the power of the Book of Mormon to bear witness of the truths that are in the Bible, and vice versa, as taught by Mormon in verse 9, above.

10 And **ye will also know that ye are a remnant of the seed of Jacob** [*that you are of Israel and can have the blessings of Abraham, Isaac, and Jacob, which are the blessings of exaltation; see Abraham 2:9–11*]; therefore **ye are numbered among the people of the first covenant** [*most likely a reference indicating that they can join those who have made and kept covenants that lead to exaltation in the highest degree of glory in the celestial kingdom; in other words, those who live in their own family units and*

[*become gods*]; and **if it so be that ye believe in Christ, and are baptized, first with water, then with fire** [*symbolic of the cleansing and "burning" out of us the sin and wickedness from our lives through the guidance and influence of the Holy Ghost*] **and with the Holy Ghost** [*the gift of the Holy Ghost, which accompanies confirmation*], **following the example of our Savior**, according to that which he hath commanded us, **it shall be well with you in the day of judgment** [*on Judgment Day*]. Amen.

MORMON 8

Mormon's son, Moroni, is the author of Mormon chapters 8 and 9. Mormon has been killed, and Moroni is finishing his father's book, the Book of Mormon within the Book of Mormon, according to instructions given to him by his father. Moroni is probably best-known to us now as the angel Moroni. He was the prophet who gave the gold plates to Joseph Smith to translate. He has been resurrected.

As we begin this chapter, it is somewhere between AD 400 and AD 421. Moroni is alone. All his family and relatives have been killed, and he has no friends and nowhere to go (verse 5). You can feel his sadness and discouragement.

In verses 1–13, Moroni describes the final scenes of his people and his father. He tells us of his circumstances now, and informs us that he and his father were both visited by the Three Nephites.

In the remainder of chapter 8 and in chapter 9, he teaches and prophesies to future generations, including us, who would be blessed to have the Book of Mormon.

1 BEHOLD **I, Moroni, do finish the record of my father, Mormon**. Behold, **I have but few things to write, which things I have been commanded by my father**.

2 And now it came to pass that **after the great and tremendous** [*huge*] **battle at Cumorah**, behold, **the Nephites who had escaped into the country southward were hunted by the Lamanites, until they were all destroyed**.

3 And **my father also was killed by them** [*the Lamanites*], and **I even remain alone to write the sad tale of the destruction of my people.** But behold, they are gone, and **I fulfil the commandment of my father. And whether they will slay me, I know not**.

4 Therefore **I will write and hide up the records in the earth**; and whither [*where*] I go it mattereth not.

Next, Moroni explains that he would write more on his father's plates, but there is not room, and he has no ore with which to make more plates for engraving. As mentioned above, one can feel the loneliness and discouragement that is upon this great prophet, Moroni. We know from the final pages of the Book of Mormon that he will live at least another twenty-one years.

5 Behold, **my father hath made this record** [*the plates of Mormon, the gold plates,*

which Moroni will finish, bury, and eventually give to Joseph Smith in 1827], **and he hath written the intent** [*purpose*] **thereof** [*see Mormon 2:17–18 and 3:17–22*]. And behold, **I would write it** [*the intent and purpose of the gold plates*] **also if I had room upon the plates**, but I have not; and ore [*rock with gold in it*] I have none, for **I am alone. My father hath been slain** [*killed*] in battle, **and all my kinsfolk** [*family, relatives*], and **I have not friends nor whither** [*anywhere*] **to go**; and **how long the Lord will suffer that I may live** [*let me live*] **I know not**.

6 Behold, **four hundred years** have passed away since the coming of our Lord and Savior [*since the birth of Christ to Mary in Bethlehem*].

7 And behold, **the Lamanites have hunted my people, the Nephites**, down from city to city and from place to place, even **until they are no more**; and great [*huge*] has been their fall; yea, **great and marvelous** [*astonishing*] **is the destruction of my people, the Nephites**.

Next, we are reminded that once the wicked have destroyed the group they were focusing on, they do not simply go home and live at peace with one another. Destroying is Satan's way, and those who follow him continue to be destroyers, no matter who or where.

8 And behold, it is the hand of the Lord which hath done it. And behold also, **the Lamanites are at war one with another**; and the whole face of this land is one continual round of murder and bloodshed; and no one knoweth the end of the war.

9 And now, behold, **I say no more concerning them**, for there are none save [*except*] it be the Lamanites and robbers that do exist upon the face of the land.

Next, Moroni informs us that the Three Nephites are the only ones left (other than himself, of course) who know about the true God.

10 And **there are none that do know the true God save it be the disciples of Jesus, who did tarry** [*remain*] in the land until the wickedness of the people was so great that the Lord would not suffer [*permit*] them to remain with the people [*see Mormon 1:13*]; and whether [*whether or not*] they be upon the face of the land no man knoweth.

11 But behold, **my father and I have seen them, and they have ministered unto us**.

Next, Moroni invites those who receive the Book of Mormon not to be critical of it because of any imperfections in it. We see some who miss the message and testimony of the Book of Mormon by setting themselves up as critics. This is a sad, sometimes everlasting mistake.

There is perhaps another message we can get, based on Moroni's counsel to avoid criticizing the delivery system for the word of God. It is that we should likewise avoid criticizing people, such as teachers, leaders, speakers, etc., who may be imperfect in their presentation of the perfect gospel. We are the losers if we fail in this area.

As pointed out next, our acceptance or rejection of the scriptures and people who give the true gospel to us seems to serve as a "judge" that determines whether we are given more truth by the Lord.

12 And **whoso** [*whoever*] **receiveth this record, and shall not condemn** [*reject, criticize*] **it because of the imperfections which are in it**, the same **shall know of greater things than these**. Behold, **I am Moroni**; and were it possible, I would make all things known unto you.

13 Behold, **I make an end of speaking concerning this people. I am the son of Mormon, and my father was a descendant of Nephi**.

Next, Moroni makes the transition between telling us of his people and the future of the gold plates, which he will later deposit in Hill Cumorah. He explains that the gold plates have no monetary value (they are not worth any money), because God will never allow anyone to get them in order to sell the gold for money.

14 And **I am the same who hideth up this record unto the Lord** [*who hides these gold plates in the Hill Cumorah in order to do the work of the Lord*]**; the plates thereof are of no worth** [*as far as money is concerned*], **because of the commandment of the Lord**. For he **truly saith that no one shall have them to get gain** [*wealth*]; **but the record thereof is of great worth** [*spiritually*]; **and whoso shall bring it to light, him** [*Joseph Smith*] **will the Lord bless**.

Next, Moroni explains that the only way the gold plates will come forth to the world will be through the gift and power of God.

15 For **none can have power to bring it to light** [*to publish it so people can read it*] **save it be given him of God**; for God wills that it shall be done **with an eye single to his glory** [*with a pure motive to do the work of God, for the benefit of others*], or the welfare of the ancient and long dispersed [*scattered*] covenant people of the Lord [*for the benefit of scattered Israel*].

16 And **blessed be he** [*Joseph Smith*] **that shall bring this thing** [*the Book of Mormon*] **to light**; for **it shall be brought out of darkness unto light, according to the word of God**; yea, **it shall be brought out of the earth** [*a reference to the fact that the Book of Mormon plates were buried in the Hill Cumorah], and it shall shine forth out of darkness [symbolic of bringing spiritual light*], and come unto the knowledge of the people; and **it shall be done by the power of God**.

Next, Moroni again cautions against being critical of the Book of Mormon, or rejecting it, because of what they consider to be faults in it.

17 And **if there be faults they be the faults of a man**. But behold, **we know no fault**; nevertheless God knoweth all things; therefore, **he that condemneth** [*criticizes and rejects it*]**, let him be aware lest he shall be in danger of hell fire**.

Next, we see a direct prophecy by Moroni, regarding those who would try to force Joseph Smith to show them the plates, or to take them from him. An account of this is given in Joseph Smith—History 1:60 in the Pearl of Great Price.

18 And **he that saith: Show unto me, or ye shall be smitten** [*show me the gold plates or I will beat you up*]**—let him beware lest he commandeth that which is forbidden of the Lord**.

Next, we have a brief reminder and warning that we will be judged by our actions and thus, in effect, will be paid back by our works. This is often referred to as the "law of the harvest;" in other words, what we "plant," we will "harvest."

19 For behold, **the same** [*anybody*] **that judgeth rashly** [*harshly*] **shall be judged rashly again; for according to his works** [*for what he does*] **shall his wages be** [*he will get paid*]**; therefore, he that smiteth shall be smitten again, of the Lord**.

Next, Moroni continues his prophetic warnings to anyone who chooses to fight the Book of Mormon and the spreading of the gospel in the last days.

20 Behold [*look at*] what the scripture says—**man shall not smite, neither shall he judge; for judgment is mine, saith the Lord, and vengeance is mine also, and I will repay**.

21 And **he that shall breathe out wrath and strifes** [*who makes threats*] **against the work of the Lord**, and against the covenant people of the Lord who are the house of Israel, **and shall say: We will destroy the work of the Lord**, and the Lord will not remember [*keep*] his covenant which he hath made unto the house of Israel [*in other words, we will keep the prophecies from being fulfilled*]—**the same is in danger to be hewn** [*cut*] **down and cast into the fire** [*like useless trees and limbs; in other words, they are in danger of being destroyed themselves*];

22 **For the eternal purposes of the Lord shall roll on, until all his promises shall be fulfilled.**

23 **Search the prophecies of Isaiah** [*for example, Isaiah 29:4, which is a prophecy of the coming forth of the Book of Mormon in the last days*]. Behold, I cannot write them [*see the reasons, in verse 5, above*]. Yea, behold I say unto you, that those saints who have gone before me [*the righteous people and prophets of the Book of Mormon*], who have possessed this land, shall cry [*shall speak out*], yea, even from the dust [*out of the ground*] will they cry unto the Lord [*their prayers for future generations of Israel will go up to God*]; **and as the Lord liveth** [*the most solemn and serious promise*] **he will remember** [*keep*] **the covenant which he hath made with them** [*that Israel will be gathered again in the last days, before the Second Coming of Christ*].

24 And **he knoweth their prayers**, that they were in behalf of their brethren. And **he knoweth their faith**, for in his name could they

remove mountains; and in his name could they cause the earth to shake; and by the power of his word did they cause prisons to tumble to the earth; yea, even the fiery furnace could not harm them, neither wild beasts nor poisonous serpents, because of the power of his word.

25 And behold, **their prayers were also in behalf of him** [*Joseph Smith*] **that the Lord should suffer** [*help*] **to bring these things forth**.

In other words, ancient prophets knew and prayed for Joseph Smith.

26 And **no one need say they shall not come** [*be fulfilled*]**, for they surely shall**, for the Lord hath spoken it; **for out of the earth** [*from Moroni to Joseph Smith*] **shall they come**, by the hand of the Lord, and **none can stay** [*stop*] **it**; and **it shall come in a day when it shall be said that miracles are done away** [*when people will say there are no such things as miracles*]; and it shall come even as if one should speak from the dead [*the Book of Mormon will be as if people who are dead are speaking to us*].

27 And **it** [*the Restoration of the gospel, including the Book of Mormon and the great gathering of Israel*] **shall come in a day when the blood of saints shall cry unto the Lord, because of secret combinations and the works of darkness** [*in other words, in a day of great wickedness and evil throughout the earth*].

28 Yea, it shall come **in a day when the power of God shall be denied**, and **churches become defiled** [*corrupted, teach many false doctrines, have no authority to perform baptisms, etc.*] **and be lifted up in the pride of their hearts**; yea, even **in a day when leaders of churches and teachers shall rise in the pride of their hearts**, even to the envying of them who belong to their churches.

29 Yea, **it shall come in a day** when there shall be heard **of fires, and tempests, and vapors of smoke in foreign lands** [*when there will be many natural disasters, and nature will be in commotion*];

30 And there shall also be heard of **wars, rumors of wars**, and **earthquakes** in divers [*various*] places.

As Moroni continues to prophesy, he describes the moral environment in the last days, which might be summarized as "anything goes."

31 Yea**, it shall come** [*the Book of Mormon will come forth*] **in a day when there shall be great pollutions** [*can include spiritual pollution as well as physical pollution in the environment*] upon the face of the earth; there shall be **murders**, and **robbing**, and **lying**, and **deceivings** [*fraud*], and **whoredoms** [*sexual immorality*], and **all manner of abominations** [*very serious sins*]**; when there shall be many who will say, Do this, or do that, and it mattereth not**, for the Lord will uphold such at the last day [*in other words, wickedness is really not that bad*]. But **wo unto such** [*big trouble will come to them*]**, for they are in the gall of bitterness** [*their lives are deeply bitter in sin*] and **in the bonds of iniquity** [*they are bound by the chains of sin*].

32 Yea, **it** [*the Book of Mormon, the restoration of the gospel, the gathering of Israel*] **shall come in a day when there shall be churches built up that shall say: Come unto me, and for your money you shall be forgiven of your sins.**

Verse 32, above, can refer to many things, including the decisions of ministers and leaders of churches to minimize standards and permit sin in order to maintain or gain membership, and thus get rich themselves. We see very few churches today who even begin to maintain the standards set by the Bible.

33 **O ye wicked and perverse** [*perverting and twisting the standards set by God*] and stiffnecked [*prideful*] people, **why have ye built up churches unto yourselves to get gain** [*to get personal wealth*]? **Why have ye transfigured** [*changed*] **the holy word of God**, that ye might bring damnation upon your souls? Behold, **look ye unto the revelations of God** [*pay close attention to what God has said*]; for behold, the time cometh at that day when all these things must be fulfilled.

As you can see, these detailed prophecies of Moroni stand as a powerful witness that the Book of Mormon is true.

34 Behold, **the Lord hath shown unto me great and marvelous things** concerning that which must shortly come, at that day [*in the last dispensation, in other words, in the time in which we are now living*] when these things **shall come forth among you**.

Next, Moroni tells us that he has seen us and our day.

35 Behold, **I speak unto you as if ye were present**, and yet ye are not. But behold, **Jesus Christ hath shown you unto me, and I know your doing.**

36 And I know that **ye do walk in the pride of your hearts; and there are none save** [*except*] **a few only who do not lift themselves up in the pride of their hearts**, unto the wearing of **very fine apparel**, unto **envying** [*jealousy*], and **strifes** [*fighting, arguing*], and **malice** [*evil desires and intentions toward others*], and **persecutions**, and **all manner of iniquities** [*wickedness*]; and **your churches**, yea, even every one, **have become polluted** [*doctrinally and spiritually*] **because of the pride of your hearts.**

In verse 37, next, Moroni gives the key as to why material things can become dangerous; namely, when we love them more than people.

37 For behold, **ye do love money**, and your **substance** [*material possessions*], and your **fine apparel** [*clothing*], and the **adorning** [*decorating*] **of your churches, more than ye love the poor** and the **needy**, the **sick** and the **afflicted** [*suffering from any kind of trouble*].

38 **O ye pollutions, ye hypocrites** [*people who want to look righteous but don't want to be righteous*], ye **teachers, who sell yourselves for that which will canker** [*who teach things for popularity, which will cause spiritual death among*

your members], **why have ye polluted the holy church of God? Why are ye ashamed to take upon you the name of Christ? Why do ye not think that greater is the value of an endless happiness than that misery which never dies—because of the praise of the world?**

39 **Why do ye adorn yourselves with that which hath no life** [*with material things and praise of wicked people, etc.*], and **yet suffer** [*let*] **the hungry, and the needy, and the naked** [*those who do not have enough clothes to stay warm, etc.*], **and the sick and the afflicted to pass by you, and notice them not?**

40 Yea, **why do ye build up your secret abominations** [*secret ways of being terribly wicked*] **to get gain** [*money, power*], **and cause that widows should mourn before the Lord, and also orphans to mourn before the Lord, and also the blood of their fathers and their husbands to cry unto the Lord from the ground, for vengeance** [*revenge*] **upon your heads**?

41 Behold, **the sword of vengeance hangeth over you** [*the Lord's law of justice is hanging over you*]; and the time soon cometh that he avengeth the blood of the saints upon you, for **he will not suffer their cries any longer** [*will not postpone justice any longer*].

MORMON 9

This last chapter of Mormon, written by his son, Moroni, could well be called "a chapter for doubters and unbelievers," in other words, for people who just plain don't believe in Jesus Christ, or strongly doubt that He ever existed or exists now. Moroni tells us in verse 1 that this is the group he is talking to. Obviously, this chapter provides valuable teachings for those of us who do believe in Christ.

Just a reminder that, on average, the Book of Mormon speaks of Christ, one way or another, every 1.7 verses. This chapter is an excellent example of how often it bears witness of the Savior.

1 AND now, **I speak also concerning those who do not believe in Christ**.

First, Moroni asks if such people will believe when they see Christ coming down from heaven at the time of His Second Coming.

2 Behold, **will ye believe in the day of your visitation** [*punishment, destruction when Christ comes again*]—behold, **when the Lord shall come**, yea, even that great day when the earth shall be rolled together as a scroll [*probably meaning when the continents come back together, see D&C 133:23 and 24*], and the elements shall melt with fervent heat, yea, in that great day **when ye shall be brought to stand before the Lamb of God** [*Jesus*]**—then will ye say that there is no God**?

3 **Then will ye longer deny the Christ, or can ye behold the Lamb of God** [*do you think you will be able to stand to look at Him*]? **Do ye suppose that ye shall dwell** [*live*] **with him** under a consciousness [*awareness*] of

your guilt? **Do ye suppose that ye could be happy to dwell with that holy Being**, when your souls are racked with a consciousness of guilt that ye have ever abused his laws?

Next, we are taught a simple fact—namely, that it would not be merciful to the wicked to allow them to live with God because they would be terribly uncomfortable and miserable living with Him. Many people fail to understand this truth.

4 Behold, I say unto you that **ye would be more miserable to dwell with a holy and just God, under a consciousness of your filthiness before him, than ye would to dwell with the damned souls in hell.**

5 For behold, **when ye shall be brought to see your nakedness** [*complete lack of valid excuses for your wicked behavior*] before God, **and also the glory of God, and the holiness of Jesus Christ, it will kindle a flame of unquenchable** [*can't be put out*] **fire upon you**.

Next, Moroni pleads with the unbelieving to change their minds.

6 O then ye unbelieving, **turn ye unto the Lord**; cry [*pray*] mightily unto the Father in the name of Jesus, that perhaps ye may be found **spotless, pure, fair, and white** [*cleansed from sin*], having been **cleansed by the blood of the Lamb** [*the Atonement of Christ*], **at that great and last day** [*on the day of Final Judgment*].

Next, Moroni specifically addresses many ministers and people in our day who claim that Biblical miracles, gifts of the Spirit, and other such blessings have been done away with by God.

Patriarchal blessings, which often specify gifts of the Spirit, are a reminder to faithful members of the Church that such things have not been done away with.

Moroni mentions many of the gifts of the Spirit (the Holy Ghost) in verse 7, next. You can also read about many of the gifts of the Spirit in D&C 46:13–25, 1 Corinthians 12:3–10, and Moroni 10:8–18.

7 And again **I speak unto you who deny the revelations of God, and say that they are done away, that there are no revelations, nor prophecies, nor gifts, nor healing, nor speaking with tongues, and the interpretation of tongues**;

8 Behold I say unto you, **he that denieth these things** [*says they do not exist*] **knoweth not the gospel of Christ**; yea, he has not read the scriptures; if so, he does not understand them.

9 For **do we not read that God is the same yesterday, today, and forever, and in him there is no variableness neither shadow of changing**?

The same gospel is used to save souls, no matter when or where. Faith, repentance, baptism, the gift of the Holy Ghost, ordinances, and doctrines are all required for salvation in celestial glory and for exaltation.

Next, Moroni emphasizes again that the gospel itself does not change. Sometimes people get confused between doctrines, principles, ordinances, policies, and procedures.

The doctrines, principles, and ordinances, such as faith, repentance, baptism, the gift of the Holy Ghost, priesthood and temple ordinances, etc., required for exaltation remain the same. Policies, such as what age young Latter-day Saints can go on missions, what age young men can be ordained to Aaronic Priesthood offices, meeting block schedules, etc., can vary from time to time and from age to age, depending on needs in the Church. All of these things are done under the direction of God.

We will now continue with Moroni emphasizing that wherever the gospel is, miracles will be also. He will go on to preach the basics of the plan of salvation, including the Creation, the Fall, and the Atonement of Christ.

This is the basic message that all people must eventually receive and understand, either on earth or in the next life, in order to have a fair opportunity to accept or reject the gospel of Christ and thus be accountable on the day of Final Judgment.

10 And now, **if ye have imagined up unto yourselves a god who doth vary** [*Who keeps changing*], **and in whom there is shadow of changing** [*even a little bit of changing*], **then have ye imagined up unto yourselves a god who is not a God of miracles**.

11 But behold, **I will show unto you a God of miracles**, even the God of Abraham, and the God of Isaac, and the God of Jacob [*in other words, the true God*]; and it is that same God **who created the heavens and the earth, and all things that in them are**.

12 Behold, **he created Adam**, and **by Adam came the fall of man**. And **because of the fall of man came Jesus Christ**, even the Father [*of our salvation*] and the Son [*because He was the Son of God and thus had power to redeem us*]; and **because of Jesus Christ came the redemption of man.**

Next, Moroni teaches that all mortals will be redeemed from physical death by the Resurrection of Christ.

13 And **because of the redemption of man, which came by Jesus Christ, they are brought back into the presence of the Lord; yea, this is wherein all men are redeemed** [*this is the way in which all people, whether righteous or wicked, are redeemed; in other words, they are all resurrected*], **because the death of Christ bringeth to pass the resurrection**, which bringeth to pass a redemption from an endless sleep, from which sleep **all** men **shall be awakened** [*resurrected*] **by the power of God** when the trump [*signaling the various resurrections; see D&C 88:98–102*] shall sound; and they shall come forth, both small and great [*people who were hardly known and people who were very well-known*], and **all shall stand before his bar** [*the judgment bar of Christ*], **being redeemed and loosed from this eternal band of death** [*being resurrected*], **which death** [*physical death*] **is a temporal death**.

Next, Moroni teaches that Christ will be our final judge. We are likewise taught this in John in the Bible:

> For **the Father judgeth no man, but hath committed all judgment unto the Son** (John 5:22).

We now continue with Moroni's teaching concerning the Final Judgment. This judgment is referred to as the "Final Judgment" because it is the one that determines our placement throughout eternity.

We have had many "partial" judgments so far in our existence. For instance, we were judged worthy to come to earth and get a body. When we die, we have a "partial" judgment to determine whether we go to paradise or prison.

Thus, the judgment spoken of here by Moroni is our "final" judgment, the one for which we have been preparing for eons of time.

14 And **then cometh the judgment of the Holy One** [*Christ*] upon them [*all who have been resurrected*]; and **then cometh the time that he that is filthy shall be filthy still**; and **he that is righteous shall be righteous still**; he that is **happy** shall be **happy still**; and he that is **unhappy** shall be **unhappy still**.

The last part of verse 14, above, is a strong reminder that if we tend to be unhappy most of the time, we ought to work on being happy and pleasant individuals.

15 And **now, O all ye that have imagined up unto yourselves a god who can do no miracles, I would ask of you, have all these things passed, of which I have spoken? Has the end come yet?** Behold I say unto you, **Nay; and God has not ceased to be a God of miracles.**

As we continue, with Moroni as our teacher, we see that pure truth is powerful logic.

16 Behold, **are not the things that God hath wrought** [*done*] **marvelous in our eyes**? Yea, and who can comprehend the marvelous works of God?

17 **Who shall say that it was not a miracle that by his word the heaven and the earth should be** [*were created*]**; and by the power of his word man was created of the dust of the earth; and by the power of his word have miracles been wrought** [*done, performed*]?

18 And **who shall say that Jesus Christ did not do many mighty miracles**? And there were **many mighty miracles wrought** [*performed*] **by the hands of the apostles.**

19 And **if there were miracles wrought then, why has God ceased to be** [*stopped being*] **a God of miracles and yet be an unchangeable Being**? And behold, I say unto you **he changeth not; if so** [*if He did*] **he would cease to be God; and he ceaseth not to be God, and is a God of miracles.**

Next, Moroni explains why there have been times when there have been no miracles. It is not because God has changed.

20 And **the reason why he ceaseth to do miracles among the children**

of men is because that they dwindle in unbelief [*they quit believing in Him*], and **depart from the right way** [*leave the gospel and the covenant path*]**, and know not the God in whom they should trust.**

21 Behold, I say unto you that **whoso believeth in Christ, doubting nothing, whatsoever he shall ask the Father in the name of Christ it shall be granted** [*given*] **him; and this promise is unto all**, even unto the ends of the earth [*to everyone everywhere on the earth*].

Next, Moroni emphasizes again that miracles do not stop where personal righteousness exists.

22 For behold, **thus said Jesus Christ**, the Son of God, **unto his disciples who should tarry** [*probably meaning the Three Nephites and John the Beloved*], yea, and also to all his disciples [*apparently those in Jerusalem; see Mark 16:15*], in the hearing of the multitude: **Go ye into all the world, and preach the gospel to every creature**;

23 And **he that believeth and is baptized shall be saved, but he that believeth not shall be damned** [*stopped in their eternal progression*];

24 And **these signs** [*miracles*] **shall follow them that believe**—in my name shall they cast out devils; they shall speak with new tongues [*languages*]; they shall take up serpents; and if they drink any deadly thing it shall not hurt them; they shall lay hands on the sick [*administer to the sick*] and they shall recover;

25 And **whosoever shall believe in my name, doubting nothing, unto him will I confirm all my words** [*I will give a personal testimony; a personal testimony of the gospel is one of the biggest and most important miracles of all*], even unto the ends of the earth.

Next, we have yet another warning to those who would scoff and mock the truths that Moroni is presenting. It is a strong warning.

26 And now, behold, **who can stand against the works of the Lord? Who can deny his sayings? Who will rise up against the almighty power of the Lord? Who will despise the works of the Lord? Who will despise the children of Christ** [*the faithful followers of Christ*]**?** Behold, all ye who are despisers of the works of the Lord, for **ye shall wonder** [*be surprised*] **and perish.**

Next, Moroni mercifully invites unbelievers to change their minds on such things and to be wise and repent.

27 O then **despise not**, and wonder not, but hearken unto the words of the Lord, and **ask the Father in the name of Jesus for what things soever** [*whatever*] **ye shall stand in need. Doubt not, but be believing**, and begin as in times of old, and **come unto the Lord with all your heart, and work out your own salvation with fear** [*deep respect for God*] **and trembling** [*humility*] **before him.**

28 **Be wise** in the days of your probation [*during your time of being tested here on earth*]; **strip yourselves of all**

uncleanness; ask not, that ye may consume it on your lusts [*don't seek signs by way of challenging God to prove He exists*], but **ask with a firmness unshaken** [*with faith and commitment*], **that ye will yield** [*give in*] **to no temptation, but that ye will serve the true and living God**.

29 **See that ye are not baptized unworthily**; see **that ye partake not of the sacrament of Christ unworthily**; but see that ye **do all things in worthiness**, and **do it in the name of Jesus Christ**, the Son of the living God; and **if ye do this, and endure to the end, ye will in nowise be cast out** [*you will be invited to enter heaven on the Final Judgment Day*].

In the final verses of this chapter, Moroni reminds us that he knows us, and he knows we will receive his words. He asks us for patience with his imperfections and to learn from them. He also explains more about the gold plates and the language used in engraving them.

30 Behold, I speak unto you as though I spake from the dead; for **I know that ye shall have my words**.

31 **Condemn me not** [*don't criticize me*] **because of mine imperfection, neither my father** [*Mormon*], **because of his imperfection, neither them who have written before him; but rather give thanks unto God that he hath made manifest unto you our imperfections, that ye may learn to be more wise than we have been**.

32 And now, behold, **we have written this record** according to our knowledge, **in the characters which are called** among us the **reformed Egyptian**, being handed down and altered [*changed*] by us, according to our manner of speech [*language*].

33 And **if our plates had been sufficiently large we should** [*would*] **have written in Hebrew**; but the Hebrew hath been altered by us also; and if we could have written in Hebrew, behold, ye would have had no imperfection in our record.

34 But **the Lord knoweth the things which we have written, and also that none other people knoweth our language;** and because that none other people knoweth our language, therefore **he hath prepared means** [*Urim and Thummim; see Mosiah 8:13; D&C 17:1; Bible Dictionary, under "Urim and Thummim"*] **for the interpretation thereof**.

It is interesting to know that there is more than one Urim and Thummim. The Prophet Joseph Smith had the one used by the Brother of Jared (see Bible Dictionary at the end of your Bible, under "Urim and Thummim").

35 And **these things are written that we may rid our garments of** [*not be held accountable for*] **the blood** [*sins*] **of our brethren, who have dwindled in unbelief** [*who have left the gospel*].

36 And behold, **these things which we have desired concerning our brethren**, yea, **even their restoration**

to the knowledge of Christ, are according to the prayers of all the saints who have dwelt in the land.

Finally, as he finishes his father's book, Moroni adds his prayers to those of previous prophets and Saints that the testimonies and teachings of the Book of Mormon will bring the blessings of the gospel of Christ to Israel in the last days.

As you know from listening to our prophets today, we are part of covenant Israel and are doing everything we can to take the gospel to all the world.

37 **And may the Lord Jesus Christ grant that their prayers may be answered according to their faith; and may God the Father remember** [*keep*] **the covenant which he hath made with the house of Israel; and may he bless them forever, through faith on the name of Jesus Christ. Amen.**

THE BOOK OF ETHER

In many ways, the book of Ether could be considered a miniature Book of Mormon. As you read it, you will be taught pretty much all of the teachings and lessons we learn from the whole Book of Mormon itself. For instance, it deals with a people who were led away from a wicked society into the promised land. They cross the ocean in ships built according to a special design revealed by God. Once in the promised land, they multiply and spread out, have righteous groups and wicked groups, have prophets and righteous leaders, have a period of 225 years of continual peace, and then have a time of constant wars and secret combinations, which lead to the extinction of the Jaredites. We are taught of Christ and the principles of salvation. We are taught faith, hope, and charity and of New Jerusalem. We are taught kindness, charity, humility, work, gratitude, and the power of righteousness on a national level. And we are given one of the most powerful sermons on the doctrine of faith found anywhere in the scriptures.

The book of Ether was abridged (see heading to Ether, chapter 1) by Moroni from engravings on twenty-four plates of pure gold, which were found by the people of Limhi (see Mosiah 8:9; 21:27). It is a record of the Jaredites, beginning at the time of the Tower of Babel (Genesis 11:1–9), probably around 2200 BC and continuing until somewhere around 120 BC, when Coriantumr became the last survivor of the Jaredites (Ether 15:29–33; Omni 1:21; Mosiah 21:26–27) other than the prophet Ether (Ether 15:33–34). Coriantumr was found by the people of Zarahemla and lived with them for nine months (Omni 1:21).

Based on the approximate dates given above, the Book of Ether probably covers close to two thousand years.

ETHER 1

In this chapter, Moroni briefly tells us how he went about giving us the Book of Ether, which is a translation of the twenty-four gold plates found by Limhi's people during the reign of King Mosiah (see Mosiah 8:9.) He gives the genealogy of the prophet Ether (who engraved the twenty-four gold plates; see Ether 1:6) and then provides a short account of origins of the people of Jared as they were led by the Lord from the wickedness of Babylon and the Tower of Babel, spoken of in the Bible in Genesis, chapter 11, verses 1–9.

Starting with verse 34, Moroni tells us that Jared and his brother and their families and friends knew that the Lord was going to confuse (scramble, mix up) the languages the people were speaking. So Jared asked his brother to pray that the Lord would not confuse the language of these men and their families and friends. Pay attention to what happened.

1 AND now **I, Moroni, proceed to give an account of those ancient inhabitants** [*the Jaredites*] **who were destroyed by the hand of the Lord** upon the face of this north country.

2 And **I take mine account from the twenty and four plates which were found by the people of Limhi** [*Mosiah 21:25–27*], which is **called the Book of Ether**.

3 And **as I suppose that the first part of this record**, which speaks concerning the creation of the world, and also of Adam, and an account from that time even to the great tower [*the Tower of Babel*], and whatsoever things transpired among the children of men until that time, **is had among the Jews** [*in records from which the Bible was derived, covering Genesis 1–10*]—

4 **Therefore I do not write those things which transpired from the days of Adam until that time** [*of the Tower of Babel*]; but they are had upon the plates [*the twenty-four gold plates of Ether*]; and whoso findeth them, the same will have power that he may get the full account [*record*].

Next, Moroni repeats that he is not giving the complete account recorded on the plates of Ether; rather, he will start with the Jaredites at the time of the Tower of Babel.

5 But behold, **I give not the full account, but a part of the account I give, from the tower down until they were destroyed**.

It is interesting that the word "descendant" (**bolded**) is used three times in place of "son" in the genealogy that follows. Perhaps this indicates a gap or a summary of generations. There are at least thirty generations from Ether back to Jared.

6 And on this wise do I give the account [*now I will proceed with my account*]. He that wrote this record was Ether, and he was a **descendant** of Coriantor.

7 Coriantor was the son of Moron.

8 And Moron was the son of Ethem.

9 And Ethem was the son of Ahah.

10 And Ahah was the son of Seth.

11 And Seth was the son of Shiblon.

12 And Shiblon was the son of Com.

13 And Com was the son of Coriantum.

14 And Coriantum was the son of Amnigaddah.

15 And Amnigaddah was the son of Aaron.

16 And Aaron was a **descendant** of Heth, who was the son of Hearthom.

17 And Hearthom was the son of Lib.

18 And Lib was the son of Kish.

19 And Kish was the son of Corom.

20 And Corom was the son of Levi.

21 And Levi was the son of Kim.

22 And Kim was the son of Morianton.

23 And Morianton was a **descendant** of Riplakish.

24 And Riplakish was the son of Shez.

25 And Shez was the son of Heth.

26 And Heth was the son of Com.

27 And Com was the son of Coriantum.

28 And Coriantum was the son of Emer.

29 And Emer was the son of Omer.

30 And Omer was the son of Shule.

31 And Shule was the son of Kib.

32 And Kib was the son of Orihah, who was the son of Jared;

By going clear back to Jared and the brother of Jared, we are now back to about 2200 BC (2,200 years before Christ was born) and not very long after the Flood. It is the time of the wicked society associated with the huge city of Babylon. We are told in the Bible Dictionary (in the back of our Bible, published by the Church), under "Babylon" or "Babel," that this city had walls 85 feet wide, 335 feet high, and 56 miles long. It was a city of terrible wickedness and pride.

At this time in history, the Lord mixed up the languages they spoke, probably so that the wicked could not work together so easily. Up to this point, we understand that everyone still spoke the same language (Genesis 11:1). The people in Babylon had determined to build a tower that would "reach unto heaven" (Genesis 11:4), no doubt as a way of showing God that they didn't need to live His gospel, perhaps in effect saying that if they build a tower high enough, the Lord couldn't destroy them again with a flood, even though He had promised not to (Genesis 9:11).

Whatever the case, we understand that the language that they were speaking before the confounding of languages was the Adamic language, or the language that Adam and Eve and their children spoke. Joseph Fielding Smith explains:

"It is stated in the Book of Ether that Jared and his brother made the request of the Lord that their language be not changed at the time of the confusion of tongues at the Tower of Babel. Their request was granted, and they carried with them the speech of their fathers, the Adamic language, which was powerful even in its written form, so that the things Mahonri wrote 'were mighty even . . . unto the overpowering of man to read them.' That was the kind of language Adam had, and this was the language with which Enoch was able to accomplish his mighty work" (Joseph Fielding Smith, *The Way to Perfection*, Genealogical Society of Utah, 1949, 69. Also quoted in the 1982 *Book of Mormon Student Manual*, sections 50–54).

We will now continue with Moroni's account of these people, focusing now on Jared and the brother of Jared, whose name we will discuss in a moment.

33 Which **Jared came forth with his brother and their families**, with

some others and their families, **from the great** [*enormous*] **tower** [*the Tower of Babel*], **at the time the Lord confounded** [*mixed up*] **the language** of the people, and swore [*gave His word*] in his wrath [*anger*] that they should be scattered upon all the face of the earth; and according to the word of the Lord the people were scattered.

Next, Jared asks his brother to pray to the Lord and request that they might be privileged to speak the same language after their languages are confused.

We get an interesting insight here from this request. It becomes clear that this mixing up of the language was prophesied in advance. Thus, Jared and his brother, their families, and righteous friends knew it was coming and asked the Lord to allow them to be able to understand each other when it happened.

34 And **the brother of Jared** being a large and mighty man, and **a man highly favored** [*blessed*] **of the Lord, Jared, his brother, said unto him: Cry** [*pray*] **unto the Lord, that he will not confound us** [*mix up our language*] **that we may not understand our words** [*so that we can't understand each other*].

35 And it came to pass that **the brother of Jared did cry** [*pray*] **unto the Lord**, and the Lord had compassion upon Jared; therefore he did not confound the language of Jared; **and Jared and his brother were not confounded** [*were still able to communicate with each other and speak the same language*].

Next, Jared asks his brother to pray to the Lord for their friends.

36 Then **Jared said** unto his brother: **Cry** [*pray*] **again unto the Lord, and it may be that he will turn away his anger from them who are our friends, that he confound not their language**.

37 And it came to pass that the brother of Jared did cry unto the Lord, and **the Lord had compassion upon their friends and their families also, that they were not confounded**.

"Mahonri Moriancumer," the actual name of the brother of Jared is not given in the Book of Mormon. It was revealed to the Prophet Joseph Smith as he was giving the infant son of Brother and Sister Reynolds Cahoon a name and a blessing. This event is recorded as follows:

"While residing in Kirtland Elder Reynolds Cahoon had a son born to him. One day when President Joseph Smith was passing his door he called the Prophet in and asked him to bless and name the baby. Joseph did so and gave the boy the name of Mahonri Moriancumer. When he had finished the blessing, he laid the child on the bed, and turning to Elder Cahoon he said, the name I have given your son is the name of the brother of Jared; the Lord has just shown [*or revealed*] it to me. Elder William F. Cahoon, who was standing near heard the Prophet make this statement to his father; and this was the first time the name of the brother of Jared was known in the Church in this dispensation" ("The Jaredites," *Juvenile Instructor*, May 1, 1892, 282).

Next, Jared asks his brother to ask the Lord as to whether they are going to have to leave their home country. The answer will be yes. Among many lessons we can learn from this is the fact that it often requires moving somewhere else and effort on our part to separate ourselves from evil.

38 And it came to pass that **Jared spake again unto his brother**, saying: Go and **inquire of the Lord whether** [*whether or not*] **he will drive us out of the land**, and if he will drive us out of the land, **cry unto him whither** [*where*] **we shall go** [*ask Him where we should go*]. And who knoweth but the Lord will carry us forth into a land which is choice above all the earth? And if it so be, **let us be faithful unto the Lord**, that we may receive it for our inheritance [*have it for our new home country*].

39 And it came to pass that **the brother of Jared did cry unto the Lord** according to that which had been spoken by the mouth of Jared.

40 And it came to pass that **the Lord did hear** the brother of Jared, and had compassion [*mercy*] upon him, **and said unto him**:

41 **Go to** [*go to work*] and **gather** together thy **flocks** [*herds of animals like sheep and goats*], both male and female, of every kind; and also of the **seed** of the earth of every kind; **and thy** [*your*] **families**; and also **Jared thy brother and his family**; and also **thy friends and their families, and the friends of Jared and their families**.

42 And **when thou hast done this thou shalt go at the head of them** [*lead them*] down into the valley which is northward. And **there will I meet thee**, and **I will go before thee** [*I will lead thee*] **into a land which is choice above all the lands of the earth**.

Joseph Fielding Smith informs us that the "land which is choice above all the lands of the earth," in verse 42, above, refers to both North and South America. He said:

"The Book of Mormon informs us that the whole of America, both North and South, is a choice land above all other lands, in other words—Zion. The Lord told the Jaredites that he would lead them to a land 'which is choice above all the lands of the earth.' (Ether 1:42.) We understand that they landed in Central America where their kingdom existed the greater part of their residence in America" (Smith, *Doctrines of Salvation*, Bookcraft, 1956, 3:73).

43 And **there will I bless thee and thy seed** [*posterity*], **and raise up** unto me of thy seed, and of the seed of thy brother, and they who shall go with thee, **a great nation**. And there shall be none greater than the nation which I will raise up unto me of thy seed, upon all the face of the earth. And thus I will do unto thee because this long time ye have cried unto me.

ETHER 2

Jared and his brother, Mahonri Moriancumer, and their families and friends were obedient to the Lord, and thus began their journey to the promised land, America.

There is symbolism in this. When we obey the commandments and instructions of God as we continue on our journey through life, we, too, are led to the "promised land;" or, in other words, the celestial kingdom, or heaven. In fact, just as the brother of Jared and his people had to pass through the water—the ocean—to get to the promised land, so also, we must pass through the waters of baptism in order to successfully arrive in the celestial kingdom.

In this chapter, we will see the Jaredites, as Jared and his family and friends are called, leave Babel as commanded. As they journey in the wilderness, they will build ships (verse 6) to cross "many waters," but this is not the journey across the ocean to America. Preparations for that voyage will begin in verse 16 when the Lord commands them to build ships like the first set they built in verse 6. In those eight ships, they will make the 344-day trip to America (see Ether 6:11).

Starting with verse 7, Moroni will teach us more about the promised land of America and will warn that those who live there "shall serve God or shall be swept off" (verse 10).

As we come to the last verses of this chapter (19–25), we will see a fascinating scene in which the brother of Jared presents three problems to the Lord regarding their journey across the ocean on the ships. First, they will need light. Second, how will they steer and in what direction? And third, they will need fresh air. The premortal Christ, also known as Jehovah in the Old Testament, will instruct him as to how to solve the problem with respect to fresh air. He, Himself, will steer them with wind and ocean currents, so that problem is solved. But He will ask the brother of Jared to come up with a solution to the problem of lighting inside the ships so they don't have to cross the ocean in the dark.

We can learn from this. The Lord gives us much by way of counsel and commandments, which, if followed, solve and take care of many situations and problems that face us during mortality. However, He also expects us to use our own brain and common sense to solve many of our problems (see D&C 58:26–27).

1 AND it came to pass that **Jared and his brother, and their families, and also the friends of Jared and his brother and their families, went down into the valley which was northward,** (and the name of the valley was Nimrod [*who was the founder of Babel, or Babylon; see Genesis 10:8–10*], being called [*named*] after the mighty hunter [*Genesis 10:9*]) **with their flocks** [*animals*] **which they had gathered together, male and female, of every kind.**

> Continuing with our symbolism (and there could be many different approaches to this), we see that the journey of these people required much work on their part. So also is it with our journey through life here on earth. We must use common sense and good judgment and do much ourselves toward gaining our salvation.

2 And **they did also lay snares** [*traps for animals to eat*] and **catch fowls** [*birds*]

of the air; and they did also prepare a vessel [*made a water tight container*], in which **they did carry with them** the **fish** of the waters.

Next, in verse 3, you will see the word "deseret," which Moroni informs us means "honey bee." You have no doubt observed that many things in our Latter-day Saint culture are named "deseret." This is the source of that name. It is associated with being industrious and everyone doing their part, like honey bees do in their hives.

3 And they did also carry with them **deseret**, which, by interpretation, is a **honey bee**; and thus **they did carry with them swarms of bees**, and all manner of that which was upon the face of the land, **seeds of every kind**.

As you can see, from the above verses, the Lord instructed the brother of Jared and his people to bring a great variety of foods and supplies with them. Their journey to the promised land was not to be a journey of barely surviving on whatever they could scrape up along the way. Rather, through their hard work, planning, and following of the Lord's instructions, their journey was to be filled with a satisfying variety and considerable enjoyment.

Such is also to be the case with our journey through life. The Lord has told us that our mortal journey should be filled with joy (2 Nephi 2:25) and has created an environment for us to live in that is designed to "please the eye and gladden the heart" (D&C 59:18). Unfortunately, some groups and individuals have interpreted the gospel to include instructions to avoid things in life that are pleasing to the God-given senses.

As we continue, remember that the Lord, with whom the brother of Jared is communicating, is the premortal Christ. Jesus is the God of the Old Testament. At this point, He still has a spirit body since He has not yet been born to Mary in order to gain a physical body. He is the God who spoke with Abraham and commanded him to sacrifice Isaac (Genesis 22). He is the God who appeared to Moses and who gave him the Ten Commandments (Exodus 19:20; 20:1–17).

Thus, it is the Savior as the premortal God of the Old Testament, a personage of spirit, who is instructing the brother of Jared.

4 And it came to pass that when they had come down into the valley of Nimrod **the Lord came down and talked with the brother of Jared**; and he was in a cloud, and the brother of Jared saw him not.

5 And it came to pass that **the Lord commanded them that they should go forth** [*travel*] **into the wilderness**, yea, into that quarter [*area of the country*] **where there never had man been**. And it came to pass that **the Lord did go before them, and did talk with them as he stood in a cloud**, and **gave directions** whither [*where*] they should travel.

A cloud is often used to represent the presence of the Lord in the Bible. (See Topical Guide under "Cloud.") In fact, at the time of the Second Coming, He will come "with clouds" (Revelation 1:7; see also D&C 34:7), which symbolizes His presence and can be symbolic of His coming and teachings and instructions during the Millennium.

6 And it came to pass that **they did travel in the wilderness** [*uninhabited land*], and **did build barges** [*not the eight ships they will cross the ocean in*], in which they **did cross many waters** [*not the ocean*], being **directed continually by the hand of the Lord**.

After they had finished this journey in barges and arrived safely on land again, the Lord required them to keep going, until they came to the ocean, at which point they again built barges or ships for their voyage to the promised land.

This may have a bit of symbolism in it; namely, that it could be tempting to stop short of our final goal (heaven), having accomplished much already. Some people spend much of their lives accomplishing good things but fail to "endure to the end" by faithfully living the gospel to the end of their lives.

7 And **the Lord would not suffer** [*permit*] **that they should stop beyond the sea** [*having already accomplished significant goals*] **in the wilderness** [*we don't know where this sea was*], **but he would** [*it was His will*] **that they should come forth even unto the land of promise** [*the land of America; symbolic of celestial glory and exaltation*], which was **choice above all other lands** [*symbolic of the best choice above all other goals*], **which the Lord God had preserved for a righteous people**.

Next, Moroni teaches us much about the "land of promise," to which the Lord was ultimately leading the Jaredites. It is America, and Moroni re-emphasizes the requirements for people and nations to continue to dwell in this "land which is choice above all other lands" (verse 10).

8 And **he had sworn in his wrath** [*made it very clear*] **unto the brother of Jared, that whoso** [*whoever*] **should possess this land of promise**, from that time henceforth [*on into the future*] and forever, **should serve him**, the true and only God, **or they should be swept off** when the fulness of his wrath [*anger*] should come upon them.

Next, Moroni defines the conditions under which a nation would be swept off of this land.

9 And now, **we can behold** [*see*] **the decrees** [*teachings*] **of God concerning this land, that it is a land of promise; and whatsoever nation shall possess it shall serve God, or they shall be swept off** when the fulness of his wrath [*God's punishments*] shall come upon them. And the fulness of his wrath cometh upon them **when they are ripened in iniquity** [*when they are so wicked that they can't be saved*].

The phrase "ripened in iniquity," as used in verse 9, above, basically means when they are hopelessly wicked, when there is not a chance for anyone born to grow up in righteousness among them. At the end of verse 10, next, Moroni repeats his definition of the conditions that must exist for a nation to be destroyed from this land of America.

10 For behold, **this is a land which is choice above all other lands**; wherefore [*therefore*] **he that doth** [*does*] **possess it shall serve God or shall be swept off**; for it is the everlasting decree of God. And **it is not until the fulness of iniquity** [*when they become completely wicked*] **among the children of the land** [*the inhabitants*], **that they are swept off.**

11 And **this** [*what Moroni is teaching, contained in the Book of Mormon*] **cometh unto you, O ye Gentiles** [*inhabitants of America; see 1 Nephi 13:14; 14:5–6; Bible Dictionary, pages 679–80*], that ye may know the decrees of God [*what God has said*]—**that ye may repent, and not continue in your iniquities** until the fulness come, **that ye may not bring down the fulness of the wrath of God upon you as the inhabitants of the land** [*for example, the Jaredites*] **have hitherto** [*up to now*] **done.**

12 Behold, **this is a choice land, and whatsoever nation shall possess it shall be free from bondage** [*being slaves*], and from **captivity**, and **from all other nations** under heaven, **if they will but serve the God of the land, who is Jesus Christ**, who hath been manifested [*shown, revealed*] by the things which we have written.

Moroni continues now with his account of the Jaredites.

13 And **now I proceed with my record**; for behold, it came to pass that **the Lord did bring Jared and his brethren forth even to that great sea which divideth the lands** [*in other words, to the ocean, which separates the continents*]. And as they came to the sea they pitched their tents; and they called the name of the place Moriancumer [*part of the name of the brother of Jared; this is significant because it is common for people to name a place for their leader*]; and they dwelt in tents, and **dwelt in tents upon the seashore for the space of four years.**

Next, the brother of Jared will be scolded for neglecting to pray and communicate with the Lord. We don't know if it had been four years since he had prayed, or a brief period in recent weeks or months. Whatever the case, one lesson learned is that we should not neglect saying our prayers.

14 And it came to pass **at the end of four years** that **the Lord came again unto the brother of Jared**, and stood **in a cloud and talked with him.** And **for** the space of **three hours did the Lord talk with the brother of Jared, and chastened** [*scolded*] **him because he remembered not to call upon the name of the Lord.**

Next we see the gift of the Atonement in action with the brother of Jared and his people. We are all reminded that the law of mercy (which means we can be forgiven of our sins because of the Atonement of Christ) can only reach so far before the law of justice (which means that we can no longer be forgiven but must be punished for our sins) must take over.

15 And **the brother of Jared repented** of the evil which he had done, and

did call upon the name of the Lord for his brethren who were with him. **And the Lord said unto him: I will forgive thee and thy brethren of their sins**; but thou shalt not sin any more, for ye shall **remember that my Spirit will not always strive with man**; wherefore, **if ye will sin until ye are fully ripe** [*until it is too late because you are completely wicked*] **ye shall be cut off from the presence of the Lord** [*your opportunity to return to live with God forever will be over; compare with D&C 76:112*]. And **these are my thoughts** [*the Lord wants us to understand His thinking so that we can exercise our agency wisely*] **upon the land which I shall give you for your inheritance; for it shall be a land choice above all other lands**.

Next, the premortal Christ commands these people to build another set of ships, in which they are to cross the ocean to America. It is a strong and simple reminder that there is a work ethic required on our part, in other words, a lot of work is required of us in order that we may someday return to heaven.

16 And the Lord said: **Go to work** and build, after the manner of barges [*the same type of ships*] which ye have hitherto [*previously*] built [*see verse 6*]. And it came to pass that **the brother of Jared did go to work, and also his brethren, and built barges** after the manner which they had built, **according to the instructions of the Lord**. And **they were small**, and they were **light upon the water**, even like unto the lightness of a fowl [*bird*] upon the water.

17 And they were built after a manner that they were **exceedingly tight, even that they would hold water like unto a dish**; and the bottom thereof was tight like unto a dish; and the sides thereof were tight like unto a dish; and the ends thereof were peaked; and the top thereof was tight like unto a dish; and the length thereof was the length of a tree; and the door thereof, when it was shut, was tight like unto a dish.

I'm hoping there will be a "celestial museum" in which we can someday see a replica of one of these little ships.

Next, the bother of Jared presents to the Lord three problems regarding the small, tight, waterproof ships. He is concerned about lighting for the interior of the barges, about how and in what direction to steer them, and about the absence of fresh air for the passengers and animals, etc. He approaches the Lord having obeyed all of the instructions he was given so far, which is a strong foundation of faith and obedience, and which brings humble confidence in approaching God for additional help.

18 And it came to pass that **the brother of Jared cried unto the Lord**, saying: **O Lord, I have performed the work which thou hast commanded me**, and I have made the barges according as thou hast directed me.

Next, tells the Lord about the three problems that still need to be overcome.

19 And behold, O Lord, **in them**

there is no light; whither shall we steer? And also we shall perish, for **in them we cannot breathe**, save it is the air which is in them; therefore we shall perish.

The Lord will answer the problems brought up by the brother of Jared as follows:

1. The problem of obtaining fresh air.
   Answer: verse 20.
2. The problem of light.
   Answer: verses 23–25; in effect, "What would you suggest?"
3. The problem of getting where they are supposed to go.
   Answer: verse 24, "I control the winds and the ocean currents. I will steer you."

20 And the Lord said unto the brother of Jared: Behold, thou shalt **make a hole in the top, and also in the bottom** [*with stoppers or plugs for them*]; and when thou shalt suffer for [*lack of fresh*] air thou shalt unstop the hole and receive air. And if it be so that the water come in upon thee, behold, ye shall stop the hole, that ye may not perish in the flood.

21 And it came to pass that **the brother of Jared did so**, according as the Lord had commanded.

22 And he cried again unto the Lord saying: O Lord, behold **I have done even as thou hast commanded me**; and I have prepared the vessels for my people, and behold **there is no light in them**. Behold, O Lord, **wilt thou suffer** [*do You want*] **that we shall cross this great water in darkness**?

23 And the Lord said unto the brother of Jared: **What will ye** [*what do you want*] **that I should do that ye may have light in your vessels** [*ships*]? For behold, **ye cannot have windows**, for they will be dashed in pieces; **neither shall ye take fire** with you, for **ye shall not go by the light of fire**.

24 For behold, ye shall be as a whale in the midst of the sea [*you will be under water much of the time*]; for the mountain waves shall dash upon you. Nevertheless, I will bring you up again out of the depths of the sea; for **the winds have gone forth out of my mouth** [*I control the winds and will steer you with them*], and also the rains and the floods have I sent forth.

25 And behold, I prepare you against these things; for ye cannot cross this great deep save I prepare you against the waves of the sea, and the winds which have gone forth, and the floods which shall come. **Therefore what will ye that I should prepare for you that ye may have light** [*what do you want Me to do to provide light for you*] when ye are swallowed up in the depths of the sea?

ETHER 3

Next, we have a marvelous chapter in which the brother of Jared will see the Savior in His premortal spirit body. You will see that our spirit bodies have the same parts that our physical bodies have.

Many lessons are taught us in this chapter. Among other things, we will be taught that it usually takes work to qualify for receiving desired blessings. We will learn about what could be termed "power prayer." Knowledge of what a spirit body looks like will be given us, and the power of faith will be taught. And we will hear once again about the Urim and Thummim.

First, we will be taught that obtaining desired blessings from God often requires work on our part. The brother of Jared is a great example of this "work ethic" principle.

Imagine how much work it would require just to be able to make the sixteen small, clear, white stones mentioned in verse 1. He would likely have to hunt and kill animals for their hides so he could make a bellows (to blow air) to heat the fire hot enough to melt the rock to form the clear, glass stones. The hides would probably have to be tanned in order to make workable bellows. Perhaps he would have to make tools and a mold in which to pour the white, hot melted rock.

Whatever the case, it would certainly require much work to form the sixteen small stones, plus the energy and effort to climb to the top of this tall mountain of "exceeding height" (verse 1) to pray and tell the Lord what he had in mind for the white stones as a means of light for the eight ships.

1 AND it came to pass that **the brother of Jared**, (now **the number of the vessels** [*ships*] which had been prepared **was eight**) **went forth unto the mount**, which they called the mount Shelem, because of its **exceeding height** [*because it was very high*], and **did molten** [*melt*] **out of a rock sixteen small stones**; and they were **white** and **clear, even as transparent** [*you can see through it*] **glass**; and **he did carry them in his hands upon the top of the mount**, **and cried** [*prayed*] **again unto the Lord, saying**:

Verses 2–5, next, are an example of powerful prayer. By studying it carefully, we can perhaps see a progression from pure humility and even some hesitancy, to a condition of pure faith and confidence in presenting a request to the Lord. Keep in mind that all such requests in prayer need to be according to the will of the Lord (see D&C 46:30; 50:30), and that we must never attempt to push God in prayer. Obviously, the Holy Ghost is directing the brother of Jared's words here.

2 O Lord, thou hast said that we must be encompassed about by the floods [*we will be covered by waves and submerged in the ocean, etc.*]. Now behold, O Lord, and **do not be angry with thy servant because of his weakness** before thee; for **we know that thou art holy** and dwellest in the heavens, and **that we are unworthy before thee**; because of the fall our natures have become evil continually; nevertheless, O Lord, **thou hast given us a commandment that we must call upon** [*pray unto*] **thee, that from thee we may receive according to our desires**.

3 Behold, O Lord, **thou hast smitten** [*punished*] **us because of our iniquity** [*sins*], and hast driven us forth, and for these many years we have been in the wilderness; **nevertheless,**

thou hast been merciful unto us. O Lord, **look upon me in pity**, and **turn away thine anger from this thy people**, and **suffer not** [*don't allow*] **that they shall go forth across this raging deep in darkness**; but **behold** [*look at*] **these things which I have molten** [*melted and formed*] **out of the rock**.

Perhaps you can feel a change in this humble man's voice as he continues in verse 4. It is a sense of confidence, brought into his soul by the approval of the Spirit as a result of his worthiness and of his openness in the previous verses.

4 And **I know, O Lord, that thou hast all power, and can do whatsoever thou wilt for the benefit of man**; therefore **touch these stones, O Lord, with thy finger**, and **prepare them that they may shine forth in darkness**; and they shall shine forth unto us in the vessels which we have prepared, that we may have light while we shall cross the sea.

5 Behold, O Lord, **thou canst do this. We know that thou art able to show forth great power**, which looks small unto the understanding of men [*which unspiritual and insensitive people would explain away and not believe came from God*].

As we continue, we see the "finger of the Lord" and learn some doctrinal details about spirits.

6 And it came to pass that when the brother of Jared had said these words, behold, **the Lord** [*the premortal Jesus Christ with His spirit body*] **stretched forth his hand and touched the stones one by one with his finger**. And **the veil** [*which keeps us from seeing God, spirits, heaven, etc.*] **was taken from off the eyes of the brother of Jared**, and **he saw the finger of the Lord**; and **it was as the finger of a man, like unto flesh and blood** [*His spirit body looked like a flesh and blood body; in other words, like our physical bodies*]; and **the brother of Jared fell down** before the Lord, for he was **struck with fear**.

As we continue, we see the Savior leading the brother of Jared through a rich learning experience, with a question and answer teaching approach. The Savior is the teacher, and Mahonri Moriancumer is the student.

Question

7 And the Lord saw that the brother of Jared had fallen to the earth; and the Lord said unto him: Arise, **why hast thou fallen**?

Answer

8 And he saith unto the Lord: **I saw the finger of the Lord, and I feared lest he should smite me** [*strike me dead*]**; for I knew not that the Lord had flesh and blood**.

Question

9 And the Lord said unto him: **Because of thy faith thou hast seen that I shall take upon me flesh and blood** [*I will receive a mortal body when I am born*]; and never has man come

before me with such exceeding faith as thou hast [*we will do more with this phrase when we get to verses 13–15*]; for were it not so ye could not have seen my finger. **Sawest thou** [*Did you see*] **more than this**?

Answer

10 And he answered: **Nay; Lord, show thyself unto me**.

Question

11 And the Lord said unto him: **Believest thou the words which I shall speak**?

Answer

12 And he answered: **Yea** [*yes*], **Lord, I know that thou speakest the truth, for thou art a God of truth, and canst not lie**.

Next, the premortal Christ actually shows Himself to the brother of Jared and introduces Himself as Jesus Christ. This is unusual, because in all other recorded appearances in the Old Testament up to this time, Christ has appeared as Jehovah, or in other words, as the God of the Old Testament under Heavenly Father's direction, without necessarily explaining that He is Jesus rather than Heavenly Father. This is called "divine investiture," which means that the Savior speaks for the Father without explaining the difference between Himself and His Father. Examples are found in Moses 6:1, 3, 27, 35; 7:35, as well as elsewhere. An example of this divine investiture in our day is found in Doctrine and Covenants 29:1, where Jesus clearly states that He is speaking, and in verses 42 and 46, where He speaks for the Father as if the Father were the one speaking.

We will continue now with this marvelous appearance to the brother of Jared.

13 And when he had said these words, behold, **the Lord showed himself unto him**, and said: Because thou knowest these things ye are redeemed from the fall [*of Adam and Eve*]; therefore ye are brought back into my presence; therefore I show myself unto you.

14 Behold, **I am he who was prepared from the foundation of the world to redeem my people** [*I am the One who was chosen in the premortal council to be the Redeemer*]. Behold, **I am Jesus Christ. I am the Father** [*the Creator; the Father or Author of your salvation; I speak for the Father*] **and the Son** [*the Son of God*]. **In me** [*through My Atonement and gospel*] **shall all mankind have life** [*eternal life; exaltation will be made available to all*], and that eternally, even **they who shall believe on my name**; and **they shall become my sons and my daughters** [*I am the "Father" of their salvation; through Me, they are born again; see Mosiah 5:7*].

15 And **never have I showed myself unto man whom I have created, for never has man believed in me as thou hast. Seest thou that ye are created after mine own image**? Yea, even **all men were created in the beginning after mine own image**.

As mentioned previously, we will spend a moment looking at the phrase "never have I showed myself unto man whom I have created," in verse 15, above.

First of all, we don't know for sure what the Savior meant by this. We will have to wait for clarification. We know from the scriptures that He had already appeared to Adam, Seth, Enoch, and Noah, who were righteous, holy prophets.

Therefore, we are left to wonder if He meant that He had never yet appeared so completely to anyone or to anybody with so much faith as the brother of Jared had. Or maybe he had never been so personal or introduced Himself as Jesus Christ. It might be that He simply meant that common, ordinary, worldly "man" had never seen Him because of his inability or unworthiness to be in the presence of God as was the brother of Jared.

Whatever the case, this was a marvelous manifestation of the premortal Christ to a humble prophet.

16 Behold, **this body, which ye now behold** [*which you are now looking at*], **is the body of my spirit**; and **man have I created after the body of my spirit** [*people's bodies look like My spirit body*]; and **even as I appear unto thee to be in the spirit will I appear unto my people in the flesh.** [*I will look like this in My mortal body.*]

Jesus seems to be speaking for the Father by way of "divine investiture" (see note after verse 12, above) when He says "and man have I created" in verse 16, above. We know that Jesus created all things under the direction of the Father, except man. We will quote from the *Doctrines of the Gospel Student Manual*, used by the Institutes of Religion of the Church, chapter 7 (**bold** added for emphasis):

"We know that Jehovah-Christ, assisted by 'many of the noble and great ones' (Abraham 3:22), of whom Michael is but the illustration, did in fact create the earth and all forms of plant and animal life on the face thereof. **But when it came to placing man on earth, there was a change in Creators**. That is, the Father himself became personally involved. All things were created by the Son, using the power delegated by the Father, except man. In the spirit and again in the flesh, **man was created by the Father. There was no delegation of authority where the crowning creature of creation was concerned**" (McConkie, *The Promised Messiah*, 62; *Doctrines of the Gospel*, 18).

Moroni now summarizes this great event.

17 And now, **as I, Moroni, said I could not make a full account of these things which are written**, therefore **it sufficeth me** [*it is enough*] **to say that Jesus showed himself unto this man in the spirit, even after the manner and in the likeness of the same body** [*like His resurrected body*] **even as he showed himself unto the Nephites**.

18 And **he ministered unto him even as he ministered unto the Nephites**; and all this, that this man might know that he was God, because of the many great works which the Lord had showed unto him.

Next, Moroni explains the power of the brother of Jared's faith, and that such faith can lead to perfect knowledge.

19 And **because of the knowledge of this man he could not be kept from beholding** [*seeing*] **within the veil** [*which normally keeps us from seeing God and spirits and angels*]; **and he saw the finger of Jesus**, which, when he saw, he fell with fear; for he knew that it was the finger of the Lord; and **he had faith no longer, for he knew, nothing doubting.**

20 Wherefore, **having this perfect knowledge of God, he could not be kept from within the veil** [*from seeing though the veil*]; **therefore he saw Jesus; and he did minister unto him.**

Next, in verses 21–28, we can learn a general lesson from a specific set of instructions from the Lord. It is that some experiences are so sacred and personal that they should only be shared with others under the direction of the Holy Ghost.

In this case, verse 21, the Savior instructs the brother of Jared not to reveal this sacred experience to anyone until He, Christ, had performed His mortal mission on earth. He is to write the experience in a language that no one can read (verse 22) by means of a Urim and Thummim (verse 23), which the Lord provides. It is interesting to know that there is more than one Urim and Thummim, and the one given to the Prophet Joseph Smith was the one used by the brother of Jared. See Bible Dictionary, at the end of the Bible published by our church, under "Urim and Thummim."

21 And it came to pass that **the Lord said unto the brother of Jared: Behold, thou shalt not suffer** [*permit*] **these things which ye have seen and heard to go forth** [*to be published*] **unto the world, until the time cometh that I shall glorify my name in the flesh**; wherefore, ye shall **treasure up the things which ye have seen and heard** [*they are for your personal benefit, for you to cherish and treasure*], and **show it to no man.**

22 And behold, **when ye shall come unto me** [*we don't know if this means just before the brother of Jared dies, or on another occasion not specifically mentioned here, when he is to meet the Savior and be given a Urim and Thummim, or what*], **ye shall write them and shall seal them up**, that no one can interpret them; for **ye shall write them in a language that they cannot be read.**

23 And behold, **these two stones** [*a Urim and Thummim*] **will I give unto thee**, and **ye shall seal them up also with the things which ye shall write.**

We assume that the things the brother of Jared wrote are contained in the sealed portion of the Book of Mormon plates, which were not translated by Joseph Smith.

24 For behold, **the language which ye shall write I have confounded** [*made so that no one else can understand it without the help of a Urim and Thummim*]; wherefore **I will cause in my own due time** [*when the time is right*] **that these stones shall magnify to the eyes of men these things which ye shall write.**

Next, the Savior showed this great prophet all things because of his tremendous faith.

25 And when the Lord had said these words, **he showed unto the brother of Jared all the inhabitants of the earth which had been, and also all that would be**; and he withheld them not from his sight, even unto the ends of the earth.

26 For he had said unto him in times before, that if he would believe in him that he could show unto him all things—it should be shown unto him; therefore **the Lord could not withhold anything from him, for he knew that the Lord could show him all things**.

27 And **the Lord said unto him: Write these things and seal them up; and I will show them in mine own due time** unto the children of men.

28 And it came to pass that **the Lord commanded him that he should seal up the two stones** [*the Urim and Thummim, which he used*] **which he had received, and show them not, until the Lord should show them unto the children of men.** [*As mentioned previously, Joseph Smith received this Urim and Thummim.*]

ETHER 4

In this chapter, the Lord will tell the brother of Jared to go back down the mountain and then to write down what he had seen when he saw the finger of the Lord and everything else he had seen.

In this chapter, Moroni will give some more information and teaching about what he told us in chapter 3. He will also teach us about faith and the importance of believing Christ.

1 AND **the Lord commanded the brother of Jared to go down out of the mount from the presence of the Lord, and write the things which he had seen** [*whether this means that he was to write them immediately, or sometime in the future after he had gone down off the mountain, we don't know*]; **and they were forbidden to come unto** [*to be revealed to*] **the children of men** [*the inhabitants of the earth*] **until after that he** [*Christ*] **should be** [*had been*] **lifted up upon the cross** [*crucified*]; and for this cause did king Mosiah keep them [*this is why King Mosiah kept them*], that they should not come unto [*be revealed to*] the world until after Christ should show himself unto his people.

2 **And after Christ truly had showed himself unto his people he commanded that they should be made manifest** [*shown so people could read about them*].

Next, Moroni reminds us that at this point in his life, the Nephites have all been destroyed or have left the true gospel and joined the Lamanites. Also, he tells us that he has written the things the brother of Jared saw on the gold plates (which Joseph Smith will receive from him).

3 And **now, after that** [*after the Savior came to the Nephites, as recorded in Third*

Nephi], **they have all dwindled in unbelief**; and **there is none save it be** [*except*] **the Lamanites**, and **they have rejected the gospel of Christ; therefore I am commanded that I should hide them up again in the earth.**

4 Behold, **I have written upon these plates** [*the gold plates, which Moroni will give to Joseph Smith*] **the very things which the brother of Jared saw**; and there never were greater things made manifest than those which were made manifest unto the brother of Jared.

In verses 5–7, Moroni tells us again that the rest of the things that the brother of Jared saw are sealed and are not to be revealed until people are ready and worthy to receive them.

Based on this and what we read in Ether, chapter 5, we understand that the things referred to by Moroni, here, are contained in the sealed portion of the Book of Mormon plates, which Moroni told Joseph Smith specifically (see Ether 5:1) not to attempt to translate.

5 Wherefore **the Lord hath commanded me to write them; and I have written them**. And **he commanded me that I should seal them up**; and **he also hath commanded that I should seal up the interpretation thereof**; wherefore [*and so*] **I have sealed up the interpreters** [*the Urim and Thummim*], **according to the commandment of the Lord**.

Next, we are told when we will be privileged to learn the contents of these sealed plates.

6 For the Lord said unto me: **They shall not go forth unto the Gentiles until the day that they shall repent of their iniquity** [*sins and wickedness*], **and become clean before the Lord**.

7 And **in that day that they shall exercise faith in me**, saith the Lord, **even as the brother of Jared did**, that they may become sanctified [*pure and holy*] in me [*through the power of the Atonement*], **then will I manifest** [*show*] **unto them the things which the brother of Jared saw, even** to the unfolding [*revealing*] unto them **all my revelations**, saith Jesus Christ, the Son of God, the Father [*the Creator*] of the heavens and of the earth, and all things that in them are.

Next, a warning from Moroni.

8 And **he that will contend** [*fight*] **against the word of the Lord, let him be accursed** [*damned; stopped in eternal progression*]; **and he that shall deny these things, let him be accursed**; for **unto them will I show no greater things, saith Jesus Christ; for I am he who speaketh.**

In verse 8, above, we are reminded that to gain additional knowledge and insights from heaven, we must be doing our best to live what we already know of the gospel.

9 And **at my command the heavens are opened and are shut; and at my word the earth shall shake; and at my command the inhabitants thereof shall pass away** [*be destroyed*], **even so as by fire**.

10 And **he that believeth not my**

words believeth not my disciples; and if it so be that I do not speak, judge ye [*you decide*]; for ye shall know that it is I that speaketh, at the last day [*when you see Me on Judgment Day*].

11 But **he that believeth these things** which I have spoken, **him will I visit** [*bless*] **with the manifestations** [*blessings and revelations*] **of my Spirit**, and he shall know and bear record. For **because of my Spirit he shall know that these things are true**; for it **persuadeth men to do good**.

12 And **whatsoever thing persuadeth men to do good is of me; for good cometh of none save it be of me. I am the same that leadeth men to all good; he that will not believe my words** [*including in the scriptures and the words of the living prophets*] **will not believe me**—that I am [*that I exist*]; and **he that will not believe me will not believe the Father who sent me**. For behold, I am the Father [*I represent the Father; Christ is the Father of our salvation; the Father or Creator of heaven and earth*], **I am the light, and the life, and the truth of the world**.

Next, the Savior invites all people to come unto Him.

13 **Come unto me, O ye Gentiles**, and I will show unto you the greater things, the knowledge which is hid up because of unbelief.

14 **Come unto me, O ye house of Israel**, and it shall be made manifest unto you how great things the Father hath laid up for you [*what great blessings Heavenly Father has for you*], from the foundation of the world [*clear from the premortal life*]; and it hath not come unto you, because of unbelief.

15 Behold, **when ye shall rend** [*tear; do away with*] **that veil of unbelief** which doth cause you to remain in your awful state of wickedness, and hardness of heart, and blindness of mind, **then shall the great and marvelous things which have been hid up from the foundation of the world from you**—yea, when ye shall call upon the Father in my name, with a broken heart and a contrite spirit, **then shall ye know that the Father hath remembered** [*is keeping*] **the covenant which he made unto your fathers, O house of Israel** [*to gather Israel and all who are willing to come, back to Christ and from Him to the Father*].

Next, Jesus speaks of the book of Revelation, written by John, which is contained in the Bible. From this context, we understand that the brother of Jared saw the things which were shown in vision to John, as did Nephi (see 1 Nephi 14:18–28). We understand that the brother of Jared's account of the things in the book of Revelation are contained in the sealed portion of the Book of Mormon plates.

16 And **then** [*when we get the sealed portion of the gold plates translated*] **shall my revelations** [*the book of Revelation*] **which I have caused to be written by my servant John** [*the Apostle*] be unfolded [*be made clear*] in the eyes of all the people. Remember, **when ye see these things** [*the Book of Mormon*],

ye shall know that the time is at hand that they [*the writings of the brother of Jared*] **shall be made manifest in very deed** [*indeed*].

Next, we are told again, as in 3 Nephi 21:1, 28, and elsewhere (see also heading to 3 Nephi 21), that the coming forth of the Book of Mormon is a sign that the Restoration of the gospel and the gathering of Israel has begun prior to the Second Coming of Christ.

17 Therefore, **when ye shall receive this record** [*the Book of Mormon*] **ye may know that the work of the Father has commenced** [*has begun*] **upon all the face of the land**.

As this chapter comes to a close, the Savior issues another invitation for all people everywhere to repent and receive the blessings of His gospel.

18 Therefore, **repent all ye ends of the earth** [*all people everywhere*], and **come unto me**, and **believe in my gospel**, and **be baptized** in my name; for **he that believeth and is baptized shall be saved**; but **he that believeth not shall be damned** [*stopped*]; and signs shall follow them that believe in my name.

19 And **blessed is he that is found faithful unto my name at the last day** [*on Judgment Day*], **for he shall be lifted up to dwell in the kingdom** [*celestial glory; exaltation*] **prepared for him from the foundation of the world** [*planned and prepared in premortality*]. And **behold it is I that hath spoken it** [*this is Christ's testimony to us*]. Amen.

ETHER 5

In this chapter, Moroni speaks directly to Joseph Smith. He warns him not to try to translate the sealed portion of the Book of Mormon plates. He also informs him that he, Joseph, will be allowed to show the gold plates to some who will serve as witnesses (verse 2), and that three witnesses will be shown the plates "by the power of God" (verse 3).

We know that in June 1829, three witnesses, Oliver Cowdery, David Whitmer, and Martin Harris, were shown the plates by the power of God (see "The Testimony of Three Witnesses" at the beginning of your Book of Mormon). As you read their testimony, you will see that an angel showed them the plates and that they heard the voice of God bearing witness that the plates were "translated by the gift and power of God." For other things that the Three Witnesses were privileged to see at this time, read Doctrine and Covenants 17:1.

We know that eight witnesses were also shown the gold plates by the Prophet Joseph Smith in June 1829. According to "The Testimony of Eight Witnesses," in the introductory pages to your Book of Mormon, their names were Christian Whitmer, Jacob Whitmer, Peter Whitmer Jun., John Whitmer, Hiram Page, Joseph Smith Sen., Hyrum Smith, and Samuel H. Smith. As you will see if you read their testimony, these eight men not only saw the set of gold plates, but they also lifted them and touched each of the translated plates. According to various accounts, the plates weighed about sixty pounds. A portion of one such account follows.

"Not long before his death, William [*Smith*] reiterated his vivid experience with the plates to interviewer J. W. Peterson. 'Bro. Briggs then handed me a pencil and asked Bro. Smith if he ever saw the plates his brother had had, from which the Book of Mormon was translated. He replied, 'I did not see them uncovered, but I handled them and hefted them while wrapped in a tow frock and **judged them to have weighed about sixty pounds**. I could tell they were plates of some kind and that they were fastened together by rings running through the back.'" (Anderson, *Investigating the Book of Mormon Witnesses*, 23)

We now continue with Moroni's instructions to Joseph Smith.

1 AND now **I, Moroni, have written the words which were commanded me, according to my memory**; and **I have told you the things which I have sealed up** [*the sealed portion of the gold plates*]; therefore **touch them not in order that ye may translate** [*don't even try to translate them*]; for **that thing** [*translating the sealed portion*] **is forbidden you**, except by and by it shall be wisdom in God [*when God decides it is time*].

2 And **behold, ye may be privileged that ye may show the plates** [*the gold plates*] **unto those** [*the Eight Witnesses*] **who shall assist** [*help*] **to bring forth this work** [*to give the world the Book of Mormon*];

3 And **unto three** [*the Three Witnesses*] **shall they be shown by the power of God**; wherefore they shall know of a surety [*for sure*] that these things are true.

4 And **in the mouth of three witnesses shall these things be established**; and the testimony of three, and this work, in the which shall be shown forth the power of God and also his word, of which the Father, and the Son, and the Holy Ghost bear record—and **all this shall stand as a testimony against the world at the last day**.

5 And **if it so be that they** [*the inhabitants of the world*] **repent and come unto the Father in the name of Jesus, they shall be received into the kingdom of God** [*heaven, celestial glory*].

In summary, Moroni challenges anyone who argues against his testimony. He leaves no doubt how strongly he feels about the truth of the work of which he is prophesying and testifying.

6 And now, **if I have no authority for these things, judge ye** [*you decide*]**; for ye shall know that I have authority when ye shall see me, and we shall stand before God at the last day** [*on the day of the Final Judgment*]. Amen.

ETHER 6

In this chapter, Jared and his brother and their families and their friends, along with their supplies, animals, and whatever else they will need, go aboard the eight small ships and make the 344-day journey to America. As you can well imagine, that is an awfully long time to be on a ship and each of the small groups on the eight ships must have had a lot of faith in God to have been able to do it.

Moroni continues to tell us the history of these Jaredites.

1 AND **now I, Moroni, proceed to give the record of Jared and his brother** [*Mahonri Moriancumer*].

2 For it came to pass after the Lord had prepared the stones [*the sixteen small stones that shined and would provide light in the ships*] which the brother of Jared had carried up into the mount, the brother of Jared came down out of the mount [*mountain*], and **he did put** forth **the stones into the vessels** which were prepared, **one in each end thereof**; and behold, **they did give light unto the vessels** [*ships*].

3 And thus **the Lord caused stones to shine in darkness, to give light unto men, women, and children, that they might not cross the great waters** [*the ocean*] **in darkness**.

4 And it came to pass that **when they had prepared all manner** [*all kinds*] **of food**, that thereby they might subsist [*survive*] upon the water, **and also food for their flocks** [*animals*] **and herds**, and whatsoever beast or animal or fowl [*bird*] that they should carry with them—and it came to pass that **when they had done all these things they got aboard of their vessels** or barges, and set forth into the sea, **commending themselves unto the Lord their God** [*turning themselves over to the Lord*].

5 And it came to pass that **the Lord God caused that there should be a furious** [*very strong*] **wind** blow upon the face of the waters, **towards the promised land**; and thus they were tossed upon the waves of the sea before the wind.

6 And it came to pass that **they were many times buried in the depths of the sea**, because of the mountain waves which broke upon them, and also the great and terrible tempests which were caused by the fierceness of the wind.

7 And it came to pass that **when they were buried in the deep there was no water that could hurt them, their vessels being tight like unto a dish**, and also they were tight like unto the ark of Noah; therefore when they were encompassed about [*surrounded*] by many waters **they did cry** [*pray*] **unto the Lord, and he did bring them forth again upon the top of the waters**.

Moroni wants us to know that prayer was a major factor in bringing them safely to the promised land.

8 And it came to pass that **the wind did never cease to blow** [*stop blowing*]

towards the promised land [*perhaps symbolizing that the help of the Lord is always there, moving us toward celestial glory*] while they were upon the waters; and thus they were driven forth before the wind.

9 And **they did sing praises unto the Lord** [*they had gratitude and optimism*]; yea, the brother of Jared did sing praises unto the Lord, and he did **thank and praise the Lord all the day long**; and when the night came, **they did not cease to praise the Lord**.

10 And **thus they were driven forth** [*pushed by the wind across the ocean*]; and **no monster of the sea could break them, neither whale that could mar** [*hurt*] **them** [*nothing could stop them, because they had followed the Lord's instructions in their preparations, and because they had put themselves in His care*]; and **they did have light continually** [*from the white stones that shined*], whether it was above the water or under the water.

11 And thus they were driven forth, **three hundred and forty and four days** upon the water.

Finally, they arrive in the promised land and immediately express gratitude for their safe arrival.

12 And **they did land upon the shore of the promised land** [*somewhere on the coast of the Americas*]. And when they had set their feet upon the shores of the promised land **they bowed themselves down upon the face of the land, and did humble themselves before the Lord, and did shed tears of joy before the Lord**, because of the multitude [*great number*] of his tender mercies over them.

Next, Moroni moves rather quickly in his summary, leading up to the issue of having a king.

13 And it came to pass that **they went forth** [*spread out*] **upon the face of the land**, and began to till the earth [*farm the ground*].

14 And **Jared had four sons**; and they were called Jacom, and Gilgah, and Mahah, and Orihah.

15 And **the brother of Jared also begat** [*had*] **sons and daughters** [*he had twenty-two children; see verse 20, below*].

16 And the friends of Jared and his brother were in number **about twenty and two souls**; and they also begat sons and daughters before they came to the promised land; and therefore **they began to be many** [*their population increased*].

17 And **they were taught to walk humbly before the Lord; and they were also taught from on high** [*from heaven*].

18 And it came to pass that **they began to spread upon the face of the land**, and to multiply and to till the earth; and they did wax [*grow*] strong in the land.

19 And **the brother of Jared began to be old**, and saw that he must soon go down to the grave [*saw that he would soon die*]; wherefore **he said unto**

Jared: Let us gather together our people that we may number [*count*] **them, that we may know of them what they will desire of us before we go down to our graves.**

20 And accordingly the people were gathered together. Now **the number of the sons and the daughters of the brother of Jared were twenty and two souls**; and **the number of sons and daughters of Jared were twelve, he having four sons.**

21 And it came to pass that **they did number their people**; and after that they had numbered them, **they did desire of them** [*they asked them*] **the things which they would that they should do before they went down to their graves.**

22 And it came to pass that **the people desired of them that they should anoint one of their sons to be a king over them.**

The request of their people to have a king was a worry to Jared and his brother. Perhaps you have noticed that whenever people have a king, they tend to think less about their own future and turn more power and responsibility over to the king. Either that, or the king takes more and more power.

Ultimately, in most cases, having a king tends to lead downhill, and this, no doubt, was one of the concerns in the minds and hearts of these two great men. You can read more about the potential problems of having a king in Mosiah 29:10–23 as King Mosiah II advises his people on the matter.

23 And now behold, **this was grievous** [*a big worry*] **unto them**. And the brother of Jared said unto them: **Surely this thing leadeth into captivity** [*having a king will lead you to having less freedom*].

24 **But Jared said unto his brother: Suffer** [*permit*] **them that they may have a king**. And therefore he said unto them: **Choose ye out from among our sons a king**, even whom ye will.

25 And it came to pass that **they chose even the firstborn of the brother of Jared**; and his name was **Pagag**. And it came to pass that **he refused** and would not be their king. And the people would that his father should constrain him [*wanted his father to force him to become their king*], **but his father would not**; and he commanded them that they should constrain no man to be their king.

26 And it came to pass that **they chose all the brothers of Pagag, and they would not** [*they all refused*].

27 And it came to pass that **neither would the sons of Jared**, even **all save** [*except*] **it were one**; and **Orihah was anointed to be king** over the people.

Orihah was a righteous man, as we see in verse 30, below, as well as in chapter 7, verse 1.

28 And **he began to reign** [*rule as king*], and **the people began to prosper** [*things went well for them*]; and they became exceedingly [*very*] rich.

Next, the brother of Jared and Jared die. It will be interesting to meet them some day.

29 And it came to pass that **Jared died, and his brother also.**

Moroni continues to teach us the principles of righteous living as he summarizes things so far, in verse 30, next.

30 And it came to pass that **Orihah did walk humbly before the Lord**, and did **remember how great things the Lord had done for his father**, and also taught his people how great things the Lord had done for their fathers [*reminded them of the many blessings from the Lord in the past so they would remember to be righteous themselves*].

ETHER 7

In chapters 7–11, Moroni will move us rather rapidly through many years of Jaredite history, occasionally stopping to give his own comments, and teaching us principles and doctrines. This is, in effect, a short course in comparison and contrast between righteous civilizations and wicked civilizations as they reject God.

We will especially be taught the effect of righteous rulers and wicked leaders upon nations. We are reminded of Doctrine and Covenants 98:9–10, as follows, about how important it is for us to select good and honorable government leaders:

9 Nevertheless, **when the wicked rule the people mourn**.

10 Wherefore [*this is why*], **honest men and wise men should be sought for diligently, and good men and wise men ye should observe to uphold**; otherwise whatsoever is less than these cometh of evil.

We will now continue, with Moroni as our teacher.

1 AND it came to pass that **Orihah did execute judgment** [*ruled with wisdom and fairness*] upon the land in righteousness all his days [*all of his life*], whose days were exceedingly many [*and he lived a very long life*].

While we don't know what the average life span among these people was, in verse 1, above, we are told that Orihah's "days were exceedingly many," leading us to believe that they were living fairly long. We may possibly get an idea of what this means in Ether 9:23–24, where we meet Coriantum's wife, who lived to be 102 years old, and Coriantum, who lived to age 142.

2 And **he begat** [*had*] **sons and daughters**; yea, he begat **thirty and one, among whom were twenty and three sons.**

3 And it came to pass that he also begat Kib in his old age. And it came to pass that **Kib** reigned in his stead [*ruled in his place*]; and Kib begat **Corihor.**

Next, Moroni shows the effect of one wicked man on what was a peaceful society. It has probably been many decades since righteous King Orihah died.

One thing we see clearly is that the wicked do not like to associate with righteous people. They usually leave and then find others who think like they do, and together, they try to impose their evil philosophies upon the righteous by force. This is Satan's way.

4 And **when Corihor was thirty and two years old he rebelled against his father**, and went over and dwelt in the land of Nehor; and he begat sons and daughters, and they became exceedingly fair [*very handsome and beautiful*]; wherefore **Corihor drew away many people after him**.

Verse 4, above, implies that the attractiveness of Corihor's sons and daughters was the motivation for many to abandon their gospel standards and move to where a worldly culture was available.

5 And **when he had gathered together an army he came up unto the land of** Moron where the king [*Kib*] **dwelt** [*lived*], and **took him captive**, which brought to pass [*fulfilled*] the saying of the brother of Jared that they would be brought into captivity [*Ether 6:23*].

6 Now **the land of Moron, where the king dwelt, was near the land which is called Desolation by the Nephites**.

7 And it came to pass that **Kib dwelt in captivity, and his people under Corihor his son, until he became exceedingly old**; nevertheless **Kib begat Shule in his old age**, while he was yet in captivity.

8 And it came to pass that **Shule was angry with his brother**; and **Shule waxed** [*grew*] **strong, and became mighty as to the strength of a man**; and he was also mighty in judgment [*he was a very capable planner, had much common sense and wisdom*].

9 Wherefore, **he** came to the hill Ephraim, and he did molten [*smelted iron*] out of the hill, and **made swords out of steel for those whom he had drawn away with him**; and **after he had armed them with swords he returned to the city** Nehor and **gave battle unto his brother Corihor**, by which means [*and that's how*] he **obtained the kingdom and restored it unto his father Kib**.

10 And now **because of the thing which Shule had done, his father bestowed upon him the kingdom**; therefore he began to reign [*rule as king*] in the stead [*place*] of his father.

Next, Moroni tells us that Shule was a righteous king. We will also see that he is capable of forgiving. He is willing to risk trusting again and forgives Corihor, who had caused so much suffering.

11 And it came to pass that **he did execute** [*carry out*] **judgment in righteousness**; and he did spread his kingdom upon all the face of the land, for the people had become exceedingly numerous [*had become a very large group*].

12 And it came to pass that **Shule also begat many sons and daughters**.

13 And **Corihor repented** of the many evils which he had done;

wherefore Shule gave him power in his kingdom.

14 And it came to pass that Corihor had many sons and daughters. And **among the sons of Corihor there was one whose name was Noah.**

15 And it came to pass that **Noah rebelled against Shule, the king, and also his father Corihor**, and **drew away Cohor his brother, and also all his brethren and many of the people.**

16 And **he gave battle unto Shule**, the king, in which **he did obtain the land of their first inheritance** [*the area where the Jaredites first landed in America*]; and he **became a king over that part of the land.**

17 And it came to pass that **he gave battle again unto** [*went to war again against*] **Shule, the king; and he took Shule, the king, and carried him away captive into Moron.**

18 And it came to pass as he was about to put him to death, **the sons of Shule crept into the house of Noah by night and slew** [*killed*] **him, and broke down the door of the prison and brought out their father, and placed him upon his throne in his own kingdom.**

19 **Wherefore** [*and so*], **the son of Noah did build up his kingdom in his stead** [*in his place*]; nevertheless they did not gain power any more over Shule the king, and the people who were under the reign of Shule the king [*a righteous king; see verse 11, above*] did prosper exceedingly and wax [*grow*] great.

Next, Moroni points out that the country has now been divided, which results in continuing war and killing. Perhaps you've noticed that unity and harmony are a major result of gospel living, and that Satan is a master at destroying it.

20 And **the country was divided**; and **there were two kingdoms, the kingdom of Shule** [*a kingdom of righteousness*], **and the kingdom of Cohor**, the son of Noah [*a kingdom of evil and wickedness*].

21 And **Cohor, the son of Noah, caused that his people should give battle unto** [*go to war against*] **Shule**, in which **Shule did beat them** and did slay [*kill*] Cohor.

Verses 22–27 are a "mini course" in the power of the gospel to restore peace to a nation. It emphasizes the importance of having national laws that allow the gospel to be preached freely.

22 And now **Cohor had a son** who was called **Nimrod**; and **Nimrod gave up the kingdom of Cohor unto Shule** [*which would promote peace but would also introduce many into righteous King Shule's kingdom who did not share the same righteous standards as Shule's people had*], and he did gain favor in the eyes of Shule; wherefore Shule did bestow great favors upon him, and he did do in the kingdom of Shule according to his desires.

It is likely, as mentioned above, that the intermixing of the people of Cohor's kingdom with the people of Shule's kingdom resulted in much apostasy and wickedness. Thus, the need for prophets to preach against the "wickedness and idolatry" referred to in verse 23, next.

23 And also **in the reign** [*rule*] **of Shule there came prophets among the people**, who were sent from the Lord, **prophesying** [*the word "prophesying," as often used in the scriptures, seems to include the concept of teaching and explaining, as well as actual prophesying of the future*] **that the wickedness and idolatry of the people was bringing a curse upon the land, and they should** [*would*] **be destroyed if they did not repent**.

As you will see, in verses 24–27, next, laws that protected the rights of the prophets to preach the gospel in public were a very necessary part of saving the nation. An important lesson is in this for us today.

24 And it came to pass that **the people did revile** [*rebel and preach*] **against the prophets**, and did **mock them**. And it came to pass that **king Shule did execute** [*carry out*] **judgment against all those who did revile against the prophets**.

25 And **he did execute** [*make*] **a law throughout all the land, which gave power unto the prophets that they should** [*could*] **go whithersoever they would** [*wherever they wanted to*]**; and by this cause** [*this is how*] **the people were brought unto repentance**.

26 And **because the people did repent of their iniquities** [*sins and wickedness*] **and idolatries** [*worshiping idols*] **the Lord did spare them**, and **they began to prosper again** in the land. And it came to pass that Shule begat sons and daughters in his old age.

As Moroni often does (and as Mormon often did), as he finishes one segment and prepares to move on to the next, he points out a particular lesson he hopes we will learn from what he has just written. In this case, it is the importance of our remembering past blessings from the Lord as a means of keeping our present lives on the covenant path in the gospel.

27 And **there were no more wars in the days of Shule**; and **he remembered the great things that the Lord had done for his fathers** [*ancestors*] in bringing them across the great deep [*the ocean*] into the promised land; **wherefore** [*therefore*] **he did execute judgment** [*carry out his duties as king*] **in righteousness all his days.**

ETHER 8

One of the most evil and powerful weapons that Satan uses against people is terrorism. It often shows up in the form of "secret combinations," or secret groups, which, in the Book of Mormon, are associated with the destruction of society and the downfall of nations.

Here, among the Jaredites, we will now see the formation of a secret combination, and Moroni will instruct us and warn against ignoring or supporting such organizations.

1 AND it came to pass that he [*Shule*] begat Omer, and **Omer reigned** [*ruled as king*] **in his stead** [*place*]. And **Omer begat Jared**; and Jared begat sons and daughters.

2 And **Jared rebelled against his father**, and came and dwelt in the land of Heth. And it came to pass that **he did flatter many people, because of his cunning** [*clever, sly*] **words, until he had gained the half of the kingdom**.

3 And when he had gained the half of the kingdom **he gave battle unto his father**, and **he did carry away his father into captivity, and did make him serve in captivity**;

4 And now, in the days of the reign of **Omer** he **was in captivity the half of his days**. And it came to pass that **he begat sons and daughters, among whom were Esrom and Coriantumr**;

5 And they **were exceedingly angry because of the doings of Jared their brother**, insomuch [*so*] that they did raise an army and gave battle unto Jared. And it came to pass that **they did give battle unto him by night**.

6 And it came to pass that when **they had slain** [*killed*] **the army of Jared they were about to slay him also; and he plead with them that they would not slay him, and he would give up the kingdom unto his father**. And it came to pass that they did grant unto him his life.

With the above verses as background, you will see that secret combinations are built upon lies. In verse 6, above, Jared promised to give the kingdom back to his father if his brothers spared his life. They agreed, and he did. But in his heart, he still wanted the kingdom with the accompanying power, glory, and wealth for himself. Thus, the stage was set for Satan to move in with his evil doctrine of secret combinations.

7 And now **Jared became exceedingly sorrowful** because of the loss of the kingdom, for **he had set his heart upon the kingdom and upon the glory of the world**.

8 Now **the daughter of Jared** being exceedingly expert [*probably means that she was very capable and cunning*], and **seeing the sorrows of her father, thought to devise** [*come up with*] **a plan whereby she could redeem the kingdom unto her father** [*get the kingdom back for her father*].

9 Now **the daughter of Jared was exceedingly fair** [*very beautiful*]. And it came to pass that **she did talk with her father, and said unto him: Whereby hath** [*what has caused*] **my father so much sorrow? Hath he not read the record** [*the first portion of the twenty-four gold plates that the Jaredites brought with them across the ocean; see Ether 1:2–4*] **which our fathers brought across the great deep**? Behold, **is there not an account concerning them of old, that they by their secret plans** [*secret combinations*] **did obtain kingdoms and great glory**?

In other words, I have read about secret combinations. Haven't you? We can use such a thing to get the kingdom back for you.

Next, we see the evil plot hatched by Jared's beautiful but wicked daughter.

10 And now, therefore, **let my father send for Akish, the son of Kimnor**; and behold, **I am fair** [*beautiful*], **and I will dance before him, and I will please him, that he will desire me to wife** [*he will want to marry me*]; wherefore if he shall desire of thee that ye shall give unto him me to wife, **then shall ye say: I will give her if ye will bring unto me the head of my father, the king.**

11 And now **Omer** [*the king, Jared's father*] **was a friend to Akish**; wherefore, **when Jared had sent for Akish, the daughter of Jared danced before him** that **she pleased him, insomuch that he desired her to wife.** And it came to pass that **he said unto Jared: Give her unto me to wife.**

12 And Jared said unto him: **I will give her unto you, if ye will bring unto me the head of my father, the king.**

Next, we see one of the evil elements of secret combinations, namely, secretly covenanting with others to protect them in murdering for purposes of gaining power and wealth. You may wish to read Moses 5:29–31, where Satan creates the first "secret combination" with Cain for the same purposes.

We are seeing this same evil and terribly destructive approach in many forms today, including terrorists groups and individuals, gangs, internet virus creators, sellers, and users of internet pornography, anonymous internet bullying, etc.

13 And it came to pass that **Akish gathered in unto the house of Jared all his kinsfolk** [*relatives*], and said unto them: **Will ye swear** [*covenant, promise*] **unto me that ye will be faithful unto me in the thing which I shall desire of you**?

14 And it came to pass that **they all sware** [*covenanted*] **unto him, by the God of heaven** [*they covenanted in the name of God to do evil, which is pure mockery of God*], **and also by the heavens, and also by the earth**, and **by their heads** [*by their own lives*], that whoso should vary [*whoever would not keep their promise*] from the assistance which Akish desired should lose his head [*be killed*]; and **whoso should divulge** [*tell anyone else*] **whatsoever thing Akish made known unto them, the same should lose his life.**

Perhaps you have noticed that Satan is the "great counterfeiter." He copies God's ways of making covenants in order accomplish his evil plans. It seems that for every good thing brought to us by a loving God, Lucifer produces a counterfeit.

For instance, God provides oaths and covenants which, if made and kept, will lead to eternal happiness in celestial glory. As an exact opposite and counterfeit, the devil sponsors secret evil oaths and covenants, which lead to destruction, both physically and spiritually.

15 And it came to pass that thus **they did agree with Akish**. And **Akish did administer unto them the oaths** which were given by them of old [*in ancient times*] who also sought power, **which had been handed down even from Cain**, who was a murderer from the beginning.

16 And **they were kept up by the power of the devil to administer these oaths unto the people, to keep them in darkness, to help such as sought power to gain power, and to murder, and to plunder** [*rob and destroy*], **and to lie, and to commit all manner of wickedness and whoredoms** [*sexual immorality*].

17 And **it was the daughter of Jared who put it into his** [*Jared's*] **heart** to search up these things of old; and **Jared put it into the heart of Akish**; wherefore, **Akish administered it** [*secret oaths and covenants*] **unto his kindred** [*relatives*] **and friends, leading them away by fair promises to do whatsoever thing he desired** [*Akish thus becomes a "type" of, or symbolic of, the devil*].

Next, in verse 18, Moroni tells us where secret combinations rank in comparison to other tools of the devil.

18 And it came to pass that **they formed a secret combination**, even as they of old; which combination is **most abominable** [*terribly evil*] **and wicked above all, in the sight of God**;

19 For **the Lord worketh not in secret combinations**, neither doth he will that man should shed blood [*commit murder*], but in all things hath forbidden it, from the beginning of man.

20 And now **I, Moroni, do not write the manner of their oaths and combinations** [*I'm not going to tell you the wording of their secret oaths and combinations*], **for** [*because*] it hath been made known unto me that **they are had among all people**, and they are had among the Lamanites.

21 And **they have caused the destruction of this people** [*the Jaredites*] of whom I am now speaking, and **also the destruction of the people of Nephi**.

Next, Moroni gives a stern warning against supporting secret combinations. We suppose that allowing them or tolerating them comes under the category of supporting them. This is a huge issue today in terms of national and international politics.

22 And **whatsoever nation shall uphold** [*support*] **such secret combinations**, to get power and gain, until they shall spread over the nation, behold, they **shall be destroyed**; for the Lord will not suffer [*allow*] that the blood of his saints, which shall be shed by them, shall always cry unto him from the ground for vengeance upon them and yet he avenge [*punish*] them not.

23 **Wherefore, O ye Gentiles, it is wisdom in God** [*it is wise in the eyes of God*] **that these things should be shown unto you, that thereby ye**

may repent of your sins, and **suffer not** [*don't permit*] **that these murderous combinations shall get above you**, which are built up to get power and gain—and the work, yea, even the work of destruction come upon you, yea, even the sword of **the justice of the Eternal God shall fall upon you, to your overthrow and destruction if ye shall suffer** [*allow*] **these things to be**.

Next, in verses 24–25, Moroni teaches us what to do if we see such things entering our society or personal lives.

24 Wherefore, the Lord commandeth you, when ye shall see these things come among you that **ye shall awake to a sense of your awful situation**, because of this secret combination which shall be among you; or wo be unto it, because of the blood of them who have been slain; for they cry from the dust for vengeance upon it, and also upon those who built it up.

25 For it cometh to pass that **whoso buildeth it up seeketh to overthrow the freedom of all lands, nations, and countries; and it bringeth to pass the destruction of all people, for it is built up by the devil, who is the father** [*the originator*] **of all lies; even that same liar who beguiled** [*deceived*] **our first parents** [*Adam and Eve*], **yea, even that same liar who hath caused man to commit murder from the beginning** [*starting with Cain, who killed his brother, Abel*]; **who hath hardened the hearts of men that they have murdered the prophets, and stoned them, and cast them out from the beginning.**

26 Wherefore, **I, Moroni, am commanded to write these things that evil may be done away, and that the time may come that Satan may have no power upon the hearts of the children of men** [*people*], **but that they may be persuaded to do good continually, that they may come unto the fountain** [*source*] **of all righteousness** [*Heavenly Father and Christ*] **and be saved.**

ETHER 9

As you may have noticed, Moroni is summarizing the history of these Jaredites as we go along, but, after he has covered quite a long time in their history, he stops and tells us what he wants us to learn from what he has just told us. He did a lot of that in chapter 8, starting with verse 19, where he told us and warned us what we should learn as far as the dangers of secret combinations are concerned. He is an inspired and powerful teacher. It will be exciting to meet him in person sometime in the next life!

In this chapter, we will see many things that we have seen in other places in the scriptures, such as the righteous being commanded to flee away from the wicked and settle elsewhere, the near complete destruction of a people through secret combinations, 225 years of righteousness combined with peace and prosperity (yes, it can be done), famine, poisonous serpents, repentance, humility, and many kinds of blessings.

First, Moroni tells us that he is now going to continue with the story of the Jaredites, after having paused in the history lesson to teach us application issues for our lives.

1 AND **now I, Moroni, proceed with my record**. Therefore, behold, it came to pass that **because of the secret combinations of Akish and his friends, behold, they did overthrow** [*took over*] **the kingdom of Omer**.

2 Nevertheless, **the Lord was merciful unto Omer** [*Jared's great-great-grandson, the great-great-nephew of the brother of Jared*], **and also to his sons and to his daughters who did not seek his destruction**.

3 And **the Lord warned Omer in a dream that he should depart out of the land**; **wherefore** [*and so*] **Omer departed out of the land with his family, and traveled many days**, and came over and passed by the hill of Shim, and came over by the place where the Nephites were destroyed, and from thence [*there*] eastward, and came to a place which was called Ablom, by the seashore, and there he pitched his tent, and also his sons and his daughters, and all his household, save [*except*] it were Jared [*his wicked son, who was trying to kill him*] and his family.

4 And it came to pass that **Jared was anointed king** [*he got what he wanted; see Ether 8:1–7*] over the people, **by the hand of wickedness** [*through evil methods*]; and **he gave unto Akish his daughter to wife**.

5 And it came to pass that **Akish sought the life of his father-in-law** [*Jared, who had entered into a secret combination with Akish to kill Jared's father, Omer; see Ether 8:10*]; and **he applied unto those whom he had sworn by the oath of the ancients** [*secret combination*], and **they obtained the head of his father-in-law** [*King Jared*], as he sat upon his throne, giving audience to his people.

6 For so great had been **the spreading of this wicked and secret society** that it had **corrupted** [*changed them to be wicked*] **the hearts of all the people; therefore Jared was murdered** upon his throne, and **Akish reigned** in his stead.

Next we see the paranoia and lack of trust that prevails in a society dominated by secret combinations.

7 And it came to pass that **Akish began to be jealous of his son** [*probably the successor to the throne*], therefore **he shut him up in prison**, and kept him upon little or no food until he had suffered death [*starved him to death*].

8 And now **the brother of him that suffered death** [*had been starved to death by his father, King Akish*], (and his name was **Nimrah**) **was angry with his father** because of that which his father had done unto his brother.

9 And it came to pass that **Nimrah gathered together a small number of men, and fled out of the land,**

and came over and dwelt with Omer [*his great-grandfather, the righteous king who had fled with his followers having been warned in a dream by the Lord; see verse 3, above*].

Next, we see King Akish lose power because his own sons follow his evil example. They bribe the people to follow them. This brings years of war, which will reduce the population in that kingdom to thirty people, plus Nimrah and the small group that followed him to live with righteous Omer (verse 9).

10 And it came to pass that **Akish begat other sons**, and **they won the hearts of the people**, notwithstanding [*in spite of the fact that*] they had sworn unto [*promised to*] him to do all manner of iniquity [*evil*] according to that which he desired [*in spite of their secret promises to support him*].

11 Now **the people of Akish were desirous for gain** [*wanted wealth and power*], even as Akish was desirous for power [*they were corrupt, just like their king*]; **wherefore** [*therefore*], **the sons of Akish did offer them money** [*bribes*], by which means they drew away the more part [*majority*] of the people after them.

12 And **there began to be a war** between the sons of Akish and Akish, **which lasted for the space of many years**, yea, unto the **destruction of nearly all the people** of the kingdom, yea, even all, **save** [*except*] it were **thirty souls**, and they who fled with the house of Omer [*verse 9*].

13 Wherefore, **Omer** [*a righteous king*] **was restored again to the land of his inheritance.**

14 And it came to pass that **Omer began to be old**; nevertheless, in his old age he begat [*had a son named*] Emer; and **he anointed Emer to be king to reign in his stead** [*place*].

In verses 15–25, we will see 225 years of peace because of the personal righteousness of the people and their kings. They will be prosperous (become wealthy) and still maintain their righteousness. They are an example that it can be done, and that prosperity doesn't necessarily have to launch nations and individuals into the "cycle of apostasy."

For a "refresher course" about the cycle of apostasy, you may wish to turn to Helaman 11:20–37 in this study guide and review the notes for those verses.

15 And **after** that **he had anointed Emer to be king he saw peace** in the land for the space of **two years**, and **he died**, having seen exceedingly many days, which were full of sorrow. And it came to pass that **Emer did reign in his stead, and did fill the steps of his father**.

16 And **the Lord began again to take the curse from off the land** [*began to bless the people and their land again*], and **the house of Emer did prosper exceedingly** under the reign of Emer; and **in the space of sixty and two years they had become exceedingly strong, insomuch that they became exceedingly rich—**

17 **Having all manner of** [*all kinds of*] **fruit**, and of **grain**, and of **silks, and of fine linen** [*nice fabric, cloth*], and of **gold**, and of **silver**, and of **precious things**;

18 And also all manner of **cattle**, of **oxen**, and **cows**, and of **sheep**, and of **swine** [*pigs*], and of **goats**, and also **many other kinds of animals** which were useful for the food of man.

19 And they also had **horses**, and **asses** [*donkeys*], and there were **elephants** and **cureloms** and **cumoms** [*we don't know what cureloms and cumoms are*]; all of which were useful unto man, and more especially the elephants and cureloms and cumoms.

20 And thus **the Lord did pour out his blessings upon this land** [*America*], **which was choice above all other lands**; and **he commanded that whoso should possess the land should possess it unto the Lord, or they should be destroyed** when they were ripened in iniquity [*completely wicked*]; for upon such, saith the Lord: I will pour out the fulness of my wrath [*anger, punishments*].

21 And **Emer did execute judgment** [*fulfill his duties*] **in righteousness** all his days, and he begat many sons and daughters; and **he begat Coriantum**, and he anointed Coriantum to reign in his stead.

22 And after he had anointed Coriantum to reign in his stead he lived four years, and he saw **peace in the land**; yea, and **he even saw the Son of Righteousness** [*the Savior*], **and did rejoice and glory in his day; and he died in peace**.

23 And it came to pass that **Coriantum did walk in the steps of his father** [*was also a righteous king*], and did build many mighty cities, and **did administer** [*provide*] **that which was good unto his people in all his days**. And it came to pass that he had no children even until he was exceedingly old.

Next, Moroni gives us an idea as to how long people lived in this era.

24 And it came to pass that **his wife died**, being an **hundred and two years old**. And it came to pass that Coriantum took to wife, in his old age, a young maid, and begat sons and daughters; wherefore **he lived until he was an hundred and forty and two years old**.

These ages are somewhat similar to others in the Bible after the flood, such as Sarah (127 years old; see Genesis 23:1) and Abraham (175 years old; see Genesis 25:7).

25 And it came to pass that **he begat Com**, and Com reigned in his stead; and he reigned forty and nine years, and **he begat Heth**; and he also begat other sons and daughters.

Next, we will see this era of peace brought to a close by wickedness and secret combinations.

26 And **the people had spread again over all the face of the land**, and **there began again to be an exceedingly great wickedness upon**

the face of the land, and **Heth began to embrace** [*accept, adopt*] **the secret plans** [*secret combinations*] again of old, **to destroy his father**.

27 And it came to pass that **he did dethrone his father, for he slew** [*killed*] **him with his own sword**; and he did reign [*rule as king*] in his stead [*place*].

As the cycle of wickedness and apostasy continues, the Lord will send prophets. When that effort is rejected, He will send famine and poisonous serpents, to humble the people. When the people begin to repent, He will send rain and prosperity will begin again.

28 And **there came prophets in the land again, crying** [*teaching and preaching*] **repentance** unto them—that they must prepare the way of the Lord **or there should come a curse upon the face of the land; yea, even there should be a great famine**, in which **they should be destroyed if they did not repent**.

29 **But the people believed not the words of the prophets**, but they cast [*threw*] them out; and some of them they cast into pits [*deep holes in the ground*] and left them to perish [*die*]. And it came to pass that **they did all these things according to the commandment of the king, Heth**.

30 And it came to pass that **there began to be a great dearth** [*drought, famine*] upon the land, and **the inhabitants began to be destroyed exceedingly fast because of the dearth, for there was no rain upon the face of the earth**.

31 And **there came forth poisonous serpents** [*snakes*] **also** upon the face of the land, **and did poison many people**. And it came to pass that **their flocks** [*animals like sheep, goats, cows, horses, etc.*] **began to flee** [*run away*] **before the poisonous serpents**, towards the land southward, which was called by the Nephites Zarahemla.

32 And it came to pass that there were **many of them** which **did perish by the way** [*along the way*]; nevertheless, there were some which fled into the land southward.

33 And it came to pass that **the Lord did cause the serpents that they should pursue them no more, but that they should hedge up** [*block*] **the way that the people could not pass**, that whoso should attempt to pass might fall by the poisonous serpents.

34 And it came to pass that **the people did follow the course of the beasts, and did devour the carcasses of them which fell by the way**, until they had devoured them all. **Now when the people saw that they must perish** [*would surely die*] **they began to repent** of their iniquities and cry unto the Lord.

35 And it came to pass that **when they had humbled themselves sufficiently** [*enough*] **before the Lord he did send rain** upon the face of the earth; and the people began to revive [*recover from the famine, from being without enough food and water*] again, and **there began to be fruit** [*food*] **in the north countries**, and in all the countries

round about. And **the Lord did show forth his power unto them in preserving them from famine**.

ETHER 10

Over fifteen generations (one "generation" is one family—for example, a mother and father and their children) are covered in this chapter. If you turn back to the genealogy listed in Ether 1:6–32, you could put a note that chapter 10 basically covers from Ether 1:13 to Ether 1:25. Many kings and kingdoms will come and go in this chapter of Moroni's history of the Jaredites. It would be easy to quickly glance over Ether 10 and get on to the next chapter. But Moroni is teaching us much with the material he has selected. Perhaps you can picture him in your mind, reading through centuries worth of records and listening for inspiration as to what should be included for our benefit in our day.

We mentioned at the beginning of Ether that the Book of Ether could almost be considered a "mini" Book of Mormon since it basically reviews all the principles and teachings of the gospel taught in the Book of Mormon itself. Likewise, this chapter could be a miniature of the "mini," a brief review of Ether. We will point out several of Moroni's teachings of the saving principles of the gospel, and, likewise, his warnings as we continue. First of all, many people died as a result of the famine sent by the Lord to humble the people according to what we read in Ether 9:28–30. Verse 1, next, is a reminder of this.

1 AND it came to pass that Shez, who was a descendant of Heth—for **Heth had perished** [*died*] **by the famine, and all his household** [*all his family, perhaps relatives also*] save [*except*] it were Shez—wherefore, **Shez began to build up again a broken people** [*the people who had been destroyed and severely hurt by the famine*].

In verse 2, Moroni reminds us that remembering the past and learning from it, as well as remembering past blessings, is a key to physical and spiritual success. (Alma 5:6 reminds us of this also.)

2 And it came to pass that **Shez did remember the destruction of his fathers**, and **he did build up a righteous kingdom**; for **he remembered what the Lord had done in bringing Jared and his brother across the deep** [*ocean*]; and **he did walk in the ways of the Lord** [*he kept the commandments of the Lord*]; and he begat [*had*] sons and daughters.

3 And **his eldest son, whose name was Shez, did rebel against him**; nevertheless, **Shez was smitten** [*killed*] **by the hand of a robber**, because of his exceeding riches, **which brought peace again unto his father**.

4 And it came to pass that **his father did build up many cities upon the face of the land, and the people began again to spread over all the face of the land**. And Shez did live to an exceedingly old age; and he begat Riplakish. And he died, and **Riplakish reigned in his stead**.

The damage done by King Riplakish, in verses 5–7, is similar to what wicked King Noah did to his people in Mosiah 11:1–15.

5 And it came to pass that **Riplakish did not do that which was right in the sight of the Lord**, for **he did have many wives and concubines** [*probably women who lived with him and committed adultery with him*], and did lay that upon men's shoulders which was grievous to be borne; yea, **he did tax them with heavy taxes**; and with the taxes **he did build many spacious buildings**.

6 And **he did erect him an exceedingly beautiful throne**; and **he did build many prisons**, and whoso [*whoever*] would not be subject unto taxes [*refused to pay taxes*] he did cast into prison; and whoso was not able to pay taxes he did cast into prison; and he did cause that they should labor continually for their support; and whoso refused to labor he did cause to be put to death [*executed*].

7 Wherefore **he did obtain all his fine work**, yea, even his **fine gold** he did cause to be refined in prison; and **all manner of fine workmanship he did cause to be wrought** [*made*] **in prison**. And it came to pass that he did afflict the people with his **whoredoms** [*sexual immorality*] **and abominations** [*all kinds of terribly evil sins*].

8 And **when he had reigned** [*ruled*] **for** the space of **forty and two years the people did rise up in rebellion against him**; and **there began to be war again in the land**, insomuch that **Riplakish was killed**, and **his descendants** [*children, grandchildren, etc.*] **were driven out of the land**.

9 And it came to pass **after** the space of **many years**, **Morianton**, (he being a descendant of Riplakish) **gathered together an army of outcasts** [*people who had been driven out of the land in verse 8, above*], **and went forth and gave battle unto the people**; and he gained power over many cities; and the war became exceedingly sore [*bad, severe*], and did last for the space of many years; and he **did gain power over all the land, and did establish himself king over all the land**.

10 And **after that he had established himself king he did ease the burden of the people** [*he reduced how much the people had to pay in taxes, etc.*], **by which he did gain favor** [*became popular*] in the eyes of the people, and they did anoint him to be their king.

Verse 11, next, is rather sad. Here is a man who apparently has many good qualities and does much good for many people but doesn't keep a major commandment of the Lord, namely, the law of chastity. He thus cuts himself off from the Spirit of the Lord (see D&C 42:23) here on earth and from salvation in celestial glory in the next life (see D&C 76:103, which says sexual immorality, unrepented of, leads to telestial glory).

11 And **he did do justice unto the people** [*he was fair with the people*]**, but not unto himself because of his many whoredoms** [*because he broke the law of chastity a lot*]; **wherefore** [*this is the*

reason that] **he was cut off from the presence of the Lord**.

12 And it came to pass that **Morianton built up many cities**, and **the people became exceedingly** [*very*] **rich under his reign** [*rule as king*], both in buildings, and in gold and silver, and in raising grain, and in flocks, and herds, and such things which had been restored unto them.

13 And **Morianton did live to an exceedingly great age** [*he lived a very long life*], and then **he begat Kim**; and Kim did reign in the stead of his father; and he did reign eight years, and his father died. And it came to pass that **Kim did not reign in righteousness, wherefore he was not favored of** [*blessed by*] **the Lord**.

14 And **his brother did rise up in rebellion against him, by which he did bring him into captivity; and he did remain in captivity all his days**; and he begat sons and daughters in captivity, and in his old age **he begat Levi**; and he died.

15 And it came to pass that **Levi did serve in captivity** after the death of his father, for the space of **forty and two years**. And he **did make war against the king of the land, by which he did obtain unto himself the kingdom**.

16 And after he had obtained unto himself the kingdom **he did that which was right in the sight of the Lord; and the people did prosper** in the land; and he did live to a good old age, and begat sons and daughters; and **he also begat Corom**, whom he anointed [*made*] king in his stead.

17 And it came to pass that **Corom did that which was good in the sight of the Lord all his days**; and he begat many sons and daughters; and after he had seen many days he did pass away, even like unto the rest of the earth; and **Kish reigned** in his stead.

18 And it came to pass that **Kish passed away** also, and **Lib reigned in his stead**.

19 And it came to pass that **Lib also did that which was good in the sight of the Lord. And in the days of Lib the poisonous serpents were destroyed** [*a curse sent by the Lord to humble the wicked; see Ether 9:31*]. Wherefore they did go into the land southward, to hunt food for the people of the land, for the land was covered with animals of the forest. And Lib also himself became a great hunter.

20 And **they built a great city by the narrow neck of land**, by the place where the sea divides the land.

21 And **they did preserve the land southward for a wilderness, to get game** [*wild animals for food*]. And the whole face of the land northward was covered with inhabitants.

22 And **they were exceedingly industrious**, and they did buy and sell and traffic one with another, that they might get gain.

23 And **they did work in all manner of ore** [*rocks from which we get metal*], and they did make gold, and silver, and iron, and brass, and all manner of metals; and they did dig it out of the earth; wherefore, they did cast up mighty heaps of earth to get ore, of gold, and of silver, and of iron, and of copper. And they did work all manner of fine work.

24 And they did have silks, and fine-twined linen; and **they did work all manner** [*all kinds of*] **of cloth**, that they might clothe themselves from their nakedness.

25 And **they did make all manner of tools** to till the earth [*to farm with*], both to plow and to sow, to reap and to hoe, and also to thrash.

26 And **they did make all manner of tools with which they did work their beasts**.

27 And **they did make all manner of weapons of war**. And they did work all manner of work of exceedingly curious workmanship.

28 And **never could be a people more blessed than were they, and more prospered by the hand of the Lord**. And **they were in a land that was choice above all lands, for the Lord had spoken it**.

29 And it came to pass that **Lib did live many years**, and begat sons and daughters; and he also **begat Hearthom**.

30 And it came to pass that **Hearthom reigned in the stead of his father**. And when Hearthom had **reigned twenty and four years**, behold, **the kingdom was taken away from him**. And he served many years in captivity, yea, even all the remainder of his days [*all of his life*].

31 And **he begat Heth**, and Heth **lived in captivity all his days**. And Heth begat Aaron, and **Aaron dwelt in captivity all his days**; and he begat Amnigaddah, and **Amnigaddah also dwelt in captivity all his days**; and he begat Coriantum, and **Coriantum dwelt in captivity all his days**; and **he begat Com**.

32 And it came to pass that **Com drew away the half of the kingdom**. And he **reigned** over the half of the kingdom **forty and two years**; and he **went to battle against the king, Amgid**, and they **fought** for the space of **many years**, during which time Com gained power over Amgid, and **obtained power over the remainder of the kingdom**.

33 And in the days of Com there began to be robbers in the land; and **they adopted the old plans, and administered oaths after the manner of the ancients** [*they enter secret combinations again, which leads to destruction; Ether 8:20–22*], and **sought again to destroy the kingdom**.

34 Now **Com did fight against them** much; nevertheless, **he did not prevail** [*win*] against them.

ETHER 11

We will continue the same format in chapter 11 as we used in chapter 10. See notes at the beginning of chapter 10.

1 AND **there came** also in the days of Com **many prophets**, and **prophesied of the destruction of that great people except** [*unless*] **they should** [*would*] **repent**, and turn unto the Lord, and forsake [*stop*] their murders and wickedness.

2 And it came to pass that **the prophets were rejected by the people**, and they fled unto Com for protection, for the people sought to destroy them.

3 And **they prophesied** [*this word includes the teaching and preaching of the gospel, as well as actual prophesying the future*] **unto Com many things; and he was blessed in all the remainder of his days** [*a reminder to us that listening to the prophets pays off wonderfully*].

4 And **he** lived to a good old age, and **begat Shiblom**; and Shiblom reigned in his stead. And **the brother of Shiblom rebelled against him**, and **there began to be an exceedingly great war in all the land**.

5 And it came to pass that **the brother of Shiblom caused that all the prophets who prophesied of the destruction of the people should be put to death**;

In other words, those who said things publicly against wicked lifestyles were not tolerated by the government.

Next, briefly and simply, Moroni points out where widespread wickedness leads a nation.

6 And **there was great calamity** [*disaster*] **in all the land**, for they had testified that a great curse should come upon the land, and also upon the people, and that **there should be a great destruction among them**, such an one as never had been upon the face of the earth, and their bones should become as heaps of earth upon the face of the land **except** [*unless*] **they should** [*would*] **repent of their wickedness**.

7 And **they hearkened not unto the voice of the Lord, because of their wicked combinations; wherefore, there began to be wars and contentions in all the land**, and also many **famines** and **pestilences**, insomuch that there was a **great destruction**, such an one as never had been known upon the face of the earth; and **all this came to pass in the days of Shiblom**.

8 And **the people began to repent of their iniquity** [*sins and wickedness*]; **and inasmuch as** [*if*] **they did the Lord did have mercy on them**.

9 And it came to pass that **Shiblom was slain** [*killed*], and Seth was brought into captivity, and did dwell in captivity all his days.

10 And it came to pass that **Ahah, his son, did obtain the kingdom**;

and he did reign over the people all his days. And he **did do all manner of iniquity in his days**, by which he did cause the shedding of much blood; and few were his days.

11 And Ethem, being a descendant of **Ahah**, did obtain the kingdom; and he **also did do that which was wicked in his days**.

12 And it came to pass that **in the days of Ethem there came many prophets**, and prophesied again unto the people; yea, **they did prophesy that the Lord would utterly destroy them from off the face of the earth except** [*unless*] **they repented of their iniquities**.

13 And it came to pass that **the people hardened their hearts** [*refused to humble themselves*], and would not hearken unto [*listen and obey*] their words; and **the prophets mourned** [*were very sad*] **and withdrew from among** [*left, went away from*] **the people**.

14 And it came to pass that **Ethem did execute judgment** [*carry out his role in government*] **in wickedness all his days** [*all his life*]; and **he begat Moron**. And it came to pass that Moron did reign in **his stead; and Moron did that which was wicked before the Lord**.

15 And it came to pass that **there arose a rebellion among the people, because of that secret combination** which was built up to get power and gain; **and there arose a mighty man among them in iniquity** [*who was very wicked*], **and gave battle unto Moron**, in which he did overthrow the half of the kingdom; and he did maintain the half of the kingdom for many years.

16 And it came to pass that **Moron did overthrow him, and did obtain the kingdom again**.

17 And it came to pass that **there arose another mighty man**; and he was a descendant of the brother of Jared.

18 And it came to pass that **he did overthrow Moron** and obtain the kingdom; wherefore, **Moron dwelt in captivity all the remainder of his days**; and **he begat Coriantor**.

19 And it came to pass that **Coriantor dwelt in captivity all his days**.

20 And **in the days of Coriantor there also came many prophets**, and prophesied of great and marvelous things, **and cried** [*taught*] **repentance unto the people**, and except they should repent the Lord God would execute judgment against them to their utter [*complete*] destruction;

21 And that **the Lord God would send or bring forth another people to possess the land**, by his power, after the manner by which [*the same way that*] he brought their fathers [*ancestors*].

22 And **they did reject all the words of the prophets, because of their secret society and wicked abominations**.

Next, we are introduced to Ether, the prophet and record keeper, who will watch and write down the final scenes of destruction among the Jaredites.

23 And it came to pass that **Coriantor begat Ether**, and he died, having dwelt in captivity all his days.

ETHER 12

This is one of the best-known chapters in the Book of Mormon. It is often quoted. In it, Moroni teaches us a wonderful and powerful lesson about faith. He also teaches how faith, hope, and charity work together to lead us to Christ and on to salvation. You have perhaps heard many quotes from it in church. Verse 27 is especially well-known. Moroni will tell us that he has seen the Savior and that Jesus is very pleasant, personable, and humble.

First, in verses 1–5, next, Moroni will introduce us to the prophet Ether.

1 AND it came to pass that **the days of Ether were** [*Ether's life took place*] **in the days of Coriantumr**; and **Coriantumr was king over all the land**.

Coriantumr will be the last survivor of the Jaredites and will be found by the people in Zarahemla and will live among them for about 9 months (see Omni 1:21).

2 And **Ether was a prophet of the Lord**; wherefore **Ether came forth in the days of Coriantumr, and began to prophesy unto the people**, for **he could not be restrained** [*no one could stop him*] **because of the Spirit of the Lord which was in him**.

3 For **he did cry** [*preach and teach*] **from the morning, even until the going down of the sun**, **exhorting** [*strongly urging*] **the people to believe in God unto repentance lest** [*for fear that*] **they should** [*would*] **be destroyed**, saying unto them that **by faith all things are fulfilled—**

4 Wherefore, **whoso believeth in God might with surety** [*certainty; confidence*] **hope for a better world** [*in the next life*], yea, even **a place at the right hand of God** [*symbolic of exaltation in the highest degree of glory in the celestial kingdom*], **which hope cometh of** [*is a result of*] **faith, maketh an anchor to the souls of men, which would make them sure and steadfast** [*steady*], **always abounding in good works** [*doing righteous acts*], **being led to glorify God** [*bring honor and joy to God; see Moses 1:39*].

5 And it came to pass that **Ether did prophesy great and marvelous things unto the people, which they did not believe, because they saw them not** [*similar to the "I won't believe it unless I see it" mentality among many today*].

Ether started us thinking about faith in the last line of verse 3, above, and spoke of hope and faith in verse 4. For the rest of the chapter, Moroni explains and teaches about what Ether said about these and other basic and very important gospel principles. Those who understand and follow are well on their way to celestial glory and exaltation.

First, Moroni gives a wonderful lesson about faith. He will teach us much about this vital gospel principle by giving us several examples.

6 And **now, I, Moroni, would speak somewhat concerning these things** [*that Ether said*]; I would show unto the world that **faith is things which are hoped for and not seen; wherefore, dispute not** [*don't argue against it*] **because ye see not, for ye receive no witness** [*solid evidence*] **until after the trial of your faith** [*a direct response to the last lines of verse 5*].

7 For **it was by faith that Christ showed himself unto our fathers** [*ancestors*], after he had risen from the dead; and **he showed not himself unto them until after they had faith in him**; wherefore, it must needs be [*it was necessary first*] that some had faith in him, for he showed himself not unto the world [*to worldly people because they did not have faith in Him*].

The appearance of Christ referred to in verse 7, above, is the appearance of the resurrected Savior in America. The showing of Himself to the world, in verse 8, next, refers to His mortal mission and Atonement.

8 But **because of the faith of men he has shown himself unto the world** [*was born and lived on earth*], **and glorified the name of** [*brought glory and honor to*] **the Father** [*by carrying out the mission given Him by the Father*], and prepared a way [*the Atonement*] that thereby others might be partakers of the heavenly gift [*including forgiveness of sins and the gift of the Holy Ghost (see Hebrews 6:4), which lead to celestial exaltation; compare with D&C 14:7; 84:24*], **that they might hope for those things which they have not seen** [*including the promised rewards for the righteous in the hereafter*].

The word "hope," as used in the Book of Mormon, is not a "wishing for" or a tentative hoping that maybe something will be obtained. It is a much stronger word than that. In Alma 58:11, "hope" is coupled with the words "assurances" and "great faith." In 2 Nephi 31:20, we see "a perfect brightness of hope" leading to "eternal life."

Thus, "hope," in a strong Book of Mormon sense, means that you can "plan on" eternal life in the presence of God because of faith in Christ.

9 **Wherefore** [*therefore*], **ye may also have hope, and be partakers of the gift, if ye will but have faith**.

Next, Moroni gives several examples of faith in action.

10 Behold **it was by faith that they of old were called after the holy order of God** [*were given the Melchizedek Priesthood; compare with Alma 13:4*].

11 Wherefore, **by faith was the law of Moses given. But in the gift of his Son hath God prepared a more excellent way** [*the gospel of Christ*]; and **it is by faith that it hath been fulfilled**.

12 For **if there be no faith among the children of men God can do no miracle among them**; wherefore, he showed not himself until after their faith.

13 Behold, **it was the faith of Alma and Amulek that caused the prison to tumble to the earth** [*Alma 14:26–27*].

14 Behold, **it was the faith of Nephi and Lehi that wrought** [*caused*] **the**

change upon the Lamanites, that they were baptized with fire and with the Holy Ghost [*summarized in Helaman 5:50–52*].

15 Behold, **it was the faith of Ammon and his brethren which wrought so great a miracle among the Lamanites** [*see Alma, chapters 17–26*].

> As you have probably noticed, many of the examples of faith, given in the above verses, show that faith is a principle of action. In other words, if you have faith in Christ, you do much, including moving out of your "comfort zone" to live the gospel and serve others. You pay tithing, go to church, keep the commandments, accept calls to serve, apologize to others for offenses, say your prayers, read the scriptures, etc. Faith requires action that goes far beyond belief. The Prophet Joseph Smith summed this up as follows:
>
> Faith is "**the principle of action in all intelligent beings**." He also said "And **as faith is the moving cause of all action in temporal concerns, so it is in spiritual**; for the Saviour has said, and that truly, that 'He that believeth and is baptized shall be saved.'" (*Lectures on Faith*, 1: 9 and 12, Deseret Book Company, 1985.)
>
> Faith is also a principle by which the powers of heaven are put into action to bless us, as illustrated by Moroni, next.

16 Yea, and even **all they who wrought** [*performed*] **miracles wrought them by faith**, even those who were before Christ and also those who were after.

17 And **it was by faith that the three disciples** [*the Three Nephites*] **obtained a promise that they should not taste of death** [*see 3 Nephi 28:7*]; and **they obtained not the promise until after their faith**.

18 And **neither at any time hath any wrought** [*performed*] **miracles until after their faith**; wherefore **they first believed in the Son of God**.

19 And **there were many whose faith was so exceedingly** [*very*] **strong, even before Christ came, who could not be kept from within the veil** [*from seeing through the veil that keeps us from seeing spirits, angels, God, etc.*], **but truly** [*literally*] **saw with their eyes** [*physical eyes*] **the things which they had beheld with an eye of faith** [*things they had believed but not seen; see verse 6*], and they were glad.

20 And behold, we have seen in this record [*the Book of Ether*] that **one of these was the brother of Jared; for so great was his faith in God, that when God put forth his finger he could not hide it from the sight of the brother of Jared**, because of his word which he had spoken unto him, which word he had obtained by faith.

21 And **after the brother of Jared had beheld** [*seen*] **the finger of the Lord, because of the promise which the brother of Jared had obtained by faith, the Lord could not withhold** [*keep back*] **anything from his sight; wherefore** [*therefore*] **he showed him all things, for he could**

no longer be kept without [*outside of*] **the veil.**

22 And **it is by faith that my fathers** [*ancestors; see Enos 1:13–16*] **have obtained the promise that these things** [*the Book of Mormon*] **should** [*would*] **come unto their brethren** [*the Lamanites*] through the Gentiles [*Joseph Smith and the members of the Church*]; **therefore the Lord hath commanded me, yea, even Jesus Christ** [*Jesus Christ Himself commanded me to prepare the gold plates to be translated and published by Joseph Smith*].

Next, Moroni gives us a rather personal insight into his own life about a time when he expressed a concern to the Savior about what he considered a serious weakness in writing on the gold plates that would later become the Book of Mormon. The Master's answer is direct and to the point, as well as comforting.

23 And **I said unto him: Lord, the Gentiles will mock at these things** [*the things that would be written in the Book of Mormon*], **because of our weakness in writing**; for Lord thou hast made us mighty in word by faith, but thou hast not made us mighty in writing; for thou hast made all this people that they could speak much, because of the Holy Ghost which thou hast given them;

24 And **thou hast made us that we could write but little**, because of the awkwardness of our hands. **Behold, thou hast not made us mighty in writing like unto the brother of Jared**, for thou madest him that the things which he wrote were mighty even as thou art, unto the overpowering of man to read them.

25 **Thou hast also made our words powerful and great, even that we cannot write them; wherefore** [*so that*], **when we write we behold** [*see*] **our weakness, and stumble because of the placing of our words; and I fear lest the Gentiles shall mock at our words.**

Next, Jesus gives His answer to Moroni regarding his concern about their weakness in writing. See verse 37 also.

26 And **when I had said this, the Lord spake unto me, saying: Fools mock** [*make fun of sacred things*], **but they shall mourn** [*be sorry that they did*]; and **my grace** [*help*] **is sufficient for the meek, that they shall take no advantage of your weakness**;

As part of the Savior's answer to Moroni, we gain one of the most famous and oft-quoted verses in the Book of Mormon, namely, verse 27, next.

It is significant to note that we are actually given weaknesses as a kindness from God. They are an important part of our schooling during this mortal life on earth. Through them we are blessed with humility, which leads to our acknowledging our dependence on Christ, which allows His grace to work with us, which leads, in turn, to strengths leading toward salvation.

27 And **if men come unto me I will show unto them their weakness. I give unto men weakness that they**

may be humble; and my grace [*help, patience*] **is sufficient** [*enough*] **for all men that humble themselves before me; for if they humble themselves before me, and have faith in me, then will I make weak things become strong unto them** [*their weaknesses will lead to great strength*].

Next, Moroni teaches us faith, hope, and charity. These are the basic character traits that lead to exaltation.

28 Behold, **I will show unto the Gentiles their weakness**, and **I will show unto them that faith, hope and charity bringeth unto me** [*bring people unto Me*]**—the fountain** [*source*] **of all righteousness.**

Next, Moroni expresses his relief at the Savior's answer to his concern, recorded in verses 23–25. Moroni is an example of the blessing of having faith in the word of the Lord. As part of his expression of gratitude to the Savior for His answer and comfort, he will support his response (that he "was comforted") with additional examples of faith from the scriptures. This could be a helpful pattern for us to follow.

29 And **I, Moroni, having heard these words, was comforted**, and said: O Lord, thy righteous will be done, for I know that thou workest unto the children of men according to their faith;

30 For **the brother of Jared said unto the mountain Zerin, Remove—and it was removed.** And **if he had not had faith it would not have moved**; wherefore **thou workest after men have faith.**

31 For thus didst thou manifest thyself unto thy disciples; for **after they had faith, and did speak in thy name, thou didst show thyself unto them in great power.**

32 And **I also remember that thou hast said that thou hast prepared a house for man, yea, even among the mansions of thy Father, in which man might have a more excellent hope**; wherefore man must hope [*includes the concept of planning on gaining exaltation because of Christ's Atonement and gospel; see notes about "hope" associated with verse 8, above*], **or he cannot receive an inheritance in the place** [*a place in heaven*] **which thou hast prepared.**

Next, Moroni teaches us about charity, defining it for us in verse 34 and showing us how necessary it is that we develop charity.

33 And again, **I remember that** thou hast said that **thou hast loved the world, even unto the laying down** [*giving*] **of thy life for the world, that thou mightest take it again** [*be resurrected*] to prepare a place for the children of men [*people*].

34 And now **I know that this love which thou hast had for the children of men is charity**; wherefore, **except men shall have charity** [*the pure love of Christ in their hearts*] **they cannot inherit** [*receive*] **that place which thou hast prepared in the mansions of thy Father** [*in heaven*].

As Moroni continues sharing with us his rather personal discussion with the Savior, he explains that he now understands that it is the Gentiles' responsibility to overlook any weaknesses in writing that could affect their response to the Book of Mormon. This principle applies to all of us, including those who attempt to discredit the Book of Mormon through academic criticism.

35 Wherefore, **I know** by this thing which thou hast said [*because of Your response to my concern about weakness in writing*], **that if the Gentiles have not charity, because of our weakness, that thou wilt prove them** [*show them that they are wrong*]**, and take away their talent** [*the blessings they could have had by accepting the Book of Mormon and the accompanying gospel of Christ*], yea, even that which they have received, and give unto them [*who do accept it*] who shall have more abundantly.

Next, we see the great charity in Moroni's heart as he prays that the gentiles will get the needed help from Christ in order to have charity. The Savior's response to him teaches a comforting lesson, namely that even if we fail to convince others of the importance of the gospel, we will still be saved through our faithfulness.

36 And it came to pass that **I prayed unto the Lord that he would give unto the Gentiles grace** [*help*], **that they might have charity.**

37 And it came to pass that the Lord said unto me: **If they have not charity it mattereth not unto thee** [*as far as your own salvation is concerned*], **thou hast been faithful; wherefore, thy garments** [*your life; "garments," are scriptural symbolism for our lives*] **shall be made clean. And because thou hast seen thy weakness thou shalt be made strong, even unto the sitting down in the place** [*exaltation in the highest degree of glory in the celestial kingdom*] **which I have prepared in the mansions of my Father** [*in heaven*].

As this chapter draws to a close, this great, lonely prophet of God says farewell to all who read his words, leaving his testimony of the Savior and pleading with us to "seek this Jesus" and the gift of the Holy Ghost, which bears continuing witness to us of the Father and the Son.

38 And now **I, Moroni, bid farewell unto the Gentiles, yea, and also unto my brethren whom I love, until we shall meet before the judgment-seat of Christ**, where **all men shall know that my garments are not spotted with your blood** [*everyone will know that Moroni tried his best to bring them to Christ, so he is not responsible if they don't make it*].

39 And **then shall ye know that I have seen Jesus**, and that **he hath talked with me face to face**, and that **he told me in plain humility**, even as a man telleth another **in mine own language**, concerning these things;

40 And **only a few have I written, because of my weakness in writing.**

41 And now, **I would commend** [*counsel, advise*] **you to seek this Jesus of whom the prophets and apostles have written, that the grace of God the Father, and also the Lord Jesus Christ, and the Holy Ghost, which beareth record of them, may be and abide in you forever**. Amen.

ETHER 13

Many people now don't even believe the Bible, or at least they ignore it and its teachings. One of the great things the Book of Mormon does is show that the Bible is true and contains the word of God, as long as it is translated correctly.

In this chapter, we have a good example of how the Book of Mormon supports the Bible and shows that it is true. On my mission, my companion and I ran into a man who had a book which tried to prove that the flood in the days of Noah in the Old Testament did not really happen. He enjoyed trying to get us to believe him. We didn't. Many people don't believe that the flood covered the whole earth as stated in the Bible in Genesis, chapters 7 and 8. Verse 2 of this chapter of Ether shows that there was a flood.

Also, in this chapter, we are taught briefly about the city of New Jerusalem, which is to be built upon the American continent (see tenth article of faith). It will become one of two world headquarters for the Savior during the Millennium (the 1,000 years of peace on earth after the Savior comes again). The other headquarters will be Old Jerusalem, which is also mentioned in this chapter. It will be built up again, and become a holy city, and a city from which the Savior will likewise reign during the Millennium.

Starting with verse 13 and continuing to the end of the chapter (and on to the end of Ether), Moroni will tell us more about Ether, who was rejected as a prophet and was forced to hide in a cave and watch and record the final destruction of the Jaredites.

1 AND **now I, Moroni, proceed to finish my record concerning the destruction of the people of whom** [*about whom*] **I have been writing** [*the Jaredites*].

> As mentioned above, verse 2, next, verifies that there was a flood that covered the whole earth, including what is now known as America.

2 For behold, they rejected all the words of Ether; for he truly told them of all things, from the beginning of man; and that **after the waters** [*of the flood*] **had receded from off the face of this land** [*America*] it became a choice land above all other lands, a chosen land of the Lord; wherefore the Lord would have [*requires*] that all men should serve him who dwell upon the face thereof;

> Next, we hear more about New Jerusalem.

3 And that **it** [*America*] **was the place of the New Jerusalem** [*as mentioned in 3 Nephi 20:22 and 21:23–24*], **which should** [*will*] **come down out of**

heaven [*see Revelation 3:12 and 21:2*], **and the holy sanctuary of the Lord** [*will be a headquarters for Jesus during the Millennium*].

4 Behold, **Ether saw the days of Christ, and he spake** [*spoke*] **concerning a New Jerusalem upon this land**.

There are three "holy cities" mentioned in scriptures in connection with the Millennium. Apostle Joseph Fielding Smith taught about these as follows (**bold** added for emphasis):

"In the day of regeneration, when all things are made new [*the Millennium*], there will be **three great cities that will be holy**. One will be **the Jerusalem of old** which shall be rebuilt according to the prophecy of Ezekiel. One will be **the city of Zion, or of Enoch**, which was taken from the earth when Enoch was translated and which will be restored; and **the city Zion, or New Jerusalem**, which is to be built by the seed of Joseph on this the American continent (*Quoting from Moses):*

"'62 And righteousness will I send down out of heaven; and truth will I send forth out of the earth, to bear testimony of mine Only Begotten; his Resurrection from the dead; yea, and also the resurrection of all men; and righteousness and truth will I cause to sweep the earth as with a flood, to gather out mine elect from the four quarters of the earth, unto a place which I shall prepare, an Holy City, that my people may gird up their loins, and be looking forth for the time of my coming; for there shall be my tabernacle, and it shall be called Zion, a New Jerusalem.

"'63 And the Lord said unto Enoch: Then shalt thou and all thy city meet them there, and we will receive them into our bosom, and they shall see us; and we will fall upon their necks, and they shall fall upon our necks, and we will kiss each other;

"'64 And there shall be mine abode, and it shall be Zion, which shall come forth out of all the creations which I have made; and for the space of a thousand years the earth shall rest.' (Moses 7:62–64.)

"After the close of the millennial reign we are informed that Satan, who was bound during the millennium, shall be loosed and go forth to deceive the nations. Then will come the end. The earth will die and be purified and receive its resurrection. During this cleansing period the City Zion, or New Jerusalem, will be taken from the earth; and when the earth is prepared for the celestial glory, the city will come down according to the prediction in the Book of Revelation" (Smith, *Answers to Gospel Questions*, 2:105).

As we continue, Moroni explains why Old Jerusalem cannot be the "New" Jerusalem.

5 And **he** [*Ether*] **spake also concerning** the house of Israel, and **the Jerusalem** [*Old Jerusalem, in the Holy Land*] **from whence** [*where*] **Lehi should** [*would*] **come**—after it should be destroyed **it should be built up again, a holy city unto the Lord**; wherefore [*therefore*], it could not be a new Jerusalem for it had been [*already existed*] in a time of old; but it should be built up again [*it will be rebuilt*], and become a holy city of the Lord; and it should be built unto [*for*] the house of Israel.

Remember, as we continue, that "New Jerusalem" refers to more than one city, depending on the context in which the term is used. (See above quote by Joseph Fielding Smith. See also Topical Guide, under "Jerusalem, New.") Verse 6, next, is referring to an actual city that will be built in Independence, Jackson County, Missouri, USA, (see D&C 42:9, 57:1–3).

6 And that **a New Jerusalem should** [*will*] **be built up upon this land** [*America*], unto the remnant of the seed of Joseph [*who was sold into Egypt; his "seed," or children, were Ephraim and Manasseh*], **for which things there has been a type.**

The word "type," as used at the end of verse 6, above, means something that is symbolic of something else. For instance, Joseph who was sold into Egypt was a "type" of Christ. (In other words, he was symbolic of Christ.) He was thirty years old when he was put in a position to save his people as prime minister of Egypt (see Genesis 41:40, 46). Jesus was thirty years of age when He began His formal mission to save His people (us). In the sacrificing of a firstborn male lamb without blemish as part of the Law of Moses, the lamb was a "type" of Christ, or in other words, symbolic of Christ. Moroni gives several "types" in verses 7–9, next.

7 For **as Joseph brought his father** [*Jacob*] **down into the land of Egypt**, even so he died there; wherefore, **the Lord brought a remnant of the seed** [*descendants; meaning Lehi and his family*] **of Joseph out of the land of Jerusalem**, that he might be merciful unto the seed of Joseph **that they should perish not** [*wouldn't die out*], **even as he was merciful unto the father of Joseph** [*Jacob*] **that he should perish not.**

8 Wherefore, **the remnant of the house of Joseph** [*Joseph's descendants*] **shall be built upon this land** [*America*]; and it shall be a land of their inheritance [*it will become their homeland, just as the land of Jerusalem was the land of inheritance for Judah, and others of Israel*]; and **they** [*Joseph's descendants*] **shall build up a holy city unto the Lord, like unto** [*a "type" of*] **the Jerusalem of old**; and they shall no more be confounded [*confused, frustrated*], until the end come when the earth shall pass away [*after the Millennium is over*].

9 And **there shall be a new heaven and a new earth**; and they shall be **like unto** [*a type of*] **the old** save [*except*] the old have passed away, and all things have become new.

Next, Moroni describes those who will be worthy to live in the city of New Jerusalem.

10 And **then cometh the New Jerusalem**; and blessed are **they who dwell therein**, for **it is they whose garments are white** [*whose lives are made pure and clean*] **through the blood of the Lamb** [*through the Atonement of Christ*]; and they are they who are numbered [*counted*] among the remnant [*the remaining part*] of the seed [*descendants*] of Joseph, who were of the house of Israel.

Next, Moroni tells us that those who live in Old Jerusalem during the Millennium will also be those (especially the Jews) who have accepted the gospel and have thus been made clean and worthy to live there.

11 And then also cometh **the Jerusalem of old**; and **the inhabitants thereof**, blessed are they, for they **have been washed in the blood of the Lamb** [*have been baptized and forgiven of their sins and made pure and clean by the Atonement of Christ*]; and they are they who were scattered and gathered in from the four quarters of the earth [*from all over the earth*], and from the north countries, **and are partakers of the fulfilling of the covenant which God made with their father, Abraham**.

Finally, as Moroni finishes summarizing what Ether taught, he explains, as taught in the above verses, that New Jerusalem will be built up first as a holy city, and then Old Jerusalem, which will fulfill the prophecy that states that the first (the Jews) will be last, and the last (the other tribes of Israel, especially Ephraim and Manasseh) will be first to be gathered in the last days. See Luke 13:30.

12 And **when these things come** [*the building of New Jerusalem, and the rebuilding and spiritualization of Old Jerusalem*], **bringeth to pass** [*fulfills*] **the scripture which saith, there are they who were first, who shall be last; and there are they who were last, who shall be first**.

Next, Moroni tells us that he is forbidden to tell us more about Ether's teachings, and so he continues with the final destruction of the Jaredites.

13 And **I was about to write more, but I am forbidden**; but great and marvelous were the prophecies of Ether; but they esteemed him as naught [*the wicked Jaredites considered him to be nothing*], and cast him out; and he hid himself in the cavity of a rock [*a cave*] by day, and by night he went forth viewing the things which should come [*were prophesied to come*] upon the people.

So far throughout the Book of Mormon, we have been given many warnings that it is possible through wickedness to get to the point where we are "past feeling" (1 Nephi 17:45). We have been warned that "the natural man is an enemy to God" (Mosiah 3:19) and have come to understand through many examples that wickedness is an enemy to wisdom and common sense.

As we continue now with the complete downfall and destruction of the Jaredite nation, perhaps you find yourself wanting to reach into the pages of the Book of Mormon and try to somehow wake these people up as to what is happening to them. Being "past feeling" seems to include being so blinded by Satan that they either can't see or don't want to acknowledge their terribly dangerous situation. Indeed, "the devil laugheth, and his angels rejoice" (3 Nephi 9:2) as people destroy each other rather than repenting and being nice.

The rest of the Book of Ether will be a sad lesson in the realities that await the wicked, both here during mortality as well as in the next life.

14 And **as he** [*the prophet Ether*] **dwelt in the cavity of a rock** [*a cave*] **he made the remainder of this record**, viewing the destructions which came upon the people, by night [*secretly going out at night to see what had happened during the day*].

15 And it came to pass that **in that same year in which he was cast out from among the people there began to be a great war** among the people, for there were many who rose up, who were mighty men, and sought to destroy Coriantumr by their secret plans of wickedness, of which hath been spoken.

> Just a reminder that Coriantumr will be the last survivor of the Jaredites and will eventually be found by Mulekites in the land of Zarahemla (see Omni 1:21).

16 And now **Coriantumr**, having studied, himself, in all the arts of war and all the cunning of the world, wherefore he **gave battle unto them who sought to destroy him**.

17 But **he repented not**, neither his fair sons nor daughters; neither the fair sons and daughters of Cohor; neither the fair sons and daughters of Corihor; and in fine [*in summary*], there were **none of the fair sons and daughters upon the face of the whole earth who repented of their sins**.

18 Wherefore, it came to pass that **in the first year that Ether dwelt in the cavity of a rock, there were many people who were slain** [*killed*] by the sword of those secret combinations, fighting against Coriantumr that they might obtain the kingdom.

19 And it came to pass that **the sons of Coriantumr fought much and bled much**.

> Next, the Lord has the prophet Ether give Coriantumr and his people yet another chance to repent. This is a reminder and an important lesson for us that the Father does everything possible to keep from losing His children. He keeps trying to save them throughout their lives. Jacob 6:4–5 emphasize this truth as follows:
>
> 4 And how merciful is our God unto us, for he remembereth the house of Israel, both roots and branches; and **he stretches forth his hands unto them** [*invites them to repent*] **all the day long** [*all their lives*]; and they are a stiffnecked and a gainsaying people; but as many as will not harden their hearts shall be saved in the kingdom of God.
>
> 5 Wherefore, my beloved brethren, I beseech of you in words of soberness that ye would repent, and come with full purpose of heart, and cleave unto God as he cleaveth unto you. And **while his arm of mercy is extended towards you in the light of the day, harden not your hearts** (Jacob 6:4–5).
>
> We will continue now with the invitation to repent and watch to see how they respond to it.

20 And in the second year **the word of the Lord came to Ether, that he should go and prophesy unto Coriantumr** that, **if he would repent, and all his household** [*everyone who lives with him*], **the Lord would give**

unto him his kingdom and spare the people—

21 **Otherwise they should be destroyed**, and **all his household save it were himself** [*Coriantumr would be the lone survivor*]. And he should [*would*] only live to see the fulfilling of the prophecies which had been spoken concerning another people [*the Nephites*] receiving the land for their inheritance; and Coriantumr should receive a burial by them; and **every soul should be destroyed save it were Coriantumr.**

22 And it came to pass that **Coriantumr repented not, neither his household, neither the people**; and the wars ceased not; and **they sought** [*tried*] **to kill Ether**, but he fled [*ran*] from before them and hid again in the cavity of the rock.

23 And it came to pass that **there arose up Shared**, and he also **gave battle unto Coriantumr; and he did beat him**, insomuch [*so*] that in the third year he did **bring him into captivity**.

24 And **the sons of Coriantumr, in the fourth year, did beat Shared**, and did obtain the kingdom again unto their father [*got the kingdom back for their father*].

25 Now there began to be **a war upon all the face of the land** [*upon the whole land*], every man with his band [*group*] fighting for that which he desired [*selfish*].

26 And **there were robbers**, and in fine [*in summary*], all manner [*all kinds*] of wickedness upon all the face of the land.

Notice how all the evil character traits sponsored by the devil are getting deeper and deeper into the lives and personalities of these people.

27 And it came to pass that **Coriantumr was exceedingly** [*very, very*] **angry with Shared**, and he went against him with his armies to battle; and they did meet in **great anger**, and they did meet in the valley of Gilgal; and the battle became exceedingly sore [*terrible*].

28 And it came to pass that **Shared fought against him for the space of three days**. And it came to pass that **Coriantumr beat him**, and did pursue him until he came to the plains of Heshlon.

29 And it came to pass that **Shared gave him battle again upon the plains**; and behold, **he did beat Coriantumr**, and drove him back again to the valley of Gilgal.

30 And **Coriantumr gave Shared battle again** in the valley of Gilgal, in which **he beat Shared and slew him**.

31 And **Shared wounded Coriantumr in his thigh**, that **he did not go to battle again for the space of two years**, in which time **all the people upon the face of the land were shedding blood** [*killing each other*]**, and there was none to restrain them.**

ETHER 14

One thing Moroni points out to us in this chapter is that as people in a nation or any group get more and more wicked, God curses them so that the things they consider to be important, material things such as tools, weapons, and other things seem to disappear. They can't hold on to them. It may be that part of the curse is fulfilled simply because wicked people are usually dishonest people, so they steal each other's things. It could also be that God makes them forget where they put their stuff so they can't find it again when they want it. Someday, we will find out more about this.

1 AND now there began to be **a great curse upon all the land because of the iniquity** [*wickedness*] **of the people**, in which, **if a man should lay his tool or his sword upon his shelf, or upon the place whither** [*where*] **he would** [*wants to*] **keep it**, behold, upon the morrow [*the next day*], **he could not find it**, so great was the curse upon the land.

2 Wherefore [*therefore*] **every man did cleave unto** [*hang onto*] **that which was his own, with his hands**, and would not borrow neither would he lend; and every man kept the hilt [*handle*] of his sword in his right hand, in the defence of his property and his own life and of his wives and children.

3 And now, **after** the space of **two years**, and after the death of Shared, behold, **there arose the brother of Shared** and he **gave battle unto** [*fought against*] **Coriantumr**, in which **Coriantumr did beat him** and did pursue him [*chased him*] to the wilderness of Akish.

4 And it came to pass that **the brother of Shared** [*Gilead; see verse 8*] **did give battle unto him in the wilderness of Akish**; and the battle became exceedingly sore [*bad, severe, intense*], and **many thousands fell** [*died*] **by the sword**.

5 And it came to pass that Coriantumr did lay siege to [*attacked them in*] the wilderness; and the brother of **Shared** did march forth out of the wilderness by night, and **slew a part of the army of Coriantumr, as they were drunken** [*while they were drunk*].

6 And **he came forth to the land of Moron, and placed himself upon the throne of Coriantumr**.

7 And it came to pass that **Coriantumr dwelt** [*lived*] **with his army in the wilderness for** the space of **two years**, in which he did receive great strength to his army [*many joined his army*].

8 Now the brother of Shared, whose name was **Gilead, also received great strength to his army, because of secret combinations**.

9 And it came to pass that **his high priest murdered him as he sat upon his throne**.

Verse 9, above, reminds us that a goal of Satan is to destroy trust in society. The opposite of this is a

"Zion" society, in which there is peace and harmony and trust (see Moses 7:18).

10 And it came to pass that **one of the secret combinations murdered him** [*the high priest who assassinated Gilead*] in a secret pass, and obtained unto himself the kingdom; and **his name was Lib**; and Lib was a man of great stature, more than any other man among all the people [*he was the largest man of all of them*].

11 And it came to pass that in the first year of Lib, **Coriantumr** came up unto the land of Moron, and **gave battle unto** [*fought against*] **Lib.**

12 And it came to pass that he fought with Lib, in which **Lib did smite upon his arm that he was wounded**; nevertheless, the army of Coriantumr did press forward upon Lib, that he fled to the borders upon the seashore.

13 And it came to pass that **Coriantumr pursued** [*chased*] **him**; and Lib gave battle unto him upon the seashore.

14 And it came to pass that **Lib did smite** [*attack and do much damage to*] **the army of Coriantumr**, that they fled again to the wilderness of Akish.

15 And it came to pass that **Lib did pursue him** until he came to the plains of Agosh. And Coriantumr had taken all the people with him as he fled before Lib in that quarter [*part*] of the land whither [*to which*] he fled.

16 And when he had come to the plains of Agosh **he gave battle unto Lib, and he smote upon** [*fought with*] **him until he died**; nevertheless, **the brother of Lib did come against Coriantumr** in the stead thereof [*in his place*], and the battle became exceedingly sore, in the which **Coriantumr fled** again before the army of the brother of Lib.

Here we are introduced to Shiz, who will fight against Coriantumr to end the final battle, completely destroying the Jaredites. Ether will still be alive to record this final, tragic, and desperate struggle (see Ether 15:29–34).

17 Now the name of the brother of Lib was called **Shiz**. And it came to pass that Shiz **pursued after Coriantumr**, and he did overthrow many cities, and he **did slay both women and children, and he did burn the cities**.

18 And **there went a fear of Shiz throughout all the land**; yea, a cry went forth throughout the land—Who can stand before the army of Shiz? Behold, he sweepeth the earth before him!

19 And it came to pass that **the people began to flock** [*come*] **together in armies, throughout all the face of the land**.

20 And **they were divided** [*Satan's goal; the opposite of the righteous unity taught by the gospel of Christ*]; and a **part of them fled to the army of Shiz, and a part of them fled to the army of Coriantumr**.

Next, Moroni teaches us again about the contrast between the beauty, pleasantness, peace, and happiness that are part of daily life in a Zion society (a society built upon keeping the laws and commandments of God) and the horror, ugliness, turmoil, and stink of wickedness. This is a major message, designed to open our eyes to the literal realities of righteousness versus wickedness. People who are wise choose righteousness.

21 And **so great and lasting had been the war**, and so long had been the scene of **bloodshed and carnage** [*mangled dead bodies*], that **the whole face of the land was covered with** the **bodies of the dead**.

22 And so swift and speedy was the war that there was **none left to bury the dead**, but they did march forth from the shedding of blood to the shedding of blood, leaving the **bodies of both men, women, and children strewed** [*scattered all over*] **upon the face of the land**, to become a prey to [*food for*] the worms of the flesh.

23 And **the scent** [*stench, smell, stink*] thereof [*of it*] went forth **upon the face of the land**, even upon all the face of the land; wherefore [*and so*] **the people became troubled by day and by night, because of the scent thereof** [*smell of it*].

As we said before, one would wish that clear, rational thinking and common sense would finally penetrate the fog and stupor of wickedness at this point. But pride and evil have become terrible masters now for these wicked people.

24 Nevertheless, **Shiz did not cease to pursue** [*stop chasing*] **Coriantumr**; for **he had sworn to avenge himself** [*had promised himself that he would get revenge*] **upon Coriantumr** of the blood of his brother [*for killing his brother, Lib; see verses 11–16*], who had been slain, **and the word of the Lord which came to Ether that Coriantumr should not fall by the sword**.

Shiz planned to make sure that Ether's prophecy that Coriantumr would not be killed would not come true, by killing him.

Next, Moroni tells us what he hopes we learn from what he is showing us here.

25 And **thus we see that the Lord did visit** [*punish*] **them in the fulness of his wrath** [*when His righteous anger was completely filled up*], and **their wickedness and abominations had prepared a way for their everlasting destruction**.

26 And it came to pass that **Shiz did pursue Coriantumr** eastward, even to the borders by the seashore, and **there he gave battle unto Shiz for** the space of **three days**.

27 And so terrible was the destruction among the armies of Shiz that **the people began to be frightened, and began to flee** before [*in front of*] the armies of Coriantumr; and they fled to the land of Corihor, and swept off the inhabitants before them, all them that would not join them.

28 And they pitched their tents in the valley of Corihor; and Coriantumr pitched his tents in the valley

of Shurr. Now the valley of Shurr was near the hill Comnor; wherefore, **Coriantumr did gather his armies together upon the hill Comnor, and did sound a trumpet unto the armies of Shiz to invite them forth to battle.**

29 And it came to pass that **they came forth, but were driven again**; and they came the second time, and they were **driven again** the second time. And it came to pass that they came again **the third time, and the battle became exceedingly sore** [*intense; severe*].

30 And it came to pass that **Shiz smote upon** [*beat upon*] **Coriantumr that he gave him many deep wounds**; and **Coriantumr**, having lost his blood, **fainted**, and was carried away as though he were dead.

Next, the battles will stop, but only temporarily.

31 Now **the loss of men, women and children on both sides was so great** [*much*] **that Shiz commanded his people that they should not pursue the armies of Coriantumr; wherefore** [*and so*], **they returned to their camp.**

ETHER 15

In this final chapter of Ether, Coriantumr will try to make peace with Shiz, but it won't work. Also, the people themselves refuse to repent. Anger toward others has taken a terrible grip on their minds. Hatred and revenge are all they are now thinking about. Satan has succeeded in getting power over them.

Imagine the prophet Ether as he stands by recording this long-prophesied, terrible destruction of his people. He would need much strength and comfort from the Lord in order to handle and endure it.

As you will see in verse 2 of this chapter, we are dealing with large numbers of people. Coriantumr had lost two million men, plus women and children. We would think that Shiz would have had similar numbers lost among his people. Altogether, we are talking millions and millions of people, a strong reminder that completely ignoring the word of the Lord can finally completely destroy nations and individuals.

At this point, Coriantumr begins to think back and remember Ether's warning and prophecy to him that if he repented, he and his people would not be killed off. But if he didn't repent, all his people would be killed, and he, himself, would live just long enough to see the people (the Nephites) who would be brought to the promised land of America to replace the Jaredites (Ether 13:20–21).

1 AND it came to pass **when Coriantumr had recovered of his wounds, he began to remember the words which Ether had spoken unto him** [*in Ether 13:20–21*].

2 **He saw that there had been slain** [*killed*] by the sword **already nearly two millions of his people**, and he began to sorrow in his heart; yea, there had been slain two millions of

mighty men, **and also their wives and their children**.

3 **He began to repent** of the evil which he had done; **he began to remember the words which had been spoken by the mouth of all the prophets**, and **he saw them** [*the prophecies*] **that they were fulfilled thus far, every whit** [*every bit*]; and his soul mourned and refused to be comforted.

Next, Coriantumr tries to make peace with Shiz, but Shiz remains hard-hearted.

4 And it came to pass that **he wrote an epistle** [*letter*] **unto Shiz, desiring him that he would spare the people, and he would give up the kingdom for the sake of the lives of the people**.

5 And it came to pass that when **Shiz** had received his epistle he **wrote an epistle unto Coriantumr, that if he would give himself up, that he might slay him with his own sword** [*probably in fulfillment of his oath to get revenge upon Coriantumr for killing his brother, Lib; see Ether 13:24 and 13:15–17*], **that he would spare the lives of the people**.

6 And it came to pass that **the people repented not of their iniquity** [*their terrible sins and wickedness*]; and **the people of Coriantumr were stirred up to anger against the people of Shiz**; and **the people of Shiz were stirred up to anger against the people of Coriantumr**; wherefore [*and so*], **the people of Shiz did give battle unto** [*fought against*] **the people of Coriantumr.**

7 And when **Coriantumr** saw that he was about to fall [*be killed*] he **fled again** before the people of Shiz.

8 And it came to pass that he came to the waters of Ripliancum, which, by interpretation, is large, or to exceed all; wherefore, when they came to these waters they pitched their tents; and **Shiz** also **pitched his tents near unto them**; and therefore on the morrow [*the next day*] they did come to battle.

9 And it came to pass that they fought an exceedingly sore battle, in which **Coriantumr was wounded again, and he** fainted with the loss of blood.

10 And it came to pass that **the armies of Coriantumr** did press upon the armies of Shiz that they **beat them**, that they caused them to flee before them; and they did flee southward, and did pitch their tents in a place which was called Ogath.

Next, the two leaders of the Jaredites, Coriantumr and Shiz, gather their followers for the final battle. It will take four years (verse 14) for this gathering. Again, we would wish that they would "wake up" to their terrible fate and repent. But such was not the case.

We saw a similar situation where people would not "wake up" among the Nephites in America before the destruction of the wicked at the time of the appearance of Christ to them. Samuel the Lamanite warned them that their money and things would "become slippery" (Helaman 13:31) and that it was "everlastingly too late" for them (Helaman 13:38) because they had "sought for happiness in doing iniquity, which thing is contrary to the nature of that righteousness which is in our great and Eternal Head." Even at the end of this severe description of their lives, these people were again invited to repent (Helaman 13:39).

Likewise, we saw the same thing happen in Mormon. And here, in Ether, we have another repetition of it. One of the obvious intentions of the Book of Mormon is to repeat messages and lessons over and over to increase our chances of understanding and applying them in our lives and being saved.

11 And it came to pass that **the army of Coriantumr did pitch their tents by the hill Ramah** [*the Jaredite name for Hill Cumorah; see Index, at the back of your Book of Mormon, under "Ramah"*]; and it was **that same hill where my father Mormon did hide up the records unto the Lord**, which were sacred.

12 And it came to pass that **they did gather together all the people upon all the face of the land**, who had not been slain, save it was [*except for*] Ether.

13 And it came to pass that **Ether did behold** [*see; observe*] **all the doings of the people**; and he beheld that the people who were for Coriantumr were gathered together to the army of Coriantumr; and the people who were for Shiz were gathered together to the army of Shiz.

14 Wherefore, **they were for the space of four years gathering together the people**, that they might get all who were upon the face of the land, and that they might receive all the strength which it was possible that they could receive.

15 And it came to pass that **when they were all gathered together**, every one to the army which he would, with their wives and their children—both **men, women and children being armed with weapons of war**, having shields, and breastplates, and head-plates, and being clothed after the manner of war—**they did march forth one against another to battle; and they fought all that day**, and conquered not.

16 And it came to pass that **when it was night** they were weary, and retired to their camps; and after they had retired to their camps **they took up a howling and a lamentation for the loss of the slain of their people**; and so great were their cries, their howlings and lamentations [*expressions of deep anguish and misery; mourning*], that they did rend [*tear*] the air exceedingly.

17 And it came to pass that **on the morrow they did go again to battle**, and great and terrible was that day; nevertheless, they conquered not, and **when the night came again they did rend the air with their cries, and their howlings, and their mournings**, for the loss of the slain of their people.

Next, Moroni teaches us what happens when people intentionally sin so long that the Spirit of the Lord is obligated to withdraw from them.

Perhaps we don't realize how important it is to have the gift of the Holy Ghost with us and to have the Light of Christ (sometimes referred to as our conscience, but it is much, much more) upon everyone who is born (John 1:9). You are seeing tragic evidence of what happens when these forces for good are taken away because of wickedness, such that the only remaining force working with the people is that of the devil. An additional example of this is found in Moroni, chapter 9.

18 And it came to pass that **Coriantumr wrote again an epistle** [*letter*] **unto Shiz**, desiring that he would not come again to battle, but that he would take the kingdom, and spare the lives of the people.

19 **But** behold, **the Spirit of the Lord had ceased striving** [*stopped working*] **with them**, and **Satan had full power over the hearts** [*the feelings and emotions*] **of the people**; for **they were given up unto** [*they had turned themselves over to*] **the hardness of their hearts**, and the **blindness of their minds** that they might be destroyed; wherefore they went again to battle.

20 And it came to pass that **they fought all that day**, and when the night came **they slept upon their swords**.

21 And **on the morrow they fought even until the night came**.

22 And when the night came they were **drunken** [*out of control*] **with anger**, even as a man who is drunken with wine; and they **slept again upon their swords** [*they kept their swords right next to them as they slept*].

Out of many millions who once lived in the Jaredite nation, they are now down to 121, plus Ether.

23 And **on the morrow they fought again**; and **when the night came they had all fallen by the sword** [*had been killed*] save it were [*except*] **fifty and two** of the people of Coriantumr, and **sixty and nine** of the people of Shiz.

24 And it came to pass that **they slept upon their swords that night**, and **on the morrow they fought again**, and they contended in their might with their swords and with their shields, all that day.

25 And **when the night came** there were **thirty and two** of the people of Shiz, and **twenty and seven** of the people of Coriantumr.

They are now down to 59, plus Ether.

26 And it came to pass that **they ate and slept, and prepared for death on the morrow** [*the next day*]. And they were large and mighty men as to the strength of men [*compared to most men*].

27 And it came to pass that **they fought for** the space of **three hours**, and they **fainted with the loss of blood**.

28 And it came to pass that when the men of Coriantumr had received sufficient strength that they could walk, they were about to flee for their

lives; but behold, **Shiz** arose, and also his men, and he **swore in his wrath** [*repeated his oath, in anger; see Ether 14:24*] **that he would slay Coriantumr** [*in defiance of the prophecy of Ether, that Coriantumr would not be killed; see Ether 13:21*] **or he would perish by the sword**.

29 Wherefore, **he did pursue** [*chased after*] **them**, and on the morrow he did **overtake them**; and **they fought again** with the sword. And it came to pass that **when they had all fallen** [*died*] **by the sword, save it were Coriantumr and Shiz**, behold **Shiz had fainted** with the loss of blood.

30 And it came to pass that when **Coriantumr** had **leaned upon his sword**, that he **rested a little**, he **smote** [*cut*] **off the head of Shiz**.

31 And it came to pass that **after he had smitten off the head of Shiz**, that **Shiz raised up on his hands and fell**; and after that he had struggled for breath, he **died**.

32 And it came to pass that **Coriantumr fell to the earth, and became as if he had no life**.

He is not dead. He will live to fulfill the prophecy of Ether (13:21) that Coriantumr will live to be buried by another people, who will have received the land of America for their inheritance. He will be found by the people of the land of Zarahemla, about one hundred to two hundred years before Christ, and will live among them for nine months; see Omni 1:21.

33 And **the Lord spake** [*spoke*] **unto Ether**, and said unto him: **Go forth**. And **he went forth, and beheld** [*saw*] **that the words of the Lord had all been fulfilled; and he finished his record**; (and the hundredth part I [*Moroni*] have not written) and he hid them in a manner that the people of Limhi did find them [*see Mosiah 8:7–11; about 121 BC*].

Next, we are privileged to read the last words of Ether and are taught a simple but important lesson, namely, that what ultimately matters is that we are worthy to return to live with God forever.

34 Now **the last words** which are **written by Ether** are these: Whether the Lord will that I be translated [*changed to keep living like the Three Nephites were*], or that I suffer the will of the Lord in the flesh, **it mattereth not, if it so be that I am saved in the kingdom of God**. Amen.

THE BOOK OF MORONI

You will see in chapter 1 that Moroni did not expect to write anything else after he finished The Book of Ether. But since he was still alive and hadn't yet been killed by the Lamanites, he decided to write a little more. The time period for this book is between 400 and 421 years after the birth of Christ—in other words, around 1,000 years after Lehi and his family left Jerusalem.

It contains ten chapters, some very short, and includes Moroni's account of his father's sermon on faith, hope, and charity (chapter 7) and two letters written by Mormon to his son, Moroni, (chapters 8 and 9).

Perhaps you have read Moroni's well-known invitation to read the Book of Mormon and to pray for a testimony from the Holy Ghost that it is true (Moroni 10:4–5).

MORONI 1

From what Moroni says in Moroni 1:1–3, and as mentioned above, we understand that he had not expected to write any more on the Book of Mormon plates (or, in other words, on the gold plates that he would give to Joseph Smith on the Hill Cumorah on September 22, 1827). He thought he was done engraving (writing on the thin gold plates) after he finished abridging or summarizing the twenty-four gold plates of Ether (about the Jaredites).

We feel his loneliness as he tells us that since he is still alive, he will try to write a few more things to the Lamanites. They are of great value to all of us.

One interesting side note is that Moroni dedicated the ground where the Manti Utah Temple now stands. We suppose that he must have "wandered" that far west during the last years of his life. A brief account of his dedicating this temple site is given as follows (**bold** added for emphasis):

"At a conference held in Ephraim, Sanpete County [Utah], June 25th, 1875, nearly all the speakers expressed their feelings to have a temple built in Sanpete County, and gave their views as to what point and where to build it, and to show the union that existed, Elder Daniel H. Wells said 'Manti,' George Q. Cannon, Brigham Young, Jr., John Taylor, Orson Hyde, Erastus Snow, Franklin D. Richards, Lorenzo Young, and A. M. Musser said 'Manti stone quarry.' I have given the names in the order in which they spoke. At 4 p.m. that day President Brigham Young said: 'The Temple should be built on Manti stone quarry.' Early on the morning of April 25th, 1877, President Brigham Young asked Brother Warren S. Snow to go with him to the Temple hill. Brother Snow says: 'We two were alone: President Young took me to the spot where the Temple was to stand; we went to the southeast corner, and President Young said: "**Here is the spot where**

the prophet Moroni stood and dedicated this piece of land for a Temple site, and that is the reason why the location is made here, and we can't move it from this spot; and if you and I are the only persons that come here at high noon today, we will dedicate this ground" (Whitney, *Life of Heber C. Kimball*, 436).

We will now continue with Moroni's introduction to his book, which is chapter one.

1 NOW **I, Moroni, after having made an end of abridging** [*summarizing, condensing*] **the account of the people of Jared** [*the Book of Ether*], **I had supposed not to have written more, but I have not as yet perished** [*died, been killed*]; and **I make not myself known to the Lamanites lest they should destroy me** [*so that they can't kill me*].

2 For behold, their wars are exceedingly [*very*] fierce among themselves; and because of their hatred **they put to death** [*kill*] **every Nephite that will not deny the Christ** [*say that there is no such thing as Christ*].

3 And **I, Moroni, will not deny the Christ; wherefore, I wander whithersoever** [*wherever*] **I can for the safety of mine own life**.

4 Wherefore [*and so*], **I write a few more things, contrary to** [*against*] **that which I had supposed**; for I had supposed not to have written any more; but I write a few more things, **that perhaps they may be of worth** [*value*] **unto my brethren** [*brothers*], **the Lamanites, in some future day**, according to the will of the Lord.

MORONI 2

The gift of the Holy Ghost is a most valuable gift from God, and Moroni wants us to understand this. In this short chapter, he tells us that Jesus laid His hands on the heads of His twelve disciples and gave them power to give the gift of the Holy Ghost to others. In chapter 10, Moroni will teach us more about the gifts of the Spirit and the blessings of following the promptings of the Holy Ghost.

In these three verses, he tells us what Jesus told the twelve Nephite disciples as He laid His hands on their heads.

1 **THE words of Christ**, which he spake [*spoke*] **unto** his disciples, **the twelve** whom he had chosen, **as he laid his hands upon them—**

2 And he called them by name, saying: **Ye shall call on the Father in my name, in mighty prayer; and after ye have done this ye shall have power that to him upon whom ye shall lay your hands, ye shall give the Holy Ghost; and in my name shall ye give it** [*do it in the name of Jesus Christ*], **for thus do mine apostles** [*this is how My Apostles in Jerusalem do it*].

3 Now **Christ spake these words unto them at the time of his first appearing** [*to the Nephites*]; and the multitude heard it not, but the disciples heard it; **and on as many as they laid their hands, fell the Holy Ghost** [*the gift of the Holy Ghost came*].

MORONI 3

Next, Moroni explains how priests and teachers are ordained. A very important message we receive from what Moroni is telling us in chapters 2–6 is that the true Church of Jesus Christ is carefully structured and organized and is a "house of order" in which priesthood ordinances must be done correctly. This includes the laying on of hands in ordaining worthy men to priesthood offices and requires the use of the name of Jesus Christ. It also includes inspiration from the Holy Ghost as to what to say by way of blessing and counsel to the person being ordained.

One other thing you might notice here is that the Nephite twelve disciples are referred to by Moroni as "elders" by Moroni. We likewise refer to our General Authorities as "Elder."

1 **THE manner** [*way*] **which the disciples, who were called the elders of the church, ordained priests and teachers**—

2 After they had prayed unto the Father in the name of Christ, **they laid their hands upon them, and said**:

3 **In the name of Jesus Christ I ordain you to be a priest, (or, if he be a teacher) I ordain you to be a teacher, to preach repentance and remission of sins through Jesus Christ, by the endurance of faith on his name to the end. Amen.**

4 And **after this manner** [*this is how*] **did they ordain priests and teachers**, according to the gifts and callings of God unto men; and **they ordained them by the power of the Holy Ghost, which was in them**.

MORONI 4

Chapters 4 and 5 give instructions on how to administer the sacrament. Remember that Moroni is telling us how the Savior organized the Church among the Nephites when he visited them after His Resurrection.

First, Moroni gives us the blessing on the bread.

1 **The manner of their elders and priests administering the flesh and blood of Christ** [*the sacrament*] unto the church; and they administered it according to the commandments of Christ; wherefore we know the manner to be true; and **the elder or priest** [*either Melchizedek Priesthood holders or priests in the Aaronic Priesthood*] **did minister it**—

2 And they did **kneel down** with the church, and **pray to the Father in the name of Christ**, **saying**:

3 **O God, the Eternal Father, we ask thee in the name of thy Son, Jesus Christ, to bless and sanctify this bread to the souls of all those who partake of it; that they may eat in remembrance of the body of thy Son, and witness unto thee, O God, the Eternal Father, that they are willing to take upon them the name of thy Son, and always remember him, and keep his commandments which he hath given them, that**

they may always have his Spirit to be with them. Amen.

MORONI 5

As you know, we now use water in place of wine when preparing and partaking of the sacrament. This is done according to the instructions of the Lord to Joseph Smith, recorded in the heading of Doctrine and Covenants section 27, as well as in verses 1–2 of that section.

The blessing on the wine (water).

1 **THE manner of administering the wine**—Behold, they took the cup, and said:

2 **O God, the Eternal Father, we ask thee, in the name of thy Son, Jesus Christ, to bless and sanctify this wine to the souls of all those who drink of it, that they may do it in remembrance of the blood of thy Son, which was shed for them; that they may witness unto thee, O God, the Eternal Father, that they do always remember him, that they may have his Spirit to be with them. Amen.**

MORONI 6

Next, Moroni tells us about the qualifications and requirements for baptism among the people of Nephi, after they were taught by the Savior at the time of His appearance to them, as recorded in Third Nephi. The requirements are the same today for baptism that works to get people back home to Heavenly Father.

1 AND **now I speak concerning baptism**. Behold, elders, priests, and teachers were baptized; and they were not baptized save [*unless*] they brought forth fruit [*works, actions*] meet [*necessary to show*] that they were worthy of it.

2 **Neither did they receive any unto baptism save** [*they didn't allow anyone to be baptized unless*] **they came forth with a broken** [*humble*] **heart and a contrite spirit** [*willing to be taught*], and **witnessed unto the church that they truly repented of all their sins.**

3 And **none were received unto baptism** [*nobody was allowed to be baptized*] **save** [*unless*] **they took upon them the name of Christ** [*agreeing to be a good example of living His gospel*], **having a determination to serve him to the end.**

In verse 4, next, Moroni teaches us three specific things that the Nephite Saints did for new members of the Church. We need to do the same things. They are:

1. They were numbered, or kept track of on the records of the Church.
2. They were named, or in other words, members became acquainted with them so they could welcome them and include them.
3. They were "nourished by the good word of God," or in other words, they continued to be taught the gospel.

These three points are **bolded** in verse 4.

4 And after they had been received unto baptism [*after they were baptized*], and were wrought upon [*worked on*] and cleansed [*made clean from their sins*] by the power of the Holy Ghost, **they were numbered** among the people of the church of Christ; and **their names were taken, that they might be remembered** and **nourished by the good word of God**, to keep them in the right way, to keep them continually watchful unto prayer, relying alone upon the merits [*qualifications*] of Christ, who was the author [*source*] and the finisher [*creator*] of their faith.

Next, Moroni tells us of the importance of attending church meetings, partaking of the sacrament, and even the necessity of church discipline, if needed, conducted by priesthood leaders.

5 And **the church did meet together oft**, to fast and to pray, and to speak one with another concerning the welfare of their souls.

6 And **they did meet together oft to partake of bread and wine** [*the sacrament*], in remembrance of the Lord Jesus.

7 And they were strict to observe that there should be **no iniquity** [*serious sin and wickedness*] **among them**; and **whoso was found to commit iniquity**, and three witnesses of the church did condemn [*witness against them*] them before the elders, and **if they repented not, and confessed not, their names were blotted out, and they were not numbered among the people of Christ** [*they were excommunicated*].

8 **But as oft** [*often*] **as they repented and sought forgiveness, with real intent** [*sincerely*], **they were forgiven**.

Verse 9, next, is similar to Doctrine and Covenants 46:2 and reminds us that this is the Lord's church and things relating to its functioning must be directed by the Holy Ghost.

9 And **their meetings were conducted** by the church after the manner of the workings of the Spirit, and **by the power of the Holy Ghost**; for as the power of the Holy Ghost led them whether to preach, or to exhort, or to pray, or to supplicate, or to sing, even so it was done.

MORONI 7

In this chapter, Moroni gives us a talk that his father, Mormon, gave to faithful members of the Church sometime during his lifetime. Mormon starts out by explaining how important faith, hope, and charity are in our lives and in the lives of people who want to get to heaven.

1 AND **now I, Moroni, write a few of the words of my father Mormon**, which he spake [*spoke*] **concerning faith, hope, and charity**; for after this manner did he speak [*this is what he said as he spoke*] unto the people, **as he taught them in the synagogue** [*in the church*] **which they had built** for the place of worship.

Mormon begins by humbly giving credit to Heavenly Father and the Savior for what he is going to say.

2 And now **I, Mormon, speak unto you**, my beloved brethren; and **it is by the grace** [*help*] **of God the Father, and our Lord Jesus Christ, and his holy will**, because of the gift of his calling unto me, **that I am permitted to speak unto you** at this time.

As mentioned above, he is speaking to faithful members of the Church.

3 Wherefore, **I would speak unto you that are of the church**, that are **the peaceable followers of Christ**, and **that have obtained a sufficient** [*enough*] **hope** [*confidence; assurance from the Holy Ghost; compare with Alma 58:11, where "hope" means "assurance"*] **by which ye can enter into the rest** [*through which you can get the peace that comes from being a faithful member of the Church*] **of the Lord**, from this time henceforth until ye shall rest [*enter into exaltation; see D&C 84:24*] with him in heaven.

4 And now my brethren, **I judge these things of you** [*I know you are moving toward heaven*] **because of your peaceable walk** [*peaceful way you live*] **with the children of men** [*with others*].

Next, Mormon will speak of motives when it comes to doing good. His sermon is an example of the fact that truth can be powerful logic. He begins by referring to a phrase that was included in the Sermon on the Mount, given by the Savior in 3 Nephi 14:20, namely, "By their fruits ye shall know them."

5 For I remember **the word of God** which **saith by their works** [*what you do, how you behave*] **ye shall know them**; for **if their works** [*actions*] **be good, then they are good also.**

6 For behold, God hath said **a man being evil cannot do that which is good**; for **if he offereth a gift, or prayeth unto God, except** [*unless*] **he shall do it with real** [*honest, sincere*] **intent it profiteth him nothing** [*it does him no good*].

7 For behold, **it is not counted unto him for righteousness** [*he does not get credit in heaven for doing good*].

8 For behold, if a man being evil giveth a gift, **he doeth it grudgingly** [*he doesn't really want to do it*]**; wherefore it is counted unto him the same as if he had retained** [*not given*] **the gift**; **wherefore** [*therefore*] **he is counted evil before God** [*he is still considered to be an evil, wicked man*].

9 And **likewise also is it counted evil unto a man, if he shall pray and not with real intent of heart** [*but not sincerely*]; yea, and it profiteth him nothing [*does him no good*], for God receiveth none such.

10 **Wherefore** [*and so*], **a man being evil cannot do that which is good**; neither will he give a good gift.

11 For behold, **a bitter fountain cannot bring forth good water; neither can a good fountain bring forth bitter water; wherefore, a man being a servant of the devil cannot follow Christ; and if he**

follow Christ he cannot be a servant of the devil.

Next, he teaches about the basic sources of good and evil.

12 Wherefore, **all things which are good cometh of** [*comes from*] **God; and that which is evil cometh of the devil**; for **the devil is an enemy unto God**, and fighteth against him continually, and inviteth and enticeth [*tempts*] to sin, and to do that which is evil continually.

13 But behold, **that which is of God inviteth and enticeth** [*encourages*] **to do good continually; wherefore, every thing which inviteth and enticeth to do good, and to love God, and to serve him, is inspired of God.**

Having clearly shown us what the sources of good and evil are, Mormon now counsels his people not to get involved in wrong thinking in this matter. Many people make the mistake of weakening gospel standards by emphasizing the good in something that is mostly evil (verse 14).

Members of the Church have the gift of the Holy Ghost to help them judge all things, and all people are blessed with the Spirit of Christ, commonly referred to as a conscience. Therefore, all people have a guidance system, which helps them choose between good and evil.

Mormon will give very simple and clear guidelines for judging between good and evil in verses 16 and 17.

14 Wherefore, **take heed** [*be careful*], my beloved brethren, **that ye do not judge that which is evil to be of God, or that which is good and of God to be of the devil.**

15 For behold, my brethren, **it is given unto you to judge, that ye may know good from evil; and the way to judge is as plain**, that ye may know with a perfect knowledge, **as the daylight is from the dark night.**

16 For behold, **the Spirit of Christ is given to every man, that he may know good from evil** [*everyone has a conscience and can tell the difference between good and evil*]; wherefore [*therefore*], **I show unto you the way to judge**; for **every thing which inviteth to do good, and to persuade to believe in Christ, is sent forth by the power and gift of Christ; wherefore ye may know with a perfect knowledge it is of God.**

17 But **whatsoever thing persuadeth men to do evil, and believe not in Christ, and deny him, and serve not God, then ye may know with a perfect knowledge it is of the devil**; for after this manner doth the devil work, for **he persuadeth no man to do good, no, not one**; neither do his angels [*the evil spirits that work with and follow the devil*]; neither do they who subject themselves unto him [*who allow him to influence them successfully*].

One principle included in this discourse on good and evil is the principle of accountability. It goes hand in hand with the gift of agency. Mormon will touch on the topic of accountability at the end of verse 18, next.

18 And now, my brethren, seeing that ye know **the light by which ye may judge**, which light **is the light of Christ**, see that ye do not judge wrongfully; **for with that same judgment which ye judge ye shall also be judged** [*you will be accountable*].

19 Wherefore, I beseech of you [*I beg you*], brethren, that ye should **search diligently in the light of Christ that ye may know good from evil**; and if ye will lay hold upon [*take hold of*] every good thing, and condemn it not [*and not reject it or criticize it*], ye certainly will be a child of Christ [*you will be a successful follower of Christ*].

Next, Mormon teaches us how faith in Christ becomes the foundation that enables us to "lay hold upon every good thing." Mormon is a master teacher and skillfully uses questions to keep his "students" involved.

20 And now, my brethren, **how is it possible that ye can lay hold upon** [*hang on to*] **every good thing**?

21 And **now I come to** that **faith**, of which I said I would speak; and **I will tell you the way whereby ye may** [*I will tell you how to*] **lay hold on every good thing**.

First, Mormon tells us why it is a good idea to trust God and believe in Christ.

22 For behold, **God knowing all things**, being from everlasting to everlasting [*God is an eternal being*], behold, he sent angels to minister unto the children of men, to make manifest concerning [*to teach them about*] the coming of Christ; and **in Christ there should come every good thing**.

23 And **God also declared unto prophets, by his own mouth, that Christ should** [*would*] **come.**

24 And behold, there were divers [*various*] ways that he did manifest [*show and teach*] things unto the children of men, which were good; and **all things which are good cometh of Christ**; otherwise men were fallen, and there could no good thing come unto them [*without Christ, we would all be lost*].

25 Wherefore, by the ministering of angels, and by every word which proceeded forth out of the mouth of God, **men began to exercise faith in Christ; and thus by faith, they did lay hold upon** [*hold on to*] **every good thing**; and thus it was until the coming of Christ.

Up until the time that Jesus actually came to earth to live, people had to live by faith that there would be a Christ.

26 And **after that he came men also were saved by faith in his name** [*after He came, people still had to exercise faith in Him*]; and **by faith, they become the sons of God** [*they become exalted; compare with D&C 76:24*]. And as surely as Christ liveth he spake these words unto our fathers, saying: Whatsoever thing ye shall ask the Father in my

name, which is good, believing that ye shall receive, behold, it shall be done unto you.

27 Wherefore, my beloved brethren, **have miracles ceased** [*see answer in verse 29, below*] because Christ hath ascended into heaven, and hath sat down on the right hand of God, to claim of the Father his rights of mercy which he hath upon the children of men?

28 For he hath answered the ends of the law [*meaning that He has satisfied the law of justice*], and **he claimeth** [*saves*] **all those who have faith in him** [*the law of mercy*]; and **they who have faith in him will cleave unto** [*hold on tightly to*] **every good thing** [*the natural outcome of having faith in Christ*]; wherefore he advocateth [*leads out in supporting*] the cause of the children of men [*he is our Redeemer; our "advocate with the Father;" see D&C 45:3–5*]; and he dwelleth [*lives*] eternally in the heavens.

29 And because he hath done this, my beloved brethren, **have miracles ceased** [*stopped*]? Behold I say unto you, **Nay** [*No*]**; neither have angels ceased to minister unto the children of men**.

30 For behold, they are subject unto him [*Christ*], **to minister according to the word of his command, showing themselves unto them of strong faith** and a firm mind in every form of godliness [*righteous living*].

Next, we are taught about the role of angels in preparing the way for all of us to be saved, if we so choose. Mormon will mention three specific duties of angels, which we will point out in the following verse by numbering.

31 And **the office of their ministry** [*their role is*] **is [*1*]** to call men unto repentance, and **[*2*]** to fulfil and to do the work of the covenants of the Father, which he hath made unto the children of men, **[*3*]** to prepare the way among the children of men, by declaring the word of Christ unto the chosen vessels of the Lord [*to appear to prophets and others*], that they may bear testimony of him.

32 And **by so doing, the Lord God prepareth the way that the residue of men** [*the rest of us*] **may have faith in Christ, that the Holy Ghost may have place in their hearts**, according to the power thereof [*to exercise His power in their lives*]; and **after this manner bringeth to pass the Father** [*this is how Heavenly Father keeps*], **the covenants which he hath made unto the children of men**.

33 And **Christ hath said: If ye will have faith in me ye shall have power to do whatsoever thing is expedient** [*necessary*] **in me** [*whatever Christ requires of us*].

34 And **he hath said: Repent all ye ends of the earth** [*everyone*], and **come unto me**, and **be baptized in my name**, and **have faith in me**, that ye may be saved.

35 And now, my beloved brethren, **if this be the case that these things are true which I have spoken unto**

you, and God will show unto you, with power and great glory at the last day, that they are true, and **if they are true has the day of miracles ceased**?

No doubt you have noticed that Mormon is emphasizing miracles. We live in a day where many people do not believe in miracles or even in God. The fact that there are miracles, including the miracle of gaining a testimony, of having prayers answered, of gaining power to forgive another, of being healed physically, etc., is a powerful witness that there is a God.

36 Or **have angels ceased to appear** unto the children of men? Or **has he withheld** [*held back*] **the power of the Holy Ghost from them**? Or will he, so long as time shall last, or the earth shall stand, or there shall be one man upon the face thereof to be saved?

37 Behold I say unto you, **Nay**; for **it is by faith that miracles are wrought** [*done*]; and **it is by faith that angels appear and minister unto men**; wherefore, **if these things have ceased wo** [*big trouble*] **be unto the children of men, for it is because of unbelief**, and all is vain [*hopeless, useless*].

38 For **no man can be saved, according to the words of Christ, save** [*unless*] **they shall have faith in his name**; wherefore, **if these things have ceased, then has faith ceased also**; **and awful is the state** [*condition*] **of man, for they are as though there had been no redemption made** [*they are as if Christ had not come and performed the Atonement*].

Next, Mormon compliments the people to whom he is speaking for having strong faith in Christ.

39 But behold, my beloved brethren, **I judge better things of you, for I judge that ye have faith in Christ because of your meekness**; for if ye have not faith in him then ye are not fit to be numbered among the people of his church.

Next, Mormon teaches us the role that hope plays in our lives as we try to live the gospel and get back to heaven. Again, he makes skillful use of questions. Remember that hope is a much stronger word in Book of Mormon usage than in our modern English usage. It reflects assurance and certainty, rather than a "wimpy hope."

40 And again, my beloved brethren, **I would speak unto you concerning hope. How is it that you can attain unto faith, save** [*unless*] **ye shall have hope**?

41 And **what is it that ye shall hope for**? Behold I say unto you that **ye shall have hope through the atonement of Christ and the power of his resurrection, to be raised unto life eternal** [*exaltation in the highest degree of glory in the celestial kingdom, or, in other words, becoming gods and living in your own family unit forever*], and **this because of your faith in him** according to the promise.

42 Wherefore, **if a man have faith he must needs** [*would have to*] **have hope**; for **without faith there cannot be any hope** [*without faith in Christ, there can be no hope for salvation*].

43 And again, behold I say unto you that **he cannot have faith and hope, save** [*unless*] **he shall be meek, and lowly of heart** [*humble, teachable, strong in keeping commitments*].

Next, Mormon brings the topic of charity into his talk. Charity is the end result of faith and hope. He will define it as the "pure love of Christ" (verse 47). It can therefore be defined as thinking as the Savior thinks and acting as the Savior acts, as taught in verse 45.

44 **If so, his faith and hope is vain** [*do him no good*], for **none is acceptable before God, save the meek and lowly in heart**; and **if a man be meek and lowly in heart, and confesses** [*acknowledges*] **by the power of the Holy Ghost that Jesus is the Christ, he must needs** [*he would have to*] **have charity**; **for if he have not charity he is nothing**; wherefore he must needs have charity.

Verse 45, next, is one of the most beautiful and oft-quoted verses in the Book of Mormon. It defines charity.

45 And **charity suffereth long** [*is patient*], **and is kind, and envieth not** [*is not jealous*], **and is not puffed up** [*is not prideful*], **seeketh not her own** [*puts others first*], **is not easily provoked** [*is not easily stirred up to anger*], **thinketh no evil** [*does not hold grudges*], **and rejoiceth not in iniquity** [*doesn't enjoy sin and wickedness*] **but rejoiceth in the truth, beareth all things** [*carries whatever responsibilities come along*], **believeth all things, hopeth all things, endureth all things** [*patiently carries the burdens of life*].

46 Wherefore [*this is why*], my beloved brethren, **if ye have not charity, ye are nothing**, for **charity never faileth** [*can mean many things, including Christlike charity never runs out; charity never fails to bring exaltation to the person who has it; charity never fails to soften your heart; and many other things*]. Wherefore, cleave [*hold tightly*] unto **charity**, which **is the greatest of all**, for all things must fail—

Next, in the first line of verse 47, Mormon gives us a beautifully simple definition of charity.

47 But **charity is the pure love of Christ**, and it endureth [*lasts*] forever; and **whoso is found possessed of it at the last day** [*whoever has it by the time they get to Judgment Day*], **it shall be well with him** [*people with charity will have a pleasant Judgment Day*].

Finally, Mormon teaches that charity is ultimately a gift from God, and that we should pray for it.

48 Wherefore, my beloved brethren, **pray unto the Father with all the energy of heart, that ye may be filled with this love** [*"the pure love of Christ," charity; see verse 47, above*], **which he hath bestowed upon** [*given to*] **all who are true followers of his Son, Jesus Christ**; that ye may become the sons of God [*a phrase meaning exaltation; compare with D&C 76:24 and Mosiah 5:7*]; **that when he** [*Christ*] **shall appear we shall be like him**, for we shall see him as he is; **that we may have this hope** [*assurance, confidence that we will be saved*]; **that we may be purified even as he is pure** [*charity is a great purifier*]. Amen.

MORONI 8

Perhaps you have heard that many churches baptize little children. You no doubt know that the Lord says not to baptize children until they are 8 years old (D&C 68:27). This chapter is a wonderful chapter which contains a letter from Mormon to his son, Moroni, telling him that baptizing little children is absolutely wrong and telling him why.

1 **AN epistle** [*letter*] **of my father Mormon, written to me, Moroni**; and it was written unto me soon after my calling to the ministry [*soon after I was called to serve the Lord*]. And **on this wise did he write unto me, saying** [*this is what he said*]:

2 **My beloved son, Moroni**, I rejoice exceedingly that your Lord Jesus Christ hath been mindful of you [*is always aware of you*], and hath called you to his ministry, and to his holy work.

3 **I am mindful** [*aware*] **of you always in my prayers**, continually praying unto God the Father in the name of his Holy Child, Jesus, that he, through his infinite [*unlimited*] goodness and grace [*power to help us*], will keep you through the endurance of faith on his name [*as you stay faithful*] to the end.

4 And now, my son, **I speak unto you concerning that which grieveth me exceedingly** [*really worries and concerns me*]; for **it grieveth me that there should disputations** [*arguments*] **rise among you** [*it really worries me that there are arguments among you on this topic*].

5 For, if I have learned the truth, there have been disputations among you **concerning the baptism of your little children**.

6 And now, my son, **I desire that ye should labor diligently** [*work hard*], **that this gross error** [*terrible mistake*] **should be removed from among you**; for, for this intent [*purpose*] I have written this epistle [*letter*].

7 For immediately after I had learned these things of [*about*] you **I inquired of** [*asked*] **the Lord** concerning the matter. And **the word of the Lord came to me by the power of the Holy Ghost, saying**:

Next, Mormon explains why little children do not need to be baptized.

8 **Listen to the words of Christ**, your Redeemer, your Lord and your God. Behold, **I came into the world not to call the righteous but sinners to repentance**; the whole [*people who are not sick*] need no physician [*doctor*], but they that are sick [*sick people are the ones who need a doctor*]; wherefore, **little children are whole**, for **they are not capable of committing sin**; wherefore **the curse of Adam** [*the accountability for sins that comes with the fall of Adam*] **is taken from them in me** [*Christ*] [*see Mosiah 3:16*], that it hath no power over them; and the law of circumcision [*part of the Law of Moses; see Genesis 17:10–12*] is done away in me.

9 And **after this manner did the Holy Ghost manifest the word of God unto me** [*this is what the Holy Ghost told me*]; wherefore [*and so*], my beloved

son, **I know that it is solemn mockery before God** [*very serious twisting of God's teachings*]**, that ye should baptize little children.**

10 Behold I say unto you that **this thing shall ye teach—repentance and baptism unto those who are accountable** [*old enough to be responsible for what they do*] **and capable of committing sin**; yea, teach parents that they must repent and be baptized, and humble themselves as their little children, and they shall all be saved with their little children.

11 And **their little children need no repentance, neither baptism**. Behold, baptism is unto [*opens the way to*] repentance to the fulfilling the commandments unto the remission of sins [*so sins can be forgiven*].

12 But **little children are alive in Christ** [*are saved by Christ's Atonement; see Mosiah 3:16*], even from the foundation of the world [*this was established in premortality*]; if not so [*if this were not the case*], God is a partial God [*a God who does not treat all people fairly*], and also a changeable God, and a respecter to persons [*treating one person differently than another, just because they are different people*]; for **how many little children have died without baptism!**

In other words, if some little children are saved because they are baptized, while others are not saved because they are not fortunate enough to be baptized, God would be showing favoritism and would not be fair.

13 Wherefore [*and so*], **if little children could not be saved without baptism, these** [*the ones who died without baptism*] **must have** [*would have*] **gone to an endless hell.**

Next, Mormon expresses very strong feelings about anyone who would claim that little children need to be baptized.

14 Behold I say unto you, that **he that supposeth that little children need baptism is in the gall of bitterness** [*has a bitter personality*] **and in the bonds of iniquity** [*is chained up by wickedness*]; **for he hath neither faith, hope, nor charity; wherefore, should he** [*if he were to*] **be cut off while in the thought, he must go down to hell.**

15 For **awful is the wickedness to suppose that God saveth one child because of baptism, and the other must perish** [*be thrown down to hell*] **because he hath no baptism.**

16 **Wo be unto them that shall pervert** [*twist and falsely change*] **the ways of the Lord after this manner** [*this way*]**, for they shall perish** [*be put in hell*] **except** [*unless*] **they repent**. Behold, **I speak with boldness**, having authority from God; and I fear not what man can do; for **perfect love casteth out** [*removes*] **all fear.**

17 And **I am filled with charity, which is everlasting love**; wherefore [*therefore*], all children are alike unto me [*I consider all children to be of equal worth*]; wherefore, I love little children

with a perfect love; and **they are all alike and partakers of salvation**.

Along with the end of verse 17, above, Doctrine and Covenants 137:10 likewise teaches the salvation of little children who die before they are old enough to be baptized.

10 And I also beheld that **all children who die before they arrive at the years of accountability are saved in the celestial kingdom** of heaven.

18 For I know that **God is not a partial God** [*does not treat people unequally*], neither a changeable being; but he is unchangeable from all eternity to all eternity.

19 **Little children cannot repent**; wherefore [*therefore*], **it is awful wickedness to deny the pure mercies of God unto them**, for they are all alive in him [*saved in heaven*] because of his mercy.

20 And **he that saith that little children need baptism denieth the mercies of Christ**, and setteth at naught [*reduces to nothing*] the atonement of him and the power of his redemption [*His power to save us*].

21 **Wo unto such, for they are in danger of death, hell, and an endless torment. I speak it boldly**; God hath commanded me. Listen unto them [*my words on this subject*] and give heed [*follow them*], or they stand against you at the judgment-seat of Christ.

22 For behold that **all little children are alive in Christ** [*are saved by Christ*], and **also all they that are without the law** [*outside of the law that requires baptism*]. For **the power of redemption cometh on all them that have no law**; wherefore, **he that is not condemned, or he that is under no condemnation, cannot repent**; and unto such baptism availeth nothing [*doesn't do any good*]—

23 But **it is mockery before God** [*making fun of God, ridiculing Him*], denying the mercies of Christ, and the power of his Holy Spirit, and putting trust in dead works.

24 Behold, my son, **this thing ought not to be**; for repentance is unto [*applies to*] them that are under condemnation [*in other words, those who are accountable*] and under the curse of a broken law [*who have broken the laws of God, in spite of their knowledge and understanding of them*].

Next, Mormon will review the first principles of the gospel, namely: faith, repentance, baptism, and the gift of the Holy Ghost, all of which lead to the forgiveness of sins.

25 And the first fruits [*the initial result*] of **repentance is baptism**; and baptism cometh by **faith** unto the fulfilling the commandments; and the **fulfilling the commandments bringeth remission of sins**;

26 And **the remission of sins bringeth meekness, and lowliness of heart** [*humility*]; and because of meekness and lowliness of heart cometh the visitation of **the Holy Ghost**, which Comforter **filleth with hope** [*fills you with confidence that you can be*

saved] and perfect love [*you feel the love of God*], which love endureth [*continues*] by diligence unto prayer [*through diligence in prayer, you can preserve this love that fills your soul*], until the end shall come [*until you have reached the goal of exaltation*], when all the saints shall dwell with God [*in celestial glory*].

27 Behold, my son, **I will write unto you again** if I go not out soon against the Lamanites. Behold, **the pride of this nation, or the people of the Nephites, hath proven** [*has caused*] **their destruction except they should repent** [*if they don't repent*].

28 **Pray for them**, my son, that repentance may come unto them. But behold, **I fear lest the Spirit hath ceased striving** [*working*] **with them**; and in this part of the land **they are also seeking to put down all power and authority which cometh from God** [*similar to many of our nation's laws and court rulings today*]; and **they are denying the Holy Ghost**.

29 And **after rejecting so great a knowledge, my son, they must perish** [*die*] **soon**, unto the fulfilling of the prophecies which were spoken by the prophets, as well as the words of our Savior himself.

30 **Farewell, my son, until I shall write unto you, or shall meet you again**. Amen.

MORONI 9

This is an awful chapter. It is an ugly chapter. When my wife and I were doing our scripture reading with our young family, we hesitated to even read this chapter as we read the Book of Mormon with them. But, since it is part of the Book of Mormon, we did.

One of the strong lessons in Moroni, chapter 9, is a warning to us and everyone else of how far down towards Satan and his evil ways people can go when they go away from God and His teachings. It is a strong warning about how important it is for us to try to live the gospel faithfully so that we can always have the Holy Ghost with us. Perhaps you've noticed that when the Spirit is with you, you have love in your heart for others.

In Ether 15:19, we were told that "the Spirit of the Lord had ceased striving with them, and Satan had full power over the hearts of the people." When this happens, the results are truly frightening and even startling. No doubt remains as to the fact that Satan has no kindness nor goodness in him, at all!

This is the second letter from Mormon to his son, Moroni.

1 MY beloved son, I write unto you again that ye may know that I am yet alive; but **I write somewhat of that which is grievous** [*very discouraging and distressing*].

2 For behold, **I have had a sore** [*terrible*] **battle with the Lamanites**, in which **we did not conquer**; and Archeantus has fallen [*been killed*] by the sword, and also Luram and Emron; yea, and **we have lost a great number of our choice men**.

3 And now behold, my son, **I fear lest the Lamanites shall destroy this people**; for **they do not repent**, and **Satan stirreth them up continually to anger one with another**.

Verse 3, above, as well as the verses that follow, remind us that Satan's way is to be constantly angry at someone, blaming them for our own inappropriate behaviors and thinking.

4 Behold, I am laboring with them continually; and **when I speak the word of God with sharpness they tremble and anger against me**; and when I use no sharpness they **harden their hearts** against it; wherefore, I fear **lest the Spirit of the Lord hath ceased** [*stopped*] **striving with them**.

5 For **so exceedingly** [*extremely*] **do they anger** [*get mad*] that **it seemeth me that they have no fear of death**; and **they have lost their love, one towards another**; and **they thirst after blood and revenge** [*they want to kill and get even*] **continually**.

Next, from the tragic setting of this chapter comes a beautiful gem of counsel that can help many who struggle with family members or acquaintances who have rebelled against the gospel. We are taught to continue trying with them.

6 And now, my beloved son, notwithstanding [*in spite of*] their hardness [*their lack of humility and spirituality*], let us labor diligently [*work hard*]; for **if we should cease to labor** [*stop working with them*], **we should be brought under condemnation** [*we would be in trouble with God*]; for **we have a labor to perform whilst in this tabernacle of clay** [*while in this mortal body*], that we may conquer the enemy of all righteousness [*Satan*], and rest our souls in the kingdom of God.

Next, Mormon will describe the total lack of feelings for others and extreme depths to which people can fall when they force the Spirit of the Lord to withdraw completely from them because of their wickedness, thus leaving the devil and his hosts without restraint in capturing their souls.

7 And **now I write somewhat concerning the sufferings of this people**. For according to the knowledge which I have received from Amoron, behold, **the Lamanites have many prisoners**, which they took from the tower of Sherrizah; and **there were men, women, and children**.

8 And **the husbands and fathers** of those women and children **they have slain** [*killed*]; and **they feed the women upon the flesh** [*bodies*] **of their husbands, and the children upon the flesh of their fathers**; and no water, save [*except*] a little, do they give unto them.

9 And notwithstanding [*in spite of*] **this great abomination** [*terrible wickedness*] of the Lamanites, **it doth not exceed** [*it is not as bad as*] **that of our people in Moriantum**. For behold, many of the **daughters of the Lamanites** have they taken prisoners; and **after depriving them of that which was most dear and precious above**

all things, which is **chastity and virtue**—

10 And after they had done this thing, **they did murder them** in a most cruel manner, **torturing their bodies even unto death** [*until they died*]; and after they have done this, they devour their flesh [*they eat them*] like unto wild beasts, because of the hardness of their hearts; and **they do it for a token** [*sign; indication*] **of bravery**.

As you are aware, the devil is the great deceiver. He is a master at fooling people. His goal is to deceive people until he gets them to think and act as he does. He was tragically successful with the people who committed the unimaginably horrible things described in the above verses.

Next, Mormon asks a series of questions about such behavior to his son, and reminds all of us how quickly Satan can strike if we give him a chance.

11 O my beloved son, **how can a people like this, that are without civilization**—

12 (And **only a few years have passed away, and they were a civil** [*peaceful and respectful*] **and a delightsome people**)

13 But O my son, **how can a people like this, whose delight is in so much abomination** [*who enjoy being so wicked*]—

14 **How can we expect that God will stay** [*hold back*] **his hand in judgment** [*punishment*] **against us** [*against our civilization*]?

15 Behold, **my heart cries: Wo unto this people. Come out in judgment, O God, and hide their sins, and wickedness, and abominations from before thy face**!

16 And again, my son, **there are many widows and their daughters who remain in Sherrizah**; and that part of the provisions which the Lamanites did not carry away, behold, the army of Zenephi has carried away, and **left** them **to wander** whithersoever [*wherever*] they can for food; and **many old women do faint** by the way **and die**.

17 And **the army which is with me is weak**; and the armies of the Lamanites are betwixt Sherrizah and me; and as many as have fled to the army of Aaron have fallen victims to their awful brutality.

18 **O the depravity** [*complete wickedness and lack of feeling for others*] **of my people! They are without order** and **without mercy**. Behold, I am but a man, and I have but the strength of a man, and I cannot any longer enforce my commands.

19 And they have become **strong in their perversion** [*doing things that are against the laws of God*]; and **they are** alike **brutal**, sparing none, neither old nor young; and **they delight in everything save** [*except*] **that which is good**; and the suffering of our women and our children upon all the

face of this land doth exceed [*is worse than*] everything; yea, **tongue cannot tell** [*we don't have words to describe it*], neither can it be written.

20 And now, my son, **I dwell no longer upon this horrible scene**. Behold, thou knowest the wickedness of this people; thou knowest that **they are without principle** [*they have no righteous standards*], and **past feeling** [*they have no conscience*]; and their wickedness doth exceed that of the Lamanites [*the Nephites have become worse than the Lamanites*].

21 Behold, my son, **I cannot recommend them unto God lest he should smite me**. [*Probably meaning that it would be mockery to ask God to save them.*]

22 **But behold, my son, I recommend thee unto God**, and I trust in Christ that thou wilt be saved; and **I pray unto God that he will spare thy life, to witness the return of his people unto him, or their utter destruction** [*Moroni did witness the complete destruction of the Nephite nation; see Mormon 8:3*]; for **I know that they must perish except** [*unless*] **they repent and return unto him**.

23 And **if they perish it will be like unto the Jaredites, because of the wilfulness** [*open rebellion*] **of their hearts, seeking for blood and revenge**.

Another major message for us, contained in verse 23, above, is the danger of seeking revenge. Such behavior drives the Spirit away and corrupts the soul.

24 And if it so be that they perish, we know that **many of our brethren have deserted over unto the Lamanites**, and many more will also desert over unto them; **wherefore** [*and so*], **write somewhat a few things, if thou art spared** [*if you are not killed*] and I shall perish and not see thee; but **I trust that I may see thee soon; for I have sacred records that I would deliver up unto thee**.

We see the tender feelings of Mormon toward his son, and he expresses love and concern that the awful scenes he has described might not be too distressing to him.

25 **My son, be faithful in Christ**; and **may not the things which I have written grieve thee** [*make you too sad*], **to weigh thee down** unto death; **but may Christ lift thee up**, and **may his sufferings and death, and the showing his body unto our fathers, and his mercy and long-suffering** [*patience*], **and the hope** [*confidence in attaining exaltation, because of Christ's Atonement*] **of his glory and of eternal life** [*exaltation*], **rest in your mind forever**.

26 And **may the grace** [*constant help and blessings*] **of God the Father**, whose throne is high in the heavens, **and our Lord Jesus Christ,** who sitteth on the right hand of his power, until all things shall become subject unto him, **be, and abide with you forever**. Amen.

MORONI 10

As Moroni says goodbye to us now, he will give us some wonderful advice about how to get a testimony that the Book of Mormon is true. You can read it in verse four. Millions of people have followed his counsel and have received such a testimony. And, hopefully, you have noticed that verse four works for us each time we are reading anywhere in the Book of Mormon. The Spirit gives us a warm, pleasant feeling and quietly teaches us and points things out as we read along. Our testimony is strengthened each time we read anywhere in the Book of Mormon.

We know from verse 1 that it is now sometime after AD 421; in other words, it has been at least 421 years from the time the sign was given (a day and a night and a day without darkness, mentioned in 3 Nephi 1:15–19). Moroni has been alone for over twenty years and is now ready to bury the gold plates in the Hill Cumorah, where they will wait for the Prophet Joseph Smith to get them from Moroni in approximately fourteen hundred years.

Moroni now gives us his final counsel.

1 **NOW I, Moroni, write somewhat as seemeth me good**; and I write unto my brethren, the Lamanites; and I would that they should know that **more than four hundred and twenty years have passed away since the sign was given of the coming of Christ** [*since the birth of Christ; see 3 Nephi 1:15–19*].

2 And **I seal up these records** [*I will deposit these gold plates in the Hill Cumorah for the Lord to keep safe*]**, after I have spoken a few words by way of exhortation** [*serious counsel*] **unto you**.

3 Behold, **I would exhort you that when ye shall read these things** [*the Book of Mormon*], if it be wisdom in God that ye should read them, **that ye would remember how merciful the Lord hath been unto the children of men** [*all people*], from the creation of Adam even down until the time that ye shall receive these things, **and ponder it in your hearts** [*so that the Holy Ghost has an opportunity to impress the importance of this upon you*].

Verses 4 and 5, next, are among the most famous verses in the Book of Mormon. They contain specific instructions for obtaining a testimony of the truth of this book of scripture, as well as all other things. Thus, they are a powerful and clear lesson in determining truth.

4 **And when ye shall receive these things, I would exhort** [*strongly counsel and urge*] **you that ye would ask God, the Eternal Father, in the name of Christ, if these things are not true; and if ye shall ask with a sincere heart, with real intent** [*determination, purpose*]**, having faith in Christ, he will manifest** [*show*] **the truth of it unto you, by the power of the Holy Ghost.**

5 **And by the power of the Holy Ghost ye may know the truth of all things.**

6 And **whatsoever** [*whatever*] **thing is good is just** [*in harmony with God's will*]

and true; wherefore [*and so you can see*], **nothing that is good denieth** [*goes against or says He doesn't exist*] **the Christ**, but acknowledgeth that he is.

As we continue, Moroni will teach us much about the role of the Holy Ghost in preparing us to be worthy of living with God forever.

7 And **ye may know that he is** [*that Christ exists*], **by the power of the Holy Ghost**; wherefore I would exhort you that ye **deny not the power of God; for he worketh by power, according to the faith of the children of men, the same today and tomorrow, and forever**.

The rules of gaining a testimony are always the same. No matter when people live on earth, a testimony is always obtained by the power of the Holy Ghost.

Next, Moroni will teach us about one of the most important manifestations of the Holy Ghost in people's lives; namely, the gifts of the Spirit. You will see what gifts of the Spirit are as Moroni mentions several of them in verses 9–19.

8 And again, **I exhort you, my brethren, that ye deny not** [*don't ignore or minimize the importance of*] **the gifts of God** [*the gifts of the Spirit; see verses 9–19*], for they are many; and they come from the same God. And **there are different ways that these gifts are administered** [*different people have different gifts; see D&C 46:11–12*]; but it is the same God who worketh all in all; and **they are given by the manifestations of the Spirit of God unto men, to profit** [*help*] **them**.

Next, Moroni will list several specific gifts of the Spirit. He will mention one in verse 14 that is not brought up in the other two main places in the scriptures where such gifts are specifically mentioned (D&C 46:13–26 and 1 Corinthians 12:3–11), namely, the gift of seeing angels. (Specific gifts are highlighted in **bold**.)

9 For behold, to one is given by the Spirit of God, that he may teach the word of **wisdom** [*the gift of being wise*];

10 And to another, that he may **teach** [*the gift of teaching*] the word of knowledge by the same Spirit;

11 And to another, exceedingly great **faith**; and to another, the gifts of **healing** by the same Spirit;

12 And again, to another, that he may work mighty **miracles**;

13 And again, to another, that he may **prophesy** concerning all things;

14 And again, to another, the **beholding** [*seeing*] **of angels and ministering spirits**;

15 And again, to another, all kinds of **tongues** [*speaking foreign languages*];

16 And again, to another, the **interpretation of languages and of divers** [*various*] **kinds of tongues** [*languages*].

In verses 17–19, Moroni summarizes his teaching about spiritual gifts, reminding us that these gifts will always be available, unless unbelief does away with them.

17 And **all these gifts come by the Spirit of Christ**; and they come unto

every man severally [*it is possible to have more than one gift of the spirit; see D&C 46:8*], according as he will.

18 And **I would exhort you, my beloved brethren, that ye remember that every good gift cometh of Christ.**

19 And I would exhort [*strongly advise*] you, my beloved brethren, that ye remember that he is the same yesterday, today, and forever, and that all **these gifts** of which I have spoken, **which are spiritual, never will be done away, even as long as the world shall stand, only** [*except*] **according to the unbelief of the children of men** [*of people*].

Many more gifts of the Spirit exist than those mentioned above and those previously given in other references. For instance, in Romans, chapter 12, we will point out some of the gifts spoken of by Paul. You will no doubt see more.

6 Having then gifts differing according to the grace that is given to us [*different gifts for each, according to God's wisdom*], whether **prophecy**, let us prophesy according to the proportion of faith;

7 Or **ministry**, let us wait on our ministering: or he that teacheth, on **teaching**;

8 Or he that exhorteth, on **exhortation** [*the gift of urging others to do right*]: he that **giveth** [*the gift of generosity*], let him do it with simplicity; he that **ruleth** [*the gift of leadership*], with diligence; he that sheweth **mercy** [*the gift of being merciful*], with **cheerfulness** [*the gift of being cheerful*].

9 Let **love be without dissimulation** [*the gift of being genuine*]. Abhor that which is evil; cleave to that which is good.

10 Be **kindly affectioned** [*the gift of being pleasant*] one to another with brotherly love; in honour **preferring one another** [*the gift of preparing the way for others; "prefer" is Old English for going before or showing the way*];

11 **Not slothful in business** [*the gift of being industrious, diligent*]; fervent in spirit; serving the Lord;

12 **Rejoicing in hope** [*the gift of optimism*]; **patient in tribulation** [*the gift of patience*]; continuing instant in prayer;

13 **Distributing to the necessity of Saints** [*the gift of helping others*]; given to **hospitality** [*the gift of being a gracious host*] (Romans 12:6–13).

Perhaps you remember that Moroni's father, Mormon, gave a wonderful talk about faith, hope, and charity, which Moroni included as Moroni, chapter seven. Here, Moroni reviews faith, hope, and charity as he teaches us how to live righteously and be faithful to God.

20 Wherefore, **there must be faith**; and if there must be faith **there must also be hope**; and if there must be hope **there must also be charity**.

21 And **except** [*unless*] **ye have charity ye can in nowise** [*no way*] **be saved in the kingdom of God; neither** can ye be saved in the kingdom of God **if ye have not faith**; **neither** can ye **if ye have no hope**.

Moroni explains "hope" as used at the end of verse 21, above. This word, as used in the Book of Mormon, means "confidence," "assurance," or "courage" (see Alma 58:11–12). You can see how this ties in with the first part of verse 22, next.

22 And **if ye have no hope ye must needs be in despair** [*in other words, if you don't have confidence that the Atonement will work for you, you will live in despair*]; and despair cometh because of iniquity [*wickedness and sin*].

One significant reason for feeling life is hopeless can be unrepented sin.

23 And Christ truly said unto our fathers: **If ye have faith ye can do all things which are expedient** [*necessary*] **unto me** [*which God requires of you*].

Next, Moroni tells us that there is only one reason why the gifts of the Spirit would ever stop working.

24 And now I speak unto all the ends of the earth [*to everybody*]—that **if the day cometh that the power and gifts of God shall be done away among you, it shall be because of unbelief**.

25 And **wo** [*big trouble*] **be unto the children of men if this be the case**; for there shall be none that doeth good among you, no not one. [*If it ever gets to this point, it will be because there is not one righteous person left on earth.*] For **if there be one among you that doeth good, he shall work by the power and gifts of God**.

Next, Moroni warns of the dangers of intentional sin and rebellion.

26 And **wo unto them who shall do these things away and die, for they die in their sins, and they cannot be saved in the kingdom of God**; and I speak it according to the words of Christ; and I lie not.

Next, we are reminded how important it is that we, ourselves, obey the teachings of the Book of Mormon.

27 And I exhort you to remember these things; for **the time speedily cometh that ye shall know that I lie not, for ye shall see me at the bar** [*the judgment bar*] **of God**; and the Lord God will say unto you: **Did I not declare** [*give*] **my words unto you, which were written by this man**, like as one crying from the dead, yea, even as one speaking out of the dust [*referring to the fact that the gold plates came out of the ground on Hill Cumorah and the Book of Mormon came from them*]?

28 **I declare these things unto the fulfilling of the prophecies.** [*The Book of Mormon is the fulfillment of prophecy.*] And behold, they shall proceed forth out of the mouth of the everlasting God; and his word shall hiss [*signal*] forth from generation to generation [*way into the future*].

29 And **God shall show unto you, that that which I have written is true**.

30 And again I would exhort [*urge*] you that ye would **come unto Christ, and lay hold upon every good gift, and touch not the evil gift, nor the unclean thing**.

By way of final farewell, Moroni pleads with all of us to come unto Christ and partake of the pleasant and beautiful blessings associated with loyalty to God. He will meet us on Judgment Day.

31 And **awake** [*wake up spiritually*], and **arise from the dust** [*shake off the past*], **O Jerusalem** [*Israel*]; yea, and put on thy beautiful garments [*put on the priesthood with its saving ordinances; see D&C 113:8*], **O daughter of Zion** [*Israel*]; and strengthen thy stakes and enlarge thy borders forever [*participate in the gathering of Israel; personally be gathered to Christ*], that thou mayest no more be confounded [*so that you are no longer confused or stopped in your eternal progression*], **that the covenants of the Eternal Father which he hath made unto thee, O house of Israel, may be fulfilled.**

32 Yea, **come unto Christ, and be perfected in him, and deny yourselves of** [*stay away from*] **all ungodliness** [*sin and wickedness*]; and **if ye shall deny yourselves of all ungodliness, and love God with all your might, mind and strength, then is his grace sufficient for you**, that **by his grace** [*His help, after all you can do; see 2 Nephi 25:23*] **ye may be perfect in Christ** [*you can be "sanctified," cleansed, and "without spot" as taught in verse 33, next*]; and **if by the grace of God ye are perfect in Christ, ye can in nowise deny the power of God.**

Next, Moroni explains what it means to be "perfect in Christ" and then says his final farewell to us. It will be a great privilege and pleasure to meet him on Judgment Day.

33 And again [*Moroni repeats for emphasis*], **if ye by the grace** [*help and blessings*] **of God are perfect in Christ, and deny not his power, then are ye sanctified** [*made clean, pure, and holy*] **in Christ by the grace of God, through the shedding of the blood of Christ** [*through the Atonement of Christ*], **which is in the covenant of the Father unto the remission** [*forgiving*] **of your sins, that ye become holy, without spot** [*made perfectly clean from sin*].

34 And **now I bid unto all, farewell.** I soon go to rest in the paradise of God, until my spirit and body shall again reunite [*until I am resurrected*], and I am brought forth triumphant through the air, to **meet you before the pleasing bar** [*judgment bar*] **of the great Jehovah** [*Christ*], **the Eternal Judge of both quick** [*the living*] **and dead.** Amen.

SOURCES

Anderson, Richard Lloyd. *Investigating the Book of Mormon Witnesses*. Salt Lake City: Shadow Mountain, 1989.

Authorized King James Version of the Bible. Salt Lake City, Utah: The Church of Jesus Christ of Latter-day Saints, 1979.

Book of Mormon Student Manual, Religion 121 and 122. Salt Lake City: The Church of Jesus Christ of Latter-day Saints, 1989.

Church History in the Fulness of Times, Religion 341–43. Salt Lake City: The Church of Jesus Christ of Latter-day Saints, 1980.

Collier, John. *The Indians of the Americas*. New York: W. W. Norton, 1947.

Dibble, Johnathan A. "Delivered by the Power of God: The American Revolution and Nephi's Prophecy." *Ensign*, October 1987.

Doctrine and Covenants Student Manual, Religion 324 and 325. Salt Lake City: The Church of Jesus Christ of Latter-day Saints, 1981.

Holland, Jeffrey R. "'This Do in Remembrance of Me.'" *Ensign*, November 1995.

Jacobs, Wilbur R. *The Frontier in American History*. Tuscon, Arizona: University of Arizona Press, 1986.

Jacobs, Wilbur R. "The Indian and the Frontier in American History—A Need for Revision." *Western Historical Quarterly*, January 1973.

Journal of Discourses. 26 vols. London: Latter-day Saints' Book Depot., 1854–86.

Kimball, Spencer W. "Our Paths Have Met Again." *Ensign*, December 1975.

Kimball, Spencer W. "The Blessings and Responsibilities of Womanhood." *Ensign*, March 1976.

Kimball, Spencer W. *The Miracle of Forgiveness*. Salt Lake City: Bookcraft, 1969.

Latourette, Kenneth Scott. *A History of the Expansion of Christianity, The Great Century*, vol. 4. New York: Harper and Brothers, 1941.

Library of Aboriginal American Literature. Edited by Daniel Garrison Brinton. 8 vols. Philadelphia: William F. Fell, 1890.

Ludlow, Daniel H. *A Companion to Your Study of The Book of Mormon*. Salt Lake City: Deseret Book, 1976.

Luther, Martin. Die Bibel (German translation of the Bible, 1545). Wheaton, Illinois: Crossway Publishing, 2009. Joseph Smith said this was the most correct of any Bible available at the time.

Maxwell, Neal A. "On Being a Light." Address delivered at the Salt Lake Institute of Religion, January 2, 1974.

Maxwell, Neal A. "According to the Desire of [Our] Hearts." *Ensign*, November 1996.

McConkie, Bruce R. *Millennial Messiah*. Salt Lake City: Deseret Book, 1983.

McConkie, Bruce R. *Mormon Doctrine*. 2nd ed. Salt Lake City: Bookcraft, 1966.

Moldenke, Harold and Alma Moldenke. *Plants of the Bible*. Mineola, New York: Dover Publications, 1986.

Nibley, Hugh. *Since Cumorah: The Book of Mormon in the Modern World*. Salt Lake City: Deseret Book, 1970.

Old Testament Student Manual, 1 Kings through Malachi, Religion 302. Salt Lake City: The Church of Jesus Christ of Latter-day Saints, 1981.

Petersen, Mark E. *The Great Prologue*. Salt Lake City: Deseret Book, 1976.

Reynolds, George and Janne M. Sjodahl. *Commentary on the Book of Mormon*. 7 vols. Salt Lake City: Deseret Press, 1976.

Richards, LeGrand. "Prophets and Prophecy." In Conference Report, October 1975; or *Ensign*, November 1975.

Richards, LeGrand. *Israel! Do You Know?* 4th ed. Salt Lake City: Shadow Mountain, 1990.

Smith, George Albert. In Conference Report, April 1918.

Smith, Joseph. *History of The Church of Jesus Christ of Latter-day Saints*. Edited by B. H. Roberts. 2d ed. rev., 7 vols., Salt Lake City: The Church of Jesus Christ of Latter-day Saints, 1932–51.

Smith, Joseph. *Messenger and Advocate*, April 1835.

Smith, Joseph. *Teachings of the Prophet Joseph Smith*. Selected and arranged by Joseph Fielding Smith. Salt Lake City: Deseret Book, 1976.

Smith, Joseph F., Anthon H. Lund, and John Henry Smith. First Presidency Statement. *Improvement Era*, August 1916.

Smith, Joseph F., John R. Winder, and Anthon H. Lund. First Presidency Message. *Messages of the First Presidency of The Church of Jesus Christ of Latter-day Saints*. 6 vols. Compiled by James R. Clark. Salt Lake City: Bookcraft, 1965.

Smith, Joseph Fielding. *Answers to Gospel Questions.* Compiled by Joseph Fielding Smith. 5 vols. Salt Lake City: Deseret Book, 1957–66.

Smith, Joseph Fielding. *Church History and Modern Revelation.* 4 vols. Salt Lake City: Deseret Book, 1947.

Smith, Joseph Fielding. *Doctrines of Salvation.* Compiled by Bruce R. McConkie. 3 vols. Salt Lake City: Bookcraft, 1954–56.

Smith, Lucy Mack. *History of Joseph Smith by His Mother.* Salt Lake City: Stevens & Wallis, 1945.

Talmage, James E. *Articles of Faith.* Salt Lake City: Deseret Book, 1981.

"The Family: A Proclamation to the World." First Presidency and Council of the Twelve Apostles. *Family Guide Book.* Salt Lake City: The Church of Jesus Christ of Latter-day Saints, 1995.

Wasserman, Jacob. *Columbus: Don Quixote of the Seas.* Translated by Eric Sutton. Boston: Little, Brown, and Company, 1930.

Young, Brigham. *Discourses of Brigham Young.* Compiled by John A. Widtsoe. Salt Lake City: Deseret Book, 1954.

NOTES

NOTES

NOTES

NOTES

NOTES

NOTES

NOTES

NOTES

NOTES

NOTES

NOTES

NOTES

NOTES

NOTES

NOTES

NOTES

ABOUT THE AUTHOR

David J. Ridges taught for the Church Educational System for thirty-five years and has taught for several years at BYU Campus Education Week. He taught adult religion classes and Know Your Religion classes for BYU Continuing Education for many years. He has also served as a curriculum writer for Sunday School, seminary, and institute of religion manuals.

He has served in many callings in the Church, including Gospel Doctrine teacher, bishop, stake president, and patriarch. He and Sister Ridges served a full-time eighteen-month mission, training senior CES missionaries and helping coordinate their assignments throughout the world.

Brother Ridges and his wife, Janette, are the parents of six children and make their home in Springville, Utah.

Scan to visit

www.davidjridges.com